New Insights in Machine Learning and Deep Neural Networks

New Insights in Machine Learning and Deep Neural Networks

Editors

Álvaro Figueira
Francesco Renna

Basel • Beijing • Wuhan • Barcelona • Belgrade • Novi Sad • Cluj • Manchester

Editors
Álvaro Figueira
Institute for Systems and
Computer Engineering
Technology and Science
Porto, Portugal

Francesco Renna
Instituto de Telecomunicações
Universidade do Porto
Porto, Portugal

Editorial Office
MDPI
St. Alban-Anlage 66
4052 Basel, Switzerland

This is a reprint of articles from the Special Issue published online in the open access journal *Mathematics* (ISSN 2227-7390) (available at: https://www.mdpi.com/journal/mathematics/special_issues/New_Insights_ML_Deep_Neural_Networks).

For citation purposes, cite each article independently as indicated on the article page online and as indicated below:

Lastname, A.A.; Lastname, B.B. Article Title. *Journal Name* **Year**, *Volume Number*, Page Range.

ISBN 978-3-0365-8982-4 (Hbk)
ISBN 978-3-0365-8983-1 (PDF)
doi.org/10.3390/books978-3-0365-8983-1

© 2023 by the authors. Articles in this book are Open Access and distributed under the Creative Commons Attribution (CC BY) license. The book as a whole is distributed by MDPI under the terms and conditions of the Creative Commons Attribution-NonCommercial-NoDerivs (CC BY-NC-ND) license.

Contents

About the Editors . . . . **vii**

Preface . . . . **ix**

Alvaro Figueira and Bruno Vaz
Survey on Synthetic Data Generation, Evaluation Methods and GANs
Reprinted from: *Mathematics* **2022**, *10*, 2733, doi:10.3390/math10152733 . . . . **1**

Marco Silva and João Pedro Pedroso
Deep Reinforcement Learning for Crowdshipping Last-Mile Delivery with
Endogenous Uncertainty
Reprinted from: *Mathematics* **2022**, *10*, 3902, doi:10.3390/math10203902 . . . . **43**

**Muhammad Kamran, Saeed Ur Rehman, Talha Meraj, Khalid A. Alnowibet and
Hafiz Tayyab Rauf**
Camouflage Object Segmentation Using an Optimized Deep-Learning Approach
Reprinted from: *Mathematics* **2022**, *10*, 4219, doi:10.3390/math10224219 . . . . **67**

Cláudia Pinheiro, Francisco Silva, Tania Pereira and Hélder P. Oliveira
Semi-Supervised Approach for EGFR Mutation Prediction on CT Images
Reprinted from: *Mathematics* **2022**, *10*, 4225, doi:10.3390/math10224225 . . . . **87**

Isack Lee and Seok Bong Yoo
Latent-PER: ICA-Latent Code Editing Framework for Portrait Emotion Recognition
Reprinted from: *Mathematics* **2022**, *10*, 4260, doi:10.3390/math10224260 . . . . **105**

**Vimala Balakrishnan, Zhongliang Shi, Chuan Liang Law, Regine Lim, Lee Leng Teh, Yue Fan
and Jeyarani Periasamy**
A Comprehensive Analysis of Transformer-Deep Neural Network Models in Twitter Disaster
Detection
Reprinted from: *Mathematics* **2022**, *10*, 4664, doi:10.3390/math10244664 . . . . **125**

Yansong Li, Paula Branco and Hanxiang Zhang
Imbalanced Multimodal Attention-Based System for Multiclass House Price Prediction
Reprinted from: *Mathematics* **2023**, *11*, 113, doi:10.3390/math11010113 . . . . **139**

**Samia Aziz, Muhammad Shahzad Sarfraz, Muhammad Usman, Muhammad Umar Aftab and
Hafiz Tayyab Rauf**
Geo-Spatial Mapping of Hate Speech Prediction in Roman Urdu
Reprinted from: *Mathematics* **2023**, *11*, 969, doi:10.3390/math11040969 . . . . **157**

Ehsan Nazari, Paula Branco and Guy-Vincent Jourdan
AutoGAN: An Automated Human-Out-of-the-Loop Approach for Training Generative
Adversarial Networks
Reprinted from: *Mathematics* **2023**, *11*, 977, doi:10.3390/math11040977 . . . . **183**

You-Liang Xie and Che-Wei Lin
Imbalanced Ectopic Beat Classification Using a Low-Memory-Usage CNN LMUEBCNet and
Correlation-Based ECG Signal Oversampling
Reprinted from: *Mathematics* **2023**, *11*, 1833, doi:10.3390/math11081833 . . . . **215**

About the Editors

Álvaro Figueira

Álvaro Figueira is an assistant professor in the Department of Computer Science, University of Porto. He obtained his BSc in Computer Science from the University of Porto, his MSc in Foundations of Advanced Information Technology from Imperial College, and a PhD in Computer Science from the University of Porto. Prof. Figueira has been principal investigator in several international projects with a focus in creating methods and techniques to analyze social media, identifying fake news, and analyzing social media publication techniques from major higher education institutions. In the last five years, Prof. Figueira has been interested in the creation and evaluation of generative synthetic data, mainly to augment the minority classes in machine learning processes. He currently serves as member of the Department's Executive Commission and as Director of the Department Master's in Data Science.

Francesco Renna

Francesco Renna is an assistant professor at the Department of Computer Science of University of Porto, Portugal. He received the Laurea Specialistica degree in telecommunication engineering and the Ph.D. degree in information engineering, both from the University of Padova, Padova, Italy, in 2006 and 2011, respectively. Between 2007 and 2022, he held visiting researcher and postdoctoral researcher positions with Infineon Technology AG, Princeton University, Georgia Institute of Technology (Lorraine Campus), Supelec, the University of Porto, Duke University, University College London, and the University of Cambridge. Since 2022, he has been a senior researcher with INESC TEC. His research interests include high-dimensional information processing, biomedical signaling, and image processing. Dr. Renna was the recipient of a Marie Sklodowska-Curie Individual Fellowship from the European Commission and a Research Contract within the Scientific Employment Stimulus program from the Portuguese Foundation for Science and Technology.

Preface

Several decades ago, linear regression models and rule-based algorithms were the primary tools in the arsenal of researchers and technologists for deciphering patterns in data and predicting outcomes. These methodologies, rooted in classical statistics and rudimentary algorithms, were effective for tackling straightforward predictive challenges but lacked the sophistication to understand complex relationships, high-dimensional data, and non-linear interactions. However, with the advent of machine learning in the late 20th century, and the subsequent rise of deep neural networks in the recent decade, the landscape dramatically shifted. These contemporary techniques, harnessing the power of advanced algorithms and vast computational resources, offer a more nuanced approach to data analysis. They now allow researchers and practitioners to delve into complex, high-dimensional spaces, making sense of data in ways that were previously thought inconceivable. As a result, they are capable of addressing challenges steeped in ambiguity and subtlety, effectively bridging the gap between raw data and human-like interpretative understanding.

In the evolving realm of machine learning and deep neural networks, research papers often converge around thematic clusters, reflecting the dominant trends and pressing challenges of the time. The following groups present a curated categorization of recent manuscripts, shedding light on the multifaceted dimensions of contemporary research in this domain.

Generative Techniques, Synthetic Data, and Advanced Feature Extraction:

Delving into the complexities of synthetic data generation, GANs, and advanced feature extraction, this cluster presents manuscripts that push the envelope of data processing and object recognition. Figueira and Vaz provide a comprehensive survey on GANs, highlighting their applications and training challenges, with an emphasis on tabular data. Lee and Yoo introduce an emotion recognition framework that leverages independent component analysis and latent codes to combat performance degradation. Nazari, Branco, and Jourdan take GAN innovations a step further with AutoGAN, which automates the GAN training process across different data modalities. Meanwhile, Kamran, Rehman, and their colleagues delve into object segmentation, proposing a sophisticated framework that harnesses parallelism in feature extraction, refining global feature maps to enhance the recognition of camouflaged objects.

Medical Innovations through Deep Learning:

Medical advancements through the lens of deep learning are the core focus of this cluster. Pinheiro, Silva, and their team introduce a semi-supervised approach that predicts EGFR mutations in lung cancer patients using 3D CT scans, merging variational autoencoders and adversarial training to improve classification. Xie and Lin pivot to cardiac health, presenting an optimized CNN for ectopic beat classification, with their correlation-based oversampling method ensuring a balanced dataset for improved performance.

Optimization and Analysis in Dynamic Environments:

These manuscripts tackle the challenges of real-world, dynamic environments through advanced machine learning techniques. Silva and Pedroso craft a deep reinforcement learning algorithm suited for the particulars of crowd shipping's last-mile delivery, demonstrating efficacy in large uncertain data instances. Balakrishnan and his team analyze the digital sprawl of Twitter, dissecting various ensemble learning models to detect disaster-related communications, highlighting the effectiveness of simpler transformer variants. Aziz's team navigates the waters of sociolinguistics, using cutting-edge vectorization techniques to predict political hate speech in Roman Urdu.

Multimodal Systems and Attention Mechanisms:

This cluster underscores the potency of multimodal data processing and attention mechanisms in modern machine learning. Li, Branco, and Zhang propose the innovative IMAS, a system that incorporates an oversampling strategy with a self-attention mechanism to refine house price prediction models. This system's capability to manage various data types underscores the potential of future multimodal systems.

This revised grouping and narrative provide a clearer representation of the manuscripts' thematic focuses within the Special Issue.

As Guest Editors of this Special Issue, we extend our sincere gratitude to the authors for their insightful contributions, to the reviewers for their constructive feedback enhancing the quality of the manuscripts, and to the administrative team at MDPI for their unwavering support in bringing this initiative to fruition, particularly to Nemo Guan for her infinite patience.

Álvaro Figueira and Francesco Renna
Editors

Review

Survey on Synthetic Data Generation, Evaluation Methods and GANs

Alvaro Figueira [1,*,†] and Bruno Vaz [2,†]

1 CRACS-INESC TEC, University of Porto, 4169-007 Porto, Portugal
2 Faculty of Sciences, University of Porto, Rua do Campo Alegre, s/n, 4169-007 Porto, Portugal; vazgbruno@gmail.com
* Correspondence: arfiguei@fc.up.pt
† These authors contributed equally to this work.

Abstract: Synthetic data consists of artificially generated data. When data are scarce, or of poor quality, synthetic data can be used, for example, to improve the performance of machine learning models. Generative adversarial networks (GANs) are a state-of-the-art deep generative models that can generate novel synthetic samples that follow the underlying data distribution of the original dataset. Reviews on synthetic data generation and on GANs have already been written. However, none in the relevant literature, to the best of our knowledge, has explicitly combined these two topics. This survey aims to fill this gap and provide useful material to new researchers in this field. That is, we aim to provide a survey that combines synthetic data generation and GANs, and that can act as a good and strong starting point for new researchers in the field, so that they have a general overview of the key contributions and useful references. We have conducted a review of the state-of-the-art by querying four major databases: Web of Sciences (WoS), Scopus, IEEE Xplore, and ACM Digital Library. This allowed us to gain insights into the most relevant authors, the most relevant scientific journals in the area, the most cited papers, the most significant research areas, the most important institutions, and the most relevant GAN architectures. GANs were thoroughly reviewed, as well as their most common training problems, their most important breakthroughs, and a focus on GAN architectures for tabular data. Further, the main algorithms for generating synthetic data, their applications and our thoughts on these methods are also expressed. Finally, we reviewed the main techniques for evaluating the quality of synthetic data (especially tabular data) and provided a schematic overview of the information presented in this paper.

Keywords: synthetic data generation; generative adversarial networks; evaluation of synthetic data

MSC: 68T07

Citation: Figueira, A.; Vaz, B. Survey on Synthetic Data Generation, Evaluation Methods and GANs. *Mathematics* **2022**, *10*, 2733. https://doi.org/10.3390/math10152733

Academic Editor: Catalin Stoean

Received: 1 July 2022
Accepted: 24 July 2022
Published: 2 August 2022

Publisher's Note: MDPI stays neutral with regard to jurisdictional claims in published maps and institutional affiliations.

Copyright: © 2022 by the authors. Licensee MDPI, Basel, Switzerland. This article is an open access article distributed under the terms and conditions of the Creative Commons Attribution (CC BY) license (https://creativecommons.org/licenses/by/4.0/).

1. Introduction

Data are ubiquitous and can be a source of great value. However, to create such value, the data needs to be of high quality. In addition, when dealing with sensitive data (e.g., medical records or credit datasets), the privacy of the data must be ensured without sacrificing quality. The lack of high-quality data and the need for privacy-preserving data has become increasingly apparent in the last few years as companies and researchers use it more and more. Synthetic data consists of artificially generated data [1] and is a quite powerful tool to overcome the two aforementioned problems. Because synthetic data are generated rather than collected or measured, they can be of much higher quality than real data. Moreover, privacy constraints can be applied so that the synthetic data does not reveal any important information, such as patients' clinical records.

Although this is a very good idea, synthetic data must be generated properly: it must be plausible and follow the underlying distribution of the original data (Synthetic data can also be generated, for example, to create video games. In this case, it may not need to resemble real-world data, but this is not the focus of our study). Therefore, the algorithms that generate it must be robust and capture the patterns in the real data. SMOTE [2] (Synthetic Minority Oversampling Technique) is one of the oldest algorithms that try to replicate a data distribution (it was proposed in 2002), apart from Random OverSampling (ROS) and other traditional algorithms such as rotation or scaling. The idea matured over the years, and several variants have been proposed [3–6]. However, it was not until the advent of Deep Learning that more promising ideas emerged, such as Variational AutoEncoders [7] (VAEs) in 2013 and, most importantly, Generative adversarial networks [8] (GANs) in 2014.

GANs are a powerful deep generative model trained with an adversarial procedure. Similar to SMOTE, GANs have undergone several modifications since they were first proposed to solve several different problems in different domains, e.g., physics [9] or healthcare [10]. However, the main focus has been on computer vision tasks where the domain consists generically of images. Nevertheless, tabular datasets are abundant, and the generation of synthetic tabular data is of great interest. For this reason, in this work, we have investigated different methods for generating synthetic data (with emphasis on tabular data), as well as the different GAN architectures that have been proposed over the years, with a particular emphasis on GANs that can generate synthetic tabular data.

Another important aspect we have studied is the evaluation of the quality of synthetic samples. As explained earlier, synthetic data can be of great use, but it is critical that such artificial data are plausible and can mimic the underlying data distribution of real datasets. Therefore, it is important to have methods to accurately assess the quality of the generated data. However, one problem that arises in such an assessment is the question of what to assess. One may want to generate synthetic data to improve the performance of a machine learning (ML) model, while others may need synthetic data with novel patterns without worrying too much about the performance of the model. Thus, depending on the problem and domain, some techniques are better suited than others. Clearly, there is not a one-size-fits-all evaluation method.

As such, we are combining a general overview of three main topics: synthetic data generation algorithms, GANs, and the evaluation of synthetic data. Moreover, we provide particular emphasis on GANs for tabular data generation, as we believe this is a not so well explored topic, unlike GANs for image generation. This can be quite convenient for new researchers in the field, as there is useful material and references in this survey. In turn, they can boost their research by having a general overview of the key breakthroughs in the field as well as an organizational and temporal summary of what has been reviewed throughout the document.

The remaining of this survey is organized as follows. Section 2 provides an overview of the current state-of-the-art in terms of research in the area and presents the major scientific key insights concerning the scientific journals publishing in the area, the most prominent authors, the scientific production, and the most cited works. Section 3 gives a comprehensive overview of how a GAN works, the main training drawbacks, the most important GAN breakthroughs, and GANs for tabular data (where they are explained with a fine level of detail). In Section 4, we survey the main methods for synthetic data generation, dividing them into standard and Deep Learning methods and giving our considerations to all of them. Then, in Section 5, we discuss the evaluation of the quality of synthetic samples. In Section 6, the information covered in the previous sections is condensed and schematized so that it becomes easier to see the big picture. Finally, in Section 7, we present the main conclusions of this survey.

2. Literature Review

To analyze the state-of-the-art in what concerns GANs used for synthetic data generation, as well as synthetic data generation methods, we collected data from four major bibliographic databases—Web of Sciences (WoS), Scopus, IEEE Xplore, and ACM Digital

Library. As such, the query used contains keywords related to both GANs (in the context of synthetic data generation) and synthetic data. The query used is shown in Listing 1.

Listing 1. Query used to search the WoS, Scopus, IEEE, and ACM databases.

(("generative adversarial network" OR "GAN" OR "adversarial neural"
OR "adversarial machine learning") AND "synthetic" AND ("sample" OR "data"))
OR ("synthetic" AND ("sample" OR "data"))

At first, running the search query without any additional filters returned a considerably high number of results in all four databases. Therefore, we determined that the query should only be applied to the title field—the number of results decreased with this restriction. Because this work is not an exhaustive literature review, the dates were also constrained to be equal to or greater than 1 January 2010, and the language in which the documents were written had to be English (however, IEEE Xplore and the ACM Digital Library did not offer this filter). Table 1 shows the filtering process just described, with the exact number of documents returned at each step.

Table 1. Filtering process. The search query in Listing 1 was used across four different databases, and three filters were applied to decrease the initial high number of results.

Database	No Filters	Field = Title	Date = 1 January 2010 to 31 December 2022	Language = English
WoS	167,419	2460	1699	1681
Scopus	1,168,662	3625	2457	2401
IEEE	44,887	731	562	No filter
ACM	31,463	65	57	No filter

Once the documents were filtered, a general analysis was conducted on the resulting dataset—2706 distinct documents were found across the four databases (see Figure 1, which shows a graphical representation of the respective databases of the filtered works).

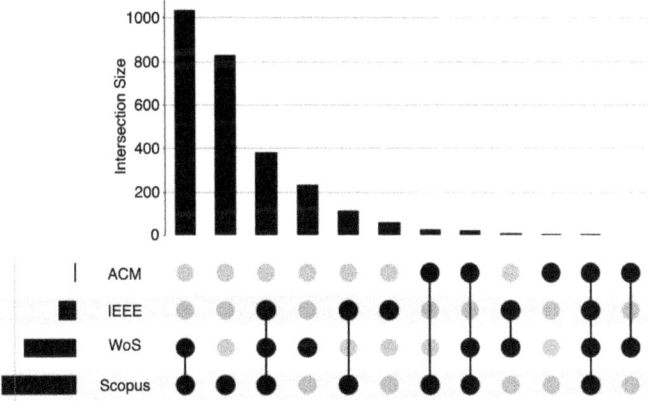

Figure 1. UpSet plot representing the number of documents in each database and the common works across the databases from the filtered results. The bar chart represents the number of documents in each database or in the intersection of databases. The plot immediately below the bar chart represents the intersection of works. If the same document was returned in the Web of Sciences, Scopus, and IEEE Xplore databases, it is denoted by black dots in the WoS, Scopus, and IEEE rows.

We start by looking at the annual scientific production (total number of works produced), the total number of citations, and the average number of citations (the total number of citations in a year, divided by the respective number of documents). Figure 2 shows three line charts, each representing the annual values of the three aforementioned measures.

Annual scientific production has been increasing over the past decade, with a massive dip only in 2022, as we are at the beginning of the year at the time of writing. The same does not happen with the number of citations, as they have been steadily decreasing since 2018. To complement these two charts, we have included another chart showing the average number of citations per year, which has been decreasing in recent years.

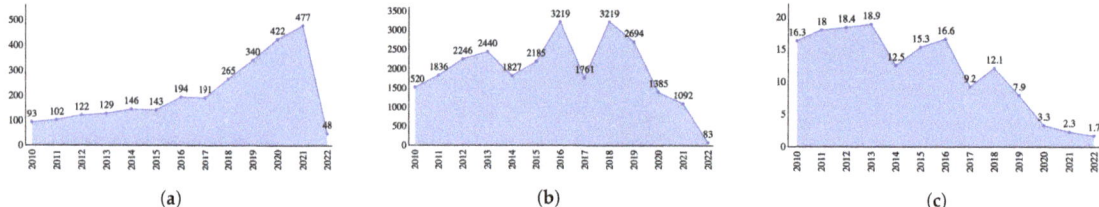

Figure 2. Line charts (filtered documents). (**a**) Total number of documents per year. (**b**) Total number of citations per year. (**c**) Average number of citations per year.

To enable new researchers in this field of studies to have an overview of the subject, showcasing the main publication sources, the most relevant authors, and the highly cited works can be quite useful. As such, the main scientific journals, books, or conferences in which the filtered documents were published are first analyzed. To support this task, a treemap was created—see Figure 3. The treemap clearly shows that Lecture Notes in Computer Science is the Series with the most published documents (from the filtered documents), with two times more documents than the next two sources, the IEEE Conferences and the Journal of Applied Remote Sensing.

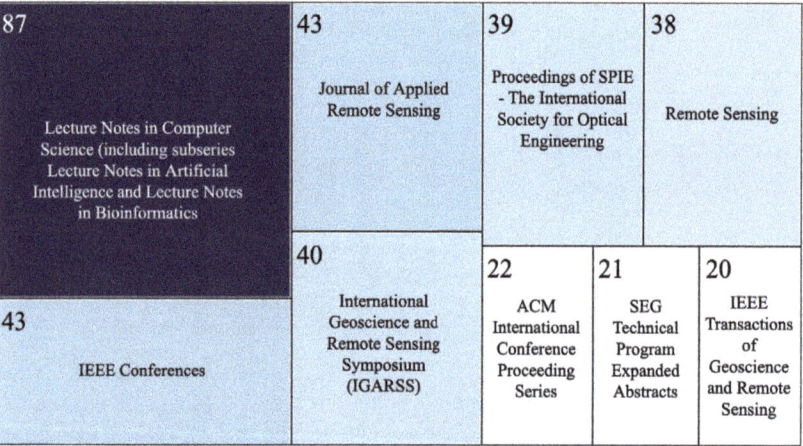

Figure 3. Treemap of the main publication sources from the filtered results.

Regarding the authors, there are three main insights that we have extracted: The authors with the highest number of publications, the ones that have been more productive in the years equal to or greater than 2020, and the ones with the most citations.

To identify the most productive authors, a plot was produced (see Figure 4) showcasing the ten authors with the most published works. As can be seen, the most productive author is Wang Y. (with 19 works), followed by Li X. (15 works) and Zhang Y. (14 works). Moreover, if the attention is shifted to the most productive authors in the years equal to or greater than 2020, Wang Y. remains the most published author, with eight works.

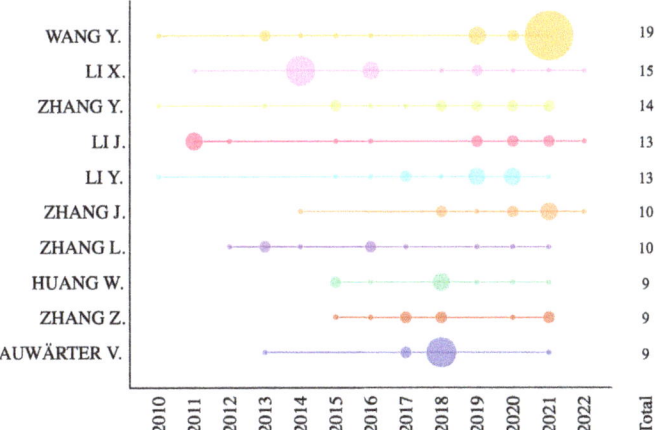

Figure 4. Most published authors. The y-axis represents the authors with the most publications by decreasing order—the total number of publications of each author is on the right. The x-axis represents the year of publication. The area of the circles is proportional to the number of publications of a given author in a given year.

Following this author is one of particular interest: Sergey I. Nikolenko, with six published works. His papers are of great interest as he writes about the early days of synthetic data, synthetic data for deep learning, and even where synthetic data is going. Moreover, he is the sole author of his published works and has also edited a book titled "Synthetic Data for Deep Learning", the text of which is based, to a considerable extent, on one of his published papers with the same name (this paper is cited at the beginning of Section 4, as it could not go unnoticed).

Interestingly enough, the authors mentioned previously are not the most cited ones. That place goes to Gupta A., Zisserman A., and Vedaldi A. with 676 citations each, followed by Alonso-Betanzos A., Sánchex-Maroño N., and Bolón-Canedo V., each with 392 citations. This happens because each triplet of authors has published a work that was heavily cited [11,12], respectively. Moreover, these are the most cited papers of the filtered results, and they are briefly described in a few lines.

To finish the authors' analysis, Table 2 contains information regarding the number of unique authors, the average number of authors per document, and a summary of the previous insights. It is interesting to note the high number of unique authors, 10,100, and that a typical paper has about four authors, on average.

Table 2. Authors' summary table.

Unique authors	10,100
Average number of authors per document	4.37
Most published works	Wang Y. (19 works) Li X. (15 works)
Most published works ($\geq$2020)	Wang Y. (6 works) Nikolenko S. I. (4 works)
Most cited	Gupta A., Zisserman A., Vedaldi A. (676 citations) Alonso A., Sánchex N., Bolón V. (392 citations)

As for the most cited publications from the filtered works, the top five are briefly described. In [11], the most cited publication, the authors generated synthetic images with text to improve text detection in natural images. In [12], a review of feature selection methods on synthetic data is presented (synthetic datasets with an increasing number of irrelevant features are generated to perform feature selection). Following these two works is [13], where a GAN is used to generate synthetic medical images to improve liver lesion classification (this work is at the top of Table 3). The next most cited paper, [14], concerns the field of remote sensing for forest biomass mapping and the importance of synthetic data in this field. Finally, in [15], the authors use synthetic data to improve seismic fault detection classification.

We have been looking for recent surveys on both synthetic data and GANs (since early 2019). Regarding the former topic, we found only one paper [16] in which the author (Nikolenko) explores the application of synthetic data outside of computer vision (currently the main area for synthetic data applications).

The latter topic is much more studied, as GANs have become increasingly important in recent years. Some of the papers focus on recent advances in GANs [17], others on the use of GANs in anomaly detection [18], or the challenges of GANs, solutions, and future directions [19]. These are not the only existing surveys concerning GANs, as this is not intended to be an exhaustive list. However, to the best of our knowledge, there is yet no work that explicitly combines and examines both topics. Therefore, this is intended to fill such a gap and provide helpful material to researchers interested in this area.

Graphical analysis was performed to identify the most common research areas, the institutions with the most publications, and those with the most citations. This analysis was performed using the Web of Sciences' results for two reasons. On the one hand, WoS is the only bibliographic database (out of the four used) that contains data on the research areas. On the other hand, institutions in the Scopus and IEEE Xplore databases are, in many cases, segmented by department, making the analysis quite difficult. However, the same does not happen in the returning records from the WoS database. In addition, the ACM Digital Library returned very few results compared to the other databases, so it is not representative of all the synthetic data research work.

When looking at the most common research areas (see Figure 5), Engineering and Computer Science are the most prominent, together accounting for about 45% of all publications. The fact that these two research areas are at the top is not surprising. However, it is interesting to note that, for example, Geology and Environmental Sciences and Ecology are the fifth and sixth most common research areas, which shows the widespread use of synthetic data in various fields.

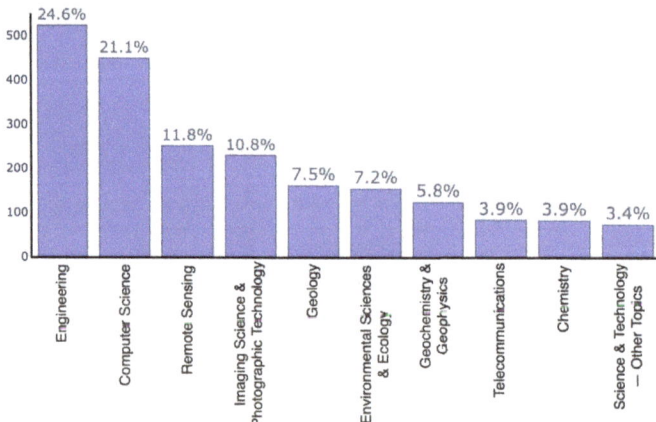

Figure 5. The top ten research areas of the filtered WoS results. The vertical axis represents the number of publications in a particular area. The percentages above the bars indicate the relative frequency of each area.

In what concerns the stronger institutions in terms of the number of publications and number of citations, two bar charts were constructed—see Figures 6 and 7. As can be seen from the plots, the most frequent institutions are from the United States—e.g., University of California, University of Texas, or NASA. As there are more institutions than research areas, the relative frequencies are smaller and closer to each other, so there is not an institution (or few institutions) that stands out as much as the research areas. Nonetheless, the University of California, the Chinese Academy of Sciences, and the CNRS are leading in terms of the number of publications and citations.

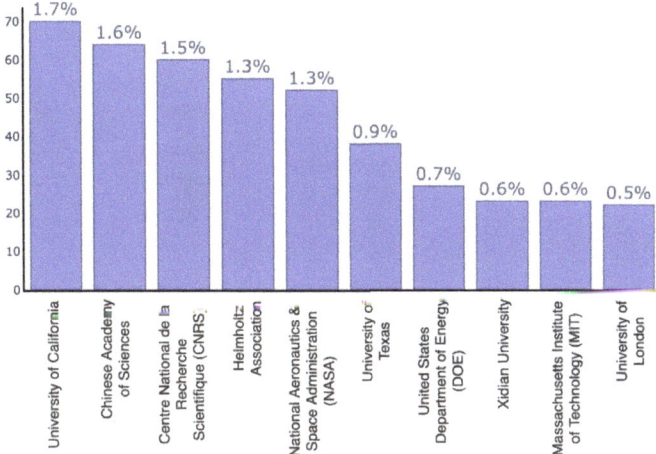

Figure 6. The institutions with the most publications from the WoS-filtered results. The vertical axis represents the number of publications. The percentages above the bars indicate the relative frequency of each institution in terms of publications.

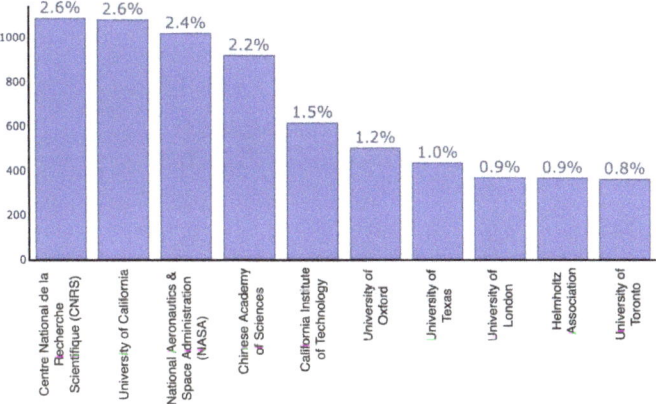

Figure 7. The institutions with more citations from the WoS-filtered results. The vertical axis represents the number of citations. The percentages above the bars indicate the relative frequency of each institution in terms of citations.

Since the main focus of this paper is to provide an overview of the literature concerning the generation of synthetic samples using GANs, a search of the most cited documents in the Web of Sciences bibliographic database on the above topic was carried out (the search was performed in the set of documents obtained after the filtering process—see Table 1). In Section 3, a comprehensive review of GANs and the most commonly used architectures are studied. Therefore, Table 3 can be supplemented by the next section.

It is interesting to note that most of the publications are from 2018 and 2019. We suspect that it took some time for GANs to mature and spread to different domains since they were first proposed in 2014. Thus, it is not far-fetched to imagine that GANs took about four years before a significant portion of the research community recognized their potential and began using them to generate synthetic data.

Table 3. Top 10 cited papers in the Web of Sciences database that use GANs.

Title	GAN Architecture	Dataset	Year	Citations
Synthetic Data Augmentation using GAN for Improved Liver Lesion Classification [13]	DCGAN	Computed tomography (CT) images of 182 liver lesions	2018	173
Learning from Synthetic Data for Crowd Counting in the Wild [20]	SSIM embedding (SE) Cycle GAN	GCC dataset, UCF CC 50, Shanghai Tech A/B, UCF-QNRF, WorldExpo'10	2019	94
Real-Time Monocular Depth Estimation using Synthetic Data with Domain Adaptation via Image Style Transfer [21]	DCGAN	KITTI, Make3D	2018	53
A Small-Sample Wind Turbine Fault Detection Method with Synthetic Fault Data using Generative Adversarial Nets [22]	CGAN	Wind turbine data collected from a wind farm in northern China	2019	44
Synthetic Data Generation for End-to-End Thermal Infrared Tracking [23]	CycleGAN, Pix2pix	KAIST, CVC-14, OSU Color Thermal, OTB, VAP Trimodal, Bilodeau, LITIV2012, VOT2016, VOT2017, ASL, Long-termInfAR	2019	40
Pixel-Wise Crowd Understanding via Synthetic Data [24]	SE CycleGAN	GCC dataset, UCF CC 50, Shanghai Tech A/B, UCF-QNRF	2021	33
Learning Semantic Segmentation from Synthetic Data: A Geometrically Guided Input-Output Adaptation Approach [25]	PatchGAN	KITTI, Virtual KITTI, SYNTHIA Cityscapes	2019	25
DeepSynth: Three-dimensional Nuclear Segmentation of Biological Images using Neural Networks Trained with Synthetic Data [26]	Spatially Constrained (SP) CycleGAN	3D biological images	2019	23
Autoencoder-Combined Generative Adversarial Networks for Synthetic Image Data Generation and Detection of Jellyfish Swarm [27]	GAN	Jellyfish images	2018	13
DP-CGAN: Differentially Private Synthetic Data and Label Generation [28]	Differentially Private Conditional GAN (DP-CGAN)	MNIST	2019	10

Unfortunately, the filtered documents lack some important works, both in terms of GAN architectures and synthetic data generation methods. Therefore, a snowballing procedure based on the references of the filtered results as well as the existing background knowledge of the authors was used to find and add relevant papers—in total, 62 extra works were found and added. These are explored in the following sections.

3. Generative Adversarial Networks

Generative adversarial networks (GANs)are a framework that uses an adversarial process to estimate generative deep learning models, proposed by Ian J. Goodfellow et al. [8] in 2014. These structures have been adapted and improved over the last years and are now very powerful. GANs are currently capable of painting, writing, composing, and playing, as we will see in this section.

Therefore, GANs are first analyzed in more detail in Section 3.1 to reveal how they work. In Section 3.2, the main training difficulties and their solutions are examined. Finally, in Section 3.3, the main GAN architectures are shown to demonstrate their capabilities, while in Section 3.4, GANs for tabular data are presented.

3.1. GANs under the Hood

A GAN is constituted by two models: a generator model G that tries to generate samples that follow the underlying distribution of the data. Nonetheless, these observations are suitably different from the ones in the dataset (i.e., they should not simply reproduce observations that already occur in the dataset). There is also a discriminator model D that, given an observation (from the original dataset or synthesized by the generator), classifies it as fake (produced by the generator) (Typically, the models used for the generator and discriminator are neural networks. As such, we normally refer to G and D as networks. However, in theory, the models need not be a neural network. Indeed, in [8], the term "model" is used. Nonetheless, they note that the "adversarial modeling framework is most straightforward to apply when the models are both multi-layer perceptrons") or real. An important thing to consider is that G and D compete against each other. While G generates similar data points to those in the original data, with the aim of deceiving the discriminator, D attempts to distinguish the generated from the real observations.

To describe in more detail how the networks are trained, the training was split into the training of the discriminator and of the generator separately. Training the discriminator consists of creating a dataset with instances generated by G and data points from the original dataset. The discriminator outputs a probability (continuous value between 0 and 1) that indicates whether a given observation came from the original data (0 means that the discriminator is 100% certain that the given example was synthesized, while 1 means the exact opposite).

The training of the generator is more complicated. G is given as the input random noise (The term *latent space* is typically used to designate G's input space.), commonly from a multivariate normal distribution, and the output is a data point with the same features of the original dataset. However, there is no dataset to inform whether a particular point in the latent space is mapped by G into a reasonable or useful example. Therefore, the generator is only provided with a value from a loss function. This is usually the binary cross-entropy (The binary cross-entropy is mathematically defined as follows $-\frac{1}{n}\sum_{i=1}^{n} y_i log(p_i) + (1 - y_i)log(1 - p_i)$ where y_i represents the label of an input sample, p_i is the probability of y_i coming from the original data, and n is the number of examples. It is a measure of the difference between the ground truth and the computed probabilities, and it is used in the case where there are only two possible outcomes—the observation came from the original data or it was synthesized by the generator) between D's output and a response vector of 1's (the instances synthesized by G are all marked as coming from the original data).

Given the discriminator's feedback, i.e., the value of the loss function, the generator attempts to improve to better fool the discriminator. As training progresses, G uses D's output to generate better examples, i.e., examples that better resemble the real data distribution. As the data produced by G becomes more realistic, D also improves so that it can better determine whether a sample is real or synthetic. As such, both networks improve each other and, ideally, G will be able to mimic the data distribution, and D will be $\frac{1}{2}$ everywhere, i.e., the probability that D distinguishes between a real observation and a generated one is as good as a random guess. In this ideal scenario, G has succeeded in recovering the distribution of the original data, completely fooling D. A GAN diagram is shown in Figure 8.

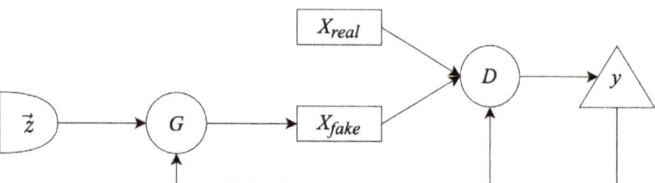

Figure 8. A GAN diagram. G is given random noise $\vec{z}$, usually from a multivariate normal distribution, to generate a set of data points, X_{fake}. D is provided with both the original data, X_{real} and the generated data. D outputs a label y, denoting if a given observation is fake (was produced by G) or real (came from the original data).

3.2. Main Drawbacks

Although plain vanilla GANs—that is, the GANs in their simplest form, as we have been explaining—are quite strong ideas, they also have disadvantages. Namely, GANs are extremely difficult to train due to a number of factors that include the loss function, hyperparameters, or a generator that can easily fool the discriminator.

Oscillatory loss (instability) is a common problem that occurs during the training process. It is characterized by wild oscillations of the discriminator's and generator's loss, which should be stable over the long term. For the training process to be effective, the loss should stabilize or gradually increase/decrease over the long term. Unfortunately, in many cases, this is not what happens. Another problem with the loss function is the lack of information it usually provides (uninformative loss). For example, a commonly used generator's loss function is the binary cross entropy. This is a disadvantage because there is no correlation between the generator's loss and the quality of the output (not only in the specific case of the binary cross entropy). Hence, the training is sometimes difficult to monitor.

Another fairly common phenomenon is that the generator finds a small number of samples that fool the discriminator—this is called mode collapse. Having found such samples, the generator will focus only on them to minimize its loss function, while the discriminator remains confused during training because it cannot distinguish whether the instances are real or synthetic. Therefore, the generator is not able to produce other examples than this limited set. Figure 9 shows an example of mode collapse in a toy dataset.

Moreover, GANs have a significant number of hyperparameters. Thus, to create a well-performing GAN, a large number of hyperparameters must be tuned. It is possible to use grid search, but only for a limited subset of hyperparameters. Otherwise, the training time will be considerably long and the resource consumption extremely high.

Finally, there is the vanishing gradient problem, which may completely stop the GAN from further training, given that the gradients can be extremely small and not allow the weights to be updated further. This can occur if the discriminator is close to optimal, which allows it to accurately discern generated samples from real ones and causes the generator's train to fail.

These are the five most common problems encountered in GAN training—oscillating loss, mode collapse, uninformative loss, vanishing gradients, and hyperparameter-tuning. The above problems are broad and independent of domain and architecture. That is, they attempt to cover the range of possible GAN training drawbacks without being too specific about the loss-function or hyperparameters used (broad); they do not depend on the particular domain, whether it is live cell images or a tabular dataset of bank fraud (domain-agnostic); and finally, they do not depend on a particular GAN architecture (architecture-agnostic).

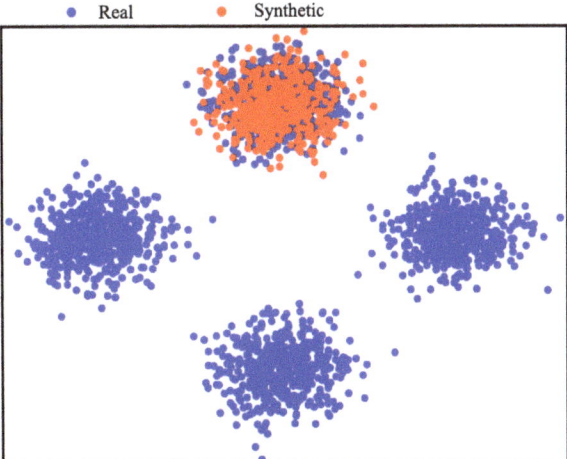

Figure 9. Graphical representation of mode collapse in a toy dataset consisting of random samples drawn from four Gaussian distributions with the same covariance matrix but different means (visible by the four separate clusters). The blue points correspond to real data points, whereas the red ones are synthesized by the generator. The generator has found a small number of samples (the ones in the upper cluster), so it does not learn beyond that. It will continue to produce samples in that range without seeing the overall distribution of the data, as it is enough to fool the discriminator.

3.3. GANs Come in a Lot of Flavours

Since GANs were proposed, many researchers have considered them a powerful tool. As a result, they have been systematically modified and improved. The architecture of a GAN can be very problem-specific, and they are often modified or fine-tuned to serve a particular purpose. Hence, the literature on them is quite extensive, and thus, only the main highlights are shown in this paper. In the following paragraphs, the GAN architectures are arranged chronologically by year (in ascending order, i.e., earlier years are shown first), so two architectures created in the same year may not be arranged by month. Nonetheless, this can show the evolution of GANs up to the time of writing (February 2022).

Conditional Generative Adversarial Network, CGAN, is a GAN variant proposed by Mehdi Mirza and Simon Osindero in [29]. Suppose one is using a vanilla GAN on an image dataset with multiple class labels (e.g., the ImageNet dataset). The GAN has been properly trained and is ready to generate synthetic samples. However, it cannot sample an image of the desired class. For example, if one wants synthetic images of cars (assuming that images of cars were used in the training data), one cannot force a vanilla GAN to do so. This happens because there is no control over the latent space representation. That is, the GAN maps point from latent space to the original domain, but the features in the latent space are not interpretable by the user. As such, one does not know from which range of points to sample in order to produce examples of a certain class. This is an obvious disadvantage of using GANs in labeled datasets. An interesting idea is to make the GAN dependent on a class label, which allows generated data to be conditioned on class labels. That is, given a labeled dataset, the CGAN is trained using the data instances and their respective labels. Once trained, the model can generate examples that depend on a class label selected by the user. For example, if a hypothetical dataset has three classes—"low", "medium", "high"—the CGAN is trained with both the instances and their associated labels. After the learning process is complete, the user can choose to generate samples of only "low" and "high" classes by specifying the desired label. A diagram representing a CGAN is shown in Figure 10.

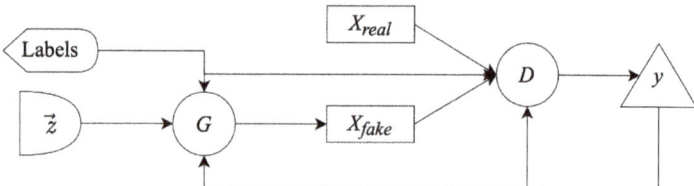

Figure 10. A diagram of a CGAN. The CGAN is similar to a vanilla GAN (see Figure 8), but the generator, G, and the discriminator, D, are conditioned on class labels.

Despite the importance of CGAN, with its clear advantage of being able to draw a sample from a user-selected class, back in 2014, the generation of synthetic images had a lot of room for improvement. As such, a growing number of GAN architectures focused on image generation were proposed in the following years.

Deep Convolutional Generative Adversarial Network, DCGAN, is a GAN architecture that combines convolutional layers (A convolutional layer is a layer that uses a convolution operation. A convolution, in terms of computer vision tasks, consists of a filter (represented by a matrix) that slides through the image pixels (also represented by a matrix) and performs matrix multiplication. This is useful in computer vision tasks because applying different filters to an image (by means of a convolution) can help, for example, detect edges, blur the image, or even remove noise), which are commonly used in computer vision tasks, with GANs. Radford et al., in [30], have brought together the success of Convolutional Neural Networks (CNNs) in supervised learning tasks with the then emerging GANs. Nowadays, the use of convolutional layers in GANs for image generation is quite common, but at that time, 2016, this was not the case. Therefore, the use of convolutional layers in the GAN structure is still a powerful tool for handling image data.

Thus, the DCGAN was able to enhance the generated images by using convolutional layers. However, the features in the latent space had no semantic meaning. That is, it was not possible to change the values of a feature in latent space and predict what that change would do to the image (e.g., rotation, widening).

Information Maximizing Generative Adversarial Network, InfoGAN, is a GAN extension proposed by Chen et al. in [31], that attempts to learn disentangled information. That is, to give semantic meaning to features in the latent space (see Figure 11). InfoGAN can successfully recognize writing styles from handwritten digits in the MNIST dataset, detect hairstyles or eyeglasses in the CelebA dataset, or even background digits from the central digit in the SVHN dataset.

The GAN architectures presented so far can be quite time-consuming and use a high amount of computing resources to train. Given a large number of hyperparameters and a large number of training samples, the training process could be prohibitively expensive due to the training time and resources required.

Coupled Generative Adversarial Networks, CoGAN, proposed in [32] by Ming-Yu Liu and Oncel Tuzel, use a pair of GANs instead of only one GAN. The CoGAN was used to learn the joint distribution of multi-domain images, which was achieved by the weight-sharing constraint between the two GANs. In addition, sharing weights requires fewer parameters than two individual GANs, which, in turn, results in less memory consumption, less computational power, and fewer resources.

The focus on image generation continued, and in 2016, the AC-GAN and the StackGAN architectures were introduced to provide improvements in synthetic image generation.

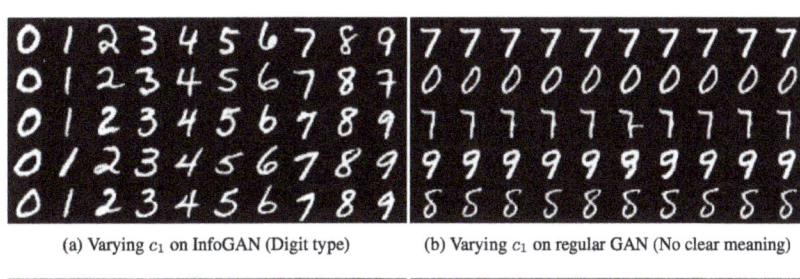

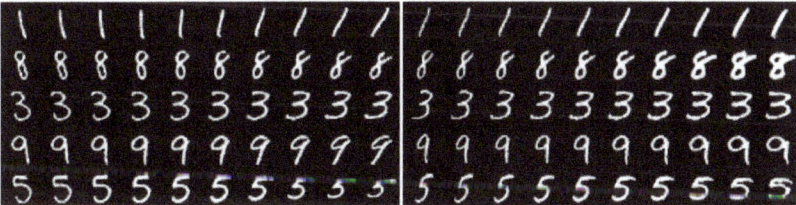

(a) Varying c_1 on InfoGAN (Digit type) (b) Varying c_1 on regular GAN (No clear meaning)

(c) Varying c_2 from -2 to 2 on InfoGAN (Rotation) (d) Varying c_3 from -2 to 2 on InfoGAN (Width)

Figure 11. The semantic meaning InfoGAN adds to the latent variables in the MNIST dataset. In (**a**), varying the latent variable c_1 leads to a digit change (from 0 to 9), while in (**b**), a regular GAN does not add meaning to its latent variables. In (**c**), the variation of c_2 leads to the rotation of digits. Finally, in (**d**), variation c_3 controls the width of the digits. Image taken from [31].

Auxiliary Classifier Generative Adversarial Network, **AC-GAN** [33], is a GAN extension proposed by Odena et al. that modifies the generator to be class dependent (it takes class labels into account) and adds an auxiliary model to the discriminator whose purpose is to reconstruct the class label. The results in [33] show that such an architecture can generate globally coherent samples that are comparable, in diversity, to those of the ImageNet dataset (see Figure 12).

Figure 12. Images of five distinct classes generated by the AC-GAN. Nowadays, the detail in the images is far superior to the one provided by the AC-GAN. Image taken from [33].

Stacked Generative Adversarial Network, **StackGAN**, proposed in [34] by Zhang et al., is another extension of GANs that can generate images from text descriptions. This generation of photorealistic images is decomposed into two parts. First, the STAGE-I GAN sketches a primitive shape and colors based on the input text. Next, the Stage-II GAN uses the same text description as the STAGE-I GAN and its output as input and generates high-resolution images by refining the output images by STAGE-I GAN. Their work has led to significant improvements in image generation.

Despite improving the quality of the generated images, adding semantic meaning to the latent features, and reducing memory consumption and training time, the training itself was still difficult due to mode collapse and uninformative loss metrics.

Wasserstein Generative Adversarial Networks, WGAN, is an alternative to traditional GAN training. The WGAN proposed by Arjovsky et al. in [35] is a GAN extension that modifies the training phase such that the discriminator, called the critic, is updated more often than the generator at each iteration i, where i is defined by the user. This change to GAN training avoids mode collapse and provides a meaningful loss metric that correlates with the generator's convergence and sample quality.

Returning to image generation, an interesting idea is to transfer an image from one area to another. For example, let us take a landscape image and "merge it" with an image of a Monet painting so that the landscape image has the style of a Monet painting.

Cycle-Consistent Generative Adversarial Network, CycleGAN, is a GAN extension for image-to-image translation without paired data. Zhu et al. proposed, in [36], an approach to translate an image from a domain X to a domain Y when no paired images are available. The CycleGAN consists of two generators, G and F, and two discriminators, D_X and D_Y. G maps an image from X to Y, and D_Y tries to determine whether it is from the original dataset or synthesized. Similarly, F maps an image from Y to X, and D_X determines whether it is real or generated by F. In addition to the four networks, the cycle consistency loss metric was also introduced to ensure that translating an image from X to Y and then from Y to X yields a very similar image to the original one. Figure 13 shows the image-to-image translation capabilities of CycleGAN.

Figure 13. Given any two image collections, the CycleGAN learns to automatically "translate" an image from one domain into the other and vice versa. Example application (bottom): using a collection of paintings of famous artists, the CycleGAN renders a user's photograph in their style. Image taken from [36].

To date, GAN architectures have focused on image generation and translation, training stabilization, and time or have been tied to class labels. Nonetheless, there is an interesting application of GANs to music generation.

Multi-track sequential GAN, MuseGAN, proposed by Dong et al. in [37] is a GAN architecture for music generation. This is quite different from generating images or videos since music has a temporal dimension, is usually composed of multiple instruments, and musical notes are often grouped into chords. Although the music generated is not as good as that produced by professional musicians, the results were quite promising, and the MuseGAN model had some interesting properties.

In late 2017 and throughout 2018, the quality of image-generated data improved greatly with the introduction of ProGAN, SAGAN, and BigGAN architectures.

Progressive growing of Generative Adversarial Networks, ProGAN, is a technique that helps stabilize GAN training by progressively increasing the resolution of generated images. Proposed in [38] by Karras et al., the ProGAN accelerates and stabilizes training by, first, constructing a generator and a discriminator that produce images with few pixels.

Then, layers corresponding to higher resolutions are added in the training process, allowing the creation of high-quality images. Figure 14 shows images generated with the ProGAN.

Figure 14. Images generated using ProGAN. Notice the level of detail when compared to the ones generated from AC-GAN (Figure 12). Image taken from [38].

Self-Attention Generative Adversarial Networks, also known as SAGAN, improve on previous GAN structures by maintaining long-range relationships within an image rather than just local points [39]. Zhang et al. have found that using spectral normalization improves the training dynamics of the generator. In addition, the discriminator can assess whether highly detailed features in distant image regions match each other. When this architecture was proposed, the authors were able to improve both the Inception Score [40] and the Fréchet Inception Distance[41] (two widely used metrics to evaluate synthetic image data) on the ImageNet dataset.

Big Generative Adversarial Network, **BigGAN**, proposed by Brock et al. [42], is a type of GAN architecture that upscales existing GAN models and produces high-quality images (see Figure 15). BigGAN has also demonstrated how to train GANs at a large scale by introducing techniques that detect training instability. At the time of BigGAN's introduction, its performance was significantly better than that of other state-of-the-art structures.

Figure 15. Class-conditional samples generated by BigGAN. Image taken from [42].

As seen previously, the image quality has improved considerably (compare Figure 12 with Figures 14 and 15, for example). However, there were still some limitations in the images generated. Although the GAN architectures provided extremely realistic images, it was still difficult to understand various aspects of the image synthesis process [43].

Style-based Generative Adversarial Networks, **StyleGAN**, proposed by Karras et al. in [43], explores an alternative generator architecture based on style transfer. The focus is not on generating more realistic images but on having better control over the generated image. This new architecture is able to learn to separate high-level features and stochastic variation. In fact, the new generator improves the quality metrics over the state-of-the-art, untangles the latent variables better, and has better interpolation properties.

Two other different ideas than those shown so far, but also very interesting, were proposed in 2019. The first is about turning a user's sketch into a realistic image. The second is about automatically completing an incomplete image in a plausible way.

GauGAN [44], a model proposed by NVIDIA Research that allows users to sketch an abstract scene and then turn it into a detailed image. Users can also manipulate the scene and label each element. This is achieved through the use of a spatially-adaptive normalization layer whose purpose is to aid in the generation of photorealistic images when a semantic layout is given as input.

Pluralistic Image Inpainting GAN, **PiiGAN**, proposed by Weiwei Cai and Zhanguo Wei [45], attempts to fill in large missing areas in an image. Unlike other Deep Learning methods that try to achieve a single optimal result, PiiGAN has a new style extractor that is able to extract the style features from the original images. As shown in [45], PiiGAN can produce images of better quality and greater variety than other state-of-the-art architectures that match the context semantics of the original image. Figure 16 shows the capabilities of PiiGAN.

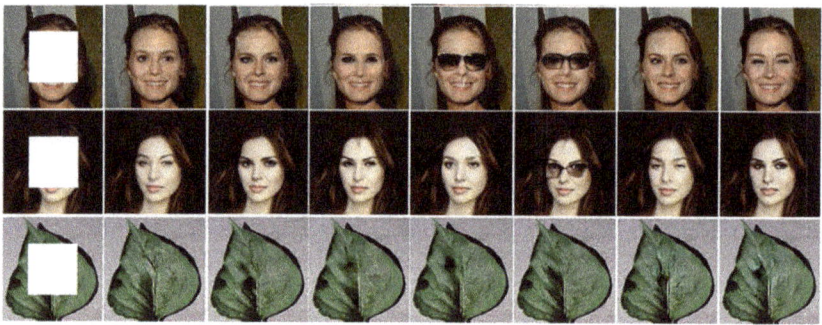

Figure 16. Examples of inpainting results produced by PiiGAN on two faces and a leaf. On the left column is the input image (with the center pixels removed). The images in the remaining columns are outputs of the PiiGAN. Image taken from [45].

A more recent architecture, introduced in 2021, is the Multy-StyleGAN, which highlights the capabilities of GANs in various image domains—in this case, biology.

Multi-StyleGAN, proposed by Prangemeier et al. [46], is a novel GAN architecture used to study the dynamic processes of life at the level of single cells. Since acquiring images to study such processes is costly and complex, the Multi-StyleGAN is a descriptive approach that simulates microscopic images of living cells. As shown by the authors, the proposed architecture is capable of capturing the underlying biophysical factors and temporal dependencies.

As shown in the previous paragraphs, the major breakthroughs of GANs are focused on imaging generation. Despite their enormous success in this area, GANs can be used in other areas as well. As can be seen in Section 3.1, there are no restrictions on whether the dataset must be an image, a video, music, or an ordinary tabular dataset. Nonetheless, different types of architectures must be considered depending on the task. Image data does not have the same characteristics as music or tabular data, so different types of layers, activation functions, or training procedures must be selected accordingly. That being said, there are some best practices that can be used depending on the data at hand, but the architecture of a GAN currently seems to be as much an art as a science. In the next subsection, we take a closer look at three GAN structures used to generate tabular data.

3.4. GANs for Tabular Data

As seen in Section 3.3, GANs are widely and successfully used for image generation tasks. However, many datasets have a tabular format, and the most popular GAN architectures cannot be used in such a setting because tabular data has unique properties.

First, continuous and categorical features are present in most tabular datasets. Since image data consists solely of numerical features (the pixels), GANs used for image generation tasks cannot accommodate the different types of variables. Second, non-Gaussian and multimodal distributions are quite common in tabular datasets. Numerical features in tabular data may have multiple modes and follow a non-Gaussian distribution, which must be considered when generating synthetic data. Third, highly imbalanced categorical variables are common. This can lead to severe mode-collapse and insufficient training for the minority classes. Finally, it is easier for a trivial discriminator to distinguish between real and fake data when it learns from sparse one-hot-encoded vectors since it takes into account the sparsity of the distribution rather than checking the overall authenticity of the sample.

In the following sections, we detail three important GAN architectures used to overcome the above problems. The TGAN architecture was introduced in 2018, followed by the CTGAN architecture in 2019, which is an evolution of the TGAN architecture and was proposed by the same authors. This was followed in 2021 by the TabFairGAN, which was intended to dethrone the two aforementioned GANs in terms of the quality of synthetic tabular data generation. We believe the detailed explanations that follow can shed some light on a topic that is as not as well disseminated in the literature, as far as we are aware—the use of GANs to generate tabular data rather than image data.

3.4.1. TGAN

TGAN was proposed in 2018 by Lei Xu and Kalyan Veeramachaneni [47] as a GAN architecture for synthesizing tabular data. Given a dataset, D, which is already split into trainset, D_{train}, and testset, D_{test}, the aim of the TGAN is twofold: given a machine learning model, its accuracy on D_{test} when trained on the D_{train} should be similar to its accuracy, also on D_{test}, but when trained using D_{synth}, which is the synthetic data (machine learning efficacy); the mutual information between each pair of columns in D and D_{synth} should be similar.

To achieve these goals, first, it is important to transform the data. A GAN usually consists of two neural networks, so it is crucial to properly represent the data before feeding it as input. This problem is addressed by applying mode-specific normalization for numerical variables and smoothing for categorical variables.

Mode-specific normalization is used to handle non-Gaussian and multimodal distributions. It fits a Gaussian mixture model (GMM), which models a distribution as a weighted sum of Gaussian distributions to each numerical variable and calculates the probability that a sample from a numerical column comes from each of the Gaussian distributions. These probabilities are then used to encode the values of the rows corresponding to the numerical features. More formally, let $\{N_1, N_2, \ldots, N_p\}$ represent the numerical columns of a tabular dataset D. A GMM with m components is fitted to each numerical variable, N_i. The means and standard deviations of the m Gaussian distribution are represented by $\mu_i^{(1)}, \mu_i^{(2)}, \ldots, \mu_i^{(m)}$ and $\sigma_i^{(1)}, \sigma_i^{(2)}, \ldots, \sigma_i^{(m)}$, respectively. The probability of $x_{i,j}$ (the value at row i and column j) coming from each of the m Gaussian distributions is given by a vector $u_{i,j}^{(1)}, u_{i,j}^{(2)}, \ldots, u_{i,j}^{(m)}$. Finally, $x_{i,j}$ is normalized as $v_{i,j} = \frac{x_{i,j} - \mu_i^{(k)}}{2\sigma_i^{(k)}}$, where $k = argmax_k u_{i,j}^{(k)}$ and $v_{i,j}$ is clipped to $[-0.99, 0.99]$, and u_i, v_i are used to encode x_i.

Smoothing of the categorical variables is achieved by representing them as one-hot-encoded vectors, adding noise to each dimension (drawn from a uniform distribution), and renormalizing the vector. After applying mode-specific normalization to the numerical columns and smoothing the categorical ones, the data are ready to be fed into the TGAN. The generator is a Long-Short Term Memory (LSTM) network that generates the numeric variables in two steps (In the first step, v_i is generated, and u_i is generated in the second step) and the categorical variables in one step. A fully connected neural network is used as the discriminator. A diagram of a TGAN is shown in Figure 17.

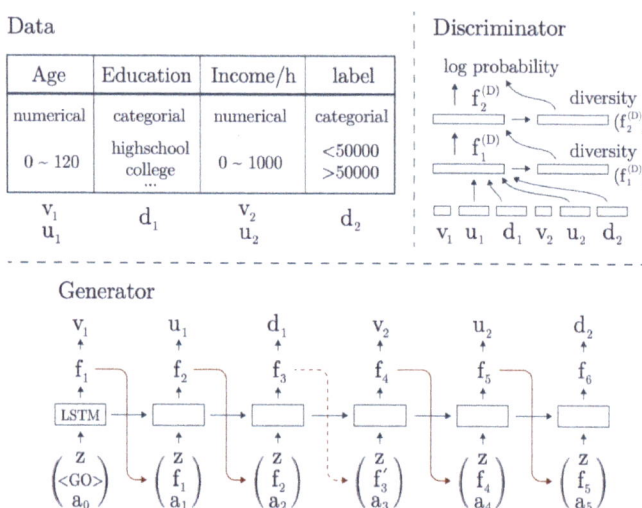

Figure 17. Diagram of a TGAN used in a toy example with 2 continuous and 2 discrete variables. Image taken from [47].

The TGAN was evaluated, in [47], with respect to machine learning efficacy and the preservation of correlation (the two aforementioned aims of the TGAN) and compared with other data synthesis models. Regarding machine learning efficacy, five models were evaluated in terms of accuracy and Macro-F1, namely, Decision Trees, Linear Support Vector Machines, Random Forests, AdaBoost, and Multi-Layer Perceptrons, on three different datasets. It was found that while the machine learning models generally performed better when trained on the real dataset, the average performance difference between the real and synthetic data was 5.7%. This suggests that the TGAN performs quite well (The authors compared the TGAN with a Gaussian Copula (GC) and a Bayesian Network (BN-Co), which showed a drop in performance of 24.9% and 43.3%, respectively). Moreover, the TGAN was able to maintain the ranking of the ML models. As for the preservation of correlation between any two pairs of variables, the TGAN was able to successfully capture this correlation.

3.4.2. CTGAN

The CTGAN, also proposed by Lei Xu and Kaylan Veeramachaneni et al. [48] in 2019, is an improvement over TGAN. The objectives of CTGAN are almost the same as those of TGAN. The difference is that CTGAN is more ambitious, and instead of just preserving the correlation between any pair of columns in the synthetic data, it aims to preserve the joint distribution of all columns.

As for the transformations of the input data, they are similar to those presented for the TGAN model. To transform the numerical columns, a variational Gaussian mixture model (VGM) is used instead of a GMM. The difference is that the VGM estimates the number of modes for each numerical column, unlike in the TGAN, where the number of modes is predefined and is the same for each numerical column. In addition, the continuous values are represented as a one-hot vector indicating the mode and a scalar indicating the value within the mode (e.g., if the VGM has an estimated three modes and a given value $x_{i,j}$ has a greater probability of coming from mode 2, then the one-hot-encoded vector would be

$\vec{\beta} = (0, 1, 0)$ and the value within the mode would be given by $a_{i,j} = \frac{x_{i,j} - \mu_2}{4\sigma_2}$, where μ_2 is the mean of the Gaussian distribution corresponding to the second mode, and σ_2 its standard deviation). The categorical features are only one-hot-encoded without adding noise.

To allow the CTGAN to deal with unbalanced discrete columns, the authors used a conditional generator that can generate synthetic rows that depend on any of the discrete columns. Further, a technique called training by sampling was proposed, allowing the CTGAN to uniformly examine all possible discrete values.

To integrate the conditional generator in the GAN architecture, it is necessary to properly prepare the input. This is accomplished by using a conditional vector, which specifies that a given categorical column must be equal to a certain value (from the set of the possible values for that particular column). Further, the generator loss is modified so that it learns to map the conditional vector into the one-hot-encoded values. The conditional vector consists of a simple transformation to the one-hot-encoded vectors. Supposing that a dataset with 3 discrete columns, $D_1 = \{0, 1, 2\}, D_2 = \{0, 1\}, D_3 = \{0, 1, 2\}$, is given, and the condition that is indicated is $D_2 = 1$, the conditional vector would be

$$\vec{cond} = (\underbrace{0, 0, 0}_{D_1}, \underbrace{0, 1}_{D_2}, \underbrace{0, 0, 0}_{D_3})$$

where the first three entries correspond to the one-hot-representation of D_1, the fourth and fifth entries correspond to the one-hot representation of D_2, and the last three entries correspond to the one-hot representation of D_3. The conditional generator is then forced to map the conditional vector into the one-hot-encoded ones by adding the cross entropy to its loss function.

Training by sampling is a technique that ensures that the conditional vector is properly sampled so that the CTGAN can uniformly examine all possible values in discrete columns. This is performed by randomly selecting a discrete column, constructing the probability mass function over the possible values for the selected column (the probability mass of each value is the logarithm of its frequency), and only then computing the conditional vector. A diagram of a CTGAN is shown in Figure 18 (the conditional generator and the discriminator are both fully-connected networks).

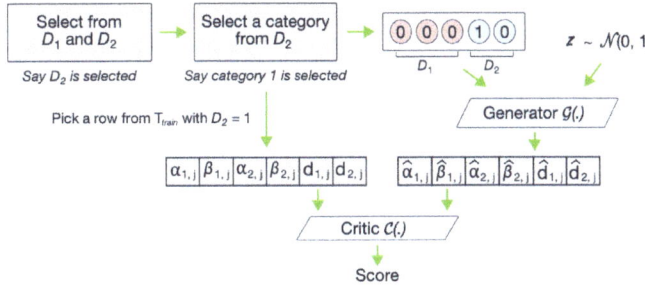

Figure 18. Diagram of a CTGAN. Image taken from [48].

To evaluate the CTGAN, the authors in [48] have used seven simulated datasets and eight real datasets. In the simulated datasets, the likelihood fitness metric was computed to evaluate performance, which is possible since the distribution of the data is known. In what concerns the real datasets, the machine learning efficacy was used to evaluate performance (it is not possible to compute the likelihood fitness metric in real datasets because the distribution of the data is unknown). The CTGAN was also compared with other generative models, namely CLBN [49], PrivBN [50], MedGAN [51], VeeGAN [52], and TableGAN [53]. It was found that in real datasets, the CTGAN outperformed all other models in terms of machine learning efficacy. In simulated datasets, the CTGAN performed quite well in terms of the likelihood fitness metric, although it was not able to outperform all other models.

Finally, an ablation study was conducted with the goal of evaluating the utility of mode-specific normalization, conditional generator, and training by sampling. The results showed that if the mode-specific normalization was replaced by either a Gaussian mixture model with five modes (GMM5), a GMM10 or a min-max normalization, the losses in performance (regarding machine learning efficacy) in the real datasets would be of −4.1%, −8.6%, and −25.7%, respectively. In what concerns the training by sampling, if removed, the performance would decrease by 17.8%. If the conditional generator was removed, the performance would drop by 36.5%. Therefore, the techniques introduced in CTGAN, namely, mode-specific normalization, training by sampling, and the conditional generator, are very important for generating high-quality tabular data.

3.4.3. TabFairGAN

TabFairGAN, proposed in 2021 by Amirarsalan Rajabi and Ozlem Ozmen Garibay [54], is a WGAN with a gradient penalty. As with TGAN and CTGAN, it is crucial to represent the data correctly before entering it as input to the TabFairGAN. Thus, Rajabi and Garibay used one-hot-encoding to represent the categorical features. A quantile transformation was used for the numerical features:

$$c'_i = \Phi^{-1}(F(c_i))$$

where c_i is the ith numerical feature, F is the cumulative distribution function (CDF) of the feature c_i, and Φ is the CDF of a uniform distribution.

In what concerns the network structure, the generator is formally described as:

$$\begin{cases} h_0 = z \\ h_1 = ReLU(FC_{l_w \to l_w}(h_0)) \\ h_2 = ReLU(FC_{l_w \to N_c}(h_1)) \oplus gumbel_{0.2}(FC_{l_w \to l_1}(h_1)) \oplus \\ \quad gumbel_{0.2}(FC_{l_w \to l_2}(h_1)) \oplus \ldots \oplus gumbel_{0.2}(FC_{l_w \to N_d}(h_1)) \end{cases}$$

where z is a latent variable drawn from a standard multivariate normal distribution, $ReLU$ is the rectified linear unit activation function, $FC_{a \to b}$ denotes a fully connected layer with input size a and output size b, l_w is the dimension of an input sample, N_c is the number of numerical columns, N_d is the number of categorical columns, l_i is the dimension of the one-hot-encoded vector of the ith categorical column, $\oplus$ denotes the concatenation of vectors, and $gumbel_\tau$ is the Gumbel softmax with parameter τ (a continuous distribution that approximates samples from a categorical distribution and uses backpropagation).

In what concerns the critic (discriminator), its architecture can be formally described as follows:

$$\begin{cases} h_0 = X \\ h_1 = LeakyReLU_{0.01}(FC_{l_w \to l_w}(h_0)) \\ h_2 = LeakyReLU_{0.01}(FC_{l_w \to l_w}(h_1)) \end{cases}$$

Here X denotes the output of the generator or the transformed real data, and $LeakyReLU_\tau$ represents the leaky rectified linear unit activation function with slope τ. Figure 19 shows a diagram of the TabFairGAN. An initial fully connected layer (with $ReLU$ activation) constitutes the generator, followed by a second layer that uses $ReLU$ for numerical attributes and Gumbel softmax for one-hot-encoding of the categorical features. In the last layer, all the attributes are concatenated, producing the final generated data. The critic is constituted by fully connected layers with the $LeakyReLU$ activation function.

TabFairGAN was evaluated in terms of machine learning efficacy (the F1-score and accuracy metrics were used) using three machine learning models, namely, decision trees, logistic regression, and multi-layer perceptron (MLP) in the UCI Adult Income Dataset. The results were compared with two other state-of-the-art models, the TGAN and the CTGAN. TabFairGAN was found to perform better than TGAN and CTGAN on all machine learning models and metrics used, with the exception of MLP, where CTGAN performed better than TabFairGAN in terms of accuracy (but not in the F1-score). Hence, the TabFairGAN is quite effective in generating data similar to the real tabular data.

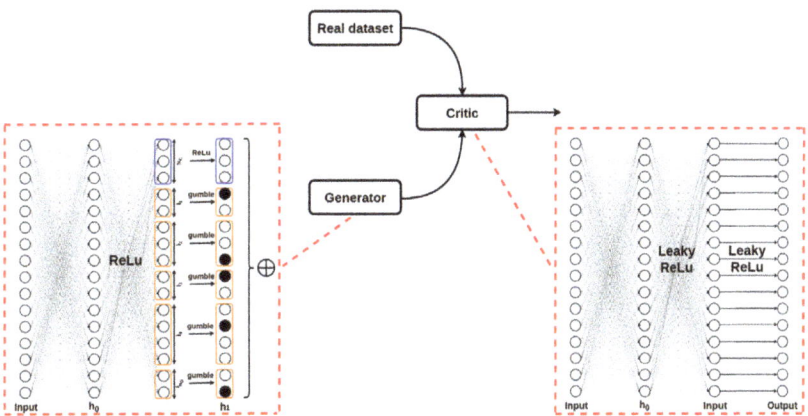

Figure 19. TabFairGAN architecture. Image taken from [54].

4. Methods for the Generation of Synthetic Samples

Synthetic data are artificially generated from real data and have the same statistical properties as real data. However, unlike real data, which are measured or collected in the real world, synthetic data are generated by computer algorithms [1,55].

According to [1], synthetic data can be generated from real data, from existing models, using expert domain knowledge, or from a mixture of these options. Synthetic samples generated from real data are obtained by creating a model that captures the properties (distribution, correlation between variables, etc.) of the real data. Once the model is created, it is used to sample synthetic data.

Synthetic data generated from existing models consist of instances generated from statistical models (mathematical models that have statistical assumptions about how the data are generated) or from simulations (e.g., game engines that create images from objects). The use of domain-specific knowledge can also be used to generate synthetic data. For example, knowledge about how the financial market behaves can be used to create an artificial dataset about stock prices. However, this requires extensive knowledge about the domain in question so that the synthetic data behaves similarly to real data.

A lot of artificial intelligence (AI) problems today arise from insufficient, poor quality, or unlabeled data. This is almost ubiquitous, as many fields of study suffer from such difficulties—e.g., physics [9,56], finance [57], health [10,58], sports [59], and agriculture [60]. As a result, there is a growing interest in the usefulness of synthetic data and the drawbacks it can overcome. An example of the usefulness of synthetic data can be found in [61], where a network trained only on synthetic data achieved competitive results when compared to a state-of-the-art network trained on real data.

In [62], the author argues that synthetic data are essential for the further development of Deep Learning and that many more potential use cases remain. He also discusses the three main directions for using synthetic data in machine learning: using synthetic data to train machine learning models and use them to make predictions in real-world data; using synthetic data to augment existing real datasets, typically used to cover underrepresented parts of the data distribution; and solving privacy or legal issues by generating anonymized data. The focus of this work is on the first two directions, with the goal of using synthetic data or augmented datasets to enhance the performance of machine learning models, so the generation of anonymized data is not addressed here.

In the following sections, several methods for generating synthetic samples are reviewed. To better organize them, they have been divided into deep learning methods and standard methods. Deep learning methods, as the name implies, use deep learning techniques to generate synthetic data. In contrast, standard methods are those that do not use deep learning.

4.1. Standard Methods

In this section, we review some of the main methods for generating synthetic data (Our focus is on tabular data, so we refrain from writing about cropping, zooming, or inverting, which are used in image data). We have called them standard methods because they were the most commonly used methods before the success of generative deep learning models. The section is organized by the level of sophistication of the algorithm. Thus, random oversampling is shown as the first algorithm, followed by SMOTE and several algorithms that improve the core idea of SMOTE (e.g., by adding safe levels or clustering). Next, cluster-based oversampling is analyzed. Finally, Gaussian mixture models are reviewed as they provide a different approach to the task of generating synthetic data.

4.1.1. Random Oversampling (ROS)

ROS adds additional observations to the dataset by randomly sampling from the minority class(es) with replacement. Probably, the simplest and most straightforward method for expanding a dataset is ROS. Nevertheless, this approach can change the data distribution. Thus, if a classifier is fed with such data, it may learn from an incorrect distribution. Moreover, since ROS duplicates observations, this technique does not create new synthetic samples but only replicates the existing ones. Therefore, more advanced techniques, such as SMOTE, had to be developed.

Examples of ROS can be found, for example, in [63], where the authors compared the use of random oversampling with random undersampling (Random undersampling is a technique that consists of randomly removing instances of the majority class so that minority classes are not underrepresented) (RUS). It has been shown that ROS gives better classification results than RUS since it does not affect the classification of the majority class instances as much as RUS, while it increases the classification of the minority class instances. Another example is shown in [64], where the authors also compare ROS and RUS. In that study, however, they concluded that ROS was surprisingly ineffective, producing little or no change in classification performance in most cases.

4.1.2. Synthetic Minority Oversampling Technique (SMOTE)

SMOTE [2] is an oversampling approach in which synthetic observations are generated (and not duplicated, as in ROS) from the minority class(es). SMOTE was inspired by a perturbation method used to recognize handwritten digits. This was a very domain-specific problem, and so were the techniques used (e.g., rotation or skew), but the authors of SMOTE generalized them to generate synthetic samples in a less application-specific way.

The algorithm works as follows. Given a data point from a minority class and its nearest neighbor from the same class, the distance between them is determined (the distance is computed as the difference between both feature vectors, the data points). This distance is multiplied by a random number between 0 and 1 and added to the selected data point. This causes the new sample to fall in the line segment between the original sample and its neighbor. The same process is repeated until the desired number of samples is reached. Figure 20 shows a toy example of an iteration of the SMOTE algorithm.

The SMOTE algorithm is quite popular in the literature. In [65], for example, the authors evaluate the use of SMOTE for high-dimensional data. It was shown that SMOTE does not attenuate the bias toward the majority class for most classifiers. However, for k-nearest neighbor classifiers based on Euclidean Distance, SMOTE may be beneficial if the number of variables is reduced by variable selection. In [66], SMOTE is combined with decision trees and bagging to address the problem of imbalanced credit evaluation of companies. The proposed framework shows good results, outperforms the five other different approaches, and overcomes the class imbalance problem. Another example of using SMOTE can be seen in [67], where SMOTE is combined with Adaboost Support Vector Machine Ensemble with time weighting (ADASVM-TW) in two different ways and evaluated in a financial dataset. The first method uses SMOTE followed by ADASVM-

TW, while the second method embeds SMOTE into the iteration of ADASVM-TW. Both approaches greatly improved the recognition performance of the minority class.

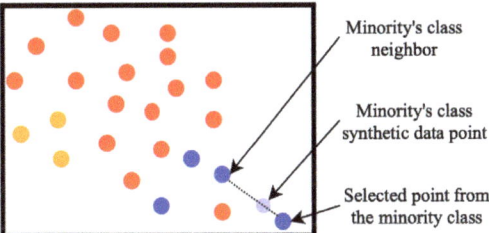

Figure 20. Toy example of the SMOTE algorithm for one iteration. The dataset has two minority classes (blue and orange) and one majority class (red). After selecting a minority class instance and its nearest neighbor, a synthetic data point is added somewhere in the line segment between them.

Although a more advanced technique than ROS, SMOTE still suffers from some problems e.g., focusing on minority class instances (thus ignoring those of the majority class) or altering the true data distribution. That being said, some informed improvements can be applied. Therefore, Borderline-SMOTE, Safe-Level-SMOTE, and ADASYN have been introduced.

4.1.3. Borderline-SMOTE

Han et al. [3] have proposed two algorithms that are a variation of SMOTE: Borderline-SMOTE1, which only oversamples the minority class(es) examples near the borderlines, and Borderline-SMOTE2, which also takes into account the majority class observations.

Borderline-SMOTE1 considers only the minority class data points that have a number of minority class neighbors in the range $[m/2, m]$, where m is defined by the user. These are the points that can be easily misclassified (the borderline data points of the minority class). After detecting such observations, SMOTE is applied to create new synthetic samples. Borderline-SMOTE2 is quite similar, with the difference that it also considers the neighbors of the majority class. According to [3], Borderline-SMOTE offers improvements over SMOTE and ROS in terms of TP-rate and F-value.

Examples of Borderline-SMOTE can be found, for example, in [68], where the authors use this method for data augmentation and evaluate its impact on an EEG (Electroencephalography) classification dataset obtained with a brain-computer interface (BCI). Borderline-SMOTE did not improve the overall classification performance but significantly increased the performance of the classifiers that produced the worst results. Another example can be found in [69], where Borderline-SMOTE was improved by using Gabriel graphs. The authors addressed the main problems of Borderline-SMOTE and were able to improve its performance on neural networks.

4.1.4. Safe-Level-SMOTE

SMOTE synthesizes minority class samples along a line connecting a minority class instance to its nearest neighbors, ignoring nearby majority class instances. Safe-Level-SMOTE [4], on the other hand, defines safe regions to prevent oversampling in overlapping or noisy regions, providing better accuracy performance than SMOTE and Borderline-SMOTE.

Each minority class example is assigned a safety level defined as the number of instances of the minority class in the k nearest neighbors, where k is specified by the user. Each synthetic instance is positioned closer to the largest safe level so that all synthetic instances are created only in safe regions. Intuitively, when given a data point, p, from the minority class and its nearest neighbor, n, (from that same class), the Safe-Level-SMOTE will generate a synthetic sample closer to p if its safe level is higher than the one of n or closer to n otherwise. That is, the synthetic sample will be closer to the data point that has more nearest neighbors from the minority class. Hence, the Safe-Level-SMOTE offers a wittier solution than the one of SMOTE, in the sense that it does not simply generate a random instance in the line segment between two minority class data points but takes into account their neighborhoods.

An example of using Safe-Level-SMOTE is shown in [70], where the authors overcome some of the difficulties of Safe-Level-SMOTE (some synthetic data points may be placed too close to nearby majority instances, which can confuse some classifiers and also the fact that it avoids using minority outcast samples for generating synthetic instances) by using two processes—moving the synthetic instances of the minority class away from the surrounding examples of the majority class and treating the outcasts of the minority class with a 1-nearest-neighbor model. Several machine learning models were evaluated with 9 UCI and 5 PROMISE datasets after using the above approach, and improvements in the F-measure were obtained.

4.1.5. ADASYN

ADASYN [5] is an oversampling algorithm that improves the learning performance of the classifiers. It uses a weighted distribution for different minority class instances that takes into account their level of difficulty for a classifier to learn—the minority class samples that have fewer minority class neighbors are harder to learn than those which have more neighbors of the same class. Thus, more synthetic samples are generated for the minority class examples that are harder to learn and less for the minority class examples that are easier to learn.

ADASYN is similar to SMOTE in the sense that it generates synthetic samples in the line segments between two minority class data points. The difference is that ADASYN uses a density distribution as a criterion to automatically determine the number of synthetic samples to generate for each instance of the minority class. Hence, the extended dataset provides a balanced representation of the data distribution and forces the classifier to pay more attention to the more difficult-to-learn examples.

The ADASYN approach is used in [71] to process an unbalanced telecommunications fraud dataset. The authors concluded that ADASYN is more beneficial than SMOTE and that accuracy, recall, and F1-measure were improved when ADASYN was used. Another example can be found in [72], where ADASYN is used this time for data augmentation in an unbalanced churn dataset. A final example is retrieved from [73], where ADASYN is used in a financial dataset. The authors note that ADASYN overcame the problem of overfitting caused by SMOTE and improved the prediction of extreme financial risk.

While ADASYN, Safe-Level, and Borderline-SMOTE are variants of SMOTE, it is also possible to not modify the SMOTE algorithm but instead use an unsupervised algorithm before performing SMOTE (or random oversampling). Clustering algorithms are a type of unsupervised algorithm that can be very useful in detecting structures in the data (e.g., divide the data into classes). When applied well, clustering algorithms can reveal hidden patterns in the dataset that were previously undetectable.

4.1.6. K-Means SMOTE

K-Means SMOTE was proposed by Last, Douzas, and Bacao in [6] and combines K-means [74], a popular clustering algorithm, with SMOTE, thereby avoiding the generation of noise and effectively overcoming the imbalances between and within classes.

K-Means SMOTE consists of three steps. First, observations are clustered using the K-means algorithm. This is followed by a filtering step in which the clusters with a small proportion of minority class instances are discarded. The number of synthetic samples to be created also depends on the cluster. That is, clusters with a lower proportion of minority class samples will have more synthesized instances. Finally, the SMOTE algorithm is applied to each of the clusters. Figure 21 shows the use of K-Means SMOTE in a toy dataset.

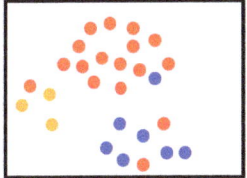 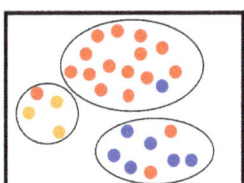 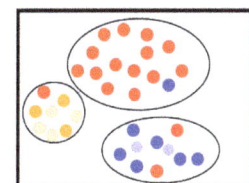

Figure 21. Toy example of the K-Means SMOTE algorithm. The left image shows the toy dataset, which consists of 3 classes: the blue and the orange are minority classes, and the red one is a majority class. The creation of clusters took place at the center. In the right picture, the clusters with a high proportion of samples from the minority class were populated with synthetic instances.

An example of the use of K-Means SMOTE can be found in [75], where the authors compared it with other methods of generating synthetic data, such as SMOTE or Borderline-SMOTE. It was shown that K-Means SMOTE is better at balancing datasets allowing machine learning models to perform better in terms of average recall, F1-score, and geometric mean.

4.1.7. Cluster-Based Oversampling

Jo and Japkowicz, in [76], address the presence of small disjuncts in the training data. Their work has shown that the loss of performance in standard classifiers is not caused by class imbalance but that class imbalance can lead to small disjuncts, which, in turn, cause the loss of performance.

The Cluster-Based Oversampling algorithm consists of clustering the data for each class, i.e., each class is clustered separately (in [76], the authors used K-Means clustering, but theoretically, any clustering algorithm can be used), and then applying ROS to each cluster. For the majority class clusters, all clusters except the largest are randomly oversampled until they have the same number of observations as the majority class cluster with the most data points. The minority class clusters are randomly oversampled until each cluster has m/N samples, where m is the number of instances of the majority class (after ROS), and N is the number of clusters of the minority class.

Cluster-Based Oversampling is similar to K-Means SMOTE in that both use clustering followed by oversampling, but they differ in some aspects. For instance, K-Means SMOTE uses a specific clustering algorithm, K-Means, and the classes are not clustered separately, while Cluster-Based Oversampling allows the user to freely choose the clustering algorithm, and the classes are clustered separately. Further, K-Means Clustering uses the oversampling SMOTE technique, while Cluster-Based Oversampling uses the ROS method.

The methods studied so far, with the exception of ADASYN, tend to neglect the distribution of the original data. Thus, a logical but different approach would be to model the underlying distribution of the data and draw a sample from it. However, estimating such a distribution is an extremely difficult problem, especially as the number of features in the data increase and simplifications need to be made.

4.1.8. Gaussian Mixture Model

A Gaussian Mixture Model (GMM) is a probabilistic model that assumes that the data can be modeled by a weighted sum of a finite number of Gaussian distributions [77]. Therefore, the resulting model is given by

$$p(x) = \pi_1 p_1(x) + \pi_2 p_2(x) + \ldots + \pi_n p_n(x)$$

where, in the univariate case, $p_i(x)$ is the probability density function of a univariate normal distribution with mean μ_i and standard deviation σ_i, π_i is the weight assigned to each $p_i(x)$, and n is the number of components. The number of components, n, is set by the user, and the parameters $\mu_1, \sigma_1, \mu_2, \sigma_2, \ldots, \mu_n, \sigma_n$, and $\pi_1, \pi_2, \ldots, \pi_{n-1}$ (The sum of all π_i equals 1, so if $n-1$ weights are estimated, the last one is equal to 1 minus their sum. That is, $\pi_j = \sum_{i \neq j}^{n} \pi_i$) are estimated, typically by an expectation-maximization algorithm—an iterative and well-founded statistical algorithm that calculates the probability that each point is generated by each component and then changes the parameters to maximize the likelihood of the data. For the multivariate case, $p_i(x)$ is replaced by a multivariate normal distribution, $N_k(\mu_i, \Sigma_i)$, where k is the dimension of the multivariate normal distribution, μ_i is now a vector of means, and Σ_i is the covariance matrix. Having determined the model, synthetic data are generated by drawing random samples from it.

An example of using GMM can be found in [78]. The authors address the problem of a lack of data in immersive virtual environments (IVEs) by using a Gaussian mixture model. The results have shown that the GMM is a good option to overcome the problem of a small sample size in IVE experiments.

4.2. Deep Learning Methods

Deep learning methods are so named because they use deep learning techniques to create new instances. Unlike standard methods, deep learning models are more difficult to understand because they are more complex and usually cannot be interpreted. In this section, we review the three main classes of deep generative models: Bayesian networks (Even though BNs may not be considered Deep Learning, they are easy generalized to Bayesian Neural Networks, which are Deep Learning structures [79], so we have included them) (BNs), autoencoders(AEs), and GANs. There are innumerable variations of these algorithms and a whole range of domain-specific architectures. It would, therefore, not be possible to list everything in the literature, so instead, a comprehensive overview is presented.

4.2.1. Bayesian Networks

A Bayesian network (also known as a belief network in the 1980s and 1990s) is a type of probabilistic graphical model that uses Bayesian inference for probability computations over a directed acyclic graph [80]. It is used to represent dependence between variables so that, essentially, any full joint probability distribution can be represented and in many cases, very succinctly [81]. In a Bayesian network, each node corresponds to a random variable (which may be discrete or continuous) and contains probability information that quantifies the effect of the parents (the nodes pointing to it) on the node. If there is a link from node x_i to node x_j, then x_i has a direct impact on x_j. Moreover, if there is a path from node x_i to node x_j (with at least one node in between), then x_i also has an influence on x_j (though not a direct influence).

As an example, suppose a certain person has an alarm system installed at home. The alarm is very good at detecting burglaries, but it also triggers for minor earthquakes. The person has asked his neighbors, John and Mary, to call him if the alarm goes off. On the one hand, however, John is more careful than Mary, so he almost always calls when he hears the alarm, but sometimes mistakes it for the phone ringing. On the other hand, Mary likes to listen to loud music, so she does not hear the alarm as often as John does. This is a simple toy example that can be modeled by a Bayesian network (see Figure 22).

The previous example is quite simple, but these structures can have many more layers, representing dependencies between multiple variables. As the number of layers increases, Bayesian networks become deep Bayesian networks. Although they played an important role in the history of deep learning (Bayesian networks were one of the first non-convolutional models to successfully allow training of deep architectures), they are rarely used nowadays [82].

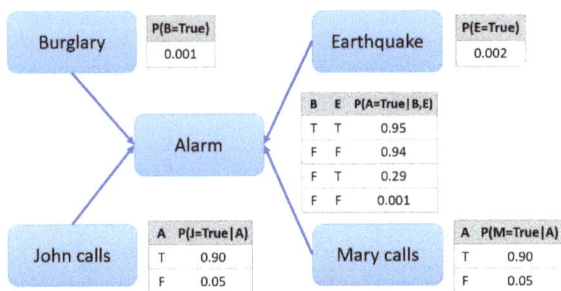

Figure 22. Toy example of a Bayesian network. A certain individual has an alarm installed at home, which fires in the case of minor earthquakes or burglaries (with a certain probability). The given individual also has two neighbors, Mary and John, who will call him in case they hear the alarm. Image adapted from [81].

An example of the use of Bayesian networks can be seen in [50], where the authors address the problem of sharing private data. A Bayesian network adds noise to the data to estimate an approximate distribution of the original data. The Bayesian network has been evaluated experimentally and found to significantly outperform existing solutions in terms of accuracy.

4.2.2. Autoencoders

An autoencoder (AE) is a special type of feedforward neural network that consists of two parts: an encoder network that learns to compress high-dimensional data into a low-dimensional, latent spacial representation (the code), and a decoder network that decompresses the compressed representation into the original domain [83]. Figure 23 shows a diagram of an autoencoder.

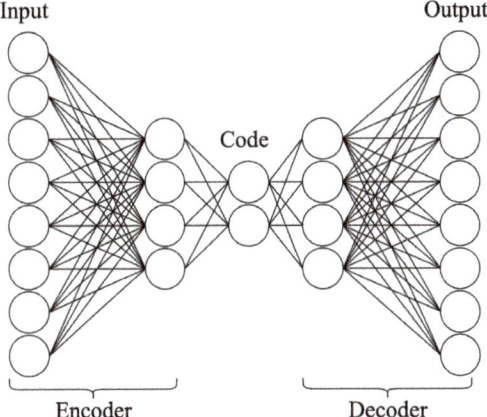

Figure 23. A diagram of an autoencoder. On the left, an example structure of an encoder is depicted. The input layer has more units than the middle layer, where the input is compressed into a lower-dimensional representation (the code). On the right, the decoder decompresses the code back to the original domain.

Formally, the encoder can be viewed as a function, $c = E(x)$, that produces a low-dimensional representation of the data, and the decoder as a function, $r = D(c)$, that produces a reconstruction of the code. The goal is not for the autoencoder to learn how to set $D(E(x)) = x$ for each input example x but rather to learn how to copy the original data only approximately, and only inputs that resemble the original data. By constraining it and forcing it to learn which aspects of the data should be prioritized, autoencoders can learn useful properties about the data (autoencoders have been on the deep learning landscape for decades and have typically been used for feature learning and dimensionality reduction) [84].

In terms of generating synthetic samples, autoencoders have some issues. First, the learned distribution of points in the latent space is undefined, i.e., when a point is sampled from the latent space and decoded to generate a new example, there is no guarantee that it is a plausible sample. Second, there is a lack of diversity in the generated samples. Finally, points belonging to the same class may have large gaps in the latent space, which can lead to poorly generated instances when samples are drawn from their neighborhood. To overcome these problems, variational autoencoders (VAEs) can be used.

Variational autoencoders were first proposed by Diederik P Kingma and Max Welling in [7] and are a natural extension of autoencoders aimed at solving the aforementioned problems. VAEs improve on vanilla autoencoders by making a few changes to the encoder and loss function:

Encoder. The encoder of a VAE maps each point in the original data to a multivariate normal distribution in the latent space, represented by the mean and variance vectors. VAEs assume that there is no correlation between two dimensions in the latent space, so the covariance matrix does not need to be calculated because it is diagonal. This small change ensures that a point, a, sampled from the neighborhood of another point, b, in the latent space, is similar to b. Thus, a point in the latent space that is completely new to the decoder will most likely still yield a correct sample.

Loss function. The VAE loss function adds the Kullback–Leibler (KL) divergence to the autoencoder reconstruction function (typically, the binary cross entropy or the root mean squared error). Formally, the KL divergence in this particular case can be written as follows.

$$KL\left(N(\mu,\sigma) \parallel N(0,1)\right) = \frac{1}{2}\sum_{i=1}^{k}(1 + log(\sigma_i^2) - \mu_i^2 - \sigma_i^2)$$

where k is the number of dimensions in the latent space. Therefore, the loss function becomes

$$L(x,\hat{x}) = RL(x,\hat{x}) + \frac{1}{2}\sum_{i=1}^{k}(1 + log(\sigma_i^2) - \mu_i^2 - \sigma_i^2)$$

where RL is the reconstruction loss, x denotes the input data, and $\hat{x}$ is the predicted output. This loss function provides a well-defined distribution (the standard normal distribution) that can be used to sample points in the latent space—sampling from this distribution most likely guarantees that the sample points are in the region from which the decoder is to decompress. Further, the gaps between points in the latent space will be smaller.

Therefore, changing the encoder mapping and adding the KL divergence to the loss function leads to a better framework for generating synthetic samples—the variational autoencoder.

The use of autoencoders to generate synthetic data is widespread in the literature. For example, in [85], the authors used a multichannel autoencoder (MCAE) to assist classifiers in the learning process. They concluded that the use of MCAE provided better feature representation. In addition, the experimental results validated their methodology for generating synthetic data. In [86], a variational autoencoder was used to address the problem of imbalanced image learning. It was shown that the VAE can generate novel samples and that it produces better results compared to other methods in several distinct datasets with different evaluation metrics. A final example of the use of autoencoders can be seen in [87], where a VAE was used to generate accident data, which was then used for data augmentation. The VAE was compared to SMOTE and ADASYN. This showed its superiority as it provided a better learning process for the classifiers and thus provided better classification metrics.

4.2.3. Generative Adversarial Networks

As shown in Section 3, GANs are a type of generative deep learning consisting of two networks: the generator, G, and the discriminator, D. The details of how they operate have already been reviewed, so we will now focus on the practical applications of such structures. Due to the usefulness of GANs in generating synthetic samples, they are widely used. Hence, it would be tedious to list them all. Therefore, only some interesting results will be shown.

In [88], the authors used a GAN to generate artificial EEG (Electroencephalography) datasets. The results presented were quite good: indeed, GANs (in this case, with convolutional layers) were able to generate brain signals similar to the real ones (obtained by EEG in multiple subjects).

Patel et al. used a CGAN for data augmentation in a signal modulation dataset used for automatic modulation classification [89]. These data were then used to improve the accuracy of a CNN classifier used as a benchmark. It was concluded that CGAN-enriched data could greatly benefit CNN-based training—it has faster convergence and lower training loss. Moreover, the more data generated by the CGAN, the better the F1-score of the CNN classifier is (the authors used 1000, 2000, 3000, 4000, and 5000 synthesized samples). Figure 24 shows the F1-score for the original and the extended dataset at different signal-to-noise ratios (SNR). Clearly, the F1-score increases at each SNR level as more synthetic samples are added to the original dataset.

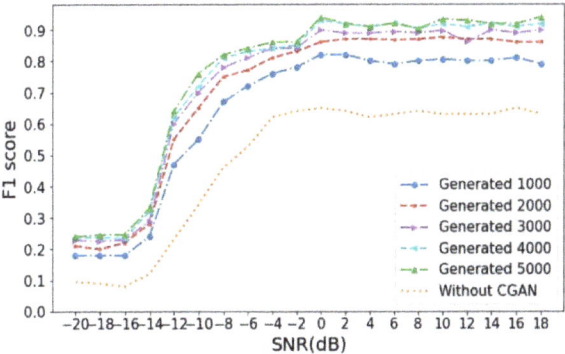

Figure 24. F1-score on the original data and on the augmented datasets (1000, 2000, 3000, 4000, and 5000 synthetic samples were added to the original data) at different SNR levels. The plot shows that, as the number of generated samples increases, the better the F1-score at each SNR level. Image taken from [89].

Another example of the use of GANs is the Multiple Fake Class GAN (MFC-GAN) ([90]). The MFC-GAN was used to handle datasets with multiple imbalanced classes by augmenting the original data with artificial samples. Four public datasets were used, MNIST, E-MNIST, CIFAR-10, and SVHN, and MFC-GAN was compared with FSC-GAN [91], AC-GAN [33], and SMOTE [2], both in terms of the quality of the generated samples and in a classification task (a baseline CNN classifier was used). It was found that MFC-GAN provided better quality generated samples and that the training time was significantly reduced compared to FSC-GAN (MNIST dataset). The results also showed that MFC-GAN performed better than SMOTE and AC-GAN on all SVHN and CIFAR-10 minority classes and in 7 of 10 E-MNIST and MNIST minority classes.

In [92], Sushko et al. proposed the One-Shot GAN, which given just one image (or video) as input, can generate images (or videos) that are significantly different from the original one. This type of GAN has improved the quality and variety of images (and videos) over previous works when only one image (or video) is available. When only small amounts of data are available, the One-Shot GAN mitigates the memorization problem (reproducing the original image) and is able to generate images that are structurally different from the original. This is extremely useful for data augmentation tasks in domains where data is very scarce and collecting it may be challenging.

A quantum GAN—*entangling* quantum GAN, EQ-GAN—was proposed in [93]. By leveraging quantum circuits' entangling (quantum entanglement is a physical phenomenon that happens when, in a set of particles, an individual particle's quantum state cannot be described independently of the state of the others, no matter how far apart they are) power, it overcomes some limitations of previously proposed quantum GANs (non-convergence due to mode collapse and a non-unique Nash equilibrium). Moreover, the authors have shown that the EQ-GAN can generate an approximate quantum random access memory (QRAM), which is required by most machine learning algorithms. They have further demonstrated an application of such a QRAM, improving the performance of a quantum neural network in a classification task.

Finally, to conclude this subsection, we show one last example. In [94], the authors have proposed the Metropolitan GAN (MetroGAN), which is used for urban morphology simulations. Recent studies have shown that GANs have the potential to simulate urban morphology, despite being a challenging task. Nevertheless, the existing GAN models are limited by the instability in model training and the sparsity of urban data, compromising their application. However, when compared to other state-of-the-art urban simulation methods—XGBoost, U-NET, and CityGAN—the MetroGAN outperforms them all in the three levels used to evaluate the results: pixel level, multi-scale spatial level, and perceptual level.

4.3. Thoughts on the Algorithms

In this section, eight techniques for data augmentation were reviewed. ROS is the most simple of them all and, therefore, is easier to implement than any of the others. However, it is a very naive approach that does not take into account the distribution of the data. Further, it disregards the majority class instances, as well as the difficulty of the classifiers in learning the decision boundaries. A simple yet more intelligent way to improve ROS is SMOTE. This technique does not replicate observations as ROS does but adds new synthetic data points to the dataset. This can make it easier for a classifier to learn from the data. Nonetheless, SMOTE does not care about changing the distribution of the data and does not consider majority class observations.

SMOTE brought a highly successful synthetic data generation method but also a lot of room for improvement. Therefore, new algorithms were created by borrowing the core idea of SMOTE, which is to add noise to the instances. Borderline-SMOTE oversamples near the borderlines to make the learning task easier for classifiers while also taking into account the majority class observations. Safe-Level-SMOTE has defined safe regions to generate better quality instances, which is an improvement over SMOTE and Borderline-SMOTE.

K-Means SMOTE first clusters the data using the K-Means algorithm and then oversamples the clusters using SMOTE, effectively overcoming the imbalances between and within classes. ADASYN is another variant of SMOTE. This method takes into account the learning difficulties of the classifiers and aims to not change the data distribution (one of the drawbacks of SMOTE). Cluster-Based Oversampling takes into account the presence of small disjuncts in the data. This algorithm is not a variant of SMOTE but a variant of ROS. Both the minority and majority classes are oversampled so that each class has the same number of instances.

Gaussian mixture models use a different approach to address the synthetic data generation task—modeling the data with a weighted sum of normal distributions. While this is usually an improvement over previous algorithms, it has two major drawbacks. First, not all datasets can be modeled with a weighted sum of the Gaussian distribution. Therefore, the use of GMM may not be the most appropriate method for generating plausible samples. On the other hand, some types of data may have categorical features. In these cases, GMM cannot be applied because the normal distribution is continuous, and it cannot model discrete variables.

BNs, AEs, and GANs are more complex techniques compared to the others. Unlike the previous methods, they use a Deep Learning approach that allows them to better learn the underlying patterns in the data and, therefore, offer higher quality synthetic patterns in most cases. Bayesian networks were widely used in the past but have fallen out of favor and are rarely used today. Autoencoders, especially variational autoencoders, are powerful generative models that have evolved and are proving useful in data generation tasks.

Nevertheless, autoencoders are not as popular and usually not as powerful as GANs. Yann LeCun has even described them as "the most interesting idea in the last 10 years in machine learning" [95]. GANs have countless different architectures, and many are yet to be created. Only a few applications of GANs for the generation of samples were shown, as it would be grueling (and probably impossible) to find and summarize all the literature on GANs and data generation. They can be quite problem-specific, so a few have been selected to show their capabilities and broad application to real-world data.

5. Synthetic Sample Quality Evaluation

Evaluating the quality of the generated samples is critical to assessing the quality of the method used to generate synthetic data. There is a huge number of evaluation techniques, so it is tedious and almost impossible to explore and describe them all. Moreover, many of these evaluation techniques are intended for specific types of data or for very specific domains. Therefore, this section focuses on evaluation methods for tabular data.

The simplest way to evaluate the quality of synthetic data is to compare their basic statistics (e.g., mean, median, standard deviation) with those of the real data. If the values are similar, it is likely that the synthetic data are similar to the real data. However, this can be misleading, as statistician Francis Anscombe showed in 1973 [96]. The Anscombe quartet includes four datasets that are nearly identical in terms of basic descriptive statistics but whose distributions are very different.

Anscombe constructed his quartet to demonstrate the importance of plotting the data when analyzing it. Back in 1973, it may have been difficult to create graphs with data, in part because of scarce and expensive computing resources. Today, however, it is quite easy, with hundreds of graphics libraries available for various programming languages. Thus, another method to evaluate the quality of synthetic data is to use graphical representations (e.g., box plots, histograms, violin plots).

Comparing the graphs of the synthetic data with the graphs of the real data provides a visual assessment of the generated data, which can also be supplemented by descriptive statistics. The Q-Q plot is a probability plot that can be particularly useful for making comparisons between two data distributions, as it plots their quantiles against each other and can, thus, evaluate the similarity between the distributions. Given the vast amounts of data available today, with datasets containing hundreds or even thousands of variables, it can be prohibitively expensive to visually represent and analyze all of the data, so other approaches to evaluate synthetic data are required.

Machine learning efficacy is another technique for evaluating synthetic data. Since many of the uses of synthetic data are to increase the performance of ML models, machine learning efficacy is used to evaluate the quality of synthetic data with respect to the performance of ML models. It consists of, given a dataset, D, already split into a trainset, D_{train}, and testset, D_{test}, comparing the performance of ML models (e.g., logistic regression, decision trees, artificial neural networks) when trained in D_{train}, and on D_{synth} (the synthetic data), and evaluated in D_{test} (see Figure 25). If the performance (e.g., in terms of accuracy, recall, precision, F1-score) of the models trained using D_{train} is similar to those trained using D_{synth}, then the synthetic data is likely to follow the underlying data distribution. In [47,48], this method was used to evaluate the performance of the TGAN and CTGAN architectures, respectively. Further, in [97], this technique was used to evaluate the forecast of emerging technologies.

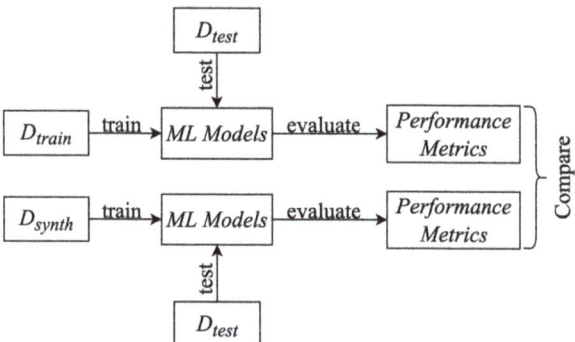

Figure 25. Machine learning efficacy diagram. The performance (accuracy, F1-score, etc.) of ML models (random forests, decision trees, etc.) in the test set, D_{test}, is compared when the models are trained on the real training data, D_{train}, and when they are trained using the synthetic data, D_{synth}.

In [98], Shmelkov et al. argue that the existing methods for evaluating synthetic samples are insufficient and need to be adapted to the task at hand. They begin by addressing two commonly used metrics, namely the Inception Score [40] and the Fréchet Inception Distance [41]. Both metrics are used for the evaluation of image-generated data and, thus, are not the focus of this work. Nonetheless, it is important to at least mention them, as they are widely used in the literature to evaluate synthetic image data.

After presenting these two metrics, the authors introduced their proposed metrics—GAN-train and GAN-test—which, although applied to image data, can also be applied to other types of data, such as tabular datasets. Moreover, despite both measures having "GAN" in their name, the synthetic samples do not need to be generated exclusively with a GAN but can also be generated with any other method. Therefore, we have slightly modified the definition of GAN-train and GAN-test given in [98] to make it more general by replacing the use of a GAN with any synthetic data generation method and the image data with any type of data (see Figure 26).

GAN-train. A classification network is trained with instances generated by a synthetic data generation method, and its performance is evaluated against a test set consisting of real-world data. This measure provides a measure of how far apart the generated and true distributions are.

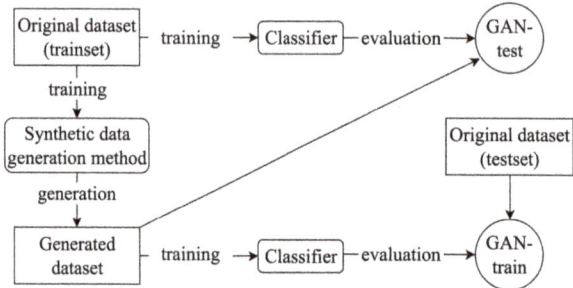

Figure 26. A diagram representing the GAN-train and GAN-test metrics. The GAN-train is a measure consisting of the accuracy of a classifier trained in the generated data and evaluated in the real data. GAN-test learns on the real data and is evaluated in the generated data. Image based on [98].

GAN-test. A classification network is trained on a real dataset and evaluated on the generated data. GAN-test provides a measure to evaluate whether the synthetic data generation method has overfitted (values significantly higher than the ones from validation accuracy) or underfitted (values significantly lower than the ones from validation accuracy) the data.

Another technique to evaluate the quality of synthetic data was proposed in [99]. The authors address the fact that most existing evaluation metrics for generative models are focused on image data and have introduced a domain and model-independent metric. The metric is three-dimensional (α-Precision, β-Recall, Authenticity), and it evaluates the fidelity, diversity, and generalization of each generative model and is independent of the domain (e.g., images or tabular data). Moreover, the three components correspond to interpretable probabilistic quantities, making it easier to detect a lack of synthetic data quality if such a problem occurs.

Fidelity. The α-Precision component measures the similarity between the generated and the real samples. Thus, values with high-fidelity correspond to realistic samples, i.e., samples that resemble those from the original dataset.

Diversity. It is not enough to have samples that resemble those from the original dataset. High-quality synthetic data must also have some diversity. The β-Recall component evaluates how diverse the generated samples are. That is, whether the generated data is diverse enough to cover the existing variability in the real data.

Generalization. Last but not least, it is essential that the generated samples are not copies of the original data. In fact, high fidelity and diversity values do not guarantee that the synthetic samples are not just copies of the original dataset. Therefore, the authenticity component is a measure of how well the model can generalize and, therefore, not overfit the real data.

The first two components are computed by embedding the real and synthetic data in hyperspheres. That is, the original data, X_r, and the generated data, X_s, are mapped from the original domain, $\mathcal{X}$, to a hypersphere of radius r, $\mathcal{S}_r$. The third component is computed by evaluating the proximity of the real data to the generated data in the embedding space using a hypothesis test. Figure 27 shows a representation of the three metrics.

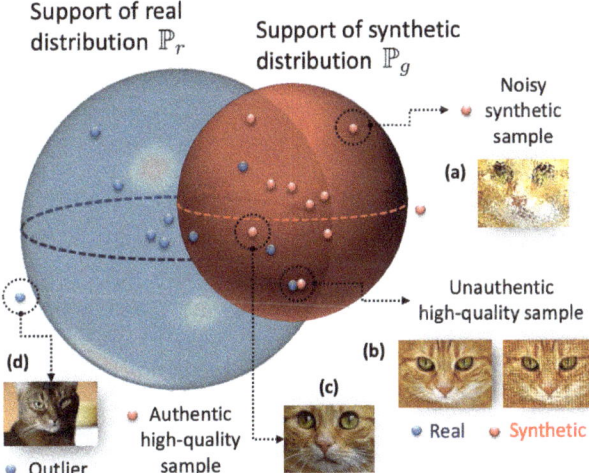

Figure 27. Representation of α-Precision, β-Recall, and Authenticity. The blue and red spheres correspond to the α- and β-supports of the real and the generated samples, respectively. Intuitively, these regions are "safe-zones" where points that lie outside the spheres are outliers, and points inside the spheres are "ordinary" samples. (**a**) Generated samples that lie outside the blue sphere are unrealistic. (**b**) Synthetic samples that are very close to real instances are inauthentic because they are almost exact copies of the real data. (**c**) Synthetic data points inside the blue sphere and without real data points near them are considered high-quality samples. (**d**) A data point outside the sphere is considered an outlier. Image retrieved from [99].

Finally, an important aspect of this metric is that, unlike the other metrics, it provides the ability to evaluate each instance. Considering this, the authors of [99] have also proposed a model-checking framework where low-quality samples (low values in some or all components) are discarded. Therefore, the final generated dataset is a "curated" version consisting only of high-quality samples.

In this section, six evaluation techniques were examined—descriptive statistics, graphical representations, machine learning efficacy, GAN-train, GAN-test, and the (α-Precision, β-Recall, Authenticity) metric. It is always good not to use only one measure and to combine at least two of them. For example, as mentioned earlier, the descriptive statistics of a generated sample may be similar to those of the real data, but the distribution of data points may be very different. Or the efficacy of machine learning might provide similar values for the models trained in the real data and those learned in the generated data, but their descriptive statistics, or graphical representations, may be very different.

Evaluating synthetic data is challenging and depends heavily on the problem at hand. Sometimes generating synthetic data can be useful to better train a classifier when there is a lack of data. In other cases, the problem might be to create simulated realities for a video game. The definition of "high-quality samples" is likely to be different in the two cases. In the first scenario, the synthetic data must be very similar to the original data for the classifier to learn a reasonable model of the real world. Therefore, the synthetic data must be closely scrutinized, and various evaluation techniques need to be used. In the latter case, the generated data need not be plausible in the human world, and less stringent criteria can be used to evaluate the quality of the samples.

Even for problems of a similar nature, the evaluation techniques may be different. Suppose there are two different classification tasks. The first is to classify a patient with cancer as "benign" or "malignant". The second task is to classify the sex of an unborn child as "male" or "female". In the first task, it is critical to generate extremely high-quality synthetic data to improve the classifiers. The data must be highly plausible and truly represent the real world. Failing to generate trustworthy synthetic data might lead doctors not to diagnose a patient with a malignant cancer, which can have serious consequences for the patient (and also for the doctor). Therefore, multiple evaluation techniques must be used to be sure that the generated data will help in the classification task and not jeopardize it.

In the second scenario, evaluation techniques to assess the quality of the generated sample may not need to be as rigorous. Improving the performance of the classifier might be useful even if it is with samples of intermediate quality so it is not necessary to analyze the synthetic data in detail. Whether the unborn child is classified as "female" or "male" does not have as much impact as a tumor being "benign" or "malignant".

6. Discussion

Given the amount of information covered in this document, it is important to schematize everything in order to have a clear overview of what was shown. For this purpose, an organizational chart (Figure 28) was created. It has been divided into two main topics, namely the methods used to generate synthetic data and the evaluation of the synthetic samples.

As for the synthetic data generation methods, they were further divided into standard and deep learning methods, as in Section 4. The standard methods include ROS, SMOTE, Borderline-SMOTE, Safe-Level-SMOTE, ADASYN, K-Means SMOTE, Cluster-Based Oversampling, and GMM. Deep learning methods consist of Bayesian networks, autoencoders, and generative adversarial networks. GANs have been further explored and are, therefore, divided into three main areas: GANs for music generation, image generation, and tabular data. As seen in Section 3.3, most GAN architectures focus on image generation, so they are better represented in the organizational chart than the other two. In addition, the CGAN and WGAN can (and should) be used in the context of tabular data, as they have useful properties. In fact, the CTGAN uses a conditional generator, which is based on the CGAN properties, and the TabFairGAN uses the WGAN with gradient penalty. Therefore, an overlapping region has been added to the organization chart to illustrate that CGAN and WGAN can be used in tabular domains.

Finally, the last part of the organizational chart consists of the evaluation techniques discussed in Section 5—descriptive statistics, graphical representations, machine-learning efficacy, GAN-train, GAN-test, and (α-Precision, β-Recall, Authenticity). They are fundamental to evaluate the quality of the generated samples and, thus, the quality of the generative models.

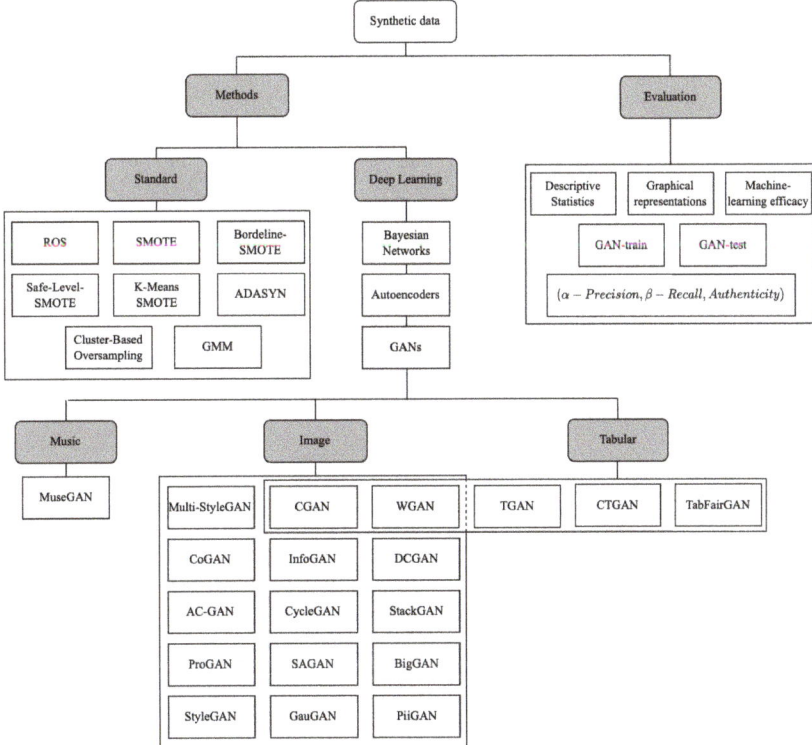

Figure 28. Organizational chart depicting several methods for the generation of synthetic samples and the evaluation techniques covered in this work.

Despite the concise representation offered by the organizational chart, it lacks a temporal dimension that can be interesting to visualize the evolution over time of the ideas that have been described. With this in mind, a timeline (Figure 29) was created. It is divided into two main themes, GAN architectures and methods for generating synthetic samples (the two themes sometimes overlap since GANs are generative models). While the topics are on the vertical axis, the horizontal axis is reserved for the temporal dimension. Given the large time span, the time axis is divided into years. We note that it is not clear when a paper on ROS, GMMs, Bayesian networks, or AEs was first published, so they are not included in the timeline.

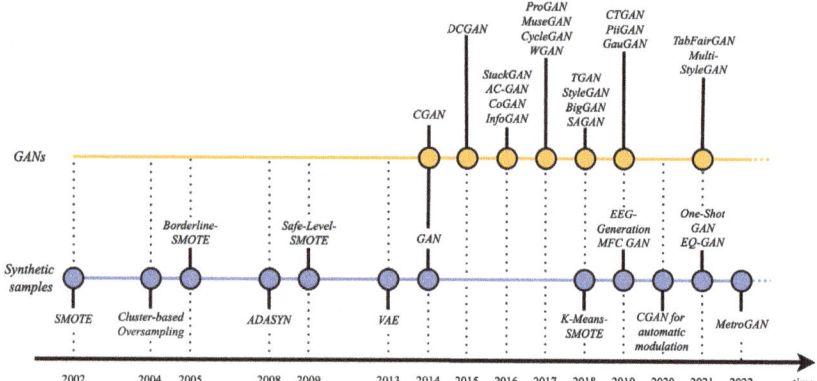

Figure 29. Timeline showing the different GAN architectures (in orange) and the generation of the synthetic sample methods (in blue) covered in this work.

Finally, a summary of the different synthetic data generation methods is given in Table 4. The methods are categorized by their type—standard or deep learning methods—and the references used throughout the document are shown in the References column.

Table 4. Summary of the synthetic data generation methods covered in this work.

Methods	Method Type	References
Random Oversampling (ROS)	Standard	[63,64]
SMOTE	Standard	[2,65–67]
Borderline-SMOTE	Standard	[3,68,69]
Safe-Level-SMOTE	Standard	[4,70]
K-Means SMOTE	Standard	[6,75]
ADASYN	Standard	[5,71–73]
Cluster-Based Oversampling	Standard	[76]
GMM	Standard	[77,78]
Bayesian Networks	Deep Learning	[50,80–82]
Autoencoders	Deep Learning	[7,83–87]
GANs	Deep Learning	[8,13,20–39,42–48,54,88–90,92–94]

7. Conclusions

To the best of our knowledge, this survey provides a comprehensive overview of the main synthetic data generation methods, the key breakthroughs in generative adversarial networks—with a special focus on GANs for tabular data—and how to assess the quality of synthetic samples. Unlike other existing surveys, e.g., [16], which focus on synthetic data, or [17], which surveys the recent advances in GANs, ours brings together both subjects.

We have provided a thorough explanation of what a GAN is, shown some of the main issues during training, the key breakthroughs in GAN architecture, and how GANs can deal with tabular data. We have also presented the more classical methods (we termed them standard methods) for the generation of synthetic samples and examples of published works showing their applicability. The same goes for deep learning methods, in which we showcased some research papers where they were used and how they work.

One of the core issues that we have come across in this work is that most research about GANs has been focused on image generation. As such, GANs for image generation tasks have been maturing and becoming more robust in the last few years. The same does not hold true for tabular data, a domain where GANs still have room for improvement.

Lastly, we showed how to evaluate the quality of synthetic data. It is crucial that the synthetic samples are of high quality, but defining them is quite problem-specific and depends on the domain.

In summary, there are four important points we have gained from this investigation. First, we have seen that Lecture Notes in Computer Science is the journal with the most publications in the area and that the authors Wang Y. and Nikolenko S. I. are of particular relevance—this may be useful for new researchers in the field to know where to find information. Second, we showed that deep learning methods were more complex than standard ones but tended to produce better results. Third, image generation has been the focus of research in GAN, while tabular data generation needs further research. Finally, evaluation techniques for synthetic data can be subjective, as they depend on the task and domain in question.

Given that three major topics were surveyed in this work—synthetic data generation methods, GANs, and synthetic data evaluation techniques, it has only been possible to cover the most important algorithms, architectures, and techniques. The literature is so vast that it would be impossible to summarize everything in a single paper. Another drawback of our study concerns the limitation of the query used (see Listing 1), since the datasets returned by it are necessarily incomplete and limited. Based on the numerous works in the literature, it is far from easy to create an all-inclusive query. This is something that could be revised and improved in future work. Nonetheless, we believe this review to be a good starting point for a new researcher in the field.

As mentioned before, one of the things that can be improved in future work is the quality of our query. Further, we want to compare the quality of the data produced by the tabular GANs outlined in Section 3.4—TGAN, CTGAN, and TabFairGAN. In order to do so, we will rely on datasets already well-established in the scientific community. Moreover, we intend to focus especially on unbalanced datasets and use machine-learning models to assess their performance in the minority class when synthetic samples are incorporated into their training.

Author Contributions: Conceptualization, A.F. and B.V.; methodology, A.F. and B.V.; software, B.V.; validation, A.F. and B.V.; formal analysis, B.V.; investigation, A.F. and B.V.; resources, B.V.; data curation, A.F. and B.V.; writing—original draft preparation, B.V.; writing—review and editing, A.F.; visualization, A.F. and B.V.; supervision, A.F.; project administration, A.F.; funding acquisition, A.F. All authors have read and agreed to the published version of the manuscript.

Funding: This research received no external funding.

Institutional Review Board Statement: Not applicable.

Informed Consent Statement: Not applicable.

Data Availability Statement: Not applicable.

Acknowledgments: This research did not receive any specific grant from funding agencies in the public, commercial, or not-for-profit sectors.

Conflicts of Interest: The authors declare no conflict of interest.

References

1. Emam, K.; Mosquera, L.; Hoptroff, R. Chapter 1: Introducing Synthetic Data Generation. In *Practical Synthetic Data Generation: Balancing Privacy and the Broad Availability of Data*; O'Reilly Media, Inc.: Sebastopol, CA, USA, 2020; pp. 1–22.
2. Chawla, N.V.; Bowyer, K.W.; Hall, L.O.; Kegelmeyer, W.P. SMOTE: Synthetic minority over-sampling technique. *J. Artif. Intell. Res.* **2002**, *16*, 321–357. [CrossRef]
3. Han, H.; Wang, W.Y.; Mao, B.H. Borderline-SMOTE: A new over-sampling method in imbalanced data sets learning. In Proceedings of the International Conference on Intelligent Computing, Hefei, China, 23–26 August 2005; pp. 878–887.
4. Bunkhumpornpat, C.; Sinapiromsaran, K.; Lursinsap, C. Safe-level-smote: Safe-level-synthetic minority over-sampling technique for handling the class imbalanced problem. In Proceedings of the Pacific-Asia Conference on Knowledge Discovery and Data Mining, Bangkok, Thailand, 27–30 April 2009; pp. 475–482.
5. He, H.; Bai, Y.; Garcia, E.A.; Li, S. ADASYN: Adaptive synthetic sampling approach for imbalanced learning. In Proceedings of the 2008 IEEE International Joint Conference on Neural Networks (IEEE World Congress on Computational Intelligence), Hong Kong, China, 1–8 June 2008; pp. 1322–1328.

6. Douzas, G.; Bacao, F.; Last, F. Improving imbalanced learning through a heuristic oversampling method based on k-means and SMOTE. *Inf. Sci.* **2018**, *465*, 1–20. [CrossRef]
7. Kingma, D.P.; Welling, M. Auto-encoding variational bayes. *arXiv* **2013**, arXiv:1312.6114.
8. Goodfellow, I.; Pouget-Abadie, J.; Mirza, M.; Xu, B.; Warde-Farley, D.; Ozair, S.; Courville, A.; Bengio, Y. Generative adversarial nets. In Proceedings of the Advances in Neural Information Processing Systems 27 (NIPS 2014), Montreal, QC, Canada, 8–13 December 2014; Volume 27.
9. Siddani, B.; Balachandar, S.; Moore, W.C.; Yang, Y.; Fang, R. Machine learning for physics-informed generation of dispersed multiphase flow using generative adversarial networks. *Theor. Comput. Fluid Dyn.* **2021**, *35*, 807–830. [CrossRef]
10. Coutinho-Almeida, J.; Rodrigues, P.P.; Cruz-Correia, R.J. GANs for Tabular Healthcare Data Generation: A Review on Utility and Privacy. In *Discovery Science*; Soares, C., Torgo, L., Eds.; Springer International Publishing: Cham, Switzerland, 2021; pp. 282–291.
11. Gupta, A.; Vedaldi, A.; Zisserman, A. Synthetic data for text localisation in natural images. In Proceedings of the IEEE Conference on Computer Vision and Pattern Recognition, Las Vegas, NV, USA, 26 June–1 July 2016; pp. 2315–2324.
12. Bolón-Canedo, V.; Sánchez-Maroño, N.; Alonso-Betanzos, A. A review of feature selection methods on synthetic data. *Knowl. Inf. Syst.* **2013**, *34*, 483–519. [CrossRef]
13. Frid-Adar, M.; Klang, E.; Amitai, M.; Goldberger, J.; Greenspan, H. Synthetic data augmentation using GAN for improved liver lesion classification. In Proceedings of the 2018 IEEE 15th International Symposium on Biomedical Imaging (ISBI 2018), Washington, DC, USA, 4–7 April 2018; pp. 289–293.
14. Koch, B. Status and future of laser scanning, synthetic aperture radar and hyperspectral remote sensing data for forest biomass assessment. *ISPRS J. Photogramm. Remote Sens.* **2010**, *65*, 581–590. [CrossRef]
15. Wu, X.; Liang, L.; Shi, Y.; Fomel, S. FaultSeg3D: Using synthetic data sets to train an end-to-end convolutional neural network for 3D seismic fault segmentation. *Geophysics* **2019**, *84*, IM35–IM45. [CrossRef]
16. Nikolenko, S.I. Synthetic Data Outside Computer Vision. In *Synthetic Data for Deep Learning*; Springer: Berlin/Heidelberg, Germany, 2021; pp. 217–226.
17. Pan, Z.; Yu, W.; Yi, X.; Khan, A.; Yuan, F.; Zheng, Y. Recent progress on generative adversarial networks (GANs): A survey. *IEEE Access* **2019**, *7*, 36322–36333. [CrossRef]
18. Di Mattia, F.; Galeone, P.; De Simoni, M.; Ghelfi, E. A survey on gans for anomaly detection. *arXiv* **2019**, arXiv:1906.11632.
19. Saxena, D.; Cao, J. Generative adversarial networks (GANs) challenges, solutions, and future directions. *ACM Comput. Surv. (CSUR)* **2021**, *54*, 1–42. [CrossRef]
20. Wang, Q.; Gao, J.; Lin, W.; Yuan, Y. Learning from synthetic data for crowd counting in the wild. In Proceedings of the IEEE/CVF Conference on Computer Vision and Pattern Recognition, Long Beach, CA, USA, 16–17 June 2019; pp. 8198–8207.
21. Atapour-Abarghouei, A.; Breckon, T.P. Real-time monocular depth estimation using synthetic data with domain adaptation via image style transfer. In Proceedings of the IEEE Conference on Computer Vision and Pattern Recognition, Salt Lake City, UT, USA, 18–23 June 2018; pp. 2800–2810.
22. Liu, J.; Qu, F.; Hong, X.; Zhang, H. A small-sample wind turbine fault detection method with synthetic fault data using generative adversarial nets. *IEEE Trans. Ind. Inform.* **2018**, *15*, 3877–3888. [CrossRef]
23. Zhang, L.; Gonzalez-Garcia, A.; Van De Weijer, J.; Danelljan, M.; Khan, F.S. Synthetic data generation for end-to-end thermal infrared tracking. *IEEE Trans. Image Process.* **2018**, *28*, 1837–1850. [CrossRef] [PubMed]
24. Wang, Q.; Gao, J.; Lin, W.; Yuan, Y. Pixel-wise crowd understanding via synthetic data. *Int. J. Comput. Vis.* **2021**, *129*, 225–245. [CrossRef]
25. Chen, Y.; Li, W.; Chen, X.; Gool, L.V. Learning semantic segmentation from synthetic data: A geometrically guided input-output adaptation approach. In Proceedings of the IEEE/CVF Conference on Computer Vision and Pattern Recognition, Long Beach, CA, USA, 15–20 June 2019; pp. 1841–1850.
26. Dunn, K.W.; Fu, C.; Ho, D.J.; Lee, S.; Han, S.; Salama, P.; Delp, E.J. DeepSynth: Three-dimensional nuclear segmentation of biological images using neural networks trained with synthetic data. *Sci. Rep.* **2019**, *9*, 18295. [CrossRef] [PubMed]
27. Kim, K.; Myung, H. Autoencoder-combined generative adversarial networks for synthetic image data generation and detection of jellyfish swarm. *IEEE Access* **2018**, *6*, 54207–54214. [CrossRef]
28. Torkzadehmahani, R.; Kairouz, P.; Paten, B. Dp-cgan: Differentially private synthetic data and label generation. In Proceedings of the IEEE/CVF Conference on Computer Vision and Pattern Recognition Workshops, Long Beach, CA, USA, 16–17 June 2019.
29. Mirza, M.; Osindero, S. Conditional generative adversarial nets. *arXiv* **2014**, arXiv:1411.1784.
30. Radford, A.; Metz, L.; Chintala, S. Unsupervised representation learning with deep convolutional generative adversarial networks. *arXiv* **2015**, arXiv:1511.06434.
31. Chen, X.; Duan, Y.; Houthooft, R.; Schulman, J.; Sutskever, I.; Abbeel, P. Infogan: Interpretable representation learning by information maximizing generative adversarial nets. In Proceedings of the 30th International Conference on Neural Information Processing Systems, Barcelona, Spain, 5–10 December 2016; pp. 2180–2188.
32. Liu, M.Y.; Tuzel, O. Coupled generative adversarial networks. *Adv. Neural Inf. Process. Syst.* **2016**, *29*, 469–477.
33. Odena, A.; Olah, C.; Shlens, J. Conditional image synthesis with auxiliary classifier gans. In Proceedings of the International Conference on Machine Learning, PMLR, Sydney, Australia, 6–11 August 2017; pp. 2642–2651.

34. Zhang, H.; Xu, T.; Li, H.; Zhang, S.; Wang, X.; Huang, X.; Metaxas, D.N. Stackgan: Text to photo-realistic image synthesis with stacked generative adversarial networks. In Proceedings of the IEEE International Conference on Computer Vision, Venice, Italy, 22–29 October 2017; pp. 5907–5915.
35. Arjovsky, M.; Chintala, S.; Bottou, L. Wasserstein generative adversarial networks. In Proceedings of the International Conference on Machine Learning, PMLR, Sydney, Australia, 6–11 August 2017; pp. 214–223.
36. Zhu, J.Y.; Park, T.; Isola, P.; Efros, A.A. Unpaired image-to-image translation using cycle-consistent adversarial networks. In Proceedings of the IEEE International Conference on Computer Vision, Venice, Italy, 22–29 October 2017; pp. 2223–2232.
37. Dong, H.W.; Hsiao, W.Y.; Yang, L.C.; Yang, Y.H. MuseGAN: Multi-track Sequential Generative Adversarial Networks for Symbolic Music Generation and Accompaniment. *arXiv* **2017**, arXiv:1709.06298.
38. Karras, T.; Aila, T.; Laine, S.; Lehtinen, J. Progressive growing of gans for improved quality, stability, and variation. *arXiv* **2017**, arXiv:1710.10196.
39. Zhang, H.; Goodfellow, I.; Metaxas, D.; Odena, A. Self-attention generative adversarial networks. In Proceedings of the International Conference on Machine Learning, PMLR, Long Beach, CA, USA, 9–15 June 2019; pp. 7354–7363.
40. Salimans, T.; Goodfellow, I.; Zaremba, W.; Cheung, V.; Radford, A.; Chen, X. Improved Techniques for Training GANs. *arXiv* **2016**, arXiv:1606.03498.
41. Heusel, M.; Ramsauer, H.; Unterthiner, T.; Nessler, B.; Hochreiter, S. GANs Trained by a Two Time-Scale Update Rule Converge to a Local Nash Equilibrium. *arXiv* **2018**, arXiv:1706.08500.
42. Brock, A.; Donahue, J.; Simonyan, K. Large scale GAN training for high fidelity natural image synthesis. *arXiv* **2018**, arXiv:1809.11096.
43. Karras, T.; Laine, S.; Aila, T. A style-based generator architecture for generative adversarial networks. In Proceedings of the IEEE/CVF Conference on Computer Vision and Pattern Recognition, Long Beach, CA, USA, 15–20 June 2019; pp. 4401–4410.
44. Park, T.; Liu, M.Y.; Wang, T.C.; Zhu, J.Y. Semantic image synthesis with spatially-adaptive normalization. In Proceedings of the IEEE/CVF Conference on Computer Vision and Pattern Recognition, Long Beach, CA, USA, 15–20 June 2019; pp. 2337–2346.
45. Cai, W.; Wei, Z. PiiGAN: Generative adversarial networks for pluralistic image inpainting. *IEEE Access* **2020**, *8*, 48451–48463. [CrossRef]
46. Prangemeier, T.; Reich, C.; Wildner, C.; Koeppl, H. Multi-StyleGAN: Towards Image-Based Simulation of Time-Lapse Live-Cell Microscopy. *arXiv* **2021**, arXiv:2106.08285.
47. Xu, L.; Veeramachaneni, K. Synthesizing tabular data using generative adversarial networks. *arXiv* **2018**, arXiv:1811.11264.
48. Xu, L.; Skoularidou, M.; Cuesta-Infante, A.; Veeramachaneni, K. Modeling tabular data using conditional gan. *arXiv* **2019**, arXiv:1907.00503.
49. Chow, C.; Liu, C. Approximating discrete probability distributions with dependence trees. *IEEE Trans. Inf. Theory* **1968**, *14*, 462–467. [CrossRef]
50. Zhang, J.; Cormode, G.; Procopiuc, C.M.; Srivastava, D.; Xiao, X. Privbayes: Private data release via bayesian networks. *ACM Trans. Database Syst. (TODS)* **2017**, *42*, 1–41. [CrossRef]
51. Choi, E.; Biswal, S.; Malin, B.; Duke, J.; Stewart, W.F.; Sun, J. Generating multi-label discrete patient records using generative adversarial networks. In Proceedings of the Machine Learning for Healthcare Conference, PMLR, Boston, MA, USA, 18–19 August 2017; pp. 286–305.
52. Srivastava, A.; Valkov, L.; Russell, C.; Gutmann, M.U.; Sutton, C. Veegan: Reducing mode collapse in gans using implicit variational learning. In Proceedings of the Advances in Neural Information Processing Systems 30 (NIPS 2017), Long Beach, CA, USA, 4–9 December 2017; Volume 30.
53. Park, N.; Mohammadi, M.; Gorde, K.; Jajodia, S.; Park, H.; Kim, Y. Data synthesis based on generative adversarial networks. *arXiv* **2018**, arXiv:1806.03384.
54. Rajabi, A.; Garibay, O.O. TabFairGAN: Fair Tabular Data Generation with Generative Adversarial Networks. *arXiv* **2021**, arXiv:2109.00666.
55. Andrews, G. What Is Synthetic Data? 2021. Available online: https://blogs.nvidia.com/blog/2021/06/08/what-is-synthetic-data/ (accessed on 14 February 2022).
56. Alanazi, Y.; Sato, N.; Ambrozewicz, P.; Blin, A.N.H.; Melnitchouk, W.; Battaglieri, M.; Liu, T.; Li, Y. A survey of machine learning-based physics event generation. *arXiv* **2021**, arXiv:2106.00643.
57. Assefa, S. Generating synthetic data in finance: Opportunities, challenges and pitfalls. In Proceedings of the International Conference on AI in Finance, New York, NY, USA, 15–16 October 2020.
58. Lan, L.; You, L.; Zhang, Z.; Fan, Z.; Zhao, W.; Zeng, N.; Chen, Y.; Zhou, X. Generative Adversarial Networks and Its Applications in Biomedical Informatics. *Front. Public Health* **2020**, *8*, 164. [CrossRef] [PubMed]
59. Chen, J.; Little, J.J. Sports camera calibration via synthetic data. In Proceedings of the IEEE/CVF Conference on Computer Vision and Pattern Recognition Workshops, Long Beach, CA, USA, 16–20 June 2019.
60. Barth, R.; IJsselmuiden, J.; Hemming, J.; van Henten, E.J. Optimising realism of synthetic agricultural images using cycle generative adversarial networks. In Proceedings of the IEEE IROS Workshop on Agricultural Robotics, Vancouver, BC, Canada, 28 September 2017; pp. 18–22.
61. Tremblay, J.; To, T.; Sundaralingam, B.; Xiang, Y.; Fox, D.; Birchfield, S. Deep object pose estimation for semantic robotic grasping of household objects. *arXiv* **2018**, arXiv:1809.10790.

62. Nikolenko, S.I. Synthetic data for deep learning. *arXiv* **2019**, arXiv:1909.11512.
63. Batuwita, R.; Palade, V. Efficient resampling methods for training support vector machines with imbalanced datasets. In Proceedings of the 2010 International Joint Conference on Neural Networks (IJCNN), Barcelona, Spain, 18–23 July 2010; pp. 1–8.
64. Drummond, C.; Holte, R.C. C4. 5, class imbalance, and cost sensitivity: Why under-sampling beats over-sampling. *Workshop Learn. Imbalanced Datasets II* **2003**, *11*, 1–8.
65. Lusa, L. Evaluation of smote for high-dimensional class-imbalanced microarray data. In Proceedings of the 2012 11th International Conference on Machine Learning and Applications, Boca Raton, FL, USA, 12–15 December 2012; Volume 2, pp. 89–94.
66. Sun, J.; Lang, J.; Fujita, H.; Li, H. Imbalanced enterprise credit evaluation with DTE-SBD: Decision tree ensemble based on SMOTE and bagging with differentiated sampling rates. *Inf. Sci.* **2018**, *425*, 76–91. [CrossRef]
67. Sun, J.; Li, H.; Fujita, H.; Fu, B.; Ai, W. Class-imbalanced dynamic financial distress prediction based on Adaboost-SVM ensemble combined with SMOTE and time weighting. *Inf. Fusion* **2020**, *54*, 128–144. [CrossRef]
68. Lee, T.; Kim, M.; Kim, S.P. Data augmentation effects using borderline-SMOTE on classification of a P300-based BCI. In Proceedings of the 2020 8th International Winter Conference on Brain-Computer Interface (BCI), Gangwon, Korea, 26–28 February 2020; pp. 1–4.
69. Riafio, D. Using Gabriel graphs in Borderline-SMOTE to deal with severe two-class imbalance problems on neural networks. In *Artificial Intelligence Research and Development, Proceedings of the 15th International Conference of the Catalan Association for Artificial Intelligence, Alicante, Spain, 24–26 October 2012*; IOS Press: Amsterdam, The Netherlands, 2012; Volume 248, p. 29.
70. Siriseriwan, W.; Sinapiromsaran, K. The effective redistribution for imbalance dataset: Relocating safe-level SMOTE with minority outcast handling. *Chiang Mai J. Sci.* **2016**, *43*, 234–246.
71. Lu, C.; Lin, S.; Liu, X.; Shi, H. Telecom fraud identification based on ADASYN and random forest. In Proceedings of the 2020 5th International Conference on Computer and Communication Systems (ICCCS), Guangzhou, China, 21–24 April 2020; pp. 447–452.
72. Aditsania, A.; Saonard, A.L. Handling imbalanced data in churn prediction using ADASYN and backpropagation algorithm. In Proceedings of the 2017 3rd International Conference on Science in Information Technology (ICSITech), Bandung, Indonesia, 25–26 October 2017; pp. 533–536.
73. Chen, S. Research on Extreme Financial Risk Early Warning Based on ODR-ADASYN-SVM. In Proceedings of the 2017 International Conference on Humanities Science, Management and Education Technology (HSMET 2017), Taiyuan, China, 25–26 February 2017; pp. 1132–1137.
74. MacQueen, J. Classification and analysis of multivariate observations. In *Proceedings of the 5th Berkeley Symposium on Mathematical Statistics and Probability*; University of California Press: Berkeley, CA, USA, 1967; pp. 281–297.
75. Sarkar, S.; Pramanik, A.; Maiti, J.; Reniers, G. Predicting and analyzing injury severity: A machine learning-based approach using class-imbalanced proactive and reactive data. *Saf. Sci.* **2020**, *125*, 104616. [CrossRef]
76. Jo, T.; Japkowicz, N. Class imbalances versus small disjuncts. *ACM Sigkdd Explor. Newsl.* **2004**, *6*, 40–49. [CrossRef]
77. Learn, S. Gaussian Mixture Models. 2022. Available online: https://scikit-learn.org/stable/modules/mixture.html (accessed on 23 February 2022).
78. Chokwitthaya, C.; Zhu, Y.; Mukhopadhyay, S.; Jafari, A. Applying the Gaussian Mixture Model to Generate Large Synthetic Data from a Small Data Set. In *Construction Research Congress 2020: Computer Applications*; American Society of Civil Engineers: Reston, VA, USA, 2020; pp. 1251–1260.
79. A Comprehensive Introduction to Bayesian Deep Learning. Available online: https://jorisbaan.nl/2021/03/02/introduction-to-bayesian-deep-learning (accessed on 11 February 2022).
80. Soni, D. Introduction to Bayesian Networks. 2019. Available online: https://towardsdatascience.com/introduction-to-bayesian-networks-81031eeed94e (accessed on 29 January 2022).
81. Russell, S.J.; Norvig, P.; Chang, M.W. Chapter 13: Probabilistic Reasoning. In *Artificial Intelligence: A Modern Approach*; Pearson: London, UK, 2022; pp. 430–478.
82. Goodfellow, I.; Bengio, Y.; Courville, A. Chapter 20: Deep Generative Models. In *Depp Learning*; MIT Press: Cambridge, MA, USA, 2016; pp. 654–720.
83. Foster, D. Chapter 3: Variational Autoencoders. In *Generative Deep Learning: Teaching Machines to Paint, Write, Compose, and Play*; O'Reilly: Sebastopol, CA, USA, 2019; pp. 61–96.
84. Goodfellow, I.; Bengio, Y.; Courville, A. Chapter 14: Autoencoders. In *Depp Learning*; MIT Press: Cambridge, MA, USA, 2016; pp. 502–525.
85. Zhang, X.; Fu, Y.; Zang, A.; Sigal, L.; Agam, G. Learning classifiers from synthetic data using a multichannel autoencoder. *arXiv* **2015**, arXiv:1503.03163.
86. Wan, Z.; Zhang, Y.; He, H. Variational autoencoder based synthetic data generation for imbalanced learning. In Proceedings of the 2017 IEEE Symposium Series on Computational Intelligence (SSCI), Honolulu, HI, USA, 27 November–1 December 2017; pp. 1–7.
87. Islam, Z.; Abdel-Aty, M.; Cai, Q.; Yuan, J. Crash data augmentation using variational autoencoder. *Accid. Anal. Prev.* **2021**, *151*, 105950. [CrossRef] [PubMed]
88. Fahimi, F.; Zhang, Z.; Goh, W.B.; Ang, K.K.; Guan, C. Towards EEG generation using GANs for BCI applications. In Proceedings of the 2019 IEEE EMBS International Conference on Biomedical & Health Informatics (BHI), Chicago, IL, USA, 19–22 May 2019; pp. 1–4.

89. Patel, M.; Wang, X.; Mao, S. Data augmentation with Conditional GAN for automatic modulation classification. In Proceedings of the 2nd ACM Workshop on Wireless Security and Machine Learning, Linz, Austria, 13 July 2020; pp. 31–36.
90. Ali-Gombe, A.; Elyan, E. MFC-GAN: Class-imbalanced dataset classification using multiple fake class generative adversarial network. *Neurocomputing* **2019**, *361*, 212–221. [CrossRef]
91. Ali-Gombe, A.; Elyan, E.; Savoye, Y.; Jayne, C. Few-shot classifier GAN. In Proceedings of the 2018 International Joint Conference on Neural Networks (IJCNN), Rio de Janeiro, Brazil, 8–13 July 2018; pp. 1–8.
92. Sushko, V.; Gall, J.; Khoreva, A. One-shot gan: Learning to generate samples from single images and videos. In Proceedings of the IEEE/CVF Conference on Computer Vision and Pattern Recognition, Nashville, TN, USA, 20–25 June 2021; pp. 2596–2600.
93. Niu, M.Y.; Zlokapa, A.; Broughton, M.; Boixo, S.; Mohseni, M.; Smelyanskyi, V.; Neven, H. Entangling quantum generative adversarial networks. *Phys. Rev. Lett.* **2022**, *128*, 220505. [CrossRef]
94. Zhang, W.; Ma, Y.; Zhu, D.; Dong, L.; Liu, Y. MetroGAN: Simulating Urban Morphology with Generative Adversarial Network. *arXiv* **2022**, arXiv:2207.02590.
95. Yann LeCun Quora Session Overview. Available online: https://www.kdnuggets.com/2016/08/yann-lecun-quora-session.html (accessed on 2 February 2022).
96. Anscombe, F.J. Graphs in statistical analysis. *Am. Stat.* **1973**, *27*, 17–21.
97. Zhou, Y.; Dong, F.; Liu, Y.; Li, Z.; Du, J.; Zhang, L. Forecasting emerging technologies using data augmentation and deep learning. *Scientometrics* **2020**, *123*, 1–29. [CrossRef]
98. Shmelkov, K.; Schmid, C.; Alahari, K. How good is my GAN? In Proceedings of the European Conference on Computer Vision (ECCV), Munich, Germany, 8–14 September 2018; pp. 213–229.
99. Alaa, A.M.; van Breugel, B.; Saveliev, E.; van der Schaar, M. How Faithful is your Synthetic Data? Sample-level Metrics for Evaluating and Auditing Generative Models. *arXiv* **2021**, arXiv:2102.08921.

Article

Deep Reinforcement Learning for Crowdshipping Last-Mile Delivery with Endogenous Uncertainty

Marco Silva [1,*] and João Pedro Pedroso [1,2]

1 Industrial Engineering and Management, Institute for Systems and Computer Engineering, Technology and Science, 4200-465 Porto, Portugal
2 Department of Computer Science, Faculty of Sciences, University of Porto, 4169-007 Porto, Portugal
* Correspondence: marco.c.silva@inesctec.pt

Abstract: In this work, we study a flexible compensation scheme for last-mile delivery where a company outsources part of the activity of delivering products to its customers to occasional drivers (ODs), under a scheme named crowdshipping. All deliveries are completed at the minimum total cost incurred with their vehicles and drivers plus the compensation paid to the ODs. The company decides on the best compensation scheme to offer to the ODs at the planning stage. We model our problem based on a stochastic and dynamic environment where delivery orders and ODs volunteering to make deliveries present themselves randomly within fixed time windows. The uncertainty is endogenous in the sense that the compensation paid to ODs influences their availability. We develop a deep reinforcement learning (DRL) algorithm that can deal with large instances while focusing on the quality of the solution: we combine the combinatorial structure of the action space with the neural network of the approximated value function, involving techniques from machine learning and integer optimization. The results show the effectiveness of the DRL approach by examining out-of-sample performance and that it is suitable to process large samples of uncertain data, which induces better solutions.

Keywords: last-mile delivery; crowd shipping; deep reinforcement learning; data-driven optimization; endogenous uncertainty

MSC: 90-08

Citation: Silva, M.; Pedroso, J.P. Deep Reinforcement Learning for Crowdshipping Last-Mile Delivery with Endogenous Uncertainty. *Mathematics* 2022, 10, 3902. https://doi.org/10.3390/math10203902

Academic Editor: Jianping Gou

Received: 26 September 2022
Accepted: 18 October 2022
Published: 20 October 2022

Publisher's Note: MDPI stays neutral with regard to jurisdictional claims in published maps and institutional affiliations.

Copyright: © 2022 by the authors. Licensee MDPI, Basel, Switzerland. This article is an open access article distributed under the terms and conditions of the Creative Commons Attribution (CC BY) license (https://creativecommons.org/licenses/by/4.0/).

1. Introduction

Last-mile delivery is a term used to define the transportation of items from a depot to a final customer destination. Last-mile delivery is evolving at a rapid rate and has become a topic of great interest due to the increase in e-commerce in recent years, making it a key differentiator among large competitors in this sector.

We study a business model where the company outsources part of the activity of delivering products to its customers to occasional drivers, also known as crowdshipping, complementing its own fleet. All deliveries are completed at the minimum total cost incurred with the company vehicles and drivers plus the compensation paid to the ODs. The company decides on the best compensation scheme to offer to the ODs at the planning stage.

Crowd-shipped delivery has been adopted as a shortcut to last-mile growth. It has been implemented under different business models depending on how the occasional drivers are engaged and managed. A survey in [1] indicates that while only 9% of retailers are using crowd-sourced providers now, one in four retailers plans to start using them in the next 12 months. It has been implemented as an enabler to same-day delivery for the last mile as can be seen in recent implementations of large companies as in [2–4].

This setting also potentiates greater efficiency by making better use of existing urban traffic flows. For example, the case of crowdshipping with in-store customers taking up delivery tasks on their way home to serve online customers. As a result of fewer freight vehicles being used, the company's costs are reduced while also benefiting society from the reduced traffic congestion.

Our setup is suitable for a same-day delivery scheme where time windows are fixed, predefined periods during the day and customers with online orders and available occasional drivers can enlist themselves in these time windows.

Crowdshipping last-mile delivery has been modeled as a variation of the vehicle routing problem (VRP) or the traveling salesman problem (TSP), under different deterministic, stochastic, and/or dynamic optimization approaches (e.g., [5–9]).

A general topic presented in these works relates to the compensation offered to occasional drivers. Choosing an appropriate compensation scheme is challenging. Different compensation schemes presented in the literature have both advantages and disadvantages associated with them. It can affect the number of available occasional drivers and also which customer locations will be assigned to occasional drivers and not to the company's drivers, affecting overall cost savings.

In general, all the compensation schemes proposed in the literature so far are static schemes (see Section 2), in the sense that the decision-maker cannot decide on different compensation rates levels paid to the occasional drivers.

In this work, a flexible compensation scheme is proposed taking into account the occasional driver's willingness to engage in a delivery task. Flexible pricing systems are still a recent subject under study in the crowdshipping literature and with only a few implementations (e.g., [10]).

We are interested in analyzing the effect of the compensation level decision not only on the solution provided to our problem but also on the complexity associated with its resolution.

We adopt a data-driven dynamic and stochastic approach where the existence of online customers' orders to be delivered, as well as the availability of occasional drivers to deliver them, are random and define scenarios on which decisions have to be made.

This problem is complex because decisions, regarding the dispatch of vehicles or occasional drivers, have to be made fast and the space to search for decisions is potentially too large. Here, we extend the work initiated in [11] and propose a deep reinforcement learning (DRL) method where we model the problem as a sequence of states connected by actions, driven by decisions, and transitions. The DRL method uses a neural network (NN) as an approximation architecture for the problem value function. Our approach is data-driven: we make use of a generative method, exploiting available scenario historical data, to generate additional scenarios, that in turn are used to train the DRL neural network.

Another key feature of our DRL approach is how we search the action (decision) space. Most reinforcement learning (RL) studies on stochastic VRPs face the challenge imposed by the combinatorial nature of state and action spaces by restricting the action space and aggregating the state space based on expert knowledge. Here, we formulate the action selection problem for each state using a recourse in a two-stage decision model where the first-stage decision is formulated as a mixed-integer optimization program. In the first stage, not only the order in which all customers will be delivered is established, as in [11], but also the best compensation to be paid for the outsourcing of each customer. The second-stage decision is made every time a scenario is revealed, and before any dispatch of fleet vehicles or ODs. The second-stage decision comprises routes defined by the recourse, where the routes follow the first-stage decision ordering but skip customers that have no online orders or customers outsourced for available ODs. Each time the vehicle capacity or the time window limit is reached, a return path to the depot is created and another route restarts from the depot if needed.

The main contributions of the approach above and the results of this work are:

- We propose a novel data-driven stochastic and dynamic approach for crowdshipping last-mile delivery, where we introduce a flexible compensation scheme, advancing the state-of-the-art in this topic.
- We experiment with generative methods to create new scenarios to train our neural network. Historical data are typically in small amounts and inadequate to evaluate

the policies of our DRL approach. We exploit the fact that there is time correlation information hidden between scenarios included in the historical data. We learn this time correlation using conditional generative adversarial networks and use them as a tool to generate scenarios to evaluate our policies.
- We present computational results on the capability of the proposed model, assuming a realistic point-of-view of correlated scenarios.

In the sequence of this work, in Section 2, we present relevant approaches to solve problem variants. In Section 3, we present our problem description and the defined model. In Section 4 we introduce the DRL method developed. Next, in Section 5, we discuss the computational results. Finally, in Section 6, we present this work's conclusions.

2. Literature Review

In the following sections, we survey relevant literature for the proposed approach. It includes not only the publications related to models for the crowdshipping of last-mile delivery, in particular in the different approaches developed to deal with the compensation of occasional drivers, but also covers the approaches for the problems where the customers are uncertain and applications of RL methods to VRPs.

2.1. Crowdshipping Routing and Compensation Schemes

In [5], the authors developed the first work on crowdshipping last-mile delivery. The authors study a deterministic approach where data such as the customers' locations, parameters used to define occasional drivers' compensation fees, and which customers an occasional driver can outsource, are used as input. The model proposed is a combination of an assignment problem for occasional drivers, with a capacitated VRP where vehicle routes are defined for customers not assigned to occasional drivers. A customer is assigned to an occasional driver only if it is overall optimal. The compensation scheme is then an important part of the proposed algorithm. In a basic variant of their problem, the compensation fee paid to an occasional driver is proportional to the distance between the depot and the customer location and does not consider the destination of the occasional driver. They argue the practical advantages of this method since the company only deals with the location of its customers, but it is non-ideal for occasional drivers because it does not consider the extra costs incurred. A variant is proposed where the occasional driver is paid proportionally to the detour from their original route between the depot and their final destination. The authors argue that this is more challenging to implement because it demands registering the occasional driver's destination. They suggest that new and innovative compensation schemes are essential to further developments on this subject.

Using the models above, the authors can exercise the potential benefits of employing occasional drivers to make deliveries. They analyze results based on: (1) the number of occasional drivers available regarding the number of customers; (2) how much flexibility exists in terms of an allowed detour from an occasional driver's original route and; (3) what compensation scheme is used and the amount an occasional driver is paid. They conclude that designing an adequate compensation scheme is one of the most important challenges for a company to define.

The authors in [8] study a dynamic and stochastic approach in which the demand, as online orders, arrives over time, as do in-store customers available to make deliveries. They present rolling horizon dispatching algorithms: one that exploits only the present state of the systems, and one that also exploits probabilistic data concerning future delivery orders and customers available to make deliveries arrivals. The compensation includes two terms. One term reflects a fixed compensation paid to in-store customers who deliver orders. The second term is proportional to the online order delivery time. Through numerical experiments, they verify that the quality of service may increase and the operational costs may decrease if the delivery capacity is augmented by the application of higher compensation fees to in-store customers. They study the sensitivity of these customers to price. Higher compensation can incur more participation but also become a less attractive alternative. As a consequence, crowdshipping may become simply the backup plan.

In [12], the authors assume occasional drivers that arrive randomly. Routes are developed for professional vehicles and the occasional drivers considering their final destination. Occasional drivers appear in defined time windows. They develop a two-stage model in which professional vehicle routes are defined in the first stage and, as occasional drivers appear, they adjust deliveries in the second stage. There is a paid penalty for customers that are not served. We note that here the uncertain event is related to the presence of a given occasional driver. Their stochastic solution is based on a scenario approach with a uniform distribution. They conduct computational experiments where they limit the size of the instances to 20 customers and 3 occasional drivers. Three alternative compensation schemes are analyzed: (1) a fixed and equal compensation fee is paid for each served request; (2) the compensation fee is proportional to the traveling distance from a pickup to the delivery location; and (3) the compensation fee is proportional to the detour distance made by the occasional driver. The computational results show that using occasional drivers can produce savings even when a suboptimal compensation scheme is used.

In an attempt to capture some randomness in the process of acceptance by occasional drivers, the authors in [6] investigate a stochastic approach to the problem. There, customers are either offered or not to potential occasional drivers and the acceptance probability is known. A heuristic is used to identify customers' orders to be offered to occasional drivers. They emphasize the relationship between the compensation offered to occasional drivers, the probability of their acceptance, and the resolution of the customer set offered to outsource. We note that here that the uncertain event is related to the customer being outsourced.

In [9], the authors assume a dynamic environment, where the solution is adjusted each time information becomes available. A service platform matches parcel delivery tasks to ad hoc drivers. An exact solution approach using a rolling horizon framework is developed. Compensations are defined as being proportional to the cost of serving all customers without occasional drivers. The authors present examples of crowdsourcing delivery platforms that offer same-day delivery and compare their respective compensation schemes that vary between hourly rates and per-package remuneration.

The section's references above provide interesting results regarding the importance of the definition of the correct compensation scheme, but they all offer post-optimal sensitivity analysis. This limitation has inspired this work to study alternatives for more flexible compensation schemes where the compensation paid to ODs can be part of the decision made by decision-makers.

A survey by [13] analyzes the status of crowdshipping and provides a classification of available platforms. The authors also review the operations research literature explicitly addressing this topic.

2.2. Routing with Customer Uncertainty

Stochastic optimization approaches to routing problems based on customer uncertainty have been studied by many authors.

A seminal work addressing routing with customer uncertainty was studied in [14]. The authors define a routing problem where only a random subset of customers are served. The problem is defined as the Probabilistic Traveling Salesman Problem. They develop closed-form expressions for the expected length of any route, given that customers' probability distributions are independent.

The study above is extended in [15], where the authors define a stochastic variant of the VRP. There, customer demands and/or customer presence are stochastic. The authors define a recourse strategy where absent or no-demand customers are skipped in pre-defined routes. Additionally, routes are split and a detour back to the depot occurs when the vehicle capacity is reached. The authors elaborate on the need to define strategic planning solutions, where an a priori service customer sequence of minimal expected length is calculated, rather than solving the problem only when the demand or presence is known. They develop closed-form expressions and algorithms to compute the expected length of an a priori sequence, given that customers' probability distributions are independent.

Branch-and-cut integer L-Shaped algorithms were developed in [16] and in [17] to solve the two models above. The authors could solve instances with up to nine uncertain customers. In [18], improvements were introduced to the branch-and-cut integer L-Shaped algorithm developing, among others, stronger lower-bounds formulations. Instances with 25 to 100 vertices and 2 to 4 vehicles were optimally solved for Poisson and normal demand distributions.

In [19], assuming stochastic demands, the authors developed a branch-cut-and-price algorithm for the VRP. They formulated it as a set partitioning model with additional constraints and improved the algorithm performance significantly. They developed the ng-routes that are used for the pricing sub-problems together with routines for 2-cycle elimination.

A branch-and-bound algorithm is developed in [20] for the probabilistic TSP, using the same concept of a priori strategy defined in [15]. They extend previous deterministic TSP algorithms, leveraging the closed expected value evaluation expression of [14]. The authors additionally present in [21] another branch-and-bound algorithm exploiting parallelization techniques and solving instances for up to 30 customers.

An approximation scheme is developed in [22] for the VRP with stochastic customers. A two-stage stochastic optimization set-partitioning formulation is presented where a set of vehicle routes serving all customer locations is defined a priori before any service request is known. The uncertain events are assumed to be independent. A column generation framework that allows for solving the problem to a given optimality tolerance is proposed. They solve instances for up to 40 customers within the time limit of six hours.

A heuristic approach for solving the VRP with stochastic demand, using a set-partitioning formulation, is presented in [23]. First, it presents a heuristic to define a good finite set of feasible routes that are used as columns to solve the problem. Furthermore, a recourse approach is developed, where vehicles can serve additional customers from failed routes before going back to the depot or they can serve customers from failed routes on a new route after going back to the depot. Instances of 75 customers are solved.

The stochastic studies in this section assume that the uncertain events are independent. In many real-life problems, although, event correlation can contain important information to be considered in the solution. These correlations are often difficult to deal with, which makes the planning problem complicated. An alternative is a modeling approach that considers the worst-case joint distribution, under the theory of Distributionally Robust Optimization (DRO—see, [24–26]). After identifying a set $\mathcal{P}$ of allowable probability distributions that include the true distribution $\mathbb{P}$, and called the ambiguity set, the objective function is reformulated concerning the worst-case expected cost over all possible distributions in the ambiguity set.

The authors in [27] present a VRP with stochastic demands with no recourse where an important feature of the methodologies presented allows random events correlation. Another characteristic is that chance constraints are used to limit the infeasibility of the routes due to capacity limits. The authors propose the use of a branch-price-and-cut algorithm. They identify that the pricing subproblem is strongly NP-hard, even if the priced routes have cycles. They identify further route relaxation alternatives and develop pricing algorithms through the use of dynamic programming. They solve instances for up to 55 customers.

In [28], the authors study a variant of the capacitated VRP with no recourse where an ambiguity set is known for the demand random vector. They also present a chance-constrained formulation and show that it can be solved with standard branch-and-cut algorithms when the ambiguity set satisfies a certain subadditivity condition.

2.3. Reinforcement Learning for Routing

Most works with an RL approach to solving the VRP interpret it as a Markov Decision Process, in which the optimal solution is viewed as a sequence of actions deciding which customer to visit according to the state revealed. They draw on the concept of policy-gradient or value-function approximation (VFA). Policy-gradient methods search directly for an optimal policy and do not have to be concerned with the value function. In general, the policy is parametrized. VFAs approximate the value of post-decision states using simulations. The values are stored usually in functions or tables. The challenge is related to the fact that the VRP, as combinatorial optimization problems in general, can have large combinatorial action spaces. The VRP high-dimensional action space turns methods that approximate state-action pair values inviable because they enumerate all possible actions. Typically, as an alternative, the action space is restricted instead.

The authors in [29] present one of the first studies involving RL methods to solve routing problems. They train a recurrent neural network for the TSP, called a pointer network. Given a set of city coordinates, it predicts a distribution over different city permutations. They developed a policy gradient algorithm to optimize the parameters of the recurrent neural network.

Motivated by the work in [29], the authors in [30] generalize to include other combinatorial optimization problems such as the VRP. They propose an alternate approach in which the policy model consists of a recurrent neural network decoder together with an attention mechanism and apply a policy-gradient approach.

An alternative to the approach of reducing the action space with VFA is presented in the work of [31]. They present a value-function-based DRL algorithm. The action selection problem is formulated as a mixed-integer optimization problem and is able to exploit the whole combinatorial action space. They focus on the Capacitated Vehicle Routing Problem. There, a capacity-constrained vehicle must be assigned one or more routes to serve customers with demands and minimize traveled distance. ReLU activations are used, exploiting the work developed in [32] for strong MILP reformulations of neural network-related problems.

With business models shifting to same-day delivery, routing problems have become increasingly stochastic and dynamic. A problem class called the stochastic dynamic vehicle routing problem (SDVRP) arises and poses new challenges as they require anticipatory real-time routing actions and static solutions are no longer adequate. Recent works have shown that RL appears to be a good solution method for dynamic combinatorial optimization as the SDVRP.

In [33], the authors present an actor-critic framework and apply a policy-based RL algorithm for the problem of pick-ups at customers with dynamic service requests. They consider dynamic requests and customer locations that are unknown in advance. They extend a policy learned for a single vehicle to all vehicles.

In [34], the authors present the first study to implement deep Q-learning methods for same-day delivery problems with a heterogeneous fleet of vehicles and drones. Their method learns the value of assigning a new customer to either drones or vehicles as well as the option to not offer service at all. They reduce the state space to a set of selected features and define it in a way to make it possible to enumerate alternative actions at the decision points.

A survey by [35] highlights the potential of RL methods applied to VRPs from the point of view of operations research and computer science communities and guide to joint approaches to overcome current obstacles. Overall, they suggest: (1) methods combining piece-wise linear neural network VFAs and solvers searching the action space; (2) policy-based methods that overcome the combinatorial action space; and (3) multi-agent RL approaches together with searching the joint action space with a global MIP.

2.4. Stochastic Optimization with Endogenous Uncertainty

The works presented in Section 2.2 are based on the assumption that the stochastic process is independent of the optimization decisions. Here, we consider the case of decision-making for an application that is not only subject to uncertainty but where decisions affect future uncertainties as well. In these cases, the uncertainty is endogenous or 'decision-dependent'.

Even though such uncertainties prevail in real-life settings, these problems have not received the deserved attention in the past, mainly because of computational burdens.

Nevertheless, considering this dependency can be an important step in improving system performance. Since the work in [36], dealing with a Markovian process, which first addresses the case with endogenous uncertainty, other approaches to this type of problem have been studied.

The authors in [37] first addressed problems with endogenous uncertainty where project decisions, instead of affecting the probability distribution themselves, give more information that is used to resolve the uncertainty instead. They assume that the cost of an item is uncertain until the moment it is produced. The probability distribution depends on which item is produced and when.

In [38], the authors address the offshore oil and gas planning problem to maximize revenues and investments over some time. The oil fields' size is not known in advance. The authors present a disjunctive formulation with non-anticipativity constraints to capture the interaction between the decisions and the resolution of uncertainty.

In [39], the authors extend the previous approach to a multistage stochastic problem for optimal production scheduling, that minimizes cost while satisfying the demand for different goods. Here, they consider endogenous uncertainty where the project decisions lead to the resolution of uncertainty.

Endogenous uncertainty has also been studied under distributionally robust optimization assumptions. Here, the set $\mathcal{P}$ of feasible probability distributions can depend on the first-stage decision variables. This leads to solving a Decision-Dependent Distributionally Robust Problem.

The authors in [40] developed a framework that includes two-stage decision-dependent distributionally robust stochastic programming as a special case and considers five types of ambiguity sets for which they offer reformulations designed for specific resolutions.

Another interesting application of endogenous uncertainty is within dynamic pricing, being a field of revenue management. Here, a company adjusts prices according to inventories left and the demand response observed. The decision to set prices at different levels influences the future demand for the products being priced. Among others, this application has been addressed under different approaches of reinforcement learning techniques (e.g., [41,42]). In fact, reinforcement learning has grown to represent a broad problem class of sequential stochastic optimal decision problems.

3. Stochastic Crowd Shipping Last-Mile Delivery with Endogenous Uncertainty

We follow [11] and define a typical setting for our problem in which a store is the location for in-store customers and also the depot from where online customer orders are dispatched. In-store customers who are available to deliver online customers' orders on their way back home are potentially offered the service. For their service, they are offered a small compensation and are referred to as ODs.

The store provides delivery services throughout fixed time windows during the day. Before each time window, and respecting a process defined by the store, a scenario is revealed with the available online customer orders, and the customers with available ODs. Based on the scenario revealed, the store decides the routes for its fleet of vehicles and which customer orders will be outsourced to ODs. This decision, in turn, defines the cost associated with that time window. The objective is to minimize the total costs in the long run.

The decision is taken in a two-stage approach, using a recourse model based on the work presented in [15] under the framework of stochastic optimization. An a priori first-stage decision is made during the store planning process, meaning that we define a solution to our problem offline, and before any delivery is initiated. Not only is the order in which all customers will be delivered established, but also the best compensation to be paid to ODs by each customer order being outsourced. This compensation is a continuous variable and may be restricted to a feasible region defined by the company. The second-stage decision is made every time a scenario is revealed, and before any dispatch of fleet vehicles or ODs. The second-stage decision defines routes that follow the first-stage decision ordering but skips customers that have no online orders and customers outsourced for available ODs. In our recourse model, the store only offers the service to the OD if it is optimal for the scenario being revealed. Additionally, each time the vehicle capacity or the time window limit is reached, a return path to the depot is created and another route restarts from the depot if needed.

The recourse model adopted brings two main advantages to our DRL method presented later in Section 4. First, it extremely reduces the action space since, in fact, only one decision, defined by the recourse, is possible at each decision point of our model. We recall that RL algorithms in general will require a small action space allowing enumeration or that is continuous. We also note that a very large action space remains to be searched during the first-stage decision, representing possible permutations of customers' delivery ordering. Second, it presents a solution that is potentially very close to the decision adopted in a reoptimization strategy, where an optimal solution is calculated each time a scenario is revealed. The authors in [15] show that, for their setup where random events associated with customers are assumed independent, both solutions are close, on average.

An important modeling feature of our implementation is that uncertainty is customer-related. We can model not only uncertainty for customers with no orders but also uncertainty related to the availability of ODs. This is an alternative to current crowdshipping last-mile delivery models, where uncertainty is related to the OD (e.g., [8,12]). This way we can reduce the complexity of the problem to beg solved since we do not deal with explicit ODs constraints, such as their quantity, capacity, and routes.

Our approach is data-driven. We assume a set of historical data is available with a sequence of scenarios expressing customer orders and ODs availability conditioned by the compensation offered.

In what follows, we detail our problem and introduce the notation used. Let $G = (V, A)$ be a directed graph, where $V = \{0, \ldots, N\}$ is the set of vertices and $A = \{(i,j) \mid i,j \in V\}$ is the set of arcs. Set V consists of a depot (vertex 0) and a subset $C = \{1, \ldots, N\}$ of customers' represented by their locations. We assume $|C| \geq 3$ to facilitate our formulations.

A non-negative cost c_{ij} and a duration in time d_{ij} are associated with each arc $(i,j) \in A$. We assume that the graph is symmetric, i.e., $c_{ij} = c_{ji}$; $d_{ij} = d_{ji}$, and they both satisfy triangular inequalities. We also assume that the company fleet vehicles are identical and can serve up to Q customers per time window and that all time window customers must be delivered within a time limit of D. There is a fixed number of K time windows during a day.

The binary vector $(\xi_1, \ldots, \xi_{2N})$ defines a scenario. The vector component $\xi_i = 1$, $i \in \{1, \ldots, N\}$ iff customer i has an online delivery order available and $\xi_i = 1$, $i \in \{N+1, \ldots, 2N\}$ iff customer (i-N) has ODs available. If $\xi_i = 0$, $i \in \{1, \ldots, N\}$, customer i will be skipped by the routes defined by the recourse. If $\xi_i = 1$ and $\xi_{i+N} = 1$, $i \in \{1, \ldots, N\}$, customer i delivery order will be considered to be delivered by an OD. If $\xi_i = 1$ and $\xi_{i+N} = 0$, $i \in \{1, \ldots, N\}$, customer i delivery order will be served by the fleet of vehicles under routes defined by the recourse.

A compensation fee f_i is defined for customer i outsourcing. We assume the compensation vector, $f \in F \subseteq \mathbb{R}_+^N$, influences the joint distribution of scenarios $\xi \in \Xi$. The feasible region F includes restrictions $f_i^{min} \leq f_i \leq f_i^{max}$, $\forall i \in C$.

We define set Ξ as the support of the joint distribution and index scenarios using indicator $w \in W = \{1, \ldots, |\Xi|\}$.

We model our problem as a Markov decision process (MDP) where there is a sequence of states connected by actions, defined by policies, rewards, and transitions, and running through episodes. A decision point $k \in \{1, \ldots, K\}$ is defined at the beginning of each time window of a day. A decision point is when a recourse action is made. In the following we consider:

States ξ^k: A state comprises all information needed to select an action and for our problem that is represented by the scenario ξ^k that presents itself right before decision point k.

Actions a^k: Action a^k implements the recourse model at each decision point k, and defines routes and ODs allocation. The actions, together with the first-stage decision vectors $z \in \mathbb{Z}^N$ and f, define a policy $\pi \in \Pi$. Element $z_i \in \{1, \ldots, N\}$ of the first-stage decision z gives the order of delivery of customer i.

Reward function $R^k(\xi^k, z, f)$: The reward function $R^k()$ expresses the immediate impact of an action a^k on the objective value of our problem. Since action a^k is a recourse under the defined policy, the reward function is dependent on z, f, and ξ^k. The reward function is defined by the cost of routes and the OD payment is defined by the recourse.

Transitions: Transitions between states are given by exogenous information and related to the time correlation between scenarios. For our model, we assume scenario ξ^k is conditioned not only by the compensation vector, f, but also by the precedent scenario ξ^{k-1}.

Episodes: An episode for our setup problem is a day at the store, composed of K time windows and K decision points. A total return TR = $\sum_{k=1}^{K} R^k(\xi^k, z, f)$ is defined for each episode.

Value function Va: A key concept of RL is the use of value functions to drive the search for good policies. In our problem, each policy π has an expected or mean total return once z and f are given. The value function Va, as a function of z and f, expresses the expected total return by applying z and f.

Objective: A solution to our problem is a policy π that assigns an ordering of customers z and a compensation vector f. The optimal solution is a policy π^* that assigns a tuple z^* and f^* and minimizes the expected total return and can be expressed by

$$(z^*, f^*) = \arg\min_{z \in \mathbb{Z}^N, f \in F} (Va(z, f) = \mathbb{E}[\sum_{k=1}^{K} R^k(\xi^k, z, f)]) \qquad (1)$$

The difficulty in dealing with scenarios is to identify the sensitivity of customers to different prices. Indeed, potentially there is not enough available data to evaluate a certain compensation scheme. Additionally, exploring odd prices can lead to unreasonable ODs reactions. On the other hand, exploiting only low prices can have undesirable consequences on the business side. For all that we apply a data augmentation technique to add newly created synthetic data from existing data (see [43]). We exploit the information contained in the historical data available by using conditional generative adversarial networks [44] to learn the time correlation between scenarios and to artificially generate the additional scenarios needed, conditioned to the compensation paid to ODs.

Our goal is to forecast new sequences of scenarios. We want to learn the predictive probability distribution over future quantities. For this purpose, we apply a probabilistic forecasting method to quantify the variance in a prediction [45].

One method for probabilistic forecasting which implies the implementation of neural networks, is the generative adversarial network (GAN). GANs are an approach to generative modeling. Generative modeling is an unsupervised learning task in machine learning that involves automatically learning the patterns in input data and which can generate outputs that could have been drawn from the original dataset. GANs train a generative model by framing the problem as a supervised learning problem with two neural network sub-models: the generator model that is trained to learn the distribution of data, and the discriminator model that tries to classify examples as either real (from the domain) or fake (generated). The two models are trained together in a zero-sum game, adversarial, until the discriminator model is fooled, meaning the generator model is generating plausible examples [46].

In [47], the authors introduce the concept of conditional GAN (cGAN) which is a GAN whose generator and discriminator are conditioned during training by using some additional information, named labels. During cGAN training, the generator learns to produce realistic examples for each label in the training dataset, and the discriminator learns to distinguish fake example-label pairs from real example-label pairs. cGAN can be used, for instance, as a method for time series forecasting if the labels are the previous time steps used to define possible realizations of the next time step of the referenced time series.

In [48], the authors also exploit the capacity of cGANs to learn the distribution of time series data, allowing the generation of synthetic scenarios from the distribution. They argue that modeling synthetic data using a GAN has been a viable response to the challenge in machine learning which is to gain access to a considerable amount of quality data.

We then opt for a probabilistic model for multivariate time-series forecasting with the use of a cGAN. With cGAN, we learn the probability distribution of one step ahead scenario ξ^{k+1} conditioned (labeled) not only to past scenario information, $\{\xi^1, \ldots, \xi^k\}$, but also to compensation fee values, f_i, defined as first-stage decisions.

4. Deep Reinforcement Learning for Stochastic Last-Mile Delivery with Crowdshipping

We implement an on-policy and ε-greedy policy iteration algorithm for value-based reinforcement learning with combinatorial actions. We leverage the strategy developed in [31] where the authors model the value function as a small NN with a fully-connected hidden layer and rectified linear unit (ReLU) activations. The NN is reformulated as a mixed-integer program, as in [32], and combined with the structure of the action space, the customers' delivery ordering, and OD compensation, for policy improvement. This, together with the recourse model defined, greatly simplifies the complexity of the policy iteration algorithm while maintaining the possibility of searching the entire first-stage decision action space.

Given a randomly chosen starter ε-soft policy π_0, where the first-stage decision can vary with probability ε, we repeatedly improve it. In the τ-th policy evaluation step, using the Monte Carlo method, we repeatedly apply the current ε-soft policy $\pi_{\tau-1}$ for episodes and average sample total returns after each episode. The episodes are defined using the sequence of scenarios provided by newly dynamically cGAN generated data, conditioned to the compensation fees defined by the policy. We use the average sample total returns provided using the Monte Carlo method to train the NN and incrementally approximate the value function Va. The NN learns by minimizing the mean-squared error (MSE) on the cumulative cost among all iterations of our algorithm.

Figure 1 defines the architecture we implement for our DRL NN. The DRL NN has as input the vectors z and f, representing the customers' delivery ordering and the ODs compensation vector; only one P hidden nodes layer with ReLU activation, and one linear output. Let $w^p \in R^{2N}$ represent the weights vector and $b^p \in R$ the bias term for the p-th hidden node. We define $w^{output} \in R^P$ and $b^{output} \in R$ analogously for the output layer.

For the DRL policy evaluation step, we now detail how cGAN data is dynamically generated and used within the Monte Carlo method. We note that the cGAN itself is trained as a previous step, using historical data, as part of the DRL algorithm. The cGAN is trained only once. By doing this, we train the cGAN's generator model to generate a new sequence of scenarios based on previous scenarios and the compensation fee defined. The cGAN's generator model is then used as part of the DRL policy evaluation step to dynamically generate a new sequence of scenarios for the execution of the Monte Carlo method at each iteration.

Figure 2 presents an overview of the cGAN. The cGAN englobes two neural networks, the generator and the discriminator. These NNs learn simultaneously in an adversarial process, with a two-player minimax game. First, we perform the conditioning by feeding the label representing the previous scenarios and compensation fees defined, into both the discriminator and generator as an additional input layer. The generator has the noise vector as input, which is sampled from a mean 0 and standard deviation 1 Gaussian distribution and forecasts ξ^{k+1} with regard to the conditioning label. The discriminator has ξ^{k+1} as input and verifies whether it is a valid value to follow the label or not. The discriminator is optimized to distinguish between generated data and real data.

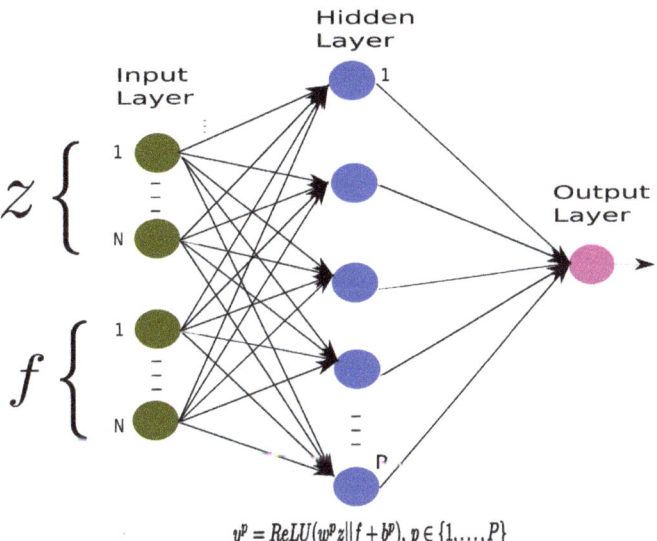

Figure 1. Fully connected neural network with one hidden layer and linear output.

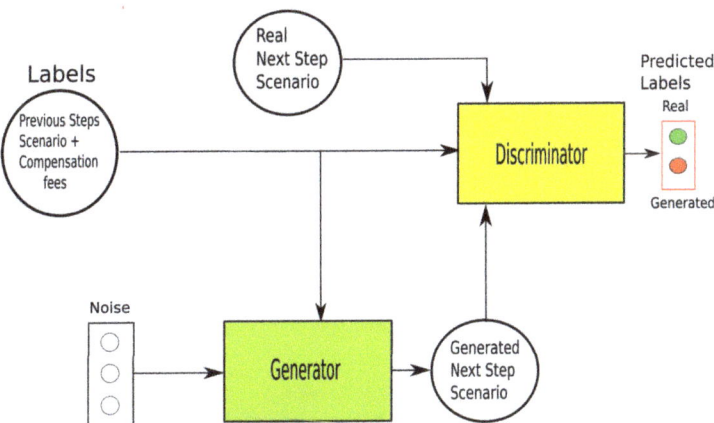

Figure 2. Conditional GAN.

The optimal generator NN models the probability distribution of ξ^{k+1}, conditioned to a label. In the end, information regarding any possible outcome can be extracted by sampling.

There are different ways to include conditional information in the neural network. Different approaches can be developed for how this information should be combined, or where in the network it should be included. Here, we include the label only in the input layer for the two networks and the representation data of the label is learned first by passing scenarios through a Long Short-Term Memory (LSTM) layer. LSTM neural networks, as introduced in [49], are distinguished by their "memory" as they take information from prior inputs to influence the current input and output.

The LSTM output is then concatenated with the compensation fee vector to finally compound the representation data.

Then, the noise vector, concatenated with the label is passed through two dense layers, leading to the predicted ξ^{k+1} value. The discriminator inputs ξ^{k+1} from the generator output or from the historical dataset concatenated with the label. This data passes a dense layer that outputs a single value specifying the output validity.

Our approach has to deal with a multivariate setting. In the multivariate setting, more complex NN architectures are needed to figure out dependencies between features. cGANs also require precise hyperparameter tuning to have a stable training process. It can be cumbersome to find adequate generator and discriminator architecture concurrently to perform adequately. To address this challenge we further adopt the cGAN training strategy of [44]. They build a probabilistic forecaster based on a deterministic forecaster using the GAN architecture. Namely, the generator model is based on the architecture and hyperparameters of the deterministic forecaster. They search a generator and discriminator architecture separately, which results in the simplification of the architecture's overall definition.

We now proceed with the policy improvement step of our DRL method. The τ-th policy improvement step involves solving the optimization problem related to (1), meaning that we find the first-stage decision to our problem that minimizes the expected total return expressed by the current approximation of the value function. Problem (1) is formulated as (see [32]):

$$\min \sum_{p=1}^{P} w_p^{output} y^p + b^{output} \tag{2}$$

$$\text{s.t. } y^p \geq \sum_{i \in \{1,\ldots,N\}} w_i^p z_i + \sum_{i \in \{N+1,\ldots,2N\}} w_i^p f_i + b^p \qquad \forall\, 1 \leq p \leq P \tag{3}$$

$$y^p \leq \sum_{i \in \{1,\ldots,N\}} w_i^p z_i + \sum_{i \in \{N+1,\ldots,2N\}} w_i^p f_i + b^p + M_-^p(1 - s^p) \qquad \forall\, 1 \leq p \leq P \tag{4}$$

$$y^p \leq M_+^p s^p \qquad \forall\, 1 \leq p \leq P \tag{5}$$

$$y^p \leq \sum_{i \in I, i \leq N} w_i^p z_i + \sum_{i \in I, i > N} w_i^p f_i - \sum_{i \in I} w_i^p L_i^p (1 - s^p) + (b^p + \sum_{i \notin I} w_i^p U_i^p) s^p \qquad \forall\, 1 \leq p \leq P,\, I \subseteq \text{supp}(w^p) \tag{6}$$

$$x_{ij} + x_{ji} = 1 \qquad \forall\, i,j \in C,\, i \neq j \tag{7}$$

$$x_{ij} + x_{jk} - x_{ik} \leq 1 \qquad \forall\, i,k,j \in C,\, i \neq j \neq k \tag{8}$$

$$z_i = 1 + \sum_{j \in V, j \neq i} x_{ji} \qquad \forall\, i \in C \tag{9}$$

$$f_i^{min} \leq f_i \leq f_i^{max} \qquad \forall\, i \in C \tag{10}$$

$$z \in \mathbb{Z}^N, f \in \mathbb{R}^N, y^p \in \mathbb{R}, s^p \in \{0,1\}, \forall\, 1 \leq p \leq P,\, x_{ij} \in \{0,1\}\, \forall\, i,j \in C,\, i \neq j \tag{11}$$

where supp(w) indicates the set of indices i such that $w_i \neq 0$ and components L_i^p and U_i^p are defined as

$$L_i^p := \begin{cases} 0, & w_i^p \geq 0, \\ N+1, & w_i^p < 0, \end{cases} \quad \text{and} \quad U_i^p := \begin{cases} N+1, & w_i^p \geq 0, \\ 0, & w_i^p < 0, \end{cases}$$

for $i \leq N$ and

$$L_i^p := \begin{cases} 0, & w_i^p \geq 0, \\ f_i^{max}+1, & w_i^p < 0, \end{cases} \quad \text{and} \quad U_i^p := \begin{cases} f_i^{max}+1, & w_i^p \geq 0, \\ 0, & w_i^p < 0, \end{cases}$$

for $i > N$.

Formulation's Big-Ms are set as $M_+^p = \max_{z \in \mathbb{Z}^N, f \in F} w^p z || f + b^p = w^p U^p + b^p$ and $M_-^p = \min_{z \in \mathbb{Z}^N, f \in F} w^p z || f + b^p = w^p L^p + b^p$, where $z || f$ is the vector resulting from the concatenation of vectors z and f and $w^p z || f$ is the inner product of vectors w^p and $z || f$. We define the N decision variables z_i, $1 \leq z_i \leq N$, giving the sequence in which customers will be delivered, a continuous variable f_i defining the compensation paid for each customer outsourced, a continuous variable y^p that models the output of the hidden node p and a binary variable s^p that indicates whether the pre-activation function is positive or negative (i.e., whether the ReLU is active or not). We also introduce variables x_{ij} to define the delivery order: $x_{ij} = 1$ if customer i precedes customer j and 0 otherwise.

This pre-activation function is enforced by the "big-M" constraints (4) and (5). The formulation is not polynomial in size, as there are exponentially many constraints of type (6), but these constraints simply strengthen the formulation.

Constraints (7) to (9) define the feasible region of all possible ordering of customers.

To be able to solve large instances and still have good solutions, we define a time limit of 1800 s to solve problem (1) at each policy improvement step and use the best solution provided until then. We apply warm start, callbacks to introduce lazy constraints and heuristics, and use only the needed half of x_{ij} variables, where $i < j$.

We warm start not only in an attempt to accelerate resolution but also to guarantee one incumbent solution. We adapt the Almost Nearest Neighbor Heuristic defined in the study of heuristic algorithms for the probabilistic TSP in [50], which considers independent marginals. We set a solution in an attempt to have a good feasible initial incumbent solution. The ordering of customers is defined by appending the customer with the lowest change in expected length from the last inserted customer to the tour. For a given set T of customers already inserted in a tour, inserting customer j with minimum cost is computed as

$$\min_{j \in C \setminus T} \sum_{i=1}^{|T|} (1-m_i)(1-m_j) c_{ij} \prod_{k=i+1}^{|T|} m_k,$$

where m_i, $i \in C$ is the marginal Bernoulli probability of the component ξ_i, $i \in C$ of the uncertain scenario vector given by the historical data. We also set $f_i = f_i^{\min}$, $\forall i \in C$.

Constraints (6) are introduced as cutting planes by lazy constraints callbacks using a linear-time separation routine as described in [32]. Heuristics callbacks introduce simple heuristics by setting variables x_{ij} as binaries and following the same customer order given by the z relaxed solution.

Algorithm 1 summarizes the steps undertaken in our policy iteration algorithm.

Algorithm 1: Policy iteration algorithm

Initialize:
  $\varepsilon \geq 0$
  $\pi \leftarrow$ an arbitrary ε-soft policy π_0 with z_0, f_0
Train cGAN using scenarios historical data
VD $\leftarrow \emptyset$ Initialize empty dataset
Repeat for each policy iteration
  Repeat for each episode:
    Generate scenarios for episode using cGAN generator model
    Generate an episode following π: $\xi^1, a^1, R^1, \ldots, \xi^K, a^K, R^K$
    TR $\leftarrow 0$
    Loop for each step of episode, $k = K, K-1, \ldots, 1$:
      TR $\leftarrow$ TR + R^k
      Append TR to Returns(z, f)
      VD(z, f) $\leftarrow$ average(Returns(z, f))
  Use VD to incrementally train the NN and approximate value function Va
  $z^*, f^* \leftarrow$ argmin Va(z, f) using Va function MIP formulation
  Define ε-soft policy π with z^*, f^*

We define two forms for the reward calculation. Here, we want an optimal assignment of ODs. To perform this exactly we first formulate it as an optimization problem. The formulation for this problem is given as

$$\min \sum_{i,j \in V, i \neq j} c_{ij} x_{ij} + \sum_{i \in C} f_i w_i$$

s.t.
$$\sum_{j \in V, i \neq j} x_{ji} = \sum_{j \in V, i \neq j} x_{ij} = v_i \quad \forall i \in C \quad (12)$$

$$\sum_{i \in C} x_{i0} - \sum_{i \in C} x_{0i} = 0 \quad (13)$$

$$v_i + w_i \leq 1 \quad \forall i \in C \quad (14)$$

$$v_i + w_i \geq \xi_i \quad \forall i \in C \quad (15)$$

$$w_i \leq \xi_i \quad \forall i \in C \quad (16)$$

$$v_i \leq \xi_i \quad \forall i \in C \quad (17)$$

$$w_i \leq \xi_{i+N} \quad \forall i \in C \quad (18)$$

$$\sum_{j \in V, i \neq j} y_{ji} - \sum_{j \in V, i \neq j} y_{ij} = v_i \quad \forall i \in C \quad (19)$$

$$\sum_{j \in C} y_{0j} = \sum_{j \in C} v_j \quad (20)$$

$$y_{i0} = 0 \quad \forall i \in C \quad (21)$$

$$y_{ij} \leq Q x_{ij} \quad \forall i, j \in V, i \neq j \quad (22)$$

$$\sum_{j \in V, i \neq j} t_{ij} - \sum_{j \in V, i \neq j} t_{ji} = \sum_{j \in V, i \neq j} d_{ij} x_{ij} \quad \forall i \in C \quad (23)$$

$$t_{0i} \geq d_{0i} x_{0i} \quad \forall i \in C \quad (24)$$

$$t_{ij} \leq (D - d_{j0}) x_{ij} \quad \forall i, j \in V, i \neq j \quad (25)$$

$$\sum_{j \in S} x_{ij} = 0 \quad \forall i \in C, S = \{j \mid z_j < z_i\} \quad (26)$$

$$\sum_{j \in S} x_{ji} \leq v_i \quad \forall i \in C; S = \{j \mid z_j < z_i]\} \quad (27)$$

$$x_{ij} \in \{0, 1\} \, \forall i, j \in V, i \neq j, y_{ij}, t_{ij} \geq 0 \, \forall i, j \in V, i \neq j \quad (28)$$

$$w_i \in \{0, 1\} \, v_i \in \{0, 1\} \, \forall i \in C \quad (29)$$

where we define variables $x_{ij} = 1$ if customer i is served by a vehicle right before j, 0 otherwise, $w_i = 1$ if customer i is served by an OD, 0 otherwise, $v_i = 1$ if customer i is served by a vehicle, 0 otherwise, y_{ij} as the accumulated capacity loaded between customer i and j and t_{ij} as the accumulated time spent between customer i and j. The objective is to minimize the total cost of routes plus OD payments. Constraints (12) and (13) are route flow conservation and should be considered every time a customer is included in a route, $v_i = 1$. Constraints (14) define that customer i is served by a vehicle, or an OD or none. Constraints (15) define that customer i is served by a vehicle or an OD if $\xi_i = 1$. Constraints (16) and (17) define that customer i is not served by an OD or a vehicle if $\xi_i = 0$. Constraints (18) define that customer i is served by an OD only if an OD is available. Constraints (19) to (22) define the capacity restrictions. Constraints (23) to (25) define the time duration restrictions. Constraints (26) and (27) guarantee that the order of first-stage decision z is respected. Here, z, f and ξ are data input to the problem. For our algorithms, we define a time limit of 600 s to solve the problem relative to this formulation and use the best solution provided until then.

As an alternative, we provide a heuristic for reward calculation where the condition to reduce cost by OD assignment is verified only locally. By Algorithm 2, customers are allocated to ODs only if the corresponding OD compensation fee is less than the vehicle cost to route from the previous to the next available customer (customers with delivery orders in the scenario being referenced).

Algorithm 2: Reward function for variant 2 of recourse model

```
Initialize:
  laststop = 0; depot
  cost = 0; cost of vehicles route
  cap = 0; accumulated capacity of a vehicle
  time = 0; accumulated time duration of a vehicle route
  continue = true; define when to stop algorithm
  bypass = false; should bypass OD available
i = 0
while continue
  i+ = 1
  if ξ[z⁻¹[i]] == 1 and (ξ[N + z⁻¹[i]] == 0 or bypass)
    bypass = false
    if time + d[laststop, z⁻¹[i]] + d[z⁻¹[i], depot] ≤ timelimit
      cost+ = c[laststop, z⁻¹[i]]; time+ = d[laststop, z⁻¹[i]]
      laststop = z⁻¹[i]; cap+ = 1
      if i == N
        cost+ = c[z⁻¹[i], depot]; continue = false
      elseif cap == Q
        cost+ = c[laststop, depot]; laststop = depot; cap = 0; time = 0
    else
      if i == N # assume 2*time from depot to i ≤ timelimit always
        cost+ = c[laststop, depot] + c[depot, z⁻¹[i]] + c[z⁻¹[i], depot]
        continue = false
      else
        cost+ = c[laststop, depot] + c[depot, z⁻¹[i]]
        time = d[depot, z⁻¹[i]]; laststop = z⁻¹[i]; cap = 1
  elseif ξ[z⁻¹[i]] == 1 and ξ[z⁻¹[i] + N] == 1
    # find next customer available
    j = i + 1
    while j ≤ N and ξ[z⁻¹[j]] == 0)
      j+ = 1
    if j ≤ N and f[z⁻¹[i]] ≤ c[laststop, z⁻¹[i]] + c[z⁻¹[i], z⁻¹[j]]
      cost+ = f[z⁻¹[i]]
      i = j − 1
    elseif j > N and f[z⁻¹[i]] ≤ c[laststop, z⁻¹[i]] + c[z⁻¹[i], depot]
      continue = false
      cost+ = f[z⁻¹[i]]
      if cap ≠ 0
        cost+ = c[laststop, depot]
    elseif j ≤ N and f[z⁻¹[i]] > c[laststop, z⁻¹[i]] + c[z⁻¹[i], z⁻¹[j]]
      bypass = true; i− = 1
    elseif j > N and f[z⁻¹[i]] ≤ c[laststop, z⁻¹[i]] + c[z⁻¹[i], depot]
      bypass = true; i− = 1
  else
    if i == N and cap ≠ 0
      cost+ = c[laststop, depot]
    if i == N
      continue = false
```

5. Experiments and Computational Results

The experiments have a three-fold objective: (1) analyze the effect of considering a flexible compensation scheme from a solution improvement perspective; (2) analyze the sensitivity of the algorithm's solution to key parameters; and (3) analyze the performance of the algorithms we have implemented.

To pursue this objective, we present in the sections below, the instances setting and the implemented benchmark algorithms.

Algorithms were developed in Python, with Keras, Tensorflow, and Docplex integrated with Cplex 12.9, running with a machine with 16 GB of RAM and Intel I7 CPU at 2.30 GHz. We present key parameters and additional architectural features defined for the DRL algorithm and used in the experiment:

- We define key parameters with default values: number of nodes of the hidden layer of the NN as 16, number of policy iterations as 15, number of historical scenarios in sequence for cGAN as 1500 and number of scenarios generated by cGAN for DRL Monte Carlo Simulation as 800,000. For some of the experiments, when specified, we change default values to analyze the sensitivity of the DRL method to these changes.
- Exploration and exploitation during training are performed by setting ε-soft policies. We set the probability of exploring $\varepsilon = 0.6$ and exploiting $1 - \varepsilon$ and decay ε over the policy iterations.
- We apply a learning rate with an exponential decay from 0.01 with the base 0.96 and the decay rate 1/6000 for updating weights.
- We pass through the entire episodes dataset 100 times (epochs) with a batch size of 100.

5.1. Instances

We generate random test instances having $|C| + 1$ vertices (depot and $|C|$ customers) for different values of $|C| \in \{10, 30, 70, 150, 300\}$. Five instances for each number of customers are generated. Results indicated by the number of customers are an average of the results of all their associated instances.

Customers' locations for each instance are assigned randomly from a grid of 100×100 possible locations. We assume that travel times and costs are deterministic and proportional to the euclidean distances between customers.

The compensation fee limits f_i^{min} and f_i^{max} for each customer i are set to the minimal and maximal detour considering all pairs of customers $r, j \in C, i \neq j \neq r$ plus a small value f^{fixed}, to avoid zero compensations, and given by $f_i^{min} = f^{fixed} + \min_{j,r \in C} c_{ji} + c_{ir} - c_{jr}$ and $f_i^{max} = f^{fixed} + \max_{j,r \in C} c_{ji} + c_{ir} - c_{jr}$.

Customers' orders and OD availability occur randomly around the day and present themselves for each time window as scenarios. We assume there is a sequence of scenarios, conditioned by compensation fee, available as data and that is sufficient to train the cGAN.

We artificially generate these scenarios for our test instances based on two probability vectors that define for each customer $i \in C$, a marginal probability m_i for his/her order, and a marginal probability o_i for the availability of an OD to attend him/her. The marginal probability o_i is dependent on the compensation fee f_i, defined as a pair (o_i, f_i).

To assure scenario consistency, the OD availability is only assigned when the respective customer is also assigned to a delivery order. To introduce a correlation between scenarios we force customers to have a maximum of one delivery order per day. We generate 1500 scenarios that are used to train the cGAN, plus 1500 scenarios that are used to simulate the solutions provided by the algorithms (out-of-sample performance). Note that the cGAN 1500 scenarios generated to simulate the solutions are, as always with the cGAN, conditioned for the compensation fees defined as first-stage solutions.

We assume that the pairs (o_i, f_i) generated are coherent, in the sense that the compensation fee influences the probability of an OD accepting to outsource.

The values m_i are assigned randomly for each instance in a range smaller than 0.3.

We set three values for f_i, $f_i = f_i^{min}$, $f_i = f_i^{max}$, $f_i = (f_i^{max} - f_i^{min})/2 + f_i^{min}$. The values of o_i are assigned randomly for each instance, according to the values of f_i. If $f_i = f_i^{min}$, then o_i is assigned in a range smaller than 0.1. If $f_i = f_i^{max}$, then o_i is assigned in a range greater than 0.3. If $f_i = f_i^{max}$, $f_i = (f_i^{max} - f_i^{min})/2 + f_i^{min}$, then o_i is assigned in a range between 0.1 and 0.3.

Each episode is composed of a delivery day with four time windows of 2 h each, and therefore, four scenarios.

The professional fleet vehicle capacity is set to $Q = \left\lfloor \frac{|C|}{3} \right\rfloor$ and the time limit of a route is given by the time windows of 2 h.

5.2. Benchmark Algorithms

We present in Table 1 a general description of the different algorithms we run our instances with.

Table 1. Algorithms.

Algorithm Code	Description
DRLV1	The DRL method presented in Section 4 with exact recourse
DRLV2	The DRL method presented in Section 4 with heuristic recourse
DRLF	The DRL method with Compensation fee fixed and set to minimum

Besides implementing algorithms DRLV1 and DRLV2 for the methods presented in Section 4, we implement algorithm DRLF to run the same instances. DRLF is the algorithm developed in [11] for the heuristic recourse. The difference is that the compensation fees are not a decision to be made. They are fixed and set to f_i^{min}, $\forall i \in C$. DRLF was implemented to allow us to verify the power of flexible compensation for our instances, running with the other algorithms.

5.3. Initial Insights

We start by gaining qualitative insights into the potential benefits of different compensation levels for crowdshipping the last-mile delivery. We want to understand the sensitivity to problem characteristics and for this, we analyze some specific toy instances.

Figure 3 presents four instances indicating six customers' positions in a graph, the best-constructed routes defined for a scenario where all customers have online orders and no ODs available, and what level of compensation was paid for each customer being outsourced, as in the solution of our DRLV1 algorithm.

For these toy examples, we assume there exist only two levels of compensation, f^0, for the lower level, and f^1 for the higher level. For compensation fees f_0 and f_1, we assume the scenarios follow a distribution probability where the Bernoulli marginals of elements $\xi_i = 1$, $i \in C$, $i \leq N$ are equal to 100 %, and the Bernoulli marginals of elements $\xi_i = 1$, $i \in C$, $i > N$ are equal to o^0 and o^1, respectively.

The level of compensation paid for each instance is indicated by the color given to the customer location in the graph, referenced by axes, being red for the higher level of compensation and green for the lower level. The depot is located at the origin of the axes. Each route is indicated also by arrows in different colors.

Below each graph, we indicate the assumptions made for vectors o^0, o^1, and capacity Q.

Our exercise here is to verify how the solution (routes and level of compensation) changes with the assumptions of o^0, o^1, f^0, f^1, and Q.

In Figure 3a customers 3 and 6 are fixed to be delivered by the professional fleet ($o_3^0 = o_3^1 = o_6^0 = o_6^1 = 0$). Since in this case Q = 4, the solution creates only two routes and leaves the two fixed customers to be delivered in sequence. We note that, since in this instance, a straight path between the depot and customer 3 can always be performed including customers 1 and 2 with no extra cost, then it was not worth offering customers 1 and 2 a higher compensation fee.

The instance in Figure 3b has the same assumptions as in Figure 3a, except that now, for the same f^1 we increase the probability o_1^1 and decrease o_5^1. A naive expectation would be that, in this case, it would continue not to be worth paying extra for customer 1 since we have a straight path to customer 3 still. Different from that, the algorithm is now able to change the route solution and will pay extra for another set of two customers only.

Now in Figure 3c, we also replicate assumptions of Figure 3a, except the capacity $Q = 2$. We see that, in this case, three customers are selected to pay extra instead of two, and the route including in sequence customers 1, 2, and 3 is not worth it anymore due to restrictions in vehicle capacity.

For Figure 3d, we just change the assumption of instance in Figure 3c and make customer 6 not fixed in this case. By doing this, the solution changes and now it is worth paying extra for all customers except the fixed customer 3.

We verify by analyzing these different examples that many things can happen and are not always intuitive. Figure 3 shows the sensitivity of the solution not only to the compensation employed but also to the many parameters used and highlights the challenge of defining an adequate compensation scheme.

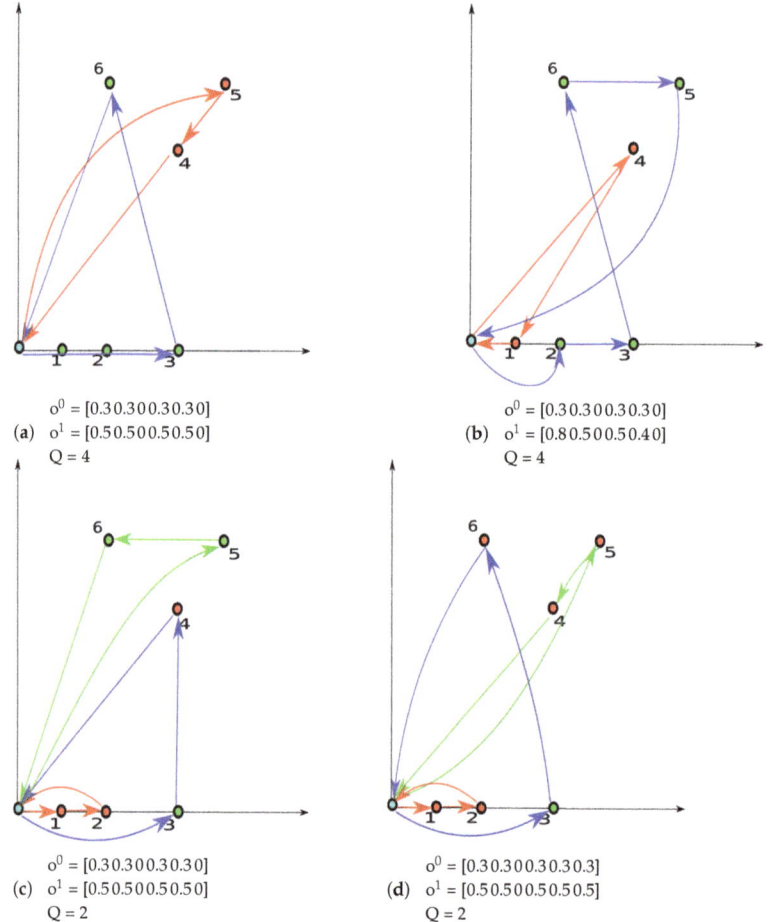

Figure 3. Initial Insights: (**a**) Instance a and optimal 2 routes; (**b**) Instance b and optimal 2 routes; (**c**) Instance c and optimal 3 routes; (**d**) Instance a and optimal 3 routes.

5.4. Solution Quality

To assess the performance of the solutions provided by the different algorithms, we simulate these solutions through various episodes using the scenarios created for this purpose, providing an out-of-sample estimate. We compare the algorithms' total cost output of this simulation.

Table 2 reports, for all instances and by the number of customers, the average percentage gap between total cost values when compared to the DRLF algorithm total cost. Overall, we observe that all algorithms provide total costs within a range of 10% of the DRLF total cost for the simulation proposed. This puts in evidence the potential of the flexible compensation scheme to improve savings. As would be expected, we also verify that the DRLV1 exact solution provided larger cost savings when compared to DRLV2.

Table 2. Solution Quality. * Results presented as percentage gap when compared to DRLF. Result = $100 * AVG((Algorithm - DRLF)/DRLF)$.

|C|	DRLV1 *	DRLV2 *
10	−5.1	−5.1
30	−5.4	−5.1
70	−9.6	−7.2
150	−7.6	−7.3
300	−7.1	−6.8

We also present in Table 3 the average percentage of ODs not accepted to outsource a customer, among those available. We present these numbers for algorithms DRLV1 and DRLF. We want to analyze if possibly increasing the compensation fee, as in the case of DRLV1, leads to an increase in the percentage of ODs not being accepted for outsourcing. An increase in the percentage of ODs not accepted could affect the success of the proposed business model. We verify by Table 3 that there is not a direct relationship between flexible compensation and the percentage of ODs accepted to outsource. Results depend on the configuration setup of each instance.

Table 3. Percentage of not accepted ODs.

|C|	DRLV1	DRLF
10	3.8	3.8
30	2.5	3.1
70	4.6	5.3
150	7.6	5.7
300	7.1	8.5

To verify the quality of the solution, we also estimate an upper bound total cost by running the out-of-sample simulation with a randomly generated first-stage solution as input. Table 4 presents the results as a percentage gap between the upper bound cost (UPPERBOUND) and DRLV1 cost. There is an average improvement of 14.48% by running DRLV1 solutions when compared to UPPERBOUND.

Table 4. DRLV1 Solution Quality. * Results presented as percentage gap when compared to UPPERBOUND. Result = $100 * AVG((DRLV1 - UPPERBOUND)/DRLV1)$.

|C|	Gap (%) *
10	−3.2
30	−11.8
70	−19.8
150	−17.5
300	−20.1

5.5. Sensitivity to Parameters Configuration

In this section, we analyze the effect of changing the number of policy iterations, the number of training scenarios, and the number of the NN hidden layer nodes on the solution quality presented as the percentage average gap between the total cost output of the simulation running the DRLV1 first-stage solution provided with new parameters, as compared to DRLV1 first-stage solution run with default parameters. We change each of the parameters independently while maintaining the other parameters as default. This is reported in Figure 4a–c, respectively.

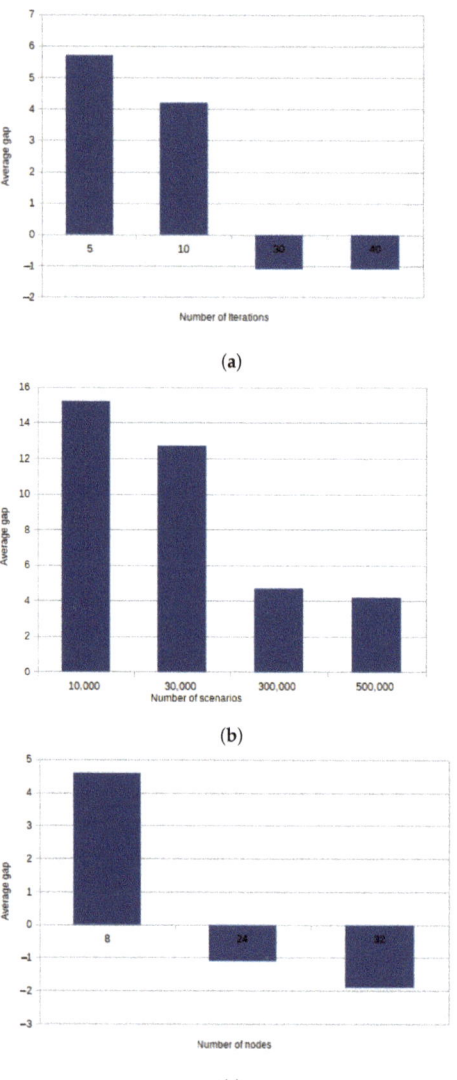

Figure 4. Sensitivity to key parameters: (**a**) Effect of number of policy iterations; (**b**) Effect of number of training scenarios; (**c**) Effect of number of NN hidden layer nodes.

In Figure 4a,b, we note that decreasing the number of training scenarios can be compensated by increasing the number of policy iterations to maintain solution quality and

Article

Camouflage Object Segmentation Using an Optimized Deep-Learning Approach

Muhammad Kamran [1], Saeed Ur Rehman [1,*], Talha Meraj [1], Khalid A. Alnowibet [2] and Hafiz Tayyab Rauf [3,*]

1 Department of Computer Science, COMSATS University Islamabad, Wah Campus, Rawalpindi 47040, Pakistan
2 Statistics and Operations Research Department, College of Science, King Saud University, Riyadh 11451, Saudi Arabia
3 Centre for Smart Systems, AI and Cybersecurity, Staffordshire University, Stoke-on-Trent ST4 2DE, UK
* Correspondence: srehman@ciitwah.edu.pk (S.U.R.); hafiztayyabrauf093@gmail.com (H.T.R.)

Abstract: Camouflage objects hide information physically based on the feature matching of the texture or boundary line within the background. Texture matching and similarities between the camouflage objects and surrounding maps make differentiation difficult with generic and salient objects, thus making camouflage object detection (COD) more challenging. The existing techniques perform well. However, the challenging nature of camouflage objects demands more accuracy in detection and segmentation. To overcome this challenge, an optimized modular framework for COD tasks, named Optimize Global Refinement (OGR), is presented. This framework comprises a parallelism approach in feature extraction for the enhancement of learned parameters and globally refined feature maps for the abstraction of all intuitive feature sets at each extraction block's outcome. Additionally, an optimized local best feature node-based rule is proposed to reduce the complexity of the proposed model. In light of the baseline experiments, OGR was applied and evaluated on a benchmark. The publicly available datasets were outperformed by achieving state-of-the-art structural similarity of 94%, 93%, and 96% for the Kvasir-SEG, COD10K, and Camouflaged Object (CAMO) datasets, respectively. The OGR is generalized and can be integrated into real-time applications for future development.

Keywords: semantic segmentation; global refinement; camouflage objects; graph fusion; edge enhancement; boundary guidance; graph convolutional network; vision transformer

MSC: 68T07

1. Introduction

In the exploration of different kinds of objects by visual observation and the process of differentiating them, most objects are efficiently observed and found easily and are thus classified as generic [1], while some hide their features [2]. Biologists declared that those objects hide their features, are difficult to recognize by a human visual sensor, and become "camouflaged". These camouflage objects, as shown in Figure 1, use the natural phenomenon of hiding features in objects using the same combination pattern of color, structure, and material to its surroundings, making its visibility and differentiation difficult—for example, a polar bear on ice, a red bee on the red carpet, an owl on a tree branch, etc. This hiding technique deceives the observer from clearly defining and exploring these objects. Therefore, it requires more boundary information about the objects to be recognized and similarities between them and their background. Some animals also take advantage of natural camouflage [3] and change their body color and structure to match their surroundings to prevent recognition by their predator. A high level of object structure and boundary information is required to find and explore these camouflage objects using computing devices as a COD [4] task. Thus, COD is a more challenging task in its data samples and techniques than salient object detection [5]. Although different applied computer vision tasks, e.g., semantic analysis, data processing, face object detection and recognition [6], and high-level understanding of image [7] and video segmentation [8], etc., helped with deep learning interpolation to solve the COD challenges.

Figure 1. Example of different camouflage objects [4].

There is still a particular area requiring further improvement regarding different groups of camouflage objects and techniques. Sometimes camouflage objects consist of multiple instances that do not have a completely singular and relevant boundary. Thus, these independent shapes are difficult to understand as a single object, e.g., the chameleon backed by a leaf as shown in Figure 2, etc.

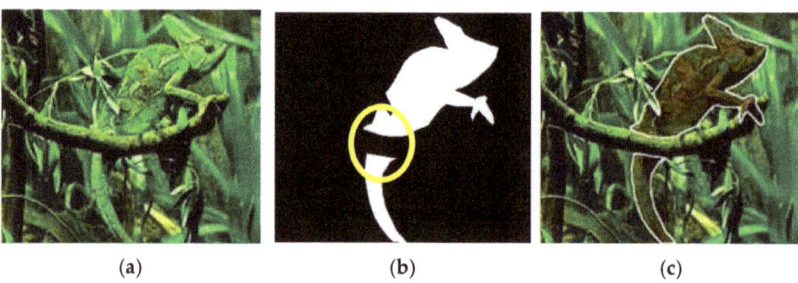

Figure 2. Occlusion in camouflage objects: (**a**) original image (The circle shows that the particular object sitting on the branch has occlusion); (**b**) ground truth label; (**c**) overlaid.

These multiple instances may differ from the other, and the complete object visualization using relevant and singular body information becomes difficult. Unlike salient object detection [5], in camouflage, the object boundary is unclear, and different separate fragments make an object more challenging. These fragments of objects need to be addressed due to the separate regions of camouflage objects in an image.

To overcome COD dataset challenges [4], many computer vision scientists and biologists have worked extensively on the goal of high-resolution image dataset collection and preparing annotations for each sample regarding each class of the camouflaged object at the object level, as shown above in Figure 2.

In [4], a significant COD10K dataset [4] was presented along with the deep learning model for a COD task. Afterward, the scientists found the flexibility to explore this dataset with multiple machine learning and deep learning methods to compare it with the methods using the generic object and the salient object dataset. In the same year, the parallel attention model [9] was proposed to speed up its performance. Recently, a modified instance-level dataset for camouflage objects was presented, and multiple prescribed methods of instance segmentation were used as frameworks. Therefore, the need for experiments on camouflage objects with high-resolution image data in such a challenging task requires the design and development of a versatile, comprehensive, and optimized approach.

As shown in Figure 3, the proposed framework contains an optimized solution using a deep learning technique with a complete training flow as described in Algorithm 1, and the optimization rule is explored in Algorithm 2. This framework follows the modular approach toward a COD task and is adopted on multiple dataset samples to ensure it outperforms previous approaches. The following contributions comprised the model's components focusing on the optimal solution. Thus, the proposed framework provides the solution for COD using three modules or sub-frameworks, i.e., global refinement, optimizer, and parallel convolution.

Algorithm 1. Optimize, Parallel Refinement.

Input:
1. Sample collection in a combined list of samples I and its target GT [I]
2. Hypothesis M with parameters w initialized with random or zero initializer.
3. Optimized process O states the member of the hypothesis function. $O \in M\ (f(x))$

Output:
1. *for* $U \leftarrow i$ *to* E *do*
2.   *for* $L \leftarrow l$ *to length* I_{train} *do*
3. $y_{pred}^{train} \leftarrow M(I_{train},\ G_{i-1}),\ O^p\left(M_i^p\right) \Rightarrow i{>}0\ |\ !\ G[\phi]$
4. $e_l^{train} = y_i^{train} - x_i^{true}$
5.   *end for*
6. $e_i^{train}/L \le e_{i-1}^{train}\ \wedge\ G_{i-1}\ |\ G_b$
7. e^{train} *minima.*
8.   *Monitor var*
9. $y_{pred}^{train} \leftrightarrow GT\ [I],\ Met\ [f, e, s]$
10. e_i^{train} *Backpropagate*
11. G_i . *Update*
12.   *end for*
13.   *In validation do*
14.   *for* $K \leftarrow k$ *to length* I_{test} *do*
15. $y_{pred}^{test} \leftarrow h(I_{test},\ G_i,\ )$
16. $e_l^{test} = y_k^{test} - x_k^{true}$
17. $\frac{e_i^{test}}{L} \le e_{i-1}^{test}$
18.   *end for*
19. *end for*

Algorithm 2. Optimization Framework

Input:
1. Initialize parameters. W, N, epochs, etc.

Output:
1. *for* $i \leftarrow 1$ *to* E *do*
2.   *for* $M \leftarrow 1$ *to length* I_{train} *do*
3.   *Convert the system into binary distribution.*
4.   *Preprocess the algorithm's parameters in all dimensions.*
5.   *Calculate fitness using the upper and lower boundary of the sample space.*
6.   *Calculate fitness by reducing error and the performance measure.*
7.   *Update all the dimensions of all the sample space*
8.   *end for*
9. *end for*

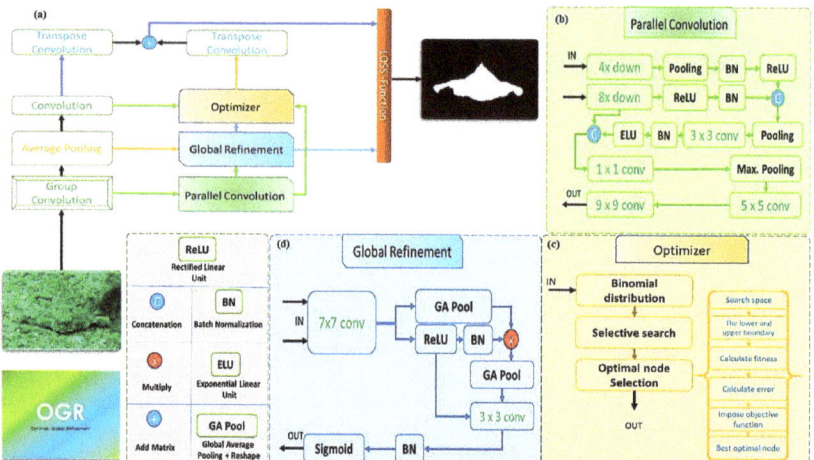

Figure 3. Optimize, Global Refinement Proposed Architecture: (**a**) Proposed Model; (**b**) Global Refinement; (**c**) Optimizer; (**d**) Parallel Convolution.

The Global Refinement Framework is proposed to utilize the ratio-dependent fusion of global features for the best alignment of the localized objects on the background map. A Parallel Convolution Framework is proposed to extract the features in parallel to make the global optimization from the parallel fused features for the best boundary construction at a low level with the least number of channels. The Optimizer Framework is proposed for the best feature channel selection and regularization. Furthermore, it helps to select the best feature matrices for the linear minimization of the loss function.

This article is composed of the following sections: Section 1 states the introduction of the domain and the problem statement that results in the proposed solution—the brief history of the domain is followed by the progressive improvement in the solution. Section 2 relates to the data, the previous methodology, and its related work. Section 3, Section 4, and Section 5 describe the proposed methodology using the mathematical model. Section 6 comprises the experiment and its results. Section 7 discusses future work and conclusions.

2. Materials and Methods

Over a decade, object detection and segmentation techniques were encouraged due to their frequent application to many real-life problems, mainly focused on the image and its pixel-wise labeling. In generic objects, labeling and prediction are comparatively easy tasks due to the discreet texture of the object and clear boundary lines to obtain the best annotations. The image's resolution is not required to be higher due to the vividness and clarity between the object and the background. However, for the COD task, the findings of the dataset are not only the depiction of the problem, but the solution faces challenging conditions in terms of the camouflage. The algorithm trained on the generic objects fails on the salient object due to the fewer features that were found, and failed to detect the camouflaged object due to having faint information of the object boundary. Therefore, the dataset and the model design are to be explored to better understand this domain and the problem statement.

This domain has a very limited collection of datasets; due to its challenging nature, the images are difficult to find and prepare, i.e., image collection and GT annotations, respectively. The CAMO dataset [10] consists of 1250 images of ecological camouflage, and the Kvasir-SEG [11] has images of medical camouflage, consisting of 1000 images. While the COD10K dataset has the natural camouflage, consisting of 10,000 images.

Many techniques in deep learning and image processing were proposed and applied specifically for camouflaged objects, and the special attention of computer vision researchers was attained. These types of objects are often hard to be recognized by humans themselves due to the complexity of their pixels and the boundary line of the distinct surface area contained within the image pixels. To express the existence of the camouflaged objects, different technologies and techniques have been promoted, as shown in Figure 4, not only to predict these features from the known data but to apply them to the unseen data. This task is classified as object detection and segmentation using specific dataset samples and algorithmic approaches.

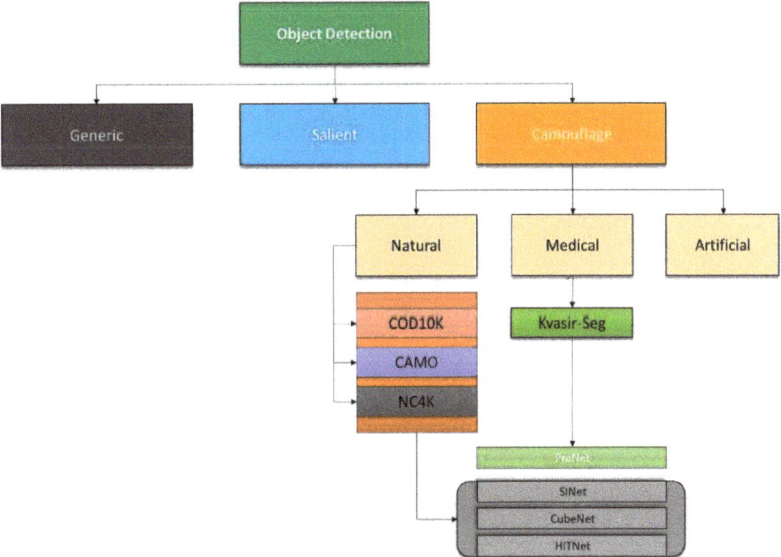

Figure 4. Object Detection Organogram.

2.1. Search and Identification

This method [4] is biologically inspired by the living predator in which, initially, a required object is searched out using the biological boundary space, having sensitive information, then the object is identified as a target for the predator. The search module uses a convolutional neural network-based inference and encloses and reduces the feature dimension of the network stream. The identification module used the block for object identification concerning the multiple evaluation functions. For this purpose, searching the identification network has resnet-50 architecture followed by the receptive field (RF) component.

The extracted features are divided for the identification module through multiple up-sampling and down-sampling serial units to be passed into the RELU activation function. The identification module has a partial decoder component (PDC) that performs element-wise multiplication to decrease the gap between the same-level features in the dual stream [12]. Hence, the designed model was accomplished with the achievement of dense feature extraction.

According to the latest research, the medical COD was explored in polyp segmentation [13], as shown in Figure 4, when a parallel reverse attention-based network [9] was utilized. Like an ordinary semantic segmentation network, it has two modules of parallel decoding and reverses the attention mechanism. The parallel decoder takes the input from a skipped serial connection of the down-sampled stream in the network, while the reverse attention is the featured mask multiplication and reversed matrix pixel decomposition followed by an up-sampled stream. The actual size is achieved after a series of up-sampled streams followed by a reverse attention module.

2.2. Boundary Guidance and Edge Enhancement

A denoised model [14] for the COD involves the removal of noise and its effects from the camouflage map in the form of uncertainty and is validated in the noisy ground truth.

The noisy labeling leads to the prediction of uncertain conditions for all types of objects and is not limited to camouflage objects. Camouflage has the particular scope to be cleaned, and handles the input and predicted weights more carefully for semantic inheritance. To achieve semantic inheritance and boundary guidance [15], as shown in Figure 5, the high-level features fused with the low-level features. These features were extracted from the independent layer and transformed into a residual channel attention block with the serial feature link to the module for each connection. Two predictions with the feature maps 3–5 and 2, with 6–8 repeating the above-mentioned process, computed the $\hat{y}^{ini}$ and $\hat{y}^{ref}$, respectively, in the 0–1 range, knowing that the $\hat{y}^{ref}$ is the final predictor. A UNet-based model [16] was proposed using the leaky ReLU [17] activation function called CODNet [18]. It uses both the predictor of $\hat{y}^{ini}$ and $\hat{y}^{ref}$ for the concatenation with the input to create a feature map as a confidence map. This confidence map is followed by the prediction of COD and ground truth of camouflage y.

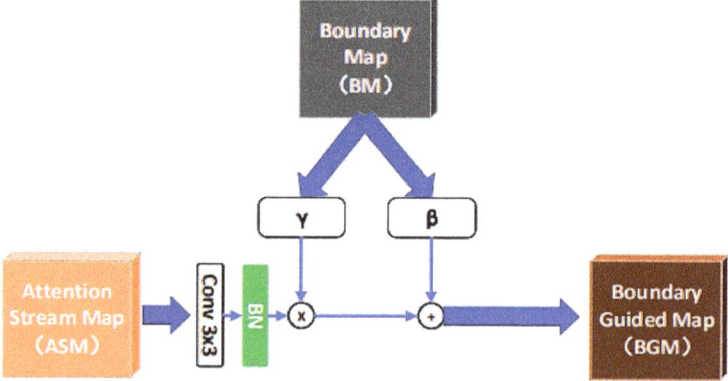

Figure 5. Boundary Guided Module [15].

The final prediction is the dynamic uncertainty precision, composed of the pixel-by-pixel distance between the actual ground truth and the confidence map of the predictor of CODNet that has two input branches. These inputs are used to adapt pixel-wise multiplication and concatenating two convolution operations following the residual block focusing on the foreground map instead of the background map. The prior edge gains the shape of the 64 channels used for the recalibration unit, and this unit is used for the refinement of the input in the decoder block instead of the fusion mechanism.

Edge-enhancement-based [19] COD tasks differentiate the traditional model approaches by modifying the sample data. The purpose is to enhance the edge information with different feature engineering techniques. A sub-edge decoder (SED) [20] is used in between the two square fusion decoders (SFD). SED uses both features, i.e., the original feature map and the fused feature map. Like most of the COD tasks, this model also uses the resnet-50 model and borrows its residual behavior to transfer to the new design. Second SFD is treated as the final camouflage map for the interaction of the loss function.

Like other COD algorithms [4,9,18], the loss function remains cooperative with the binary cross-entropy and IoU. This edge enhancement further undergoes feature-based optimization with respect to the object. The binary pixel-wise classification algorithms have the potential to be estimated by the edge dataset. The notable COD10K dataset [4] contains the edge information for all the camouflage objects and instances. These samples are to be used with edge-based classification or boundary regression using the values of the edge.

2.3. Vision Transformer in COD

The latest research found the transformer-based model's [21] interaction with the computer vision tasks led to the basic encoder and decoder network in semantic or instance segmentation to the transformer module. The process modified the basic design of the feed-forward neural network with the refinement of feedback [22] that was attained from the loss function after the complete input inferences. The feed-forward block utilized the transformer model, and the training went iteratively backward, followed by the refinement of the effect of the loss function. A pyramid vision transformer [23] was used for the feature extraction and fed to the feedback block in which the layer is concatenated with the input. These feedback blocks were followed by some basic blocks.

The basic block consists of the convolutional layer in series with the multiplication of the fully connected layer. This output is provided to the iteration feedback module in which the data flow is controlled by the loss function with the Intersection over Union (IoU) and binary-weighted cross-entropy, as shown in [4,9,18,20].

2.4. Graph and Search Fusion in COD

A graph convolutional network (GCN) was mutually applied for edge- and region-based feature learning. The image features populated for the mutual graph learning [24] technique have a task-specific block of the extracted feature. A graph fusion [25] was implied between the inference stream of the extracted feature tensor F_1 followed by the basic block and the definite forward iteration Y^{iii} of the network to obtain a resultant named Y'. These resultants were forwarded to the loss function and named iterative feedback loss to evaluate the network and update the training.

The instance-level method to separate the object in a single frame needs more attention and technical methodology. Camouflage fusion learning was performed to efficiently solve instance segmentation tasks. For this purpose, a search-based model was used with all the samples of the input images. The instance-level methodology was achieved using a vision transformer as well as multiple well-known methods, including Mask RCNN [26], Cascade Mask RCNN [27], MS RCNN [28], RetinaMask [29], CenterMask [30], YOLACT [31], SOLO [32], BlendMask [33] with ResNet50 [34], ResNet101-FPN [34] and ResNetXt101-FPN [35]. The framework [36] completes its task in two stages. Firstly, the instance segmentation model is trained using this loss function, and secondly, the search algorithm trained the predictor to choose the best instance in the segmentation model.

Hence, these techniques are for camouflage object and instance detection tasks. For this purpose, remarkable work also has been observed in the dataset collection and its preparation. However, there is still a need to fill the gap in the dataset collection and algorithm design to solve the task of COD. The search-based model combines instance search model implementations with the dual loss binary cross-entropy. The search for the best weightage of the image sample is imposed for updating the waiting list of the sample image, in this instance, with the use of the segmentation model.

3. Parallel Convolution Framework (PCF)

The PCF acquires the group convolution blocks input and surpasses it to the global refinement and optimizer. In PCF, the group convolved input g_{conv} is separated in two parallel paths for discreet structural feature extraction, and the channel outputs are concatenated in the $Conc_1$ states as shown in Equation (1).

$$Conc_1 = (P_1 \mathbb{C} P_2) \qquad (1)$$

$$P_1 = \varphi \left(Bn(Max(4 \times Conv (g_{conv}))) \right) \qquad (2)$$

$$P_2 = \varphi \left((8 \times Conv (g_{conv})) + Bn \right) \qquad (3)$$

P_1 shows the pooled and batch normalization path that is concatenated with the unpooled path P_2, as shown in Equations (2) and (3). The $Conc_1$ is responsible for the serial path ω_3 That is activated with the ELU activation function $\mathcal{E}$ and initial features f_1. ω_3 is followed by the batch normalization layer and its pooled and convolved $Conc_1$ input as shown in Equation (6).

$$Conc_2 = (f_1 \mathbb{C} \, \omega_3) \qquad (4)$$

$$f_1 = P_2 - \varphi \, (\, Bn(.)) \qquad (5)$$

$$\omega_3 = \mathcal{E} \, (Bn(\, Max(\, Conc_1) + Conv)) \qquad (6)$$

In Equation (4), $Conc_2$ is the concatenated output of the serial path ω_3 and initial features f_1. Initial features f_1 are composed of $8 \times Conv$ of a group of convolved input g_{conv}, as shown in Equations (3) and (5). The final output of the ρ is retrieved after the series of convolution operations, as described in Equation (7).

$$\rho = Conc_2 + Max \, (Conv) + Conv_{k=1}^2 \qquad (7)$$

Here, ρ is transferred to the global refinement and optimizer module independently. In the global refinement, the parallel convolved input is mixed with the average pooled input and passed to the optimizer.

4. Global Refinement Framework (GRF)

In this section, a global refinement framework is presented that employs the feature refinement of pooled input P_i and the convolved input C_i states from the average of g_{conv} and ρ, respectively, as shown in Equation (8). This P_i is composed of the average of the group convolution feature g_{conv}, as shown in Equation (9).

$$\Re^{\mathcal{G}} \, (P_i \oplus C_i) \qquad (8)$$

$$P_i = avg \, (g_{conv}) \qquad (9)$$

$\Re^{\mathcal{G}}$ is the refined global function that handles two flows of stream, i.e., normal flow v_{in} and the vectorized flow Φ_{in}. The normal flow is activated with the ReLU and surpasses the batch normalization layer. Both flows are multiplied with the 1×1 index ratio, as shown in Equation (10).

$$\omega_1 = \sum_{i=1}^{l} v_{in}^i \odot \Phi_{in}^i \qquad (10)$$

The first serial part ω_1 shows the partial vectorized multiplication, and the output is converted to the global average pooling layer, taking the v_{in} as convolved input stream and Φ_{in} as the pooled input stream is explored in Equations (11) and (12).

$$v_{in} = \varphi \, (Conv \, (C_i) + Bn) \qquad (11)$$

$$\Phi_{in} = \aleph_{avg} \, (Conv \, (P_i)) \qquad (12)$$

φ shows the activation function on the convolved input flow after convolution as $Conv$, and batch normalization as Bn make the output as v_{in}. $\aleph_{avg}$ shows the global average pooling after the convolution on the pooled input. ω_1 is reshaped from the vector to two-dimensional vector space $\mathbb{R}^2$ to apply the convolution with the concatenation of activated convolved input as $v_{in} - Bn$ is shown in Equations (14) and (15).

$$\omega_2 = \left(v_p \, \mathbb{C} \, \Phi_p \right) \qquad (13)$$

$$v_p = Conv(\, (v_{in} - Bn) \qquad (14)$$

$$\Phi_p = \aleph_{avg} \left(\mathbb{R}^2 \, (\omega_1) \right) \qquad (15)$$

The second serial part ω_2 shows the output from the concatenation of partial convolved and partial pooled inputs as v_p and Φ_p, respectively, as shown in Equation (13). The final output of this framework is attained after passing the batch normalization Bn and sigmoid activation Sig to ϖ_2, as shown in Equation (16).

$$\Re^{\mathcal{G}} = Sig\left(Bn\left(\varpi_2\right)\right) \quad (16)$$

The objective of the global refinement module is to expand the global features by index-wise multiplication in a two-dimensional vector space and normalization of features with the average pooling and sigmoid activation function. The globally refined output is transferred to the optimizer module and the cost function. In the optimizer module, the best channels are selected for the best position of the feature matrices.

5. Optimizer Framework (OF)

In OF, channel-wise optimization is proposed for the best channel selection to avoid the overfitting and complexity of the training model. The optimizer framework $\mathcal{O}$ is composed of three major tasks, i.e., binomial distribution, selective search, and optimal channel selections.

$$\iota = \mathbb{R} \left| \sum \rho + \Re^{\mathcal{G}} + Conv \right| \quad (17)$$

It takes the input ι from the parallel convolved ρ, globally refined $\Re^{\mathcal{G}}$ and simple convolution input as shown in Equation (17) and the input is transformed to the linear vector space $\mathbb{R}$.

The binomial distribution β having a lower boundary ℓ_d and the upper boundary ℓ_u, takes the vectorized input ι and formats the values in 0 and 1, as shown in Equation (18). The purpose of these binary values transformation is to make the decision effectively for the selective search. This selective search works efficiently on the one-dimensional binary values β by ordering the distribution in ascending order $0 \leq i \leq n$, $\lambda_0^n \because \lambda_i \in \beta$.

$$\beta = \varphi\left(\iota, [\ell_d, \ell_u]\right) \quad (18)$$

The optimal feature selection takes the inner boundary values from β and calculates the fitness function Y for the searched instances λ_0^n as shown in Equation (19). The Y calculates the error e of λ_0^n and updates the cost using the objective function o as shown in Equations (21) and (22). For error calculation in λ_0^n, mean squared error (MSE) for the regression values and the objective function is expanded using the best instance value raisebox1 1 as shown in Equation (20).

$$Y = \sum_{k=1}^{l} (e + o), \quad \lambda_k^n = 1 \quad (19)$$

$$1 = (\lambda_0^n = 1) \quad (20)$$

$$e - MSE\left(a + b\lambda_k^n\right) \quad (21)$$

$$o = a \times e + (1-a) \times \left(\frac{1}{dim_0\left(\lambda_k^n\right)}\right) \quad (22)$$

l shows the number of iterations for the fitness function, composed of the error calculation and the objective function. The samples at a higher position, correspond to the fitness evaluation and are selected from β. The best features f_b from the λ_k^n are selected based on high boundary values as shown in Equation (23).

$$f_b = \begin{cases} \beta_i = 1 & \lambda_k^n = 1 \\ \beta_i = 1 & otherwise \end{cases} \quad (23)$$

The f_b and $Conv$ are transferred to the convolutional transpose layer and added to make a single flow τ_f as shown in Equation (24) to the cost function. The MAE is used as a cost function C_m of the model in which τ_f and ground truth G, as shown in Equation (25).

$$\tau_f = transConv(f_b) \oplus transConv(Conv) \tag{24}$$

$$C_m = MAE\left(\tau_f, G\right) \tag{25}$$

transConv is transpose convolution that is applied to the best feature's output and convolved output to get the contracted feature map.

6. Experiments and Results

The proposed model is applied in the experimental setup by using PyTorch with the Adam Optimizer. The training batch size was experienced on the 8 and 12 and found the results were better on batch size 8 with the initial learning rate of 1×10^{-4}. The whole training time was almost 60 min for the 10 epochs. The experiment was performed on the platform of 12 CPUs and 1280-core graphic processors on all the datasets, and the image size was maintained at $352 \times 352 \times 3$. This input size of the model is further used in preprocessing, cleaning, and enhancement of the model. The preprocessing was performed for data normalization and defining the parameter of the input shape from the raw data. A pixel value normalization was also used on the model input gate from its minimum to maximum range. This input was forwarded to the model for feature extraction, and the results were compared with the predefined results to train the model. The evaluation time on this framework is 83.3 ms/sample.

The CAMO dataset [10] consists of generic camouflage objects that are dependent upon the specific situation or condition, as shown in Figure 6a. COD10K [4] contains 10,000 images, as shown in Figure 6b, in which 5066 are defined as camouflaged, 3000 background, and 1934 as non-camouflaged. It occupies the 78 sub-classes of biological camouflage. The collection of the 10,000 images includes 6000 for training and the remaining 4000 samples for testing purposes. The Kvasir-SEG dataset [11] is the medical camouflage dataset with a gastrointestinal binary segmented area designed for polyp segmentation. It has 1000 samples with the ground truth provided, a very small dataset of images. The provided annotations were generated for the images as shown in Figure 6c, and the images were collected through biomedical sources. This dataset was beyond consideration in the COD domain, but due to its application in the medical field, it is an important camouflage dataset, and researchers have been utilizing it for experiments.

Mean absolute error (MAE) [37] is the simplest cost function to evaluate the two values, i.e., predicted and actual. As shown in Equation (26), the formula is the qualitative measurement of the two values concerning the observed samples. The formula explains the difference between the actual and predicted value and the mean to the total number of observations.

$$MAE = \frac{\sum_{i=1}^{n} |y_i - x_i|}{n} \tag{26}$$

The precision [38] formula is modified with the average précised class on the predicted class with the True Positive *TP* and False Positive *FP*.

$$S - Measure(x, y) = \frac{(2\,\mu_x\,\mu_y + c1)(2\,\sigma_{xy} + c2)}{\left(\mu_x^2,\ \mu_y^2 + c1\right)\left(\sigma_x^2 + \sigma_y^2 + c2\right)} \tag{27}$$

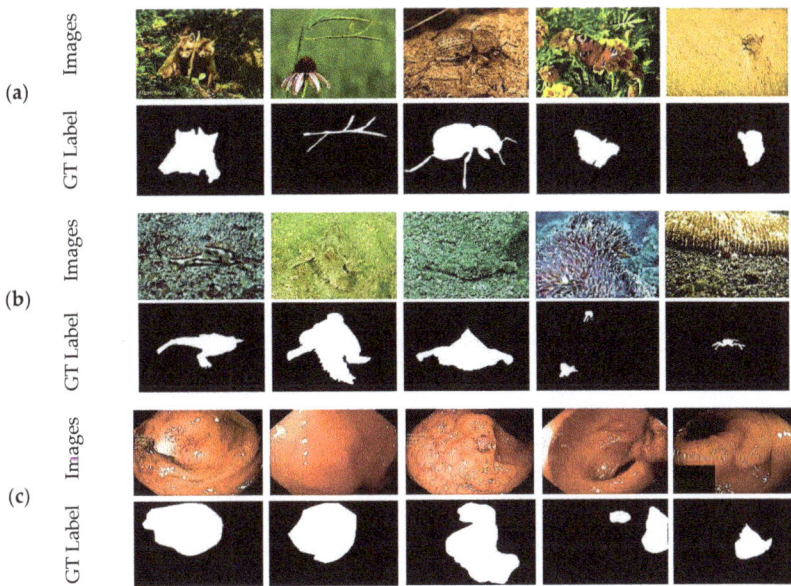

Figure 6. Camouflage Dataset Image Samples (**a**) COD10K (**b**) CAMO (**c**) Kvasir-SEG.

The structure similarity index measure [39] is described in Equation (27) as the *S-Measure* uses the average of x, y position as μ_x μ_y, variance of x, y and covariance of x and y σ_x^2, σ_y^2, σ_{xy}. L as dynamic range, $c1$ and $c2$ constant as bits per pixel, 0.01 and 0.03 by default, respectively. This is a performance metric of two binary maps of predicted and true to find the similarity of the structure.

$$F_\beta = \left(1 + \beta^2\right) \frac{Precision \cdot Recall}{\beta^2 \cdot Precision + Recall} \quad (28)$$

The F-measure beta [40] is denoted by F_β, the binary map using the *Precision (avg)* and *Recall* as described in Equation (28). It uses the beta constant β to control the complete and detection co-factors. The beta constant is 1 by default in order to have smoothness detection.

$$E - measure = \frac{1}{w \times h} \sum_{x=1}^{w} \sum_{y=1}^{h} \varnothing FM.(x,y) \quad (29)$$

It [41] is a binary map performance metric denoted by *E-Measure* dependent on the ground truth *GT* and foreground map *FM* bias metric $\varnothing FM$ as shown in Equation (29). With the weight w and height h of the foreground map, the alignment measurement is accomplished at the x and y position of the pixel.

The experimental procedure was initially adopted and performed using the benchmark publicly available dataset and the pre-trained model. Furthermore, all the datasets are trained and tested using the proposed framework and compared with the existing methods. The experiments and comparative results are presented in the following order:

1. Experiments on benchmark datasets using baseline and pretrained methods;
2. Experiments on benchmark datasets using the proposed method;
- Comparison of the proposed method with baseline and pretrained results;
- Comparison of the proposed method with the state-of-the-art method's results.

6.1. Experiment 1 on Pretrained Models

6.1.1. CAMO + COD10K Datasets—In the Light of Composite Experiments

These large-scale datasets need to explore predefined random methods. Firstly, the dataset is tested with binary accuracy and the Dice coefficient with the binary cross-entropy loss function. The model used for these performance measures was polyp segmentation based on the area color.

Experiments show that the results are about 10% in the ten epochs, even when transfer learning is performed. Furthermore, the cost function is very high. The efficient segmentation net has also been used to tackle these problems. The dataset is measured upon the binary accuracy performance metric as well. The loss or the cost function was still binary cross-entropy.

The graph in Figure 7a,b shows that the dice coefficient increases after 20+ epochs, while the loss is reduced, as shown in the figure, which is more costly than the model taking a significant amount of time to be trained, as one iteration takes 30 min to 60 min due to a large number of samples in the dataset. The same behavior has been identified in the other performance metric and the loss function applied to this model. The UNET model [16] and FCN [42] with the VGG16 pre-trained backbone [43] are also used with this dataset, but the same behavior of the model was observed. This limitation needs to be addressed to explore the dataset's nature. The proposed model and its experiments are conducted to understand that refinement is needed for some spatial feature extraction processes and optimization. The experiment as mentioned above shows the behavior of the dataset before the benchmark pre-trained models.

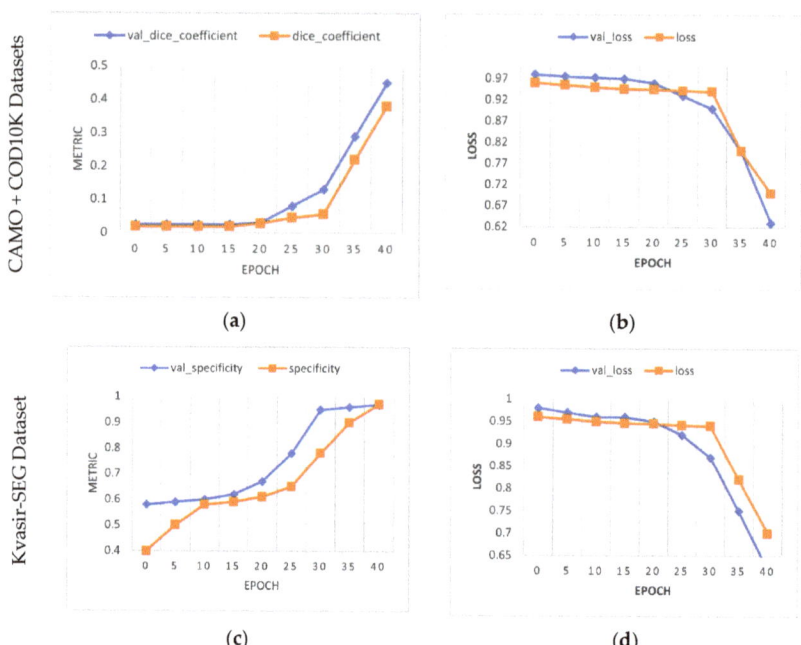

Figure 7. CAMO + COD10K, and Kvasir-SEG Datasets, Combined Experiments on training and validation dataset: (**a**) dice coefficient; (**b**) binary cross-entropy loss; (**c**) specificity; (**d**) binary cross-entropy loss.

6.1.2. Kvasir-SEG—In the Light of Composite Experiments

The experimental results on the ground truth and texture of the sample were achieved due to less complexity. The dataset was trained on the same set of hyperparameters and other dataset behavior such as sample size, batch size, and the transformation applied. The tabular data show the experiments based on the three datasets and their training with the composite and proposed model architecture, as shown in Table 1. The specificity was used as the performance metric with built-in accuracy metric binary accuracy and the loss function of binary cross-entropy due to the binary segmentation of the dataset using the image samples and binary ground truth, as shown in Figure 7c,d. The analyses of all of the experiments using different deep-learning algorithms and the proposed model indicate the achievement of optimization.

Table 1. Comparison of the proposed method with pre-trained UNet and VGG-16.

Algorithm	Epochs				Dataset	Remarks
	6	10	20	20+		
UNET (Modified)	4%	2%	8%	12%+	CAMO	-
	3%	2%	7%	10%+	COD10K	-
	52%	60%	67%	70%+	Kvasir-SEG	-
VGG 16 pretrained backbone	1%	3%	6%	12%+	CAMO	-
	2%	4%	5%	10%+	COD10K	-
	55%	56%	65%	70%+	Kvasir-SEG	-
Optimize Global Refinement	70%	96%	-	-	CAMO	
	91%	94%	-	-	COD10K	Optimized
	87%	93%	-	-	Kvasir-SEG	

6.2. Experiment 2 Using OGR Framework

The training and validation graph based on the performance and the loss function is to be demonstrated to visualize the experimental achievements. The proposed model was applied to the three datasets, including CAMO, COD10K, and Kvasir–Seg, respectively. These datasets are from different branches of image segmentation.

6.2.1. Experiments on CAMO Dataset

The benefit of an average number of samples with the binary generated a mask of almost ~1250 and was trained with the proposed architecture and attained the desired results. In the preprocessing stage, the transformation was used on the image samples to exploit the flip, translate, and rotate parameters. The image samples were then passed to the proposed architecture of the semantic segmentation model to train the samples with masks. The MAE was a loss function for the model backpropagation and updating the weights.

In some experiments, the loss function was reduced by the iteration or epochs, but the accuracy was not attained. Additionally, in the iteration where the trainable parameters do not reduce the loss function, validation accuracy of >90% was achieved. Such behavior of the loss function on training and validation shows the inconsistency in the data samples. The CAMO dataset [10] has generalized camouflage, which is not only limited to natural camouflage but also contains situational or other camouflage. The Adam optimizer initialized with zero gradients showed the independent behavior of the model inference. The model's training sample showed some accuracy reduction, but on the test set, remarkable model behavior was observed. The strategy was observed in that the MAE was working independently, and the model parameter metrics were saying something else. The validation of the situation-based camouflage has the same impact on the model behavior in terms of inference and learning. The model was repeatedly trained on this dataset, wherein the Adam optimizer, variational accuracy and loss are better than the training accuracy and loss, which is very common.

The graph as shown in Figure 8 describes that the model validation accuracy has sudden behavioral learning, which is somehow a fair condition and the cause of dataset complexity, as well as learning rate (initially 0.001) for 10 epochs, and the 70 | 30% train–test ratio.

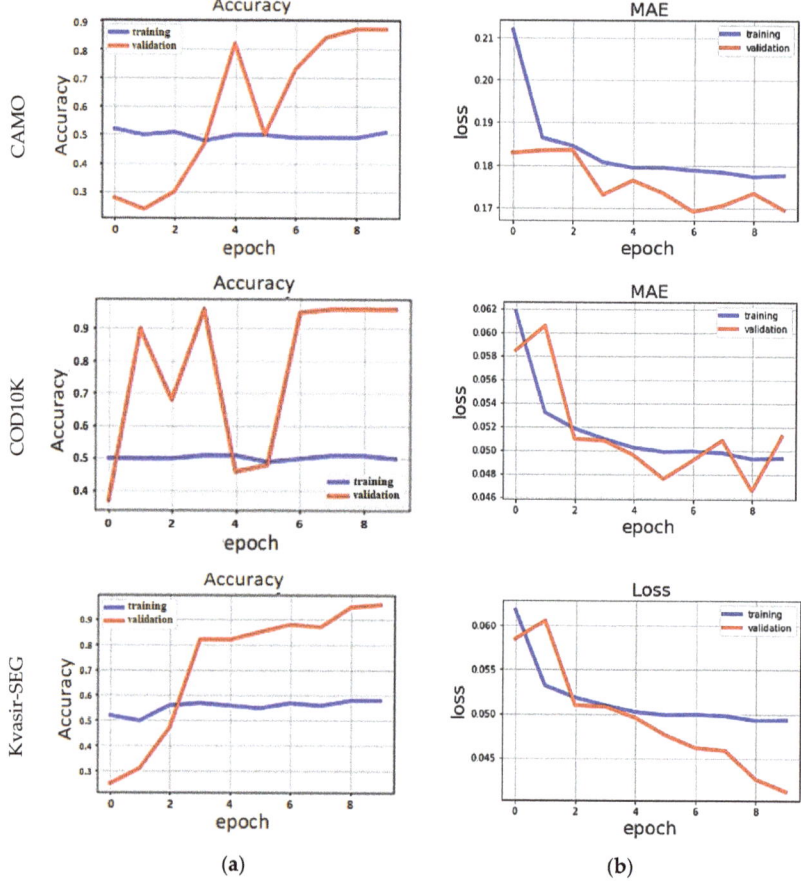

Figure 8. Training and validation graph on CAMO, COD10K, Kvasir-SEG on training and validation dataset: (**a**) binary accuracy; (**b**) mean absolute error loss.

6.2.2. Experiments on COD10K

This is a large dataset with high-resolution images for training (352 × 352), and the Adam optimizer was used for the learning rate control. With the loss function of MAE, the network was trained in 10 iterations. This dataset is complex in that the predefined model, such as UNeT, only brings an accuracy of 50%. The technique of parallel convolution and the optimizer function caused the dataset to have the highest accuracy. The learning parameters of the model remained at zero for each batch size until the model obtained the best results independent of the iterations. In another setting, the model optimizer became iterative of the previous epoch. The batch size of 2 and 3 was the only possible option for the machine to have an offline experiment of the proposed model.

The training results of the proposed model were explored in graph form, and the quantitative analysis of this dataset with the previous technique was in tabular form. The data was in the binary polyp segmentation type despite multiple instances. The concept of the existence and non-existence of the camouflage was used to keep the model smooth and less burdened. The data loader identified with the normalization and the preprocessing of the input sample image. The model is trained on the condition to reduce the loss function and the performance measurement. The training direction is independent of the metrics used in this model. The graph shows the accuracy, the losses, and the effect of the reducing loss function, which was very low on this dataset. The constant lowering of the cost function can result in accuracy loss independent of the iterations and dependent on the data samples. As shown, the proposed model was trained on this dataset with the Adam optimizer, a variational learning rate initially at 0.001 with ten epochs, and 70|30% and 80|20% train–test ratios.

6.2.3. Experiments on Kvasir–Seg Dataset

The rarely used dataset used as camouflage is the polyp segmentation of gastrointestinal with the relevant segmentation mask. This dataset is based on binary polyp segmentation and was passed to the proposed model. The data is biological, so the behavior is different for the validation. The settings of the model hyperparameters were not changed to see the model's behavior for each dataset under the same circumstances. The preferred input size was 256 × 256 instead of 352 × 352. The optimizer was changed to RMSProp to show the dataset variations and the effect of the dataset sample on the model.

The comparison of multiple datasets is shown in Table 2. The binary segmentation was performed with batch sizes of 2 and 3, respectively. The learning iteration was 10, and the train–test ratios were 80|20% and 90|10% due to the 1000 samples.

Table 2. Comparison of the proposed OGR w.r.t Baselines Camouflage models and datasets.

Baseline	Dataset	↑$S_{measure}$	↑$E_{measure}$	↑$F_{measure}$	↓MAE
SiNet	CAMO	0.751	0.771	0.606	0.100
	COD10K	0.869	0.891	0.740	0.044
	Kvasir-SEG	-	-	-	-
PraNET	CAMO	-	-	-	-
	COD10K	-	-	-	-
	Kvasir-SEG	0.915	0.948	0.915	0.030
CubeNet	CAMO	0.788	0.850	0.788	0.085
	COD10K	0.795	0.864	0.644	0.041
	Kvasir-SEG	-	-	-	-
CANet	CAMO	0.799	0.770	0.865	0.075
	COD10K	0.809	0.885	0.703	0.035
	Kvasir-SEG	-	-	-	-
Pyvit+GCN	CAMO	0.544	0.902	0.801	0.057
	COD10K	0.868	0.932	0.798	0.024
	Kvasir-SEG	-	-	-	-
Proposed	CAMO	0.962	0.951	0.8952	0.0362
	COD10K	0.94	0.9353	0.8426	0.0402
	Kvasir-SEG	0.936	0.957	0.922	0.0258

Figure 9 shows the experiment results performed using three different datasets and validation and the training graphs that were generated. The loss function is also presented for comparative analysis of all the metrics. In this section, tables and charts are shown concerning the different datasets and the comparison with the previous benchmark techniques/algorithms based on the standard performance measures. The detailed information in the form of the graph is shown in Figure 9a–c, showing the performance of the proposed model and the dominancy of all the previously proposed algorithms for accuracy gain and cost reduction, while Figure 10 shows the prediction result on the COD10K dataset.

For a comprehensive analysis, a discussion of the different performance metrics is shown in Table 2. In light of the following experiments and discussion, the loss function and MAE analysis found that accuracy was not attained, despite lowering the cost function. The lowering of MAE should increase the accuracy of the model. In the model's controlling phase of the training, only the cost function can play a role in updating the gradient of the model's parameters. The cost function is responsible for the model training control and the parameters update. The observations indicate that lowering the cost function led to sudden changes in accuracy, which is very dangerous.

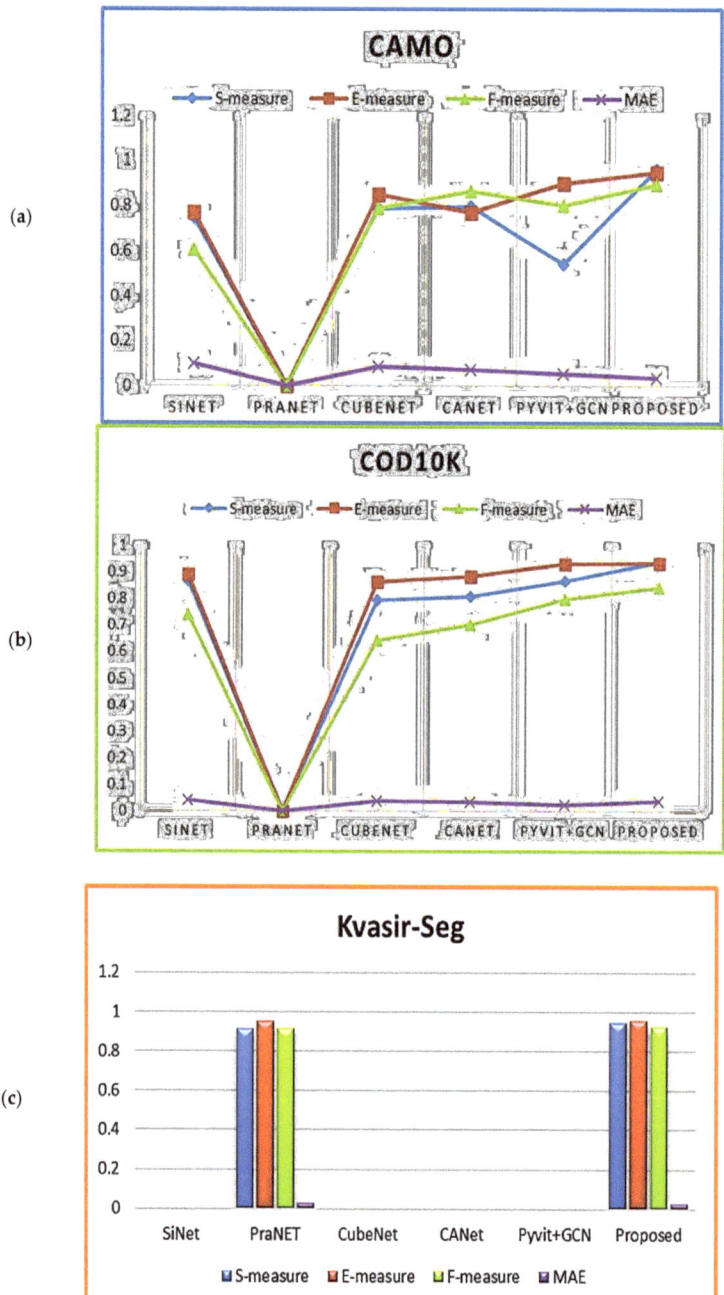

Figure 9. Comparative Analysis of multiple datasets: (a) CAMO; (b) COD10K; (c) Kvasir-SEG.

Figure 10. Prediction Results of OGR on COD10K: (**a**) Sample Images; (**b**) GT Label; (**c**) Predicted Label.

6.3. Comparison Results

Due to the very small number of samples in the past, the accuracy achievement and the deep learning strategy were hard to be accomplished. The large-scale working of the COD10K shows the way of interaction in the different parameters of exploration. A fully convolutional-based network has been applied so far in this type of dataset due to the image and the ground truth availability. The results indicated that the SINet achieved results of almost 86%, 86%, 75%, and 77% for the CHAMELEON, CAMO, and COD10K, respectively, with the different experiments of dataset generalization, meaning the different combinations of the multiple datasets, as shown in Table 3.

Another experiment was conducted but without the large-scale dataset (COD10K); it involved the internal body camouflage (Kvasir-SEG), and the results could reach91%. Then, multiple models, e.g., parallel attention-based, Pyramid transformer-based, and pre-trained backbone with resnet50, were used with the multiple datasets, and average scores of 91.5%, [92%, 84%, 86%, 87%], [87%, 78%] were achieved. Comparing these results with this study to further analyze this method is necessary. The proposed framework attained accuracy results of **96.2%**, **94.1%**, and **93.4%** on the CAMO, COD10K, and Kvasir-SEG datasets, respectively.

This section described the results of the previous study with another study in terms of quantitative analysis. The methods used in previous research were useful to this study by way of comparison.

Table 3. Comparison of different state-of-the-art methods, datasets, and their results.

References	Methods	Dataset	Results
[4]	A resnet50-CNN model with Search and Identification deep models	CHAMELEON, CAMO, COD10K	86.9%, 75.1%, 77.1%
[9]	PraNet	Kvasir-SEG	91.5%
[18]	A resnet50-CNN model with CANet	CHAMELEON CAMO, COD10K, NC4K	90.1%, 80.7%, 83.2%, 85.7%
[24]	Mutual GCN	CHAMELEON CAMO, COD10K	89.3%, 77.5%, 81.4%
[20]	A resnet50-CNN model with CubeNet	CHAMELEON CAMO, COD10K	87.3%, 78.8%, 79.5%
[25]	Pyramid vision Transformer + GCN fusion	CHAMELEON CAMO, COD10K, NC4K	92.2%, 84.4%, 86.8%, 87.0%
[36]	ResNet50,101-FPN, ResNetXt101-FPN with CFL	CAMO++, COD10K (Instance)	33.6% 31.4%
Proposed Model	Optimized Parallel Refinement	CAMO COD10K Kvasir-SEG	96.2% 94.1% 93.4%

7. Conclusions and Future Work

This study presents an optimization technique for COD tasks and a comparative analysis with the previous study. The dataset was used with the same parameters as previously used. The preprocessing techniques, e.g., transformation, image enhancement, noise removal, etc., are used in some experiments. The proposed model works efficiently and provides an optimal solution to the problem of camouflaged object detection. The performed experiments used to benchmark and publicly available datasets on pre-trained models, benchmark models, and the proposed model, indicating that the proposed model was the best in terms of the mentioned datasets concerning performance optimization and accuracy of the model. The training epochs, efficient learning, and optimization are best for the previously defined architecture. This study explored the comparative results of the experiment of the previous study with the performance of the proposed model.

The identification of the loss function is very important for model performance.

It can be further improved by selecting the best loss function for the specific model. The model can be generalized further, and the combined dictionary keys in the model can be modified for a better solution. This technique can also be optimized by combining supervised and unsupervised methods. The advancement in the run-time inference and the comparative analysis of the samples can also be enhanced.

Author Contributions: Conceptualization, M.K., S.U.R. and K.A.A.; Formal analysis, M.K.; Funding acquisition, K.A.A.; Methodology, M.K., S.U.R., T.M., K.A.A. and H.T.R.; Software, M.K., S.U.R., T.M. and H.T.R.; Supervision, S.U.R. and H.T.R.; Visualization, S.U.R., T.M. and K.A.A.; Writing—original draft, M.K., S.U.R., T.M., K.A.A. and H.T.R.; Writing—review and editing, M.K., S.U.R., T.M. and H.T.R. All authors have read and agreed to the published version of the manuscript.

Funding: The authors extend their appreciation to King Saud University, Saudi Arabia, for funding this work through the Researchers Supporting Project number (RSP-2021/305), King Saud University, Riyadh, Saudi Arabia.

Data Availability Statement: Not applicable.

Acknowledgments: The authors extend their appreciation to King Saud University, Saudi Arabia, for funding this work through Researchers Supporting Project number (RSP-2021/305), King Saud University, Riyadh, Saudi Arabia.

Conflicts of Interest: The authors declare no conflict of interest.

References

1. Horikawa, T.; Kamitani, Y. Generic decoding of seen and imagined objects using hierarchical visual features. *Nat. Commun.* **2017**, *8*, 15037. [CrossRef]
2. How, M.J.; Santon, M. Cuttlefish camouflage: Blending in by matching background features. *Curr. Biol.* **2022**, *32*, R523–R525. [CrossRef]
3. Soofi, M.; Sharma, S.; Safaei-Mahroo, B.; Sohrabi, M.; Organli, M.G.; Waltert, M. Lichens and animal camouflage: Some observations from central Asian ecoregions. *J. Threat. Taxa* **2022**, *14*, 20672–20676. [CrossRef]
4. Fan, D.-P.; Ji, G.-P.; Sun, G.; Cheng, M.-M.; Shen, J.; Shao, L. Camouflaged object detection. In Proceedings of the IEEE/CVF Conference on Computer Vision and Pattern Recognition, Seattle, WA, USA, 13–19 June 2020; pp. 2777–2787.
5. Borji, A.; Cheng, M.-M.; Hou, Q.; Jiang, H.; Li, J. Salient object detection: A survey. *Comput. Vis. Media* **2019**, *5*, 117–150. [CrossRef]
6. Shah, J.H.; Sharif, M.; Raza, M.; Murtaza, M.; Rehman, S.U. Robust Face Recognition Technique under Varying Illumination. *J. Appl. Res. Technol.* **2015**, *13*, 97–105. [CrossRef]
7. Yasmeen, U.; Shah, J.H.; Khan, M.A.; Ansari, G.J.; Rehman, S.U.; Sharif, M.; Kadry, S.; Nam, Y. Text Detection and Classification from Low Quality Natural Images. *Intell. Autom. Soft Comput.* **2020**, *26*, 1251–1266. [CrossRef]
8. Wang, H.; Jiang, X.; Ren, H.; Hu, Y.; Bai, S. Swiftnet: Real-time video object segmentation. In Proceedings of the IEEE/CVF Conference on Computer Vision and Pattern Recognition, Nashville, TN, USA, 20–25 June 2021; pp. 1296–1305.
9. Fan, D.P.; Ji, G.P.; Zhou, T.; Chen, G.; Fu, H.; Shen, J.; Shao, L. Pranet: Parallel reverse attention network for polyp segmentation. In Proceedings of the International Conference on Medical Image Computing and Computer-Assisted Intervention, Lima, Peru, 4–8 October 2020; Springer: Berlin/Heidelberg, Germany, 2020; pp. 263–273.
10. Le, T.-N.; Nguyen, T.V.; Nie, Z.; Tran, M.-T.; Sugimoto, A. Anabranch network for camouflaged object segmentation. *Comput. Vis. Image Underst.* **2019**, *184*, 45–56. [CrossRef]
11. Jha, D.; Smedsrud, P.H.; Riegler, M.A.; Halvorsen, P.; Lange, T.D.; Johansen, D.; Johansen, H.D. Kvasir-seg: A segmented polyp dataset. In Proceedings of the International Conference on Multimedia Modeling, Daejeon, Korea, 5–8 January 2020; Springer: Berlin/Heidelberg, Germany, 2020; pp. 451–462.
12. Zou, Z.; Shi, Z.; Guo, Y.; Ye, J. Object detection in 20 years: A survey. *arXiv* **2019**, arXiv:1905.05055.
13. Dong, B.; Wang, W.; Fan, D.P.; Li, J.; Fu, H.; Shao, L. Polyp-pvt: Polyp segmentation with pyramid vision transformers. *arXiv* **2021**, arXiv:2108.06932.
14. Tian, C.; Fei, L.; Zheng, W.; Xu, Y.; Zuo, W.; Lin, C.-W. Deep learning on image denoising: An overview. *Neural Netw.* **2020**, *131*, 251–275. [CrossRef]
15. Zhu, H.; Li, P.; Xie, H.; Yan, X.; Liang, D.; Chen, D.; Wei, M.; Qin, J. I Can Find You! Boundary-Guided Separated Attention Network for Camouflaged Object Detection. *AAAI* **2022**, *36*, 3608–3616. [CrossRef]
16. Ronneberger, O.; Fischer, P.; Brox, T. U-net: Convolutional networks for biomedical image segmentation. In Proceedings of the International Conference on Medical Image Computing and Computer-Assisted Intervention, Munich, Germany, 5–9 October 2015; Springer: Berlin/Heidelberg, Germany, 2015; pp. 234–241.
17. Dubey, A.K.; Jain, V. Comparative Study of Convolution Neural Network's ReLu and Leaky-ReLu Activation Functions. In *Applications of Computing, Automation and Wireless Systems in Electrical Engineering*; Springer: Berlin/Heidelberg, Germany, 2019; pp. 873–880.
18. Liu, J.; Zhang, J.; Barnes, N. Confidence-Aware Learning for Camouflaged Object Detection. *arXiv* **2021**, arXiv:2106.11641.
19. Luthra, A.; Sulakhe, H.; Mittal, T.; Iyer, A.; Yadav, S. Eformer: Edge Enhancement based Transformer for Medical Image Denoising. *arXiv* **2021**, arXiv:2109.08044.
20. Zhuge, M.; Lu, X.; Guo, Y.; Cai, Z.; Chen, S. CubeNet: X-shape connection for camouflaged object detection. *Pattern Recognit.* **2022**, *127*, 108644. [CrossRef]
21. Han, K.; Wang, Y.; Chen, H.; Chen, X.; Guo, J.; Liu, Z.; Tang, Y.; Xiao, A.; Xu, C.; Xu, Y.; et al. A survey on visual transformer. *arXiv* **2020**, arXiv:2012.12556.
22. Le, T.-H.; Dai, L.; Jang, H.; Shin, S. Robust Process Parameter Design Methodology: A New Estimation Approach by Using Feed-Forward Neural Network Structures and Machine Learning Algorithms. *Appl. Sci.* **2022**, *12*, 2904. [CrossRef]
23. Wang, W.; Xie, E.; Li, X.; Fan, D.-P.; Song, K.; Liang, D.; Lu, T.; Luo, P.; Shao, L. Pyramid Vision Transformer: A Versatile Backbone for Dense Prediction without Convolutions. In Proceedings of the IEEE/CVF International Conference on Computer Vision, Montreal, QC, Canada, 10–17 October 2021; pp. 548–558. [CrossRef]
24. Zhai, Q.; Li, X.; Yang, F.; Chen, C.; Cheng, H.; Fan, D.P. Mutual graph learning for camouflaged object detection. In Proceedings of the IEEE/CVF Conference on Computer Vision and Pattern Recognition, Nashville, TN, USA, 20–25 June 2021; pp. 12997–13007.
25. Hu, X.; Fan, D.P.; Qin, X.; Dai, H.; Ren, W.; Tai, Y.; Wang, C.; Shao, L. High-resolution Iterative Feedback Network for Camouflaged Object Detection. *arXiv* **2022**, arXiv:2203.11624.

26. He, K.; Gkioxari, G.; Dollár, P.; Girshick, R. Mask r-cnn. In Proceedings of the IEEE International Conference on Computer Vision, Venice, Italy, 22–29 October 2017; pp. 2961–2969.
27. Cai, Z.; Vasconcelos, N. Cascade r-cnn: Delving into high quality object detection. In Proceedings of the IEEE Conference on Computer Vision and Pattern Recognition, Salt Lake City, UT, USA, 18–23 June 2018; pp. 6154–6162.
28. Huang, Z.; Huang, L.; Gong, Y.; Huang, C.; Wang, X. Mask scoring r-cnn. In Proceedings of the IEEE/CVF Conference on Computer Vision and Pattern Recognition, Long Beach, CA, USA, 15–20 June 2019; pp. 6409–6418.
29. Fu, C.Y.; Shvets, M.; Berg, A.C. RetinaMask: Learning to predict masks improves state-of-the-art single-shot detection for free. *arXiv* **2019**, arXiv:1901.03353.
30. Lee, Y.; Park, J. Centermask: Real-time anchor-free instance segmentation. In Proceedings of the IEEE/CVF Conference on Computer Vision and Pattern Recognition, Seattle, WA, USA, 13–19 June 2020; pp. 13906–13915.
31. Bolya, D.; Zhou, C.; Xiao, F.; Lee, Y.J. Yolact: Real-time instance segmentation. In Proceedings of the IEEE/CVF International Conference on Computer Vision, Seoul, Korea, 27 October–2 November 2019; pp. 9157–9166.
32. Wang, X.; Kong, T.; Shen, C.; Jiang, Y.; Li, L. Solo: Segmenting objects by locations. In Proceedings of the European Conference on Computer Vision, Glasgow, UK, 23–28 August 2020; Springer: Berlin/Heidelberg, Germany, 2020; pp. 649–665.
33. Chen, H.; Sun, K.; Tian, Z.; Shen, C.; Huang, Y.; Yan, Y. Blendmask: Top-down meets bottom-up for instance segmentation. In Proceedings of the IEEE/CVF Conference on Computer Vision and Pattern Recognition, Seattle, WA, USA, 14–19 June 2020; pp. 8573–8581.
34. He, K.; Zhang, X.; Ren, S.; Sun, J. Deep residual learning for image recognition. In Proceedings of the IEEE Conference on Computer Vision and Pattern Recognition, Las Vegas, NV, USA, 27–30 June 2016; pp. 770–778.
35. Xie, S.; Girshick, R.; Dollár, P.; Tu, Z.; He, K. Aggregated residual transformations for deep neural networks. In Proceedings of the IEEE Conference on Computer Vision and Pattern Recognition, Honolulu, HI, USA, 21–26 July 2017; pp. 1492–1500.
36. Le, T.N.; Cao, Y.; Nguyen, T.C.; Le, M.Q.; Nguyen, K.D.; Do, T.T.; Tran, M.T.; Nguyen, T.V. Camouflaged Instance Segmentation In-the-Wild: Dataset, Method, and Benchmark Suite. *IEEE Trans. Image Process.* **2021**, *31*, 287–300. [CrossRef]
37. Chai, T.; Draxler, R.R. Root mean square error (RMSE) or mean absolute error (MAE)?—Arguments against avoiding RMSE in the literature. *Geosci. Model Dev.* **2014**, *7*, 1247–1250. [CrossRef]
38. Henderson, P.; Ferrari, V. End-to-End Training of Object Class Detectors for Mean Average Precision. In *Asian Conference on Computer Vision*; Springer: Cham, Switzerland, 2016; pp. 198–213. [CrossRef]
39. Wang, Z.; Bovik, A.; Sheikh, H.; Simoncelli, E. Image Quality Assessment: From Error Visibility to Structural Similarity. *IEEE Trans. Image Process.* **2004**, *13*, 600–612. [CrossRef] [PubMed]
40. Margolin, R.; Zelnik-Manor, L.; Tal, A. How to evaluate foreground maps? In Proceedings of the IEEE Conference on Computer Vision and Pattern Recognition, Columbus, OH, USA, 23–28 June 2014; pp. 248–255.
41. Fan, D.-P.; Gong, C.; Cao, Y.; Ren, B.; Cheng, M.-M.; Borji, A. Enhanced-alignment Measure for Binary Foreground Map Evaluation. *arXiv* **2018**, arXiv:1805.10421. [CrossRef]
42. Long, J.; Shelhamer, E.; Darrell, T. Fully convolutional networks for semantic segmentation. In Proceedings of the IEEE Conference on Computer Vision and Pattern Recognition, Boston, MA, USA, 7–12 June 2015; pp. 3431–3440.
43. Simonyan, K.; Zisserman, A. Very deep convolutional networks for large-scale image recognition. *arXiv* **2014**, arXiv:1409.1556.

Article

Semi-Supervised Approach for EGFR Mutation Prediction on CT Images

Cláudia Pinheiro [1,2], Francisco Silva [1,3], Tania Pereira [1,*] and Hélder P. Oliveira [1,3]

1 INESC TEC—Institute for Systems and Computer Engineering, Technology and Science, 4200-465 Porto, Portugal
2 FEUP—Faculty of Engineering, University of Porto, 4200-465 Porto, Portugal
3 FCUP—Faculty of Science, University of Porto, 4169-007 Porto, Portugal
* Correspondence: tania.pereira@inesctec.pt

Abstract: The use of deep learning methods in medical imaging has been able to deliver promising results; however, the success of such models highly relies on large, properly annotated datasets. The annotation of medical images is a laborious, expensive, and time-consuming process. This difficulty is increased for the mutations status label since these require additional exams (usually biopsies) to be obtained. On the other hand, raw images, without annotations, are extensively collected as part of the clinical routine. This work investigated methods that could mitigate the labelled data scarcity problem by using both labelled and unlabelled data to improve the efficiency of predictive models. A semi-supervised learning (SSL) approach was developed to predict epidermal growth factor receptor (*EGFR*) mutation status in lung cancer in a less invasive manner using 3D CT scans.The proposed approach consists of combining a variational autoencoder (VAE) and exploiting the power of adversarial training, intending that the features extracted from unlabelled data to discriminate images can help in the classification task. To incorporate labelled and unlabelled images, adversarial training was used, extending a traditional variational autoencoder. With the developed method, a mean AUC of 0.701 was achieved with the best-performing model, with only 14% of the training data being labelled. This SSL approach improved the discrimination ability by nearly 7 percentage points over a fully supervised model developed with the same amount of labelled data, confirming the advantage of using such methods when few annotated examples are available.

Keywords: semi-supervised learning; adversarial training; generative adversarial networks; medical image analysis; genotype prediction

MSC: 68T01; 68T07; 68T20

1. Introduction

According to the 2019 report of the World Health Organization [1], trachea, bronchus and lung cancer deaths are ranked as the 6th leading cause of death worldwide. Although it was not the most common cancer in terms of new cases in 2020, lung cancer was, by far, the most lethal cancer in the same year [2]. When diagnosed at an early stage, this ailment can present a favourable prospect, with 5-year survival rates around 60% for localised cancer (limited to the lungs) [3]; however, early-stage detection remains challenging, with more than half of all cases being diagnosed when cancer has already spread to other organs, with a corresponding 5-year survival rate of only 6% [3]. For this reason, it is crucial to work on individualised treatments according to lung cancer type and stage, leaving behind the traditional approaches relying almost exclusively on chemotherapy and radiotherapy treatments for patients with advanced disease. Targeted therapies have emerged as a strategy to enhance the outcome of lung cancer, improving patient survival. Some gene mutations linked to lung cancer have already been identified, with epidermal growth factor receptor (*EGFR*) and Kirsten rat sarcoma viral oncogene homolog (*KRAS*) being the most common ones. Due to their prevalence, they are important biomarkers to be identified, although only *EGFR* has approved targeted therapies. Consequently, assessing *EGFR* mutation has become a determinant step when deciding on the possible treatments for each individual, enabling more effective patient management in precision medicine. *EGFR* mutations are usually detected using DNA extracted from tumour tissue samples obtained during biopsy or resection; however, this method is an invasive procedure with clinical implications. In this context, the need to find alternative less-invasive methods to determine gene mutation status arises. Computer-aided diagnosis (CAD) systems can play an essential role in this assessment. These systems allow clinicians to have more information (often not accessible to the human eye) to support decision-making. Therefore, the analysis of medical images such as computed tomography (CT) scans may be the key to overcoming the aforementioned problem. Medical images have already proven to be able to provide valuable information on the understanding of biological characteristics of cancer and on tumour genomic profiling [4–6]. Moreover, previous works have highlighted and revealed the connection between *EGFR* mutation status (mutant or wild-type/non-mutant) and CT scan imaging phenotypes [7–9] using supervised approaches. By establishing this link, some light is shed on a less invasive way of identifying mutations driving cancer; however, studies so far were limited to the small size of the available datasets with the *EGFR* mutation information.

Some studies have developed machine learning (ML) models to predict *EGFR* mutation status using features extracted from different ROIs. Pinheiro et al. [9] used different combinations of input features, obtaining the highest value of the averaged area under the curve (AUC) of 0.7458 ± 0.0877 with hybrid semantic features (features describing not only the nodule but also other lung structures than the nodule). Having shown the importance of a holistic lung analysis, Morgado et al. [10] presented an approach extending the latter by assessing *EGFR* mutation status using radiomic features extracted from the entire volumetric region of the lung containing the tumour instead of focusing on the nodule region only. The best-performing model recorded an average AUC of 0.737 ± 0.018. Deep learning (DL) models have shown to be able to capture relevant information and patterns directly from images, avoiding all the feature engineering processes. An end-to-end pipeline based on DL was presented by Wang et al. [11] using only the tumour-region CT images, which were previously manually identified. The developed model comprised two subnetworks. The first one shares the same structure with the first 20 layers in DenseNet, with weights acquired from the ImageNet dataset [12] in a transfer learning manner. The second subnetwork was trained with a dataset consisting of nearly 15,000 CT images to identify the *EGFR* mutation status. With this DL model, an AUC of 0.85 was achieved. Using a 3D perspective of the nodules, Zhao et al. [13] developed a 3D DenseNet framework to analyse cubic patches containing the tumour region in an end-to-end approach, attaining an AUC of 0.758. Although these studies cannot be directly compared, as they used fairly different methodologies, a tendency is evident: a holistic assessment can provide more discriminative information relating to the alterations induced by this mutation, and DL methods seem to be able to capture these patterns. These aspects are fundamental when assessing mutation status through CT images since it is not yet fully known which structures/tissues can exhibit alterations induced by genetic mutations; therefore, the entire image might contain many mineable data.

Some of the presented works considered ROIs containing only the nodule [11,13], although studies so far have demonstrated that a holistic analysis is able to provide better results. Other studies were usually limited to the small size of the available datasets with the *EGFR* mutation information [9,10]. More robust and reliable models could be developed if more data were used. Despite the availability of larger datasets with CT scans, they lack the intended labels. This is a recurrent problem in medical imaging analysis due to the evident difficulty in collecting such labels, since the process is expensive, time-consuming, and oftentimes requires additional invasive exams, as is the case when collecting labels regarding mutations that drive cancer. For this reason, the usage of semi-supervised learning (SSL) techniques, which make use of a combination of labelled and unlabelled data, going further than traditional supervised approaches, comes as a solution to overcome the problem of scarcity of annotated data and might enhance the predictive abilities of the models.

In recent years, several SSL methods have been proposed, and some works have already applied these approaches in medical imaging in order to deal with the small proportion of labelled data in the training datasets. Martins and Silva [14] used a teacher-student-based pipeline in the classification of chest X-ray images, intending to evaluate the improvement in the performance of a DL model when additional unlabelled data is used. The registered performance gain was higher when smaller datasets were used, with enhancements going as high as around 7 percentage points with only 2% of labelled data when compared to the fully supervised counterpart. Similar comparative studies were performed by Sun et al. [15] and Al-Azzam and Shatnawi [16] regarding breast cancer diagnosis in digital mammography using a graph-based approach and a self-training technique, respectively. Exploiting the power of adversarial training, Das et al. [17] and Xie et al. [18] proposed semi-supervised adversarial classification models for different tasks: breast cancer grading through histopathological images and classifying lung nodules as benign and malignant on chest CT scans, respectively. The results revealed excellent performances, with AUCs above 0.90 in both studies.

The current work intends to use a semi-supervised learning approach to predict *EGFR* mutation status using CT images. This study represents the first implementation of SSL dedicated to such a complex biomarker prediction. The mutation status prediction is not possible to identify via the human naked eye, which implies no visible features in the image related to the genotype. However, deep learning models can capture more abstract features that can be used for mutation status prediction. Additionally, the extremely small datasets with this kind of label information have limited the prediction capacity of the learning models due to the variability of the cases that not are covered by the current labeled dataset, which is expected to be an overfitting issue for the supervised learning models. SSL algorithms attempt to create more robust predictive models by taking advantage of a broader set of data and using information that unlabelled data are able to provide. Exploiting the power of adversarial training, the approach used consists of combining a variational autoencoder (VAE) and adversarial training, intending that the features extracted from unlabelled data to discriminate images can help in the classification task. This method is expected to significantly reduce the necessary labelled data required to train such a classification model. The development of this methodology contributes to: supporting medical decision-making in the use of targeted therapies by providing a method for lung cancer characterisation; the development of a DL classification model with a small labelled dataset; and the comparison of important aspects when developing such classification models, including losses applied and tackling imbalanced datasets and different proportions of an unlabelled set.

2. Material and Methods

2.1. Datasets

Two datasets with CT images were used to develop the proposed work: one including clinical data with the *EGFR* mutation status label, and the other without this label. A detailed description of each dataset is provided hereafter.

2.1.1. NSCLC-Radiogenomics Dataset

The NSCLC-Radiogenomics dataset [19] is a publicly available collection developed from a cohort of 211 NSCLC patients, comprising clinical and imaging data. The records were acquired between 2008 and 2012 and are related to patients from the Stanford University School of Medicine and the Palo Alto Veterans Affairs Healthcare System. This is a unique dataset containing imaging data paired with genomic data, including mutation status information for *EGFR* (172 patients, 43 mutant and 129 wild-type), *KRAS*

(171 patients, 38 mutant and 133 wild-type), and *ALK* (157 patients, 2 translocated and 155 wild-type). In addition to CT and PET/CT scans, this dataset provides semantic annotation of the tumours in a controlled vocabulary and binary tumour masks. The latter result from a manual delineation made by a radiation oncologist. From the NSCLC-Radiogenomics dataset, just 117 patients were considered, as only these suited the following inclusion criteria: having an *EGFR* mutation test result, having an available CT scan, and binary tumour masks. The CT scans contained in this database were acquired using different CT scanners and imaging protocols, resulting in a slice thickness variation from 0.625 to 3 mm (with a median value of 1.5 mm) and an X-ray tube current from 124 to 699 mA (with a mean value of 220 mA) at 80–140 kVp (mean value: 120 kVp) [19]. From this dataset, just 117 patients were considered in the present work, and regarding the distribution of the *EGFR* mutation status for this subset, the wild-type is predominant, with mutants representing $\approx$ 20% and the wild-type representing $\approx$ 80% of the cases.

2.1.2. National Lung Screening Trial (NLST) Dataset

The National Lung Screening Trial (NLST) [20] was a randomised trial of lung cancer screening tests with 53,454 registered participants between 2002 and 2004. All the subjects were individuals considered at high risk: smokers or former smokers, with ages between 55 and 74 and at least a 30 pack-year smoking history. The study aimed to evaluate the clinical effectiveness of lung screening with chest CT. Screenings took place from 2002 to 2007 at 33 medical institutions in the United States. From the cohort, 26,722 participants were randomly assigned to screening with low-dose CT, and 26,732 were assigned to screening with chest radiography. Participants were offered three exams (T0, T1, and T2) performed annually, with the first (T0) being done soon after enrolment. All abnormalities found in the exams were recorded, and, for a CT scan to be considered positive (suspicious for lung cancer), the radiologist had to observe a non-calcified nodule or mass of at least 4 mm diameter or other suspicious findings for lung cancer. The confirmation of lung cancer was made by the NLST through medical records abstraction, and participants diagnosed with this disease did not undergo any posterior screening test in this trial. In these cases, information was documented in an additional dataset containing data about each confirmed lung cancer case, including tumour size and location. The latter encompasses the following: carina, left hilum, lingula, left lower lobe, left main stem bronchus, left upper lobe, mediastinum, right hilum, right lower lobe, right middle lobe, right main stem bronchus, right upper lobe, other and unknown. All screening examinations were performed in line with a standard protocol, which specified acceptable machine characteristics and acquisition variables, resulting in a variation of the slice thickness from 1.0 to 2.5 mm and of the tube current-time product from 40 to 80 mAs with 120 to 140 kVp of voltage [20,21]. With the data collected in this trial, one of the most extensive chest CT datasets publicly available was built. The NLST database also includes clinical data, which, along with the images, are only available for researchers through the Cancer Data Access System https://cdas.cancer.gov/plco/ (accessed on 5 February 2022). Out of the 26,722 patients assigned to screening with CT, only 1089 had a confirmed cancer diagnosis, and, from those, just 622 had paired image data. This last subset was the initial collection of data considered in this work, and, due to not carrying information regarding the *EGFR* mutation status, was the unlabelled set.

2.2. Data Pre-Processing

Considering the different acquisition protocols present in both datasets, the following pre-processing techniques were employed to reduce their effect on the learning process (Figure 1). First, the distance between adjacent pixels was set at 1 mm, with further resizing to a 256 $\times$ 256-pixel resolution. Then, the pixel intensities were converted to Hounsfield units (HU) by applying a linear transformation using *min-max* normalisation. Values under -1000 HU, which corresponds to air density, were assigned to 0, and values above 400 HU, which relates to the density of hard tissues, were assigned to 1.

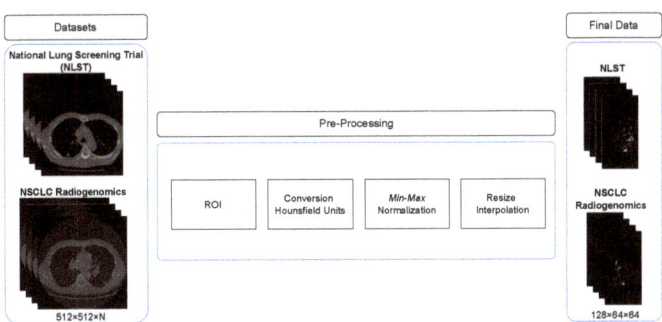

Figure 1. Overview of the pipeline developed for preprocessing the images from the two datasets.

Previous works identified the importance of not restricting the analysis to the nodule structure [22]. Additionally, the use of more "established" regions of interest for EGFR prediction in this SSL approach makes it easier to compare with the literature. The performed study used a holistic approach based on the entire lung containing the nodule in confirmed lung cancer cases. The binary masks for the lungs were obtained using a lung segmentation algorithm [22]. For the NSCLC-Radiogenomics dataset, binary masks for the nodule were available. The NLST dataset only provided the size of the tumours, the corresponding locations, and the CT scan slice number containing the largest nodule diameter. Based on the available information, each scan was cropped to the lung containing the nodule. Since the carina is located at the base of the trachea (the area where the trachea splits into the left and right bronchus), and the mediastinum is also located in the region that separates the lungs, individuals that only presented tumours in these locations were excluded. Moreover, one case was found in which both lungs exhibited primary tumours. In this situation, the two lungs were considered distinct samples (as if they belonged to different patients). This resulted in a total of 574 volumes.

In this work, it is intended to take as input 3D volumes providing information about the lung as a whole. For this reason, data uniformisation was an essential step, as CT scans from the considered datasets had a varying number of slices: from 245 to 635 in the NSCLC-Radiogenomics and between 46 and 545 in the NLST dataset. Therefore, to obtain volumes with the same number of slices, a standard depth of 64 was selected. Considering this value, the only CT scan with an inferior slice number was excluded from the NLST data collection. Additionally, the axial image size was also a challenge due to resource limitations. Therefore, each cropped slice was resized to half its size by interpolation, with (128×64) being the final axial image size. To achieve the desired standard depth, two different strategies were tested:

- Rescaling the volume, using interpolation, by a scaling factor given by

$$factor = \frac{desired\ depth}{scan\ depth} \qquad (1)$$

where the *desired depth* was set to 64 and the *scan depth* represents the number of slices of the CT scan;
- Selecting 64 uniformly spaced slices, simulating a wider space between slices. In this selection, it was imposed that the slice containing the maximum nodule mask area was included.

After the pre-processing steps, the final number of considered images from each dataset, according to the aforementioned inclusion criteria, are summarised in Table 1.

Table 1. Number of CT scans considered from each dataset.

Dataset	EGFR Mutation Status	# CT scans Considered
NSCLC-Radiogenomics	Available	117
NLST	Unavailable	574

2.3. Learning Models

In this study, learning models were developed for a more robust classification model for *EGFR* mutation status assessment using CT scan images as input in a combination of labelled and unlabelled data. To achieve this, the power of adversarial training was explored using a combination of an SSL generative adversarial network (GAN) and a VAE.

Autoencoders, an efficient feature extraction method, are neural networks used to learn lower-dimensional codifications (latent space) to, afterwards, generate input reconstructions. Their architecture comprises two networks: an encoder and a decoder. The former transforms the input data into an encoded representation, and the latter reconstructs, as closely as possible, the original input from the low-dimensional latent space. Thus, the decoder acts similarly to a GAN generator, projecting a low-dimensional vector to an image. A shortcoming of this kind of representation learning algorithm is that it does not allow the generation of new samples as it uses a deterministic approach. VAEs [23], generative models with a similar structure to autoencoders and a solid probabilistic foundation, replace the encoded representation by a stochastic sampling operation, learning, instead, the parameters of a probability distribution using a Bayesian approach. As the posterior distribution $p(z|x)$ (where z are the latent variables and x is the input) is an intractable probability distribution, using this variational inference, the encoder learns $q(z|x)$, a simpler and tractable distribution [24]. Typically, $q(z|x)$ is a Gaussian.

Proposed Method

In this study, the proposed method encompasses two main structures connected by a shared network: a VAE and a semi-supervised GAN, where the decoder of the VAE acts as the GAN generator, as illustrated in Figure 2.

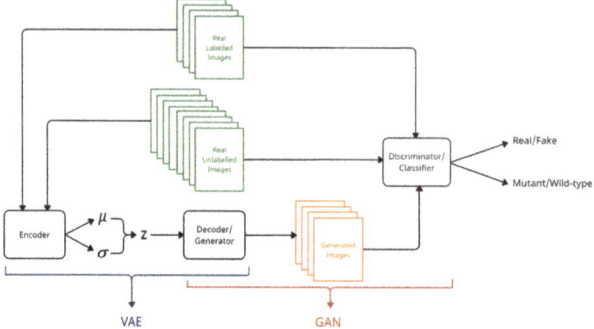

Figure 2. Proposed method, which consists of two main structures linked by a shared network: a VAE and a semi-supervised GAN, with the VAE decoder acting as the GAN generator.

The discriminator has two different outputs, both for binary classification tasks: one for the likelihood of an image being a real CT (belonging to the training data) or a generated one, and the other to classify labelled data as *EGFR* mutant or wild-type. In fact, this can be seen as having a discriminator and a classifier with a common backbone and two different output layers. The encoder of the VAE receives as input CT scan images from the training set (both labelled and unlabelled) and maps them to a distribution, providing as outputs two vectors: one representing the mean (μ) and the other representing the log-variance (σ) of $q(z|x)$. Latent vectors z, sampled from these distributions, are passed to the decoder/generator that maps the code to an image. In the generation of each of these samples z, a reparameterisation must be performed to enable backpropagation [23]. Thus, the variable z can be obtained by $z = \mu + \sigma \odot \epsilon$, where $\odot$ represents the element-wise product, and ϵ is an auxiliary noise variable (the stochastic component), $\epsilon \sim \mathcal{N}(0, 1)$. The reconstructed and original images are then provided as input to the discriminator/classifier, whose role is to undertake the two classification tasks mentioned above. To stabilise the training of the generator, avoiding a faster convergence of the discriminator early in training, the VAE part was initially fixed to be trained alone, giving the decoder/generator a better starting position.

The proposed VAE and GAN architectures were largely based on the deep convolutional generative adversarial network (DCGAN) [25]. In the case of the VAE base architecture, which was kept unchanged during the experiments and is represented in Figure 3, the encoder is similar to the DCGAN discriminator, and the decoder is similar to the DCGAN generator. Considering the GAN architecture, only a scheme of the discriminator base architecture is represented in Figure 4.

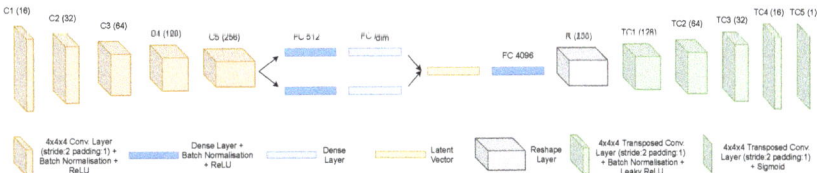

Figure 3. Proposed VAE architecture. As can be seen, the encoder is composed of five convolution blocks (C1 to C5) and two bottleneck dense layers. Each convolution block comprises convolutional layers with an increasing number of filters, with each one followed by a rectified linear unit (ReLU) activation function and batch normalisation [26]. To reduce the size of each feature map by half, $4 \times 4 \times 4$ kernels with a stride of 2 and a padding of 1 were used. To reconstruct the original input, a latent vector with the size of the latent dimension (l_{dim}) is passed to a dense layer to, afterwards, be reshaped into 256 activation maps. This is used as input to four transposed convolution blocks (TC1 to TC4), each one composed of a $4 \times 4 \times 4$ transposed convolutional layer, with a decreasing number of filters with a stride of 2 and a padding of 1, followed by a Leaky ReLU activation (with a negative slope of 0.2) and batch normalisation. The last transposed convolutional layer (TC5) is followed by a sigmoid activation function to ensure that all output pixel values belong to the original range of values [0, 1].

Additionally, a slight variation of the base architecture was tested, as depicted in Figure 4, by adding into each classification head another dense layer with a smaller number of neurons than those used in the previous layer.

Before this final base architecture was achieved, a different design for the discriminator was tested using an approach introduced by Salımans et al. [27]. The main difference between the two implementations concerned the output layer: instead of having two output layers, a single one was used with two nodes (the same number of classes in the initial supervised classification problem), and, therefore, a Softmax activation function. The unsupervised classification task used the outputs before the activation function, and a normalised sum of the exponential outputs was calculated, returning the probability of the input being fake [27].

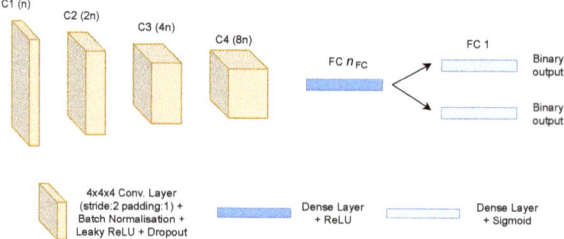

Figure 4. Proposed discriminator architecture. As illustrated, this network embodies four blocks of convolutional layers with $4 \times 4 \times 4$, a stride of 2 and a padding of 1 for down-sampling, as well as one dense layer in the backbone followed by two classification heads. Each convolutional layer is followed by batch normalisation and uses Leaky ReLU (with a negative slope of 0.2) as the activation function. A dropout layer [28] was added after each of these convolutional blocks to decrease the number of trainable parameters, reducing overfitting. This regularisation strategy, which consists of randomly dropping out neurons during training with a certain defined probability, has the additional benefit of promoting a more robust feature extraction. Similarly to the decoder network, the number of filters increases as the network becomes deeper. Lastly, a dense layer with a variable number of neurons was included prior to the classification heads.

2.4. Training

For all the experiments performed, the labelled dataset considered was randomly split into two different sets: one for training (80%) and the other for testing (20%). With this, different training and testing groups are achieved within each random split. Given the small dimension of the dataset, only a train and test split (i.e., no validation sets created) was performed, allowing more data to be added to the training set. The divisions are performed independently, restarting all the model parameters at each one, which ensures there is no data leakage. The unlabelled set utilised was added to the training set, and the model was trained until the classifier (the discriminator) converged. To achieve a model that was as robust as possible without drawing conclusions based on a possibly biased test set and to explore data variance, 10 different random train-test splits were performed. During this training and testing process, different evaluation metrics were computed and averaged over the 10 random splits: AUC, precision, sensitivity and specificity.

2.5. Experiment Design

Different experiments were conducted in order to test some possible solutions for the model described above. In addition to hyperparameter tuning, different discriminator network architectures were tested, as well as some variations to the loss functions.

2.5.1. Loss Functions

During the training process, different loss functions were tested for the optimisation of all the networks involved, trying to find the best way to combine the VAE with the GAN with the best possible performance.

Discriminator

Starting with the discriminator, the loss functions considered for the optimisation of this network comprised an adversarial loss and a supervised classification loss used separately or combined using the average (both options were tested). In the adversarial part, as proposed in the original GAN paper [29], the goal of the discriminator is to maximise the function presented below:

$$\mathcal{L}_{adversarial} = \mathbb{E}_{x \sim p_{data}(x)}[\log D(x)] + \mathbb{E}_{z \sim p_z(z)}[\log(1 - D(G(z)))] \qquad (2)$$

where $\mathbb{E}_{x \sim p_{data}(x)}$ and $\mathbb{E}_{z \sim p_z(z)}$ are the expected values over the real data inputs and over the fake images $G(z)$, respectively; $D(x)$ is the discriminator probability estimation that a real image x is real; $G(z)$ is the generator output for a given input z, and $D(G(z))$ is the discriminator probability estimation that an image produced by the generator is real.

Additionally, another version of Equation (2) was tested by adding another term. The goal was to enforce the discriminator to distinguish not only images generated from latent vectors sampled from the distributions outputted by the encoder but also from random noise vectors sampled from a Gaussian distribution. Hence, the alternative adversarial loss to be maximized is given by:

$$\mathcal{L}_{adversarial} = \mathbb{E}_x[\log D(x)] + \mathbb{E}_z[\log(1 - D(G(z)))] + \mathbb{E}_{z_p}[\log(1 - D(G(z_p)))] \quad (3)$$

with $z_p \sim \mathcal{N}(0, 1)$. The supervised classification loss considered was the binary cross-entropy (BCE) loss:

$$\mathcal{L}_{BCE} = -\frac{1}{N}\sum_{i=1}^{N}(Y_i \cdot \log \hat{Y}_i + (1-Y_i) \cdot \log(1-\hat{Y}_i)) \quad (4)$$

where Y_i is the ground truth label, $\hat{Y}_i$ is the predicted probability for the ith image, and N is the mini-batch size. Moreover, we also tested if the addition of a manifold regularisation term would improve the overall performance. A manifold regularisation, $\Omega_{manifold}$, should enforce the discriminator to yield similar features for nearby points in the latent space.

$$\Omega_{manifold} = \left\| D(G(z)) - D(G(z + \delta \cdot 1 \times 10^{-5})) \right\|, \delta \sim \mathcal{N}(0, 1) \quad (5)$$

Decoder/Generator

For the optimisation of the decoder/generator, different combinations of loss functions (C_1, C_2 and C_3) were tested and are now described (in the equations that follow, the parameter λ represent loss weights, and the reduction or aggregation method selected is the mean):

(C_1) with a loss function composed of a reconstruction term $\mathcal{L}_{reconstruction}$ (Equation (6))—in this case, the mean squared error (MSE) between the decoder reconstruction $\hat{x}$ and the original input x, and a generator term, $\mathcal{L}_{adversarial}$. The latter is determined by maximising the log-probability of the discriminator by considering generated images as belonging to the training data or, analogously, minimizing the log-probability of the discriminator by correctly classifying fake images. This was done by applying the loss introduced by Goodfellow et al. [29] given by Equation (7) or, alternatively, the non-saturating version (Equation (8)). In such a case, the decoder/generator loss is provided by Equation (9);

$$\mathcal{L}_{reconstruction} = \frac{1}{N}\sum_{i=1}^{N}(x - \hat{x})^2 \quad (6)$$

$$\mathcal{L}_{adversarial} = \mathbb{E}_{z \sim p_z(z)}[\log(1 - D(G(z)))] \quad (7)$$

$$\mathcal{L}_{adversarial} = \mathbb{E}_{z \sim p_z(z)}[-\log(D(G(z)))] \quad (8)$$

$$\mathcal{L}_{generator} = \lambda \cdot \mathcal{L}_{reconstruction} + \mathcal{L}_{adversarial} \quad (9)$$

(C_2) maintaining the same reconstruction loss mentioned above (6) and substituting the adversarial loss (Equation (8)) with the feature matching loss, introduced by Salimans et al. [27], where the generator is encouraged to synthesise data that minimises the statistical difference between the features of the real and fake data on an intermediate layer of the discriminator. Therefore, this loss is defined as follows:

$$\mathcal{L}_{feature\ matching} = \left\|\mathbb{E}_{x \sim p_{data}} f(x) - \mathbb{E}_{z \sim p_z(z)} f(G(z))\right\|^2 \tag{10}$$

where $f(x)$ represents activations on an intermediate layer of the discriminator. Consequently, in this case,

$$\mathcal{L}_{generator} = \lambda \cdot \mathcal{L}_{reconstruction} + \mathcal{L}_{feature\ matching} \tag{11}$$

(C_3) inspired by Larsen et al. ([30]), using the feature matching loss (Equation 10) instead of a reconstruction loss combined with an adversarial loss achieved by:

$$\mathcal{L}_{adversarial} = \mathbb{E}[log(1 - D(G(z)))] + \mathbb{E}[log(1 - D(G(z_p)))] \tag{12}$$

where z_p is a sample from the prior $\mathcal{N}(0,1)$. For this situation,

$$\mathcal{L}_{generator} = \lambda \cdot \mathcal{L}_{feature\ matching} + \mathcal{L}_{adversarial} \tag{13}$$

Encoder

Similarly to the decoder/generator optimisation, distinct combinations (C_1) and (C_2) were tested for this network (in the equations that follow, the parameter γ represent loss weights, and the reduction or aggregation method selected is the mean):

(C_1) with the traditional VAE loss, which incorporates both a reconstruction loss (6) and a latent loss $\mathcal{L}_{prior}$ (Equation (14)), the Kullback–Leibler (KL) divergence loss or relative entropy. The latter is a statistical measure and quantifies the distance between two probability distributions [31], in this case, the distribution of the encoder output and a Gaussian of mean 0 and variance 1. Therefore, for this situation, the encoder loss can be obtained by Equation (15), a loss similar to the one used in β-VAE [32] but, in this case, varying $\frac{1}{\beta}$ instead;

$$\begin{aligned}\mathcal{L}_{prior} &= \mathbb{D}_{KL}(q(zx)\,\mathcal{N}(0,1))\\ &= -\frac{1}{2}\sum_{i=1}^{N}(1 + log\,(\sigma^2) - \sigma^2 - \mu^2)\end{aligned} \tag{14}$$

$$\mathcal{L}_{encoder} = \gamma \cdot \mathcal{L}_{reconstruction} + \mathcal{L}_{prior} \tag{15}$$

(C_2) replacing the previously mentioned reconstruction term by the feature-matching loss (Equation (10)) while maintaining the KL divergence loss. Thus, in this case,

$$\mathcal{L}_{encoder} = \gamma \cdot \mathcal{L}_{feature\ matching} + \mathcal{L}_{prior} \tag{16}$$

2.5.2. Hyperparameters

The described networks required careful hyperparameter optimisation for fine-tuning. Table 2 presents the list of values considered for the hyperparameter manual search applied.

As the training sets used included different proportions of labelled and unlabelled data, it was decided to keep the same ratio in the mini-batch size. That is, if the used training set had, for instance, a proportion of 15% of annotated data and the remaining 85% of data without a label, the mini-batch comprised data with a similar division.

Table 2. List of values used for hyperparameter optimisation in the SSL model.

Hyperparameter	Values
Mini-batch size	8, 16, 32
Dropout discriminator	0.3, 0.4, 0.5
Learning rate discriminator	$1 \times 10^{-5}, 2 \times 10^{-5}, 5 \times 10^{-5}, 1 \times 10^{-4}, 3 \times 10^{-4}, 1 \times 10^{-3}$
Learning rate VAE	$1 \times 10^{-5}, 1 \times 10^{-4}, 2 \times 10^{-4}, 1 \times 10^{-3}$
Optimisers	Adam, AdamW, SGD [a]
Weight decay	$1 \times 10^{-7}, 1 \times 10^{-4}, 1 \times 10^{-3}, 1 \times 10^{-2}$
Momentum	0.1, 0.5, 0.9
l_{dim}	128, 256, 512
n [b]	16, 32, 64
n_{FC} [c]	512, 1024
γ	1, 5
λ	5, 10, 15

[a] Stochastic gradient descent. [b] Number of filters in the first hidden layer of the discriminator network. [c] Number of neurons in the dense layer of the discriminator network.

2.5.3. Imbalanced Data

As usually occurs when dealing with medical diagnosis, the labelled datasets have an uneven class distribution, with the mutant type as the underrepresented class. If a classification model were built with this imbalance without any further attention given, the model would tend to be biased towards the negative classification, failing to capture the minority class. To tackle this, two strategies were tested:

- **Oversampling** the minority class by applying data augmentation techniques—horizontal and vertical flips, random rotation, and adding Gaussian noise on-the-fly, that is, without physically storing transformed images. Instead, in each mini-batch, the same number of samples for each class is used, allowing repetition of the minority samples and applying transformations to 75% of them;
- **Using a weighted loss function** during training, including in the classification loss an argument with class weights given by $\left[\frac{n_0}{n_0}, \frac{n_0}{n_1}\right]$, where n_0 represents the number of examples in the negative class (the majority class) and n_1 represents the number of examples in the positive class (the minority class) in the training set.

2.5.4. Distribution of Unlabelled Data

A final experiment relates to the percentage of unlabelled data used. To evaluate the performance when different amounts of data without labels are used to build the SSL approach, once a final model was achieved, the number of utilised training samples from the NLST dataset was reduced. Training the model using the entire NLST subset summarised in Table 1 corresponds to a percentage of around 14% of labelled data, as presented in Table 3. To investigate if a variation in the unlabelled dataset size would affect the classification performance and up to which point, different values for the percentage of NLST data used were tested: 100% (the base model), 80%, 60%, and 40%. To provide different percentages of unlabelled data to each model, random splits of the full unlabelled dataset were performed according to the desired proportion. For instance, for a percentage of 80%, the dataset was randomly divided into two groups (of 80% and 20%), giving as input to the model the intended percentage, being, in this case, the remaining 20% of data discarded. The corresponding proportions of labelled and unlabelled data used for developing the models are detailed in Table 4.

Table 3. Percentage of labelled data when using the entire NLST dataset.

Dataset	Available # Samples	# Samples for Training	% Labelled Data
NSCLC-Radiogenomics	117	94	14.07%
NLST	574	574	

Table 4. Proportions of labelled and unlabelled data for different NLST data percentages.

% NLST Considered	% Labelled Data	% Unlabelled Data
100	14	86
80	17	83
60	21	79
40	29	71

3. Results

Numerous experiments were performed, and the best outcomes were provided when using the base architecture for the discriminator represented in Figure 4, with the following combination of loss functions:

- Discriminator—using the $\mathcal{L}_{adversarial}$ depicted in Equation (3) and the $\mathcal{L}_{BCE}$ propagated separately through the network;
- Decoder/generator—applying the $\mathcal{L}_{generator}$ summarised in Equation (13);
- Encoder—optimised with the $\mathcal{L}_{encoder}$ presented in Equation (16).

The base model with the best performance was obtained with the set of hyperparameters presented in Table 5. The model with all these settings defined was trained in the remaining scenarios: tackling the imbalance present in the labelled set by oversampling or by using a weighted loss; rescaling the image depth by interpolation or by selecting 64 linearly separated slices; and adding a manifold regularisation term (Equation (5)) to the discriminator loss.

Table 5. Set of hyperparameters that led to the best-performing SSL model.

Hyperparameter	Values
Mini-batch size	32
Dropout discriminator	0.5
Learning rate discriminator	1×10^{-5}
Learning rate VAE	2×10^{-4}
Optimisers	Adam
Weight decay	1×10^{-4}
l_{dim}	128 [a]
n [b]	64
n_{FC} [c]	512
γ	5
λ	10

[a] As no significant differences between the three tested values were found, a size of 128 was selected to reduce the number of trainable parameters. [b] Number of filters in the first hidden layer of the discriminator network. [c] Number of neurons in the dense layer of the discriminator network.

3.1. Ablation Studies

3.1.1. Imbalanced Data and Rescaling the Depth of the Volumes

Starting with the strategy to overcome the imbalance found in the dataset, Table 6 presents the achieved performances when considering the two tested approaches. The results are also discriminated by the technique used to rescale the depth of the considered volumes. Using a weighted loss function instead of oversampling the minority class provided better results, which was more noticeable when the rescaling of the number of slices per image was performed with interpolation, registering an AUC of 0.701 ± 0.114 averaged over 10 random train-test splits. Thus, in the results provided hereafter, this was the technique applied.

Table 6. Performance results for the *EGFR* mutation prediction when considering different strategies to handle imbalanced data. The evaluation metrics are presented as mean ± standard deviation averaged over 10 random train-test splits.

Strategy Imbalanced	Image Depth Rescaling	AUC	Precision	Sensitivity	Specificity
Weighted loss	Interpolation	**0.701 ± 0.114**	0.425 ± 0.140	**0.660 ± 0.254**	0.742 ± 0.134
	Linearly spaced	0.597 ± 0.106	0.302 ± 0.087	0.500 ± 0.248	0.693 ± 0.121
Oversampling	Interpolation	0.610 ± 0.071	**0.433 ± 0.227**	0.420 ± 0.189	**0.800 ± 0.129**
	Linearly spaced	0.592 ± 0.106	0.420 ± 0.287	0.300 ± 0.241	0.884 ± 0.077

3.1.2. Add a Manifold Regularisation Term

When evaluating the effect of adding a manifold regularisation term to the discriminator loss, the results show that such a term is more advantageous when the strategy used for rescaling is the selection of linearly separated slices, as detailed in Table 7. While with the interpolation method, the model achieved worse performance, using a manifold regularisation with the former strategy increases the average AUC from 0.5974 ± 0.1060 to 0.6274 ± 0.1372.

Table 7. Performance results when considering the addition of a manifold regularisation term to the discriminator loss.

Image Depth Rescaling	AUC	Precision	Sensitivity	Specificity
Interpolation	**0.665 ± 0.125**	**0.367 ± 0.134**	**0.640 ± 0.250**	0.690 ± 0.140
Linearly spaced	0.627 ± 0.137	0.350 ± 0.216	0.460 ± 0.284	**0.795 ± 0.101**

3.1.3. Proportions of Unlabelled Data

Lastly, different percentages for the NLST data were tested. The results for the two models that achieved better results in the previous experiments are detailed in Tables 8 and 9. It should be noticed that a fully supervised model (using exclusively labelled data) is only presented in Table 8, since the addition of the manifold regularisation was added upon the SSL approach. As can be observed, reducing the amount of unlabelled data given as input to the models results in slightly worse performances. The variation between different percentages (80%, 60% and 40%) is almost inexistent when no manifold regularisation is applied, being small when this term is added. Nevertheless, utilising unlabelled data, even if in smaller amounts, provides better models than not using them at all.

Table 8. Performance results for different percentages of the unlabelled dataset used when considering a weighted loss function.

	Percentage Unlabelled Dataset Used				
Metric	100%	80%	60%	40%	0% [a]
AUC	**0.701 ± 0.114**	0.659 ± 0.120	0.651 ± 0.1101	0.655 ± 0.153	0.632 ± 0.063
Precision	**0.424 ± 0.140**	0.388 ± 0.188	0.343 ± 0.124	0.368 ± 0.153	0.286 ± 0.042
Sensitivity	0.660 ± 0.254	0.560 ± 0.265	0.560 ± 0.265	0.620 ± 0.244	**0.800 ± 0.155**
Specificity	0.742 ± 0.134	**0.758 ± 0.158**	0.737 ± 0.125	0.689 ± 0.134	0.463 ± 0.131

[a] Fully supervised model—baseline model.

Table 9. Performance results for different percentages of the unlabelled dataset used when considering a weighted loss function and a manifold regularisation term.

Metric	Percentage Unlabelled Dataset Used			
	100%	80%	60%	40%
AUC	**0.665 ± 0.125**	0.631 ± 0.120	0.618 ± 0.105	0.613 ± 0.130
Precision	0.367 ± 0.134	**0.388 ± 0.188**	0.348 ± 0.108	0.333 ± 0.115
Sensitivity	**0.640 ± 0.250**	0.560 ± 0.265	0.520 ± 0.223	0.500 ± 0.272
Specificity	0.689 ± 0.140	0.726 ± 0.148	0.726 ± 0.123	**0.726 ± 0.112**

The addition of the unlabeled data does not produce a monotonic increase in the performance; however, there is a more marked increase with the addition of all the unlabeled data, which seems that the final addition of the data brings some variability relevant to the learning model to improve the capability of the prediction.

The combination that achieved the best results was using a weighted loss function to tackle the imbalance of the labelled data without adding a regularisation term, with a mean AUC of 0.701 ± 0.114, as illustrated in the mean ROC curve of Figure 5 with the baseline method.

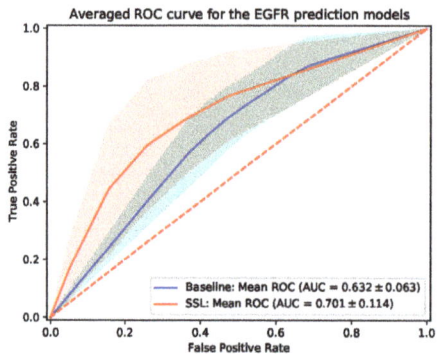

Figure 5. Averaged ROC curve for *EGFR* mutation status prediction with the baseline and best-performing SSL model. For each train-test split, the ROC curve is computed. The blue and orange lines represent the arithmetic average ROC curve for each model, and the shaded areas depict the corresponding standard deviation. The red dashed line illustrates the ROC curve of an at-chance classifier.

4. Discussion

Although this SSL approach contains architectural blocks with generative purposes, the discriminative part was the most exploited here. Not only was the quality of the generated images not expected to be very close to real (mostly due to the choice of $\mathcal{L}_{generator}$), their reality was not aimed at, since that would mean that the concrete imaging manifestations associated with *EGFR* mutation status would be accurately found, which we did not expect in advance given its extreme difficulty. Instead, we focused on finding regularities at a lower level using the feature space extracted by the discriminator. Furthermore, as stated in [33], when it comes to semi-supervised tasks using GANs, good classification performance is not compatible with a realistic generator output. Using feature matching results in better semi-supervised learning performances but, as a drawback, generates worse images.

The results of this research display the difficulty of detecting relevant and significant features that could be related to *EGFR* mutation status. Conditioned by the limited amount of labelled data available, we tried to achieve a more robust classification model by incorporating unlabelled data in a semi-supervised approach. Even with this extra data without annotation, the task has proven to be quite challenging and susceptible to the train-test split variations, as can be observed by the high values of standard deviation across all experiments. This high variation can also be a consequence of the small number of included *EGFR* mutant patients (23 cases), with it being desirable to add extra samples of this class to verify if the variation would be reduced.

When tackling the imbalance present in the data, using a weighted loss function proved to be a better approach when compared to oversampling the minority class. This has the additional benefit of reducing the required training time as the number of images is fewer. Undersampling the majority class was never an option in this work given that one is dealing with the problem of data scarcity, and dismissing valuable data seems counterintuitive.

When using the full unlabelled dataset instead of only a portion of it, the model benefits more from the additional information provided by this data collection. Furthermore, the increased performance is even more notorious when comparing the model with a fully supervised baseline, which uses only the labelled data as input. A direct comparison with related works concerning the effect of such variations cannot be made given that, traditionally, the variation of the labelled-unlabelled data proportions is performed by adding labels to the desired part of the unannotated data and not by removing data without labels, as was tested in this study.

The manifold regularisation term aimed to approximate the information extracted by the discriminator according to how closely the data points were located in the latent space (space mapped by the generative encoder). However, the demonstrated decrease in discriminative performance (although not significant) can be possibly explained by the idea that close latent data points actually belonged to different classes, which could be related to the difficulty of correctly approximating the Bayesian posterior for such a complex task: this approximation implies navigating through explainable factors that are not well-known by clinicians yet and with a vast space of complex structures within the lung that can possibly be wrongly associated with EGFR mutation status.

Regarding related works in *EGFR* assessment in lung cancer CT scans, to the best of our gathered knowledge, no other research has attempted a 3D deep learning approach using the entire lung volumetric region in a semi-supervised fashion. Furthermore, SSL methods are typically tested using extended labelled datasets and by simply removing the label of a significant portion of the data, simulating the existence of a large unlabelled set. Approaches that combine different datasets in a similar way as presented in this work are difficult to find. Additionally, no study was found combining the two datasets used in this task (NSCLC-Radiogenomics and NLST). Silva et al. [34] developed a DL model based on transfer learning methods using 2D CT scan slices from the NSCLC-Radiogenomics dataset. Utilising the analysis of the lung containing the nodule as ROI, a mean AUC of 0.68 ± 0.08 was achieved. Comparing the results, the developed SSL approach was able to slightly increase this performance using the same labelled dataset.

Although the performance results obtained in this work are promising but still not very good, they are aligned with the performance obtained in the previous works. The current work suffers from the inability to find concrete visual manifestations associated with EGFR mutation status, which represents a transversal challenge in any machine learning application. The susceptibility against spurious correlations when trying to extract these very complex relations is often manifested by overfitting and lack of performance stability (here shown by the high variation in test set results), something that is only emphasized when dealing with smaller sets of training data. The possibility of bringing more semantic discriminative information to decisions, which by being connected with the feature extractor will influence what is being captured as relevant or not, might be a further alternative to enhance the generalization power of the system.

Limitations

No direct comparison can be made in terms of state-of-the-art results since some methodologies use feature engineering processes; others that use end-to-end DL models develop them with large, non-public datasets.

Another important aspect relates to the combination of two different datasets that may have different characteristics. These may include distinct stages of cancer that might be translated into different visual manifestations of the target variable. By combining distinct datasets, it is assumed that such manifestations, to exist, are similar in terms of image patterns, though there is still no clear evidence that this happens.

The developed work was constrained by hardware limitations, which, when analysing images in a 3D perspective, may be cumbersome given the density of the networks involved. If this problem could be overcome, it would be helpful to explore, in the future, more complex architectures that might be able to capture more abstract patterns, given the demonstrated complexity of the task. Furthermore, although features extracted from the unlabelled data to discriminate images helped when classifying scans as mutant or wild-type, more samples from the minority class, which included only 23 images, would probably be needed for a more accurate model.

VAE was implemented in adversarial training, and various percentages of unlabeled data were tried to train the model. However, other SSL methods, such as co-training or graph-based methods, can be implemented in the future, and their capacity to predict EGFR mutation status can be compared.

Overfitting is always a concern for small datasets. Some strategies were implemented to mitigate this effect, such as dropout and weight decay; however, with such a small training dataset, overfitting still occurred to some extent.

Despite not reaching remarkable results, the developed work may be seen as a stepping stone from which subsequent works can improve upon the highlighted limitations.

5. Conclusions

A personalised treatment plan presents the opportunity to improve lung cancer patient outcomes. In the era of precision medicine, the identification of driver mutations in lung cancer brought new treatment options and helped increase the overall survival rates. For this reason, a complete cancer characterisation is of the utmost importance to choose the best treatment for each individual. This opens doors to the use of artificial intelligence, which is gaining ground in the medical field as the utilisation of images such as computed tomography scans has already proven to allow the detection of relevant patterns and relations. Despite the success of deep learning models when it comes to analysing such medical images, the lack of labelled data makes their development difficult.

This study aimed to provide an end-to-end lung cancer characterisation by analysing the entire volumetric region of the lung containing the nodule, using CT images, in a semi-supervised approach. The method employed to integrate both labelled and unlabelled data consisted of a combination of a VAE and a GAN. The best-performing classification model achieved a mean AUC of 0.701 ± 0.114. Despite not largely improving the performance results in this task, the utilisation of the additional unlabelled dataset brought more discriminative power to the model. This was further evidenced by the increase in terms of performance when more unlabelled data were used, resulting in an improvement of circa 7 percentual points in the mean AUC compared to a fully supervised model developed with the same labelled set. It should be noticed that the best model was built only with 14% of the data containing a label. Adding an unlabelled dataset, in an SSL fashion, improved the performance of the predictive deep learning model, allowing the development of a better-performing end-to-end model with a reduced amount of labelled data.

Author Contributions: C.P., F.S., T.P., and H.P.O. conceived the study and designed the methodology. F.S. performed data curation. C.P. developed the software, performed the analysis of the results, and drafted the manuscript. All authors provided critical feedback and contributed to the final manuscript. All authors have read and agreed to the published version of the manuscript.

Funding: This work is financed by National Funds through the Portuguese funding agency, FCT-Foundation for Science and Technology Portugal, within project LA/P/0063/2020, and a PhD Grant Number: 2021.05767.BD.

Data Availability Statement: We acknowledged the National Cancer Institute for the access of National Lung Screening Trial (NLST) dataset, and The Cancer Imaging Archive (TCIA) Public Access for the publicly available Non-Small Cell Lung Cancer (NSCLC)-Radiogenomics Database used in this work.

Conflicts of Interest: The authors declare no conflict of interest.

References

1. The Top 10 Causes of Death. Available online: https://www.who.int/news-room/fact-sheets/detail/the-top-10-causes-of-death (accessed on 30 October 2021).
2. Cancer Today-International Agency for Research on Cancer. Available online: https://gco.iarc.fr/today/home (accessed on 7 March 2022).
3. Siegel, R.L.; Miller, K.D.; Fuchs, H.E.; Jemal, A. Cancer Statistics, 2021. *CA A Cancer J. Clin.* **2021**, *71*, 7–33. [CrossRef] [PubMed]
4. Aerts, H.J.; Velazquez, E.R.; Leijenaar, R.T.; Parmar, C.; Grossmann, P.; Cavalho, S.; Bussink, J.; Monshouwer, R.; Haibe-Kains, B.; Rietveld, D.; et al. Decoding tumour phenotype by noninvasive imaging using a quantitative radiomics approach. *Nat. Commun.* **2014**, *5*, 4006. [CrossRef] [PubMed]
5. Gillies, R.; Boellard, R.; Dekker, A.; Aerts, H.J.W.L. Radiomics: Extracting more information from medical images using advanced feature analysis. *Eur. J. Cancer* **2012**, *48*, 441–446. [CrossRef]
6. Gillies, R.J.; Kinahan, P.E.; Hricak, H. Radiomics: Images are more than pictures, they are data. *Radiology* **2016**, *278*, 563–577. [CrossRef] [PubMed]
7. Bodalal, Z.; Trebeschi, S.; Nguyen-Kim, T.D.L.; Schats, W.; Beets-Tan, R. Radiogenomics: Bridging imaging and genomics. *Abdom. Radiol.* **2019**, *44*, 1960–1984. [CrossRef]
8. Digumarthy, S.R.; Padole, A.M.; Gullo, R.L.; Sequist, L.V.; Kalra, M.K. Can CT radiomic analysis in NSCLC predict histology and EGFR mutation status? *Medicine* **2019**, *98*, e13963. [CrossRef]
9. Pinheiro, G.; Pereira, T.; Dias, C.; Freitas, C.; Hespanhol, V.; Costa, J.L.; Cunha, A.; Oliveira, H.P. Identifying relationships between imaging phenotypes and lung cancer-related mutation status: EGFR and KRAS. *Sci. Rep.* **2020**, *10*. [CrossRef]
10. Morgado, J.; Pereira, T.; Silva, F.; Freitas, C.; Negrão, E.; de Lima, B.F.; da Silva, M.C.; Madureira, A.J.; Ramos, I.; Hespanhol, V.; et al. Machine Learning and Feature Selection Methods for EGFR Mutation Status Prediction in Lung Cancer. *Appl. Sci.* **2021**, *11*, 3273. [CrossRef]
11. Wang, S.; Shi, J.; Ye, Z.; Dong, D.; Yu, D.; Zhou, M.; Liu, Y.; Gevaert, O.; Wang, K.; Zhu, Y.; et al. Predicting EGFR mutation status in lung adenocarcinoma on computed tomography image using deep learning. *Eur. Respir. J.* **2019**, *53*, 1800986. [CrossRef]
12. Russakovsky, O.; Deng, J.; Su, H.; Krause, J.; Satheesh, S.; Ma, S.; Huang, Z.; Karpathy, A.; Khosla, A.; Bernstein, M.S.; et al. ImageNet Large Scale Visual Recognition Challenge. *CoRR* **2014**, *115*, 211–252.
13. Zhao, W.; Yang, J.; Ni, B.; Bi, D.; Sun, Y.; Xu, M.; Zhu, X.; Li, C.; Jin, L.; Gao, P.; et al. Toward automatic prediction of EGFR mutation status in pulmonary adenocarcinoma with 3D deep learning. *Cancer Med.* **2019**, *8*, 3532–3543. [CrossRef]
14. Martins, R.A.P.; Silva, D. On Teacher-Student Semi-Supervised Learning for Chest X-ray Image Classification. In *Anais do 15 Congresso Brasileiro de Inteligência Computacional*; Filho, C.J.A.B., Siqueira, H.V., Ferreira, D.D., Bertol, D.W., de Oliveira, R.C.L., Eds.; SBIC: Joinville, Brazil, 2021; pp. 1–6. [CrossRef]
15. Sun, W.; Tseng, T.L.B.; Zhang, J.; Qian, W. Enhancing deep convolutional neural network scheme for breast cancer diagnosis with unlabeled data. *Comput. Med Imaging Graph.* **2017**, *57*, 4–9. [CrossRef]
16. Al-Azzam, N.; Shatnawi, I. Comparing supervised and semi-supervised Machine Learning Models on Diagnosing Breast Cancer. *Ann. Med. Surg.* **2021**, *62*, 53–64. [CrossRef]
17. Das, A.; Devarampati, V.K.; Nair, M.S. NAS-SGAN: A Semi-supervised Generative Adversarial Network Model for Atypia Scoring of Breast Cancer Histopathological Images. *IEEE J. Biomed. Health Inform.* **2021**, *26*, 2276–2287. [CrossRef]
18. Xie, Y.; Zhang, J.; Xia, Y. Semi-supervised adversarial model for benign–malignant lung nodule classification on chest CT. *Med Image Anal.* **2019**, *57*, 237–248. [CrossRef]
19. Bakr, S.; Gevaert, O.; Echegaray, S.; Ayers, K.; Zhou, M.; Shafiq, M.; Zheng, H.; Benson, J.A.; Zhang, W.; Leung, A.N.; et al. A radiogenomic dataset of non-small cell lung cancer. *Sci. Data* **2018**, *5*, 180202. [CrossRef]
20. Reduced Lung-Cancer Mortality with Low-Dose Computed Tomographic Screening. *N. Engl. J. Med.* **2011**, *365*, 395–409. [CrossRef]
21. Aberle, D.R. The National Lung Screening Trial: Overview and Study Design. *Radiology* **2010**, *258*, 243.
22. Silva, F.; Pereira, T.; Morgado, J.; Cunha, A.; Oliveira, H.P. The Impact of Interstitial Diseases Patterns on Lung CT Segmentation. In Proceedings of the 2021 43rd Annual International Conference of the IEEE Engineering in Medicine & Biology Society (EMBC), Guadalajara, Mexico, 1–5 November 2021; pp. 2856–2859. [CrossRef]
23. Kingma, D.P.; Welling, M. Auto-Encoding Variational Bayes. *arXiv* **2013**, arXiv:1312.6114.
24. Doersch, C. Tutorial on Variational Autoencoders. *arXiv* **2016**, arXiv:1606.05908.
25. Radford, A.; Metz, L.; Chintala, S. Unsupervised Representation Learning with Deep Convolutional Generative Adversarial Networks. *arXiv* **2015**, arXiv:1511.06434.

26. Ioffe, S.; Szegedy, C. Batch Normalization: Accelerating Deep Network Training by Reducing Internal Covariate Shift. In Proceedings of the 32nd International Conference on Machine Learning, Lille, France, 6–11 July 2015; Bach, F., Blei, D., Eds.; PMLR: Lille, France, 2015; Volume 37, pp. 448–456.
27. Salimans, T.; Goodfellow, I.; Zaremba, W.; Cheung, V.; Radford, A.; Chen, X.; Chen, X. Improved Techniques for Training GANs. In Proceedings of the Advances in Neural Information Processing Systems; Lee, D., Sugiyama, M., Luxburg, U., Guyon, I., Garnett, R., Eds.; Curran Associates, Inc.: Red Hook, NY, USA, 2016; Volume 29.
28. Srivastava, N.; Hinton, G.; Krizhevsky, A.; Sutskever, I.; Salakhutdinov, R. Dropout: A Simple Way to Prevent Neural Networks from Overfitting. *J. Mach. Learn. Res.* **2014**, *15*, 1929–1958.
29. Goodfellow, I.; Pouget-Abadie, J.; Mirza, M.; Xu, B.; Warde-Farley, D.; Ozair, S.; Courville, A.; Bengio, Y. Generative Adversarial Nets. In Proceedings of the Advances in Neural Information Processing Systems, Montreal, QC, Canada, 8–13 December 2014; Ghahramani, Z., Welling, M., Cortes, C., Lawrence, N., Weinberger, K., Eds.; Curran Associates, Inc.: Red Hook, NY, USA, 2014; Volume 27.
30. Larsen, A.B.L.; Sønderby, S.K.; Winther, O. Autoencoding beyond pixels using a learned similarity metric. In Proceedings of The 33rd International Conference on Machine Learning, New York, NY, USA, 20–22 June 2015.
31. Cover, T.M.; Thomas, J.A. *Elements of Information Theory*, 2nd ed.; Wiley Series in Telecommunications and Signal Processing; Wiley-Interscience: Hoboken, NJ, USA, 2006.
32. Higgins, I.; Matthey, L.; Pal, A.; Burgess, C.P.; Glorot, X.; Botvinick, M.M.; Mohamed, S.; Lerchner, A. beta-VAE: Learning Basic Visual Concepts with a Constrained Variational Framework. In Proceedings of the ICLR, Toulon, France, 24–26 April 2017.
33. Dai, Z.; Yang, Z.; Yang, F.; Cohen, W.W. Good semi-supervised learning that requires a bad gan. *Adv. Neural Inf. Process. Syst.* **2017**, *30*, 3270.
34. Silva, F.; Pereira, T.; Morgado, J.; Frade, J.; Mendes, J.; Freitas, C.; Negrão, E.; De Lima, B.F.; Silva, M.C.D.; Madureira, A.J.; et al. EGFR Assessment in Lung Cancer CT Images: Analysis of Local and Holistic Regions of Interest Using Deep Unsupervised Transfer Learning. *IEEE Access* **2021**, *9*, 58667–58676. [CrossRef]

Article

Latent-PER: ICA-Latent Code Editing Framework for Portrait Emotion Recognition

Isack Lee and Seok Bong Yoo *

Department of Artificial Intelligence Convergence, Chonnam National University, Gwangju 61186, Republic of Korea
* Correspondence: sbyoo@jnu.ac.kr; Tel.: +82-625303437

Abstract: Although real-image emotion recognition has been developed in several studies, an acceptable accuracy level has not been achieved in portrait drawings. This paper proposes a portrait emotion recognition framework based on independent component analysis (ICA) and latent codes to overcome the performance degradation problem in drawings. This framework employs latent code extracted through a generative adversarial network (GAN)-based encoder. It learns independently from factors that interfere with expression recognition, such as color, small occlusion, and various face angles. It is robust against environmental factors since it filters latent code by adding an emotion-relevant code extractor to extract only information related to facial expressions from the latent code. In addition, an image is generated by changing the latent code to the direction of the eigenvector for each emotion obtained through the ICA method. Since only the position of the latent code related to the facial expression is changed, there is little external change and the expression changes in the desired direction. This technique is helpful for qualitative and quantitative emotional recognition learning. The experimental results reveal that the proposed model performs better than the existing models, and the latent editing used in this process suggests a novel manipulation method through ICA. Moreover, the proposed framework can be applied for various portrait emotion applications from recognition to manipulation, such as automation of emotional subtitle production for the visually impaired, understanding the emotions of objects in famous classic artwork, and animation production assistance.

Keywords: generative adversarial network; latent code; portrait emotion recognition; independent component analysis

MSC: 68T45

1. Introduction

In computer vision, facial expression analysis is an exciting research subject. Given that the input to the intelligent system is a facial image, facial expression recognition (FER) [1–5] is an essential visual recognition method to recognize emotions. In addition, FER has wide applications in the real world, such as autonomous vehicle driver monitoring, psychiatric treatments, education, and human-computer interaction. The deep neural network [6] has recently exhibited considerable performance in image recognition challenges. Furthermore, convolutional neural network (CNN) methods [7–17] are well-known deep learning techniques that automatically extract deep feature representations, as depicted in Figure 1.

The input space (i.e., a two-dimensional picture) is converted to a high-dimensional feature representation vector that captures the semantics of the input image for any visual recognition system with a defined set of classes. By combining features from lower to higher levels, deep CNN-based algorithms extract spatial characteristics that represent the abstract semantics of the input image. These extracted features reduce the amount of

information through a pooling layer. Then, the pooling layer is flattened into the form of a single vector through a fully connected layer. Therefore, a softmax function computes a probability distribution over all classes in the last stage. The softmax function expression for the *i*-th class is written as follows:

$$softmax(x_i) = \frac{e^{x_i}}{\sum_{j=1}^{k} e^{x_j}} \text{ for } i = 1, \ldots, k, \quad (1)$$

where *k* denotes the number of classes. Thereafter, similar to the mean squared error (*MSE*) loss, training proceeds to reduce the difference between the predicted class and ground truth through the loss function. The function expression is written as follows:

$$MSE = \frac{1}{n} \sum_{k=1}^{n} (y_k - \widetilde{y_k})^2, \quad (2)$$

where *n* is the number of batch images, y_k denotes the ground truth, and $\widetilde{y_k}$ represents the predicted class. Figure 1 depicts this process graphically. Although CNN-based approaches have achieved promising accuracy in authentic facial photograph images, FER is still considered a challenging task in various portrait applications, such as the emotional recognition of famous drawings, paintings, cartoons, and animated films. In previous studies, the model has been designed to recognize facial expressions well when learning using actual photograph images. However, suppose that only the existing method of extracting feature maps through the CNN is used for portrait images that lack color information or have weak details compared to natural images, for example, cartoons, drawings, and paintings. In that case, the previous methods suffer severe emotion recognition performance degradation. Due to this problem, a model with acceptable expression recognition performance in various styles is needed. However, most of the current expression recognition research focuses on authentic-photograph images.

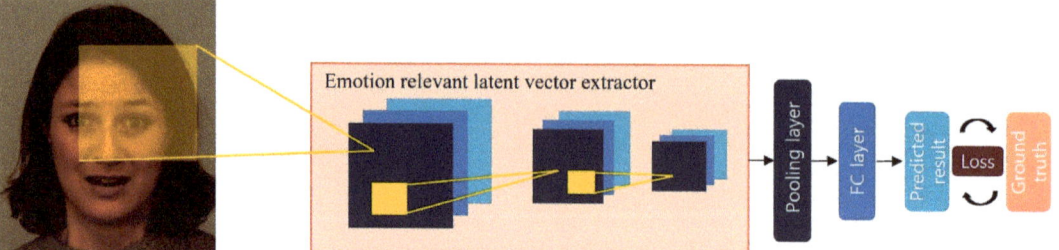

Figure 1. Typical emotion recognition model overview using a convolutional neural network (CNN).

To solve this problem, we propose a portrait emotion recognition (PER) framework using the latent code (Latent-PER), which is information extracted from the generated image. The latent code was edited using a new method based on independent component analysis (ICA) [18]. In this approach, we focus on the disentanglement and editability properties of generative adversarial network (GAN) [19] inversion. In the GAN, the disentanglement characteristic guarantees independence between styles without losing basic information when generating face images. Editability enables manipulation or editing concerning a specific attribute, allowing the latent code to be selectively used by excluding or retaining the information in emotion recognition models. The proposed method uses ICA [20] in the latent domain to determine elements that correlate highly with facial expression information. To facilitate analysis via ICA, we establish a statistically favorable situation.

For photographs of the same person, the information on the appearance is statistically similar. Furthermore, since facial expressions are made differently, information on facial expressions is statistically different. A dataset with the same object with different emotions is used to address this. Through an eigenvector that can classify the latent codes of these images, we find elements related to emotions in the entire latent code. In addition, specific information in the latent code is used attentively to train the FER models. As illustrated in Figure 2a, the general emotion recognition method uses an image with entangled features and thus conditions, such as resolution and illumination of the input image are critical.

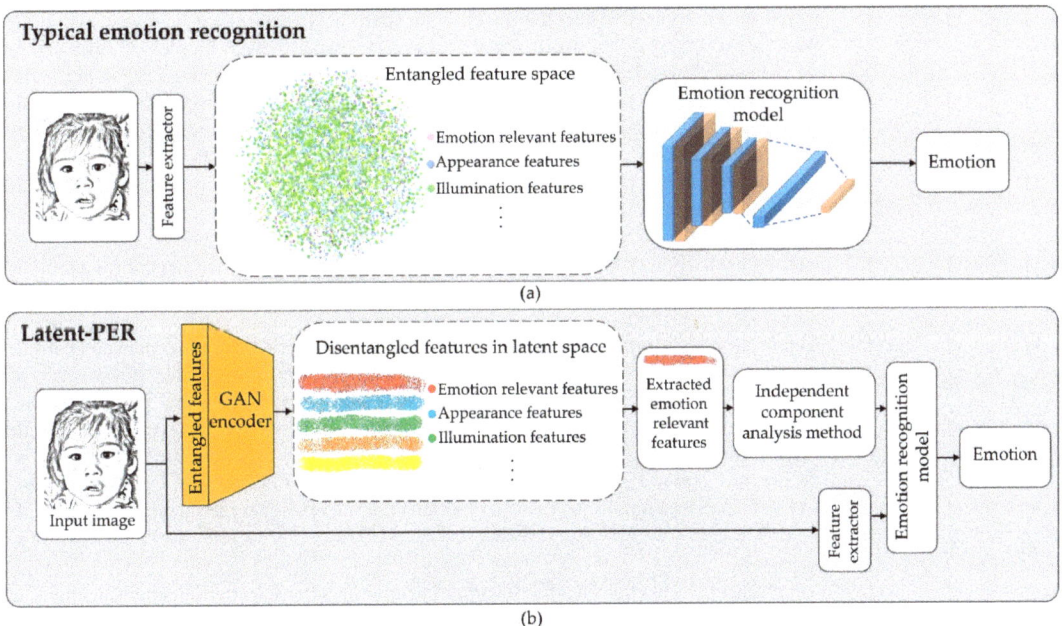

Figure 2. (**a**) Typical emotion recognition method using entangled features. (**b**) Latent-PER, which utilizes ICA-latent code with portrait image.

In contrast, as shown in Figure 2b, latent code-based approach disentangles information from the input image. The Latent-PER is a plug-and-play framework that employs disentangled features using a GAN inversion encoder on existing models. These two modules use images and latent codes to improve facial emotion recognition performance in portrait images with various styles and real photograph images.

Based on the above, the main contributions of this work can be summarized as follows:

1. We observe that existing authentic-photograph image-based models do not perform adequately in portrait images with various styles and propose a plug-and-play framework to prevent performance degradation in existing models.
2. We propose a latent code-based approach that disentangles the irrelevant emotional features of the image. Latent-PER provides robustness to various portrait image domains, such as drawings and paintings.
3. We propose a latent code editing method that rectifies the latent code to improve the PER performance by applying an eigenvector extracted using ICA. This eigenvector can also be employed for image manipulation while changing only relevant features.

2. Related Work

2.1. Facial Expression Recognition

Using FER, computers can better understand human behavior or communicate with people. The first FER system based on optical flow was introduced in 1991. Recent advances in deep learning have improved FER systems, and it is now possible to perform feature extraction and expression classification using a neural network. A FER system typically consists of three stages: Face detection, feature extraction, and expression recognition.

Although it varies from model to model, in face detection, several face detectors, such as MTCNN [21], FFHQ [22], and Dlib [23] are used to locate faces in complex scenes. Detected faces can be aligned further.

Various methods have been created to capture facial geometry and appearance features brought on by facial expressions. According to Fasel [24], a shallow CNN is robust to facial positions and scales. Using deep CNNs for feature extraction, Tang [9] and Kanou [25] and Ge et al. [26] pointed out that classification through SVM has lower performance than the CNN method. For this reason, they proposed a CNN-based facial expression recognition model. Kanou et al. [25] won in the FER challenges, respectively. An identity-aware CNN was created by Meng et al. [27] to discriminate between expression-related and identity-related information simultaneously. To determine the relative weights of several convolutional receptive fields in the network, Li et al. [28] proposed a multi scale CNN using an attention method. Wen et al. [29] proposed multiple cross-attention heads and ensured that they capture useful aspects of facial expressions without overlapping. Farzaneh et al. [30] proposed selecting a subset of significant feature components adaptively for improved discrimination. Moreover, Zhang et al. [31] used ResNet as the backbone to address the uncertainty problem in FER and proposed several uncertainty learning methods. Xu et al. [32] proposed a flexibly asymmetrical neural representation of facial expression recognition. Most studies [33–38] of facial expression recognition tasks developed with a focus on authentic-photograph images. Moetesum et al. [39] proposed an expression recognition method for sketch, but it is designed for images, such as emoticons. For this reason, when the existing model is applied to other style images, performance degradation occurs, and a new approach to solve this problem has not been proposed. Our proposed Latent-PER is a plug-and-play framework that employs disentangled features using a GAN inversion encoder on existing models.

2.2. Latent Space Embedding via GAN Inversion

Recent research has demonstrated that, as a result of picture production, GANs efficiently encode various semantic information in latent space [40]. Various manipulation techniques have been developed to extract and manipulate picture properties. Mirza et al. [41] trained early on creating conditional images, allowing for manipulating a specific picture property. Chrysos et al. [42] proposed a conditionally robust GAN network. Through latent spatial mapping, this network has significantly improved the image creation performance that meets the desired conditions. Abdal et al. [43] analyzed three semantic editing procedures that may be used on vectors in the latent space. Shen et al. [44] used principal component analysis (PCA) and a data-driven approach to determine the most important directions. In addition, Park et al. [38] provided a straightforward yet efficient method for conditional continuous normalizing flows in the GAN latent space conditioned by attribute features. However, these latent code manipulations are only relevant to pictures created by GANs that have already been trained, not to any actual image. We propose a novel manipulation method in the present study to discover the direction that correlates with the accuracy of face emotion identification.

Additionally, we demonstrate the value and necessity of latent code modification by demonstrating FER evaluations. The GAN inversion uses a pretrained generator to map an actual image into a latent space. Inversion must be semantically meaningful to perform editing and consider reconstruction performance. Zhu et al. [45] proposed a domain-guided encoder and domain-regularized optimizer to achieve semantically significant inversion. Furthermore, Tov et al. [46] studied the distortion, perception, and editability characteristics of high-quality inversion and demonstrated their inherent tradeoffs. Encoders generally learn to reduce distortion, which measures how close the input and target images are in the RGB and feature domains. He et al. [47] proposed an architecture that self-learns to separate and encode these unimportant variations. The advantage of the GAN-based encoder is disentanglement. Herein, we analyze this by applying ICA. As a result, it is effectively managed through an eigenvector, which expresses independent characteristics.

3. Method

This section describes the method proposed in this research for PER. The overall architecture of Latent-PER is presented in Figure 3. After facial detection and alignment, an image is inputted into a typical model and GAN-based encoder. The first module for the proposed method is the extraction of latent code through the GAN-based encoder to analyze and use it for learning. The second module is a typical model. Although the number of final features differs for each model, it is usually configured to output features through CNN. We propose a plug-and-play framework; therefore, any model the user desires can be used. Furthermore, in the third module, the concat layer combines the extracted latent code with the output value from the used model. The difference between prediction and ground truth is learned through MSE loss of Equation (2). The three modules are collaboratively learned.

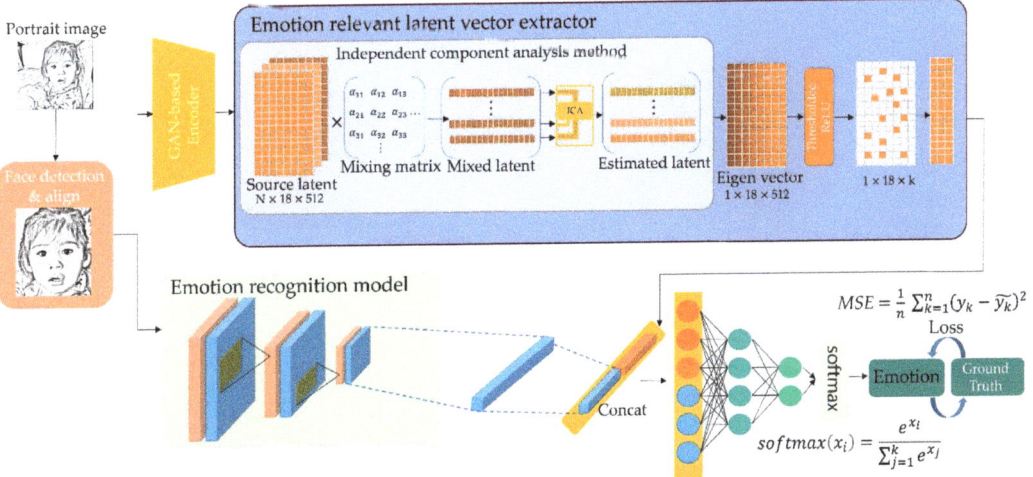

Figure 3. Overview of the proposed Latent-PER.

3.1. Conversion to Portrait-Style Images

We changed all the datasets we used to a drawing style following the aim of this work: PER. Figure 4 reveals that converting authentic-photograph images to a pencil drawing style is a five-step process. First, it converts the real photograph image to grayscale as follows:

$$imgGray = 0.2989 \times R + 0.5870 \times G + 0.1140 \times B, \qquad (3)$$

where R, G, and B are the values for red, green, and blue in the same pixel, respectively.

Second, the converted grayscale image is inverted through a bitwise not operation as follows:

$$img\_Invert_{(2)} = 1 - imgGray_{(2)}, \qquad (4)$$

where $imgGray_{(2)}$ represents the binary version of $imgGray$.

Third, $img\_Invert_{(2)}$ is converted to decimal and Gaussian blur is applied to this converted image using the Gaussian function:

$$G(x,y) = \frac{1}{2\pi\sigma^2} e^{-\frac{x^2+y^2}{2\sigma^2}}, \qquad (5)$$

where x denotes the distance from the origin in the horizontal axis, y denotes the distance from the origin in the vertical axis, and σ represents the standard deviation of the Gaussian distribution.

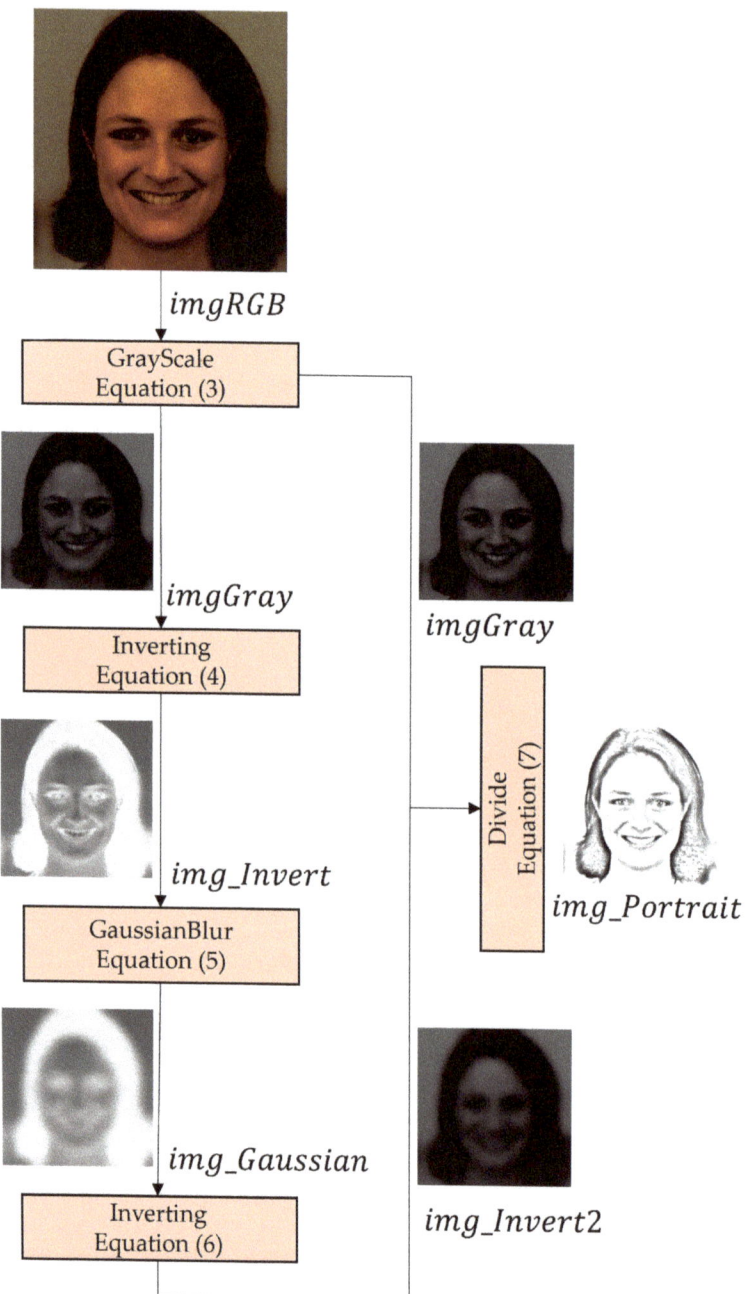

Figure 4. Conversion process of photographs to portrait drawing styles.

Fourth, the Gaussian blurred image is inverted again through a bitwise not operation as follows:

$$img\_Invert2_{(2)} = 1 - img\_Gaussian_{(2)}, \qquad (6)$$

where $img\_Gaussian_{(2)}$ represents the binary version of $img\_Gaussian$ obtained from Gaussian blurring as in Equation (5).

Fifth, the grayscale image converted to decimal is divided with this inverted image as follows:

$$img\_Portrait = img\_Gray\ /\ img\_Invert2, \tag{7}$$

where $img\_Invert2$ represents the decimal version of $img\_Invert2_{(2)}$.

To create drawing-style images, we set the kernel size in order that the edges are not blurred significantly. A larger kernel size of the Gaussian blur results in a more blurred image and the loss of detailed features. A kernel size of 3×3 or 5×5 is sufficient for small images but less effective for large images. Therefore, an appropriate kernel size is selected according to the size of the dataset. As a result, the photographs are converted into a portrait drawing-style, as shown in Figure 4.

3.2. Emotion Relevant Latent Code Extractor

3.2.1. Independent Component Analysis

As illustrated in Figure 5, ICA determines the same basis vector as the PCA. However, PCA finds the eigenvector in the direction with the most significant variance. Therefore, it is primarily used for dimension reduction. In contrast, ICA determines the basis vector that best represents each independent component. Therefore, it is suitable for the task since it is possible to determine an independent eigenvector for emotions using a data-driven approach from data with the same object with different emotions. In general, singular value decomposition and PCA are often used for manipulation in the GAN, which is suitable for diversifying the change in the generated image through the change in the latent code. However, we used the ICA method to locate the eigenvector representing the independent component rather than the basis vector with the most significant variance. The proposed Latent-PER uses eigenvectors. We only determined the index of the latent code that can change the facial expression.

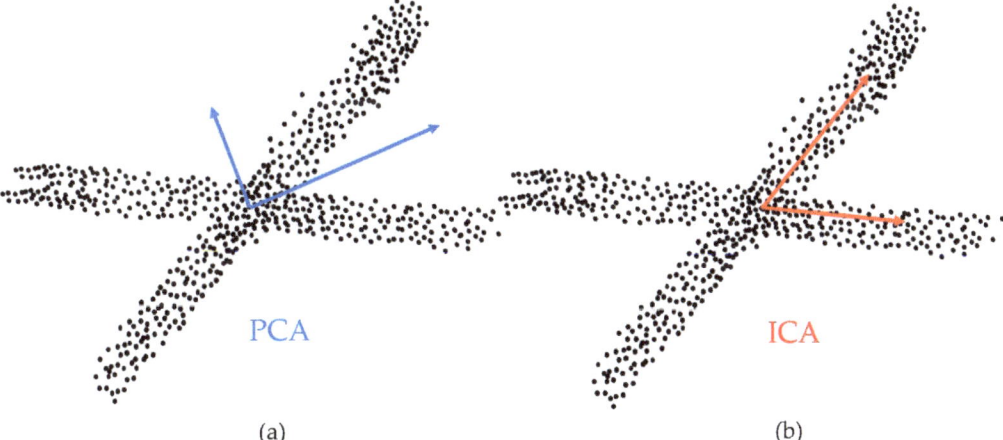

Figure 5. Visualization of eigenvectors after analyzing linear mixed signals using (**a**) PCA and (**b**) ICA.

Closely related to the problem of blind source separation, the goal of ICA is to decompose the observed signal into a linear combination of unknown independent signals, where s is the unknown source signal vector, and x is the vector of the observed mixture. If $\mathbf{A}$ is an unknown mixing matrix, the mixture model is written as follows:

$$x = \mathbf{A}s, \tag{8}$$

where **A** is an unknown non-square matrix that combines the components of the source s. Finding the mixing matrix **A** (more precisely, the inverse of **A**) is the aim of ICA to recover the original signal s from the observed data x. We can recover the underlying source $\hat{s}$ from the linearly converted data by building a new matrix **W** as follows:

$$\hat{s} = \mathbf{W}x. \tag{9}$$

The goal of ICA is to determine an unmixing matrix **W** that approximates $\mathbf{A}^{-1}$, resulting in $\hat{s} \approx s$. In addition, **A** can be divided into simpler pieces using a linear algebra singular value decomposition technique:

$$\mathbf{A} = \mathbf{U}\sum \mathbf{V}^T, \tag{10}$$

where $\mathbf{U} \in \mathbb{R}^{N \times M}$ and $\mathbf{V} \in \mathbb{R}^{M \times M}$ are matrices with orthogonal columns and Σ is diagonal. A straightforward transformation of the probabilities reveals that $\mathbf{V}^T$ is Gaussian with covariance.

3.2.2. Emotion-Relevant Latent Code Extractor

We propose a latent code extractor that can extract semantically meaningful information from the latent code. Figure 6 displays a method of extracting facial expression-related information using a dataset with the same object with different facial expressions. Therefore, the latent code for the external information of the same person is very similar. However, since the facial expressions are different, the location where the most significant difference appears in the latent code of the same person is facial expression-related information. For this reason, the Karolinska Directed Emotional Faces (KDEF) dataset is primarily used to analyze the latent code.

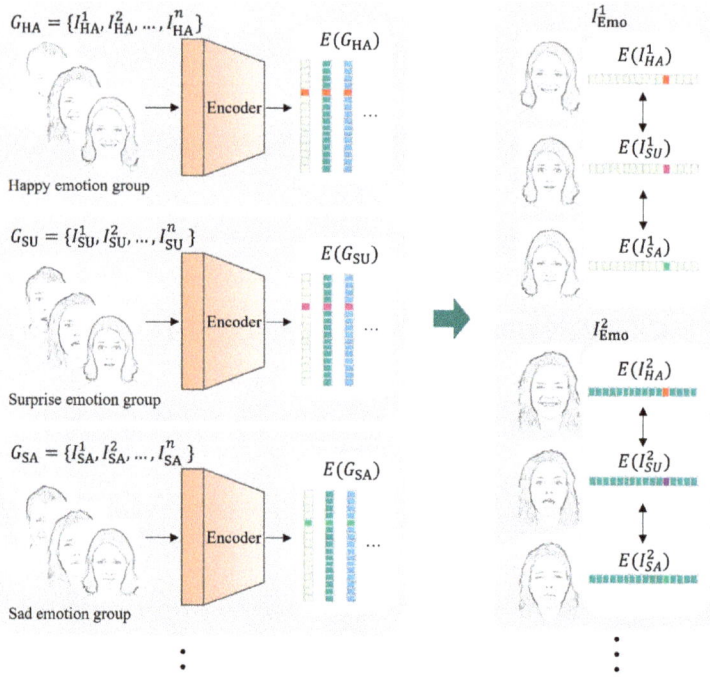

Figure 6. Explanatory diagram of latent code analysis through ICA.

The detailed process is described as follows. First, the image is inputted into the GAN-based encoder through facial detection and alignment. Through this process, the image is converted into latent code, which is an array of real numbers. The converted latent code contains information that can generate an input image. It can be estimated that the index of the latent code that can change the expression in the image as a result of creation contains information on the expression of the image. We used images of the same object but with different expressions to determine these indices. Since the images display the same face, the appearance information in the latent code is very similar, but the expression-related information differs since the expressions are different. As shown in Figure 6, we divide the groups by emotion. G_{HA} indicates a group whose label is happy, and G_{SU} indicates a group whose label is surprising. The upper subscript of I^1_{HA} distinguishes objects, and the lower subscript indicates emotion. Therefore, I^1_{HA} indicates the happiness emotion image of person 1. E indicates encoding, and $E(G_{HA})$ indicates the latent code of the encoded happiness group. The extracted latent codes for each object are compared. I^1_{EMO} indicates seven emotional latent codes for an object. Since the appearance information will be similar, the part with a large difference in the latent code is information related to expressions. This point uses ICA to determine the eigenvector that best distinguishes each independent component. The latent code corresponding to each expression can be distinguished through the ICA eigenvector. An index with a large value may be considered related to the expression. In contrast, an index with a small value is evaluated as external information irrelevant to the expression. This part can be verified qualitatively through the visual results.

Figure 7 presents the activation function for latent code editing, thresholded rectified linear unit (ReLU). The *Thresholded ReLU* [48] is designed to preserve the value when it exceeds the reference value, except when it is less than the reference value:

$$Thresholded\ ReLU(x) = \begin{cases} x & x \geq h \\ 0 & x < h \end{cases} \quad (11)$$

where h denotes the threshold value the user correctly specifies after analyzing the dataset.

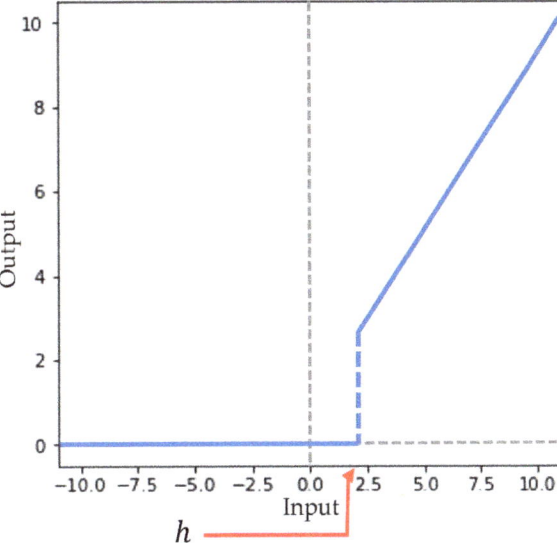

Figure 7. Transformation activation function for latent code editing with the *Thresholded ReLU*.

It is not necessary to use the entire eigenvector. Therefore, eigenvectors are filtered by the *Thresholded ReLU*. The reference value is the optimal value for each dataset, but we used the average as the reference value. As a result, index values related to facial expressions are extracted from the latent code and used for learning.

Furthermore, as this result is important information related to facial expressions, it qualitatively proves that facial recognition performance increases when used for model training. Therefore, the emotion-relevant latent code extractor extracts expression-related information from the entire latent code and edits and manipulates it. First, it can improve expression recognition performance. Second, a novel manipulation method through ICA is suggested.

3.3. Combination Module of Existing Model and Emotion Relevant Features

Existing conventional models typically have a similar structure. Most CNN-based models are converted into high-dimensional feature representation vectors using the CNN. By integrating features from lower to higher levels, CNN-based algorithms extract spatial characteristics that represent the abstract semantics of the input image. Through a pooling layer, these extracted features lower the amount of information. Then, the layer is flattened into a single vector using a fully connected layer. In the final step, the softmax function computes the probability distribution for all classes.

However, unlike the typical method, we propose to additionally use latent code containing information that can generate images for training. Moreover, the advantage of the proposed plug-and-play framework is that it can be used regardless of any existing model. Therefore, it is possible to use the existing emotion recognition model, or another model suggested by the user in the module. The critical point is that the performance is best when using the plug-and-play framework we propose in combination rather than when only the corresponding model is used.

The number of features extracted through the existing model varies slightly from model to model, but the proposed framework combines any number of features with the modified latent code. The tensors combine the features extracted through the existing CNN-based model with the expression-related latent code extracted only from the expression-related information. In the method in Section 3.2, the tensors output one tensor through two fully connected layers. Emotions are inferred through these processes.

4. Experimental Results

4.1. Datasets and Setting

4.1.1. Portrait Emotion Recognition

The Real-World Affective Faces Database (RAF-DB) [49] contains 29,670 facial images acquired from the Internet using crowd-sourcing techniques. About 40 skilled people annotated this database with simple or complicated expressions. In this study, 12,271 images were used for training and 3068 for testing, each containing one of the seven basic facial expressions (i.e., neutral, happy, surprised, sad, angry, disgust, and fear).

The Extended Cohn-Kanade (CK+) [50] dataset contains 593 video sequences from 123 participants ranging in age from 18 to 50 years old and of various genders and nationalities. Each film presents a facial transition from neutral to a targeted peak emotion, captured at 30 frames per second with a resolution of 640 × 490 or 640 × 480 pixels. Three hundred and twenty-seven of these movies have been labeled with one of seven expression classes: Anger, contempt, disgust, fear, happiness, sorrow, and surprise. The CK+ database, which is used in the majority of facial expression classification methods, is largely recognized as the most frequently used laboratory-controlled facial expression classification database available.

The KDEF [51] is a set of 4900 images of human facial expressions. The photograph images represent 70 people with seven emotional expressions. Each expression is viewed from five viewpoints.

4.1.2. Face Image Generation

The Flickr-Faces-HQ (FFHQ) [22] only provides face images without labels for facial expressions. This database consists of 70,000 high-quality PNG images at 1024 × 1024 resolution and contains considerable variation in age, ethnicity, and image background. This dataset is not intended for facial recognition but is widely used in generative learning research.

4.1.3. Manipulation

Most datasets for FER consist of different objects. However, a dataset with the same object but different facial expressions is required to extract information related only to facial expressions in the latent code. Therefore, the KEDF dataset comprising the same object with different facial expressions is used for ICA.

4.2. Evaluation of Latent-PER on General Models

We quantitatively evaluated performance improvement through Latent-PER. As shown in Table 1, we compared the emotion recognition performance of the portrait drawing image using several state-of-the-art models and the emotion recognition performance of the proposed plug-and-play framework applied to the existing model. The performance of the proposed Latent-PER has the highest accuracy compared to most others, indicating the superiority of the framework. The function expression of the *PercentagePoint* is written as follows:

$$PercentagePoint = F - O, \qquad (12)$$

where F denotes final percentage value, O denotes original percentage value. We use the percentage point as an indicator of performance improvement and the unit of *PercentagePoint* is %p. To evaluate the recognition accuracy of individual classes, we present the confusion matrices obtained with the Latent-PER framework for the RAF-DB dataset in Figure 8.

Table 1. Portrait emotion recognition performance according to the presence or absence of Latent-PER using latent codes. The dataset uses RAF-DB, CK+, and KDEF. The performance is compared through the existing state-of-the-art models, DAN, DACL, and RUL.

Dataset	Method	DAN [21]	DACL [22]	RUL [23]
RAF-DB	Without Latent-PER	74.0%	70.4%	67.7%
	With Latent-PER	84.3% (10.3%p ↑)	82.8% (12.4%p ↑)	78.2% (10.5%p ↑)
CK+	Without Latent-PER	63.7%	67.1%	42.3%
	With Latent-PER	73.4% (9.7%p ↑)	70.1% (3%p ↑)	70.3% (28%p ↑)
KDEF	Without Latent-PER	81.3%	84.6%	72.8%
	With Latent-PER	84.2% (2.9%p ↑)	85.8% (1.2%p ↑)	83.0% (10.2%p ↑)

Latent-PER improves the recognition accuracy of all classes of the three FER datasets compared to the existing methods. The detailed analysis results for each dataset for each model are as follows. First, the RAF-DB dataset for the DAN model and the Latent-PER are compared. As shown in Figure 8, the precision for happiness tends to be the highest among all emotions. When comparing the accuracy between models, an overall performance improvement occurs in all emotions. In particular, the precision for neutral and fear increased by 21%p and 19%p, respectively, exhibiting the most significant performance improvement. In addition, DAN mistakenly recognized fear as a surprise due to the enlarged mouth. Furthermore, the accuracy of disgust, anger, and sad emotions, which had poor performance, increased by 13%p, 14%p, and 17%p, respectively.

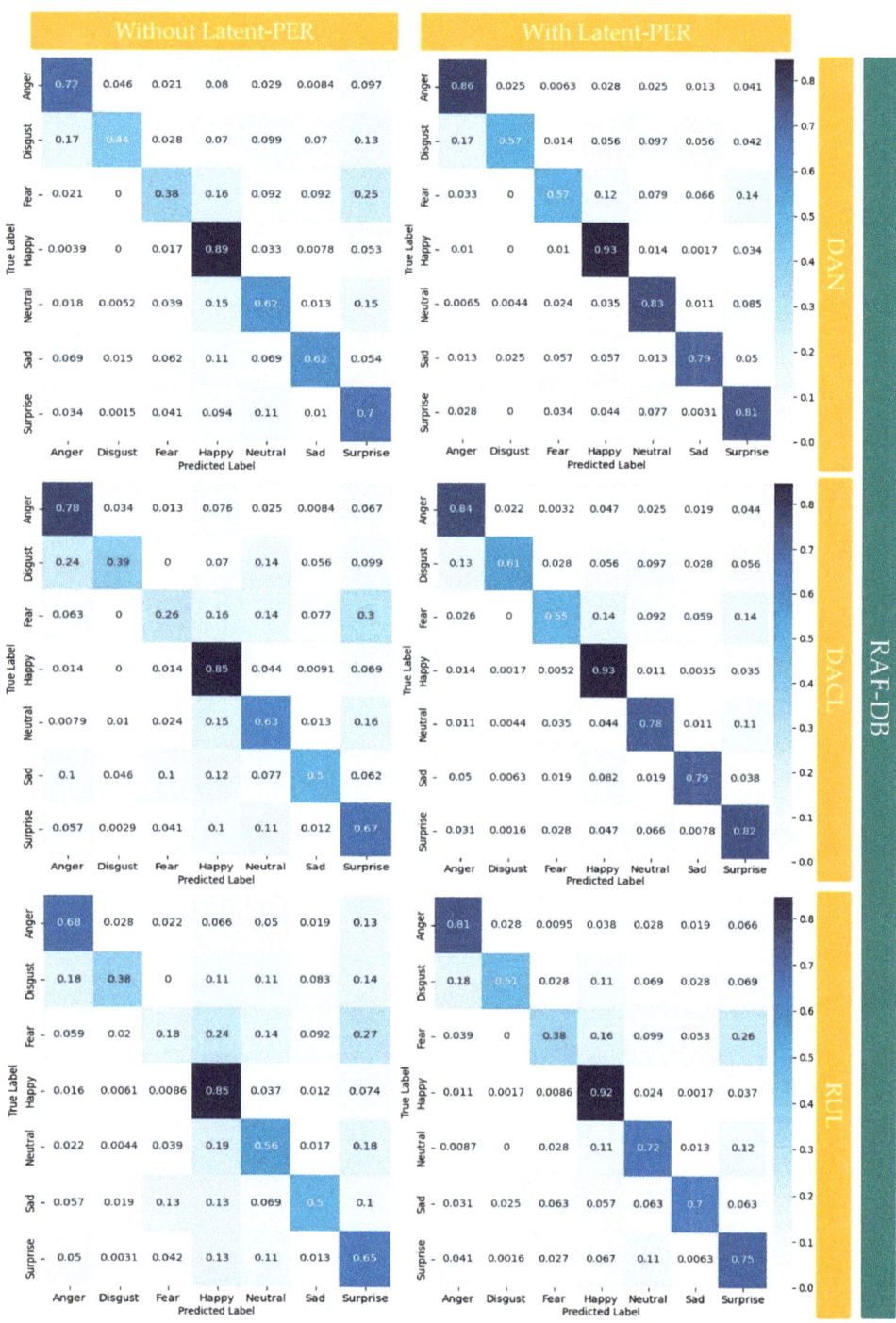

Figure 8. Performance comparison on RAF-DB dataset using confusion matrices without and with Latent-PER.

Similarly, this trend is also observed in DACL, and the precision for fear increased by 29%p with Latent-PER compared to DAN. In addition, the precision of the disgust emotion is 22%p lower in DACL compared to Latent-PER since the disgust emotion was mistakenly recognized as anger. Furthermore, the accuracy of neutral and sad, which had poor performance, increased by 15%p and 29%p, respectively. Happiness is rarely perceived as sadness, but errors concerning happiness and neutrality and regarding fear and surprise are common in existing models. Therefore, most of the recognition performance for facial expressions with ambiguous elements between facial expressions is lowered. In the case of RUL, there was the most significant difference between the case where Latent-PER was used and the case where it was not. In particular, in the previous two models, happiness was recognized well, whereas, in RUL, the emotion recognition performance of fear was not good. Moreover, the misjudgment rate for sadness and fear was high, and it can be seen that this part was significantly improved when Latent-PER was applied. In the case of fear, the precision of RUL is only 18%. In contrast, the precision of RUL with Latent-PER shows 38% performance. The precision of RUL with Latent-PER shows performance improvements of 13%p and 20%p in disgust and sad emotions, respectively. Furthermore, the accuracy of neutral, fear, anger, and surprise which had poor performance, increased by 16%p, 20%p, 13%p, and 10%p, respectively. Since Latent-PER learns through independent components between features, disentangled features learned from entangled features space can be used. Therefore, it performs better on ambiguous expression elements, as shown in Figures 9 and 10. As shown in Figure 9, the precisions of fear and sad emotions are very low in the case of DAN. Fear and sad emotions are often misjudged as a surprise. In contrast, DAN with Latent-PER presents 44%p and 22%p higher percentage points than basic DAN in fear and sad emotions, respectively. DACL with Latent-PER shows 25%p and 9%p higher percentage points than the base DACL in fear and sad emotions, respectively. In addition, RUL provides lower precision of all emotion on CK+ dataset. However, RUL with Latent-PER presents about 46%p and 47%p higher percentage points than basic RUL in fear and sad emotions, respectively. However, failure examples are observed for neutral emotion in the CK+ dataset, as shown in the results of most models with Latent-PER. The CK+ dataset has various emotional intensities. When the happy emotion with very weak intensity is included in the dataset, neutral can be recognized as happy. To solve this problem, if data preprocessing is performed on these weak emotions, the emotion recognition accuracy for neutral can be improved. Overall, our framework shows performance gains of 9.7%p, 3%p, and 28%p, respectively, for DAN, DACL, and RUL models using CK+ dataset.

4.3. Ablations Study

4.3.1. Latent Code Editing

In this paper, the parts related to facial expressions are extracted from the entire latent code using the ICA method. Seven emotional images are converted for one object into latent code using the KDEF dataset. The ICA algorithm extracts an eigenvector that can classify the latent code for each emotion. As depicted in Figure 11, a single latent code is created by mixing the latent code for all emotions through the mixing matrix of the source latent code. From this, one latent code is classified into seven original latent codes. If the value of the eigenvector is large, there is a significant correlation between the index and the expression, and when it is small, the correlation with the expression is also small. As illustrated in Figures 6 and 12, we edited the latent code based on certain thresholds to avoid using index information that is irrelevant to the expression for training.

Figure 9. Performance comparison on CK+ dataset using confusion matrices without and with Latent-PER.

Figure 10. Visual prediction results of examples on CK+ dataset without and with Latent-PER.

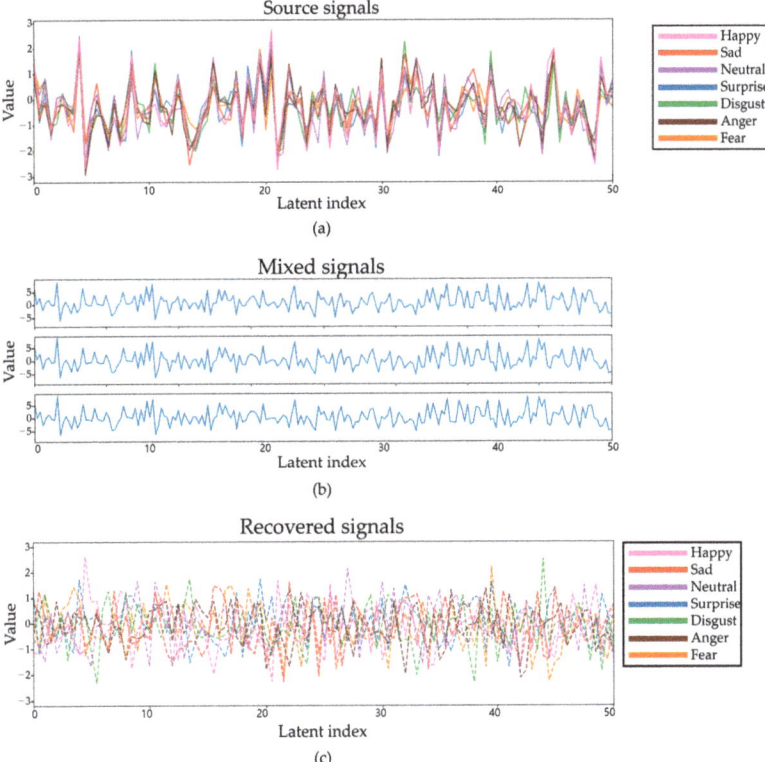

Figure 11. Example of an ICA solution that restores independent components. (**a**) Source information entered as input. It is mixed as in (**b**) through the mixing matrix and divided into independent signals as in (**c**) through ICA.

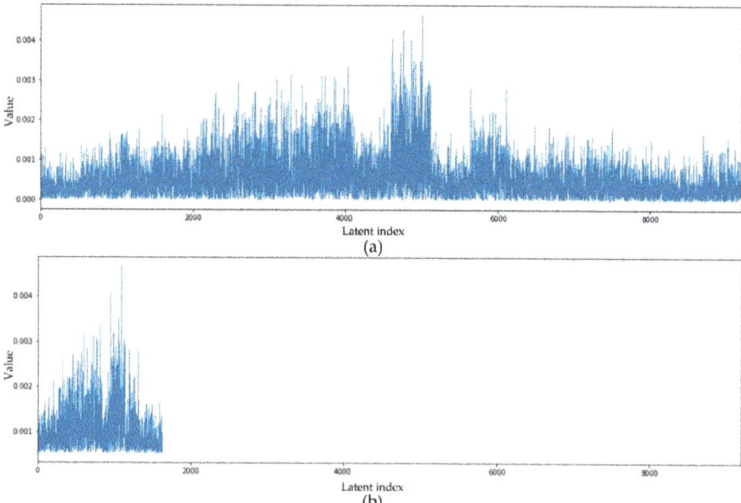

Figure 12. Visualization of the rectified eigenvector excluding information unrelated to the expression: (**a**) Entire eigenvector and (**b**) rectified eigenvector.

We quantitatively and qualitatively prove the correlation between these eigenvectors and expressions. For the quantitative proof, as shown in Tables 2–4, the editing hidden code for learning provides higher accuracy than the emotion recognition performance when the entire latent code is used. In particular, when the mean is filtered by the threshold, only about 17% of the information is used. However, the accuracy is higher than using the entire latent code.

Table 2. Portrait emotion recognition performance of latent code editing on the RAF-DB validation set in terms of accuracy.

Threshold (h)	Number of Tensors	DAN	RUL	DACL
0	Full latent code (9126 tensor)	82.7%	84.7%	78.2%
Median	Edited latent code (2194 tensor)	83.5% (0.8%p ↑)	85.2% (0.5%p ↑)	80.8% (2.6%p ↑)
Mean	Edited latent code (1638 tensor)	84.2% (1.5%p ↑)	85.8% (1.1%p ↑)	83.0% (4.8%p ↑)

Table 3. Portrait emotion recognition performance of latent code editing on the CK+ validation set in terms of accuracy.

Threshold (h)	Number of Tensors	DAN	RUL	DACL
0	Full latent code (9126 tensor)	72.1%	63.0%	68.0%
Median	Edited latent code (2194 tensor)	72.6% (0.5%p ↑)	68.2% (5.2%p ↑)	69.2% (1.2%p ↑)
Mean	Edited latent code (1638 tensor)	73.4% (1.3%p ↑)	70.3% (7.3%p ↑)	70.1% (2.1%p ↑)

Table 4. Portrait emotion recognition performance of latent code editing on the KDEF validation set in terms of accuracy.

Threshold (h)	Number of Tensors	DAN	RUL	DACL
0	Full latent code (9126 tensor)	83.2%	77.0%	81.2%
Median	Edited latent code (2194 tensor)	84.0% (0.8%p ↑)	78.2% (1.2%p ↑)	82.0% (0.8%p ↑)
Mean	Edited latent code (1638 tensor)	84.3% (1.1%p ↑)	78.4% (1.4%p ↑)	82.8% (1.6%p ↑)

For qualitative proof, the original latent code is changed to the greatest extent possible as the rectified eigenvector obtained through the above method, and an image is generated through a generator. If the information in the latent code is unrelated to the expression, such as hair length and skin color, an image with a changed appearance is created. However, if it is related to the expression, only the expression changes are disentangled while maintaining the existing appearance. For this proof, the degree of emotion was controlled by calculating the eigenvector in the latent code for a specific emotion. Figure 13 confirms that the proposed method changes the facial expression while disentangling the expression data and maintaining the appearance information. Our proposed manipulation method can be applied to various image styles, such as painting, drawing, and cartoon. The task of facial expression recognition using the proposed latent code and facial expression manipulation via eigenvectors can help in automating animation emotion caption generation tasks and in supporting existing expensive animation production systems.

Figure 13. Emotional intensity manipulation based on latent code change.

4.3.2. Complexity

The model weight sizes for DAN, DACL, and RUL are approximately 150, 400, and 380 MB, respectively. Our proposed Latent-PER model is a plug-and-play framework for the existing facial expression recognition model. Therefore, as shown in Table 5, it requires more computing resources as additional encoders. For this reason, additional inference time is required the average 6 ms than the existing model.

Table 5. Comparison of computational complexity of various methods.

Method	Inference Time (ms)	Model Weight Size (MB)
DAN	6	150
DAN + Latent-PER	12	270
DACL	43	400
DACL + Latent-PER	49	520
RUL	42	380
RUL + Latent-PER	48	500

4.3.3. Limitation

Our method can have limitations in terms of computational complexity. Since it is a GAN-based method, the inference time is larger than a typical CNN-based method. Therefore, in the future work, additional network compression is needed to reduce the inference time to reduce the weights of the GAN-based method. Additionally, since a GAN-based encoder is used, it must be aligned to the input image to show the complete estimation performance. If face-occluded images are inputted into facial expression recognition models, the model suffers severe performance degradation. To address this problem, a GAN-based image recovery method can be applied. Moreover, if we develop this research, it becomes possible to recognize emotions in all existing image styles from the viewpoint of emotion recognition. Furthermore, from the viewpoint of manipulation, many computer vision researchers are currently interested in generative models. If manipulation through the proposed ICA is further developed, an actor's acting can be assisted through manipulation in making a movie, and for animation, the existing production work can be simplified.

5. Conclusions

Applying conventional emotion recognition models to portrait images presents unacceptable accuracy. In this case, it is significantly inaccurate to recognize the emotion of a style face different from the actual image, such as a famous drawing, painting, or animation. Emotion recognition in portraits is clearly necessary, but most of the papers focus on authentic-photograph images. Therefore, we propose a specialized model.

We propose a plug-and-play-style portrait emotion recognition framework to solve this problem by adding the existing model to the proposed method that transforms the input image into latent code via a GAN-based encoder. This approach is a first in the FER. In this latent code, only information related to portrait emotion is edited in the ICA method, and only the extracted information is used for training along with the existing model. The manipulation method we proposed is the first approach that applied ICA to latent code editing. We observe considerable performance improvement with the proposed method. Moreover, we quantitatively and qualitatively prove that we extracted only expression-related information in the latent code. Through this, we propose a novel method to manipulate visually independent components from the generative learning of the GAN.

Author Contributions: Conceptualization, S.B.Y.; methodology, I.L. and S.B.Y.; software, I.L.; validation, I.L.; formal analysis, I.L. and S.B.Y.; investigation, I.L. and S.B.Y.; resources, I.L. and S.B.Y.; data curation, I.L. and S.B.Y.; writing—original draft preparation, I.L. and S.B.Y.; writing—review and editing, I.L. and S.B.Y.; visualization, S.B.Y.; supervision, S.B.Y.; project administration, S.B.Y.; funding acquisition, S.B.Y. All authors have read and agreed to the published version of the manuscript.

Funding: This work was supported by the National Research Foundation of Korea (NRF) grant funded by the Korea government (MSIT) (NRF-2020R1A4A1019191) and the Industrial Fundamental Technology Development Program (No. 20018699) funded by the Ministry of Trade, Industry & Energy (MOTIE) of Korea.

Data Availability Statement: Not applicable.

Conflicts of Interest: The authors declare no conflict of interest.

References

1. Tian, Y.; Kanade, T.; Cohn, J.F. Facial Expression Recognition. In *Handbook of Face Recognition*; Springer London: London, UK, 2011; pp. 487–519.
2. Shan, C.; Gong, S.; McOwan, P.W. Facial Expression Recognition Based on Local Binary Patterns: A Comprehensive Study. *Image Vis. Comput.* **2009**, *27*, 803–816. [CrossRef]
3. Zhao, G.; Pietikainen, M. Dynamic Texture Recognition Using Local Binary Patterns with an Application to Facial Expressions. *IEEE Trans. Pattern Anal. Mach. Intell.* **2007**, *29*, 915–928. [CrossRef] [PubMed]
4. Zhi, R.; Flierl, M.; Ruan, Q.; Kleijn, W.B. Graph-Preserving Sparse Nonnegative Matrix Factorization with Application to Facial Expression Recognition. *IEEE Trans. Syst. Man Cybern. Part B* **2011**, *41*, 38–52. [CrossRef]
5. Zhong, L.; Liu, Q.; Yang, P.; Liu, B.; Huang, J.; Metaxas, D.N. Learning Active Facial Patches for Expression Analysis. In Proceedings of the 2012 IEEE Conference on Computer Vision and Pattern Recognition, Providence, RI, USA, 16–21 June 2012; pp. 2562–2569.
6. Szegedy, C.; Toshev, A.; Erhan, D. Deep Neural Networks for Object Detection. *Adv. Neural Inf. Process. Syst.* **2013**, *26*, 2553–2561.
7. LeCun, Y.; Boser, B.; Denker, J.S.; Henderson, D.; Howard, R.E.; Hubbard, W.; Jackel, L.D. Backpropagation Applied to Handwritten Zip Code Recognition. *Neural Comput.* **1989**, *1*, 541–551. [CrossRef]
8. Simonyan, K.; Zisserman, A. Very Deep Convolutional Networks for Large-Scale Image Recognition. In Proceedings of the 3rd International Conference on Learning Representations, Guilin, China, 19–20 May 2018.
9. Tang, Y. Deep Learning Using Linear Support Vector Machines. *arXiv* **2013**, arXiv:1306.0239.
10. Hong, Y.; Lee, S.; Yoo, S.B. AugMoCrack: Augmented Morphological Attention Network for Weakly Supervised Crack Detection. *Electron. Lett.* **2022**, *58*, 651–653. [CrossRef]
11. Lee, S.-J.; Yun, J.-S.; Lee, E.J.; Yoo, S.B. HIFA-LPR: High-Frequency Augmented License Plate Recognition in Low-Quality Legacy Conditions via Gradual End-to-End Learning. *Mathematics* **2022**, *10*, 1569. [CrossRef]
12. Yun, J.-S.; Yoo, S.-B. Single Image Super-Resolution with Arbitrary Magnification Based on High-Frequency Attention Network. *Mathematics* **2022**, *10*, 275. [CrossRef]
13. Lee, S.; Yun, J.S.; Yoo, S.B. Alternative Collaborative Learning for Character Recognition in Low-Resolution Images. *IEEE Access* **2022**, *10*, 22003–22017. [CrossRef]
14. Lee, S.-J.; Yoo, S.B. Super-Resolved Recognition of License Plate Characters. *Mathematics* **2021**, *9*, 2494. [CrossRef]
15. Yun, J.-S.; Na, Y.; Kim, H.H.; Kim, H.-I.; Yoo, S.B. HAZE-Net: High-Frequency Attentive Super-Resolved Gaze Estimation in Low-Resolution Face Images. *arXiv* **2022**, arXiv:2209.10167.
16. Hong, Y.; Yoo, S.B. OASIS-Net: Morphological Attention Ensemble Learning for Surface Defect Detection. *Mathematics* **2022**, *10*, 4114. [CrossRef]
17. Yun, J.-S.; Yoo, S.B. Infusion-Net: Inter- and Intra-Weighted Cross-Fusion Network for Multispectral Object Detection. *Mathematics* **2022**, *10*, 3966. [CrossRef]
18. Hyvärinen, A.; Jarmo, H.; Patrik, O. *Hoyer Independent Component Analysis. Natural Image Statistics*; Springer: London, UK, 2009; Volume 529.
19. Goodfellow, I.; Pouget, A.J.; Mirza, M.; Xu, B.; Warde-Farley, D.; Ozair, S.; Courville, A.; Bengio, Y. Generative Adversarial Networks. *Commun. ACM* **2020**, *63*, 139–144. [CrossRef]
20. Mase, K. Recognition of Facial Expression from Optical Flow. *IEICE Trans. Inf. Syst.* **1991**, *74*, 3474–3483.
21. Xiang, J.; Zhu, G. Joint Face Detection and Facial Expression Recognition with MTCNN. In Proceedings of the 2017 4th International Conference on Information Science and Control Engineering, Changsha, China, 21–23 July 2017; pp. 424–427.
22. Karras, T.; Laine, S.; Aila, T. A Style-Based Generator Architecture for Generative Adversarial Networks. In Proceedings of the IEEE/CVF Conference on Computer Vision and Pattern Recognition, Long Beach, CA, USA, 15–20 June 2019; pp. 4401–4410.
23. King, D.E. Dlib-Ml: A Machine Learning Toolkit. *J. Mach. Learn. Res.* **2009**, *10*, 1755–1758.
24. Fasel, B. Robust Face Analysis Using Convolutional Neural Networks. In Proceedings of the Object Recognition Supported by User Interaction for Service Robots, Quebec City, QC, Canada, 11–15 August 2002; pp. 40–43.

25. Kanou, S.E.; Ferrari, R.C.; Mirza, M.; Jean, S.; Carrier, P.-L.; Dauphin, Y.; Boulanger-Lewandowski, N.; Aggarwal, A.; Zumer, J.; Lamblin, P. Combining Modality Specific Deep Neural Networks for Emotion Recognition in Video. In Proceedings of the 15th ACM on International Conference on Multimodal Interaction, Sydney, Australia, 9–13 December 2013; pp. 543–550.
26. Ge, H.; Zhu, Z.; Dai, Y.; Wang, B.; Wu, X. Facial Expression Recognition Based on Deep Learning. *Comput. Methods Programs Biomed.* **2022**, *215*, 106621. [CrossRef]
27. Meng, Z.; Liu, P.; Cai, J.; Han, S.; Tong, Y. Identity-Aware Convolutional Neural Network for Facial Expression Recognition. In Proceedings of the 2017 12th IEEE International Conference on Automatic Face & Gesture Recognition, Washington, DC, USA, 30 May–3 June 2017; pp. 558–565.
28. Li, Z.; Wu, S.; Xiao, G. Facial Expression Recognition by Multi-Scale CNN with Regularized Center Loss. In Proceedings of the 2018 24th International Conference on Pattern Recognition, Beijing, China, 20–24 August 2018; pp. 3384–3389.
29. Wen, Z.; Lin, W.; Wang, T.; Xu, G. Distract Your Attention: Multi-Head Cross Attention Network for Facial Expression Recognition. *arXiv* **2021**, arXiv:2109.07270.
30. Farzaneh, A.H.; Qi, X. Facial Expression Recognition in the Wild via Deep Attentive Center Loss. In Proceedings of the 2021 IEEE Winter Conference on Applications of Computer Vision, Waikoloa, HI, USA, 3–8 January 2021; pp. 2401–2410.
31. Zhang, Y.; Wang, C.; Deng, W. Relative Uncertainty Learning for Facial Expression Recognition. *Adv. Neural Inf. Process. Syst.* **2021**, *34*, 17616–17627.
32. Xu, P.; Peng, S.; Luo, Y.; Gong, G. Facial Expression Recognition: A Meta-Analytic Review of Theoretical Models and Neuroimaging Evidence. *Neurosci. Biobehav. Rev.* **2021**, *127*, 820–836. [CrossRef]
33. Ruan, D.; Yan, Y.; Lai, S.; Chai, Z.; Shen, C.; Wang, H. Feature Decomposition and Reconstruction Learning for Effective Facial Expression Recognition. In Proceedings of the IEEE/CVF Conference on Computer Vision and Pattern Recognition, Nashville, TN, USA, 20–25 June 2021; pp. 7660–7669.
34. Li, B.; Lima, D. Facial Expression Recognition via ResNet-50. *Int. J. Cogn. Comput. Eng.* **2021**, *2*, 57–64. [CrossRef]
35. Zhao, Z.; Liu, Q.; Zhou, F. Robust Lightweight Facial Expression Recognition Network with Label Distribution Training. *Proc. AAAI Conf. Artif. Intell.* **2021**, *35*, 3510–3519. [CrossRef]
36. Pham, L.; Vu, T.H.; Tran, T.A. Facial Expression Recognition Using Residual Masking Network. In Proceedings of the 2020 25th International Conference on Pattern Recognition, Milan, Italy, 10–15 January 2021; pp. 4513–4519.
37. Liu, C.; Hirota, K.; Ma, J.; Jia, Z.; Dai, Y. Facial Expression Recognition Using Hybrid Features of Pixel and Geometry. *IEEE Access* **2021**, *9*, 18876–18889. [CrossRef]
38. Park, S.-J.; Kim, B.-G.; Chilamkurti, N. A Robust Facial Expression Recognition Algorithm Based on Multi-Rate Feature Fusion Scheme. *Sensors* **2021**, *21*, 6954. [CrossRef] [PubMed]
39. Moetesum, M.; Aslam, T.; Saeed, H.; Siddiqi, I.; Masroor, U. Sketch-Based Facial Expression Recognition for Human Figure Drawing Psychological Test. In Proceedings of the 2017 International Conference on Frontiers of Information Technology, Islamabad, Pakistan, 18–20 December 2017; pp. 258–263.
40. Lee, I.; Yun, J.-S.; Kim, H.H.; Na, Y.; Yoo, S.B. LatentGaze: Cross-Domain Gaze Estimation through Gaze-Aware Analytic Latent Code Manipulation. *arXiv* **2022**, arXiv:2209.10171.
41. Mirza, M.; Osindero, S. Conditional Generative Adversarial Nets. *arXiv* **2014**, arXiv:1411.1784.
42. Chrysos, G.G.; Kossaifi, J.; Zafeiriou, S. Robust Conditional Generative Adversarial Networks. International Conference on Learning Representations. *arXiv* **2018**, arXiv:1805.08557.
43. Abdal, R.; Qin, Y.; Wonka, P. Image2StyleGAN: How to Embed Images into the StyleGAN Latent Space? In Proceedings of the IEEE/CVF International Conference on Computer Vision, Seoul, Republic of Korea, 27 October–2 November 2019; pp. 4432–4441.
44. Shen, Y.; Gu, J.; Tang, X.; Zhou, B. Interpreting the Latent Space of GANs for Semantic Face Editing. In Proceedings of the IEEE/CVF Conference on Computer Vision and Pattern Recognition, Seattle, WA, USA, 13–19 June 2020; pp. 9243–9252.
45. Zhu, J.; Shen, Y.; Zhao, D.; Zhou, B. In-Domain GAN Inversion for Real Image Editing. In Proceedings of the European Conference on Computer Vision (ECCV), Glasgow, UK, 23–28 August 2020; pp. 592–608.
46. Tov, O.; Alaluf, Y.; Nitzan, Y.; Patashnik, O.; Cohen-Or, D. Designing an Encoder for StyleGAN Image Manipulation. *ACM Trans. Graph.* **2021**, *40*, 1–14. [CrossRef]
47. He, Z.; Spurr, A.; Zhang, X.; Hilliges, O. Photo-Realistic Monocular Gaze Redirection Using Generative Adversarial Networks. In Proceedings of the IEEE/CVF International Conference on Computer Vision, Seoul, Republic of Korea, 27 October–2 November 2019; pp. 6932–6941.
48. Konda, K.; Memisevic, R.; Krueger, D. Zero-Bias Autoencoders and the Benefits of Co-Adapting Features. *arXiv* **2014**, arXiv:1402.3337.
49. Li, S.; Deng, W.; Du, J. Reliable Crowdsourcing and Deep Locality-Preserving Learning for Expression Recognition in the Wild. In Proceedings of the 2017 IEEE Conference on Computer Vision and Pattern Recognition, Honolulu, HI, USA, 21–26 July 2017; pp. 2584–2593.
50. Lucey, P.; Cohn, J.F.; Kanade, T.; Saragih, J.; Ambadar, Z.; Matthews, I. The Extended Cohn-Kanade Dataset (CK+): A Complete Dataset for Action Unit and Emotion-Specified Expression. In Proceedings of the 2010 IEEE Computer Society Conference on Computer Vision and Pattern Recognition—Workshops, San Francisco, CA, USA, 13–18 June 2010; pp. 94–101.
51. Calvo, M.G.; Lundqvist, D. Facial Expressions of Emotion (KDEF): Identification under Different Display-Duration Conditions. *Behav. Res. Methods* **2008**, *40*, 109–115. [CrossRef] [PubMed]

Article

A Comprehensive Analysis of Transformer-Deep Neural Network Models in Twitter Disaster Detection

Vimala Balakrishnan [1,*], Zhongliang Shi [1], Chuan Liang Law [2], Regine Lim [1], Lee Leng Teh [1], Yue Fan [1] and Jeyarani Periasamy [3]

[1] Faculty of Computer Science and Information Technology, Universiti Malaya, Kuala Lumpur 50603, Malaysia
[2] Malayan Banking Berhad, Kuala Lumpur 50050, Malaysia
[3] Faculty of Data Science and Information Technology, INTI International University, Nilai 71800, Malaysia
* Correspondence: vimala.balakrishnan@um.edu.my

Abstract: Social media platforms such as Twitter are a vital source of information during major events, such as natural disasters. Studies attempting to automatically detect textual communications have mostly focused on machine learning and deep learning algorithms. Recent evidence shows improvement in disaster detection models with the use of contextual word embedding techniques (i.e., transformers) that take the context of a word into consideration, unlike the traditional context-free techniques; however, studies regarding this model are scant. To this end, this paper investigates a selection of ensemble learning models by merging transformers with deep neural network algorithms to assess their performance in detecting informative and non-informative disaster-related Twitter communications. A total of 7613 tweets were used to train and test the models. Results indicate that the ensemble models consistently yield good performance results, with F-score values ranging between 76% and 80%. Simpler transformer variants, such as ELECTRA and Talking-Heads Attention, yielded comparable and superior results compared to the computationally expensive BERT, with F-scores ranging from 80% to 84%, especially when merged with Bi-LSTM. Our findings show that the newer and simpler transformers can be used effectively, with less computational costs, in detecting disaster-related Twitter communications.

Keywords: disaster; Twitter; deep neural network; transformers; ensemble

MSC: 68-04

1. Introduction

Social media has become a common place for people to seek information and help during emergencies and major crises, particularly during natural disasters such as storms, tsunamis, earthquakes, flood, etc., by sharing posts in the forms of images, texts, and videos [1,2]. The platforms have a developing role in how people communicate and respond to disasters, providing a network to seek help; gain information, guidance and reassurance; and respond to help requests. For instance, social media posts requesting aid and support were found to have superseded the emergency (911) phone system during the 9/11 American "natural disaster" [3]. Similarly, "#SOSHarvey" and "#HelpHouston" were found to be trending during Hurricane Harvey and were used to flag people who needed help/rescue [3].

Twitter, in particular, has been shown to be popular in generating disaster-related content, with users tweeting information about affected people and infrastructure damage that are sometimes very useful for aid and rescue teams, government, and private disaster relief organizations rendering assistance to those in need. The social media platform is known for its ability to communicate quickly across space supporting victims and disaster response, directing resources, and highlighting what the affected community prioritizes in a disaster [2–6]. As a matter of fact, Twitter is regarded as the 'most useful social media tool', particularly for natural disasters [2,6,7]. Despite its popularity, tweets are limited in terms of their length, and thus tend to be more challenging (e.g., sparse, more abbreviations, etc.), thus making it difficult to differentiate if a specific communication (i.e., tweet) is related to a disaster or not.

Social Media and Disaster Detection

Although the data generated by social media platforms such as Twitter are ubiquitous, extracting useful and relevant information is not only a tedious task, but nearly impossible due to their enormous volume and velocity, thus making automatic disaster detection and classification models feasible solutions [2,7–9]. With the advent of artificial intelligence (AI), evidence exists showing that approaches such as machine and deep learning can be effectively used to detect information related to natural disasters, based on social media communications [7]. A search of the literature on the application of AI and social media in disaster-related events revealed several aspects investigated by research scholars, including damage assessments [10,11], enhancing or promoting situational awareness [5,6], using sentiment for disaster predictions [8,12,13], and disaster classification/detection models focusing on differentiating informative and non-informative content [2,8,9,14], the latter of which is the focus of the present study. For example, the authors of [10] used a semi-supervised approach to evaluate the damage extent indicated by Twitter communication during the Hong Kong and Macau typhoons in 2017, whereas the authors of [12] used a big data driven approach for disaster response through sentiment analysis, with the results indicating a lexicon-based approach to be more suitable in analyzing the needs of the people during a disaster.

Numerous studies were found to have used the traditional machine learning algorithms, such as support vector machine (SVM), naïve Bayes, decision tree, and logistic regression, etc., with promising results [15–18]. More recent studies utilized deep learning algorithms such as the convolutional neural network (CNN) and the recurrent neural network (RNN) [19–21]; however, most of them were based on the context-free word embedding techniques, such as Word2Vec. In this technique, the context in which a word is used is disregarded. For example, "*#RockingBand, fire and smoke on stage, having a blast at this concert!!!*" indicates that the user is having a great time at a concert despite the use of words such as "fire," "smoke," and "blast." The tweet is not disaster-related; however, a context-free word embedding technique will likely classify the tweet as such, due to the occurrence of these words. To address this issue, some studies refined the models' performance using a contextual or transformer-based word embedding technique, that is, bidirectional encoder representations from transformers (BERT) [8,9,22–25]. However, studies exploring these transformers, including BERT variants such as RoBERTa, AlBERT, and ELECTRA, for example, are scant, despite the growing popularity of these contextual word embedding techniques and their positive results [22,26].

To close this gap and to further extend the current literature, we aim to explore several well-known deep learning algorithms, especially neural network (NN) models and transformer-based word embedding techniques, to identify the best/optimal ensemble solutions in detecting Twitter disaster-related communications. The main contributions of this study are as follows:

- We explore, implement, and compare the transformer-based embedding techniques, including the base model and its simpler variants, in detecting disaster using a real-life Twitter dataset;
- We implement the various transformers with several well-known NN models, and identify the best/optimal combination in detecting disasters via Twitter.

From the above-mentioned comparisons and analyses, the study offers evidence and support to alternative solutions, including the use of the simpler and more cost-effective transformer variants in effectively detecting disaster-related communication on social media.

The remainder of the paper is structured as follows: related studies employing deep learning approaches, using both context-free and contextual based techniques, are reviewed in Section 2, followed by the methods adopted to achieve the main objective of this study. Section 4 provides the results and a discussion, and the conclusion is provided in Section 5, along with limitations and ideas for future directions.

2. Related Work

Deep learning models are generally based on supervised models requiring large amounts of labeled data, often yielding more accurate results, albeit being computationally expensive [14,26]. Popular examples of deep NN models include CNN, RNN, and long short-term memory (LSTM), among others. A search of the literature revealed several studies exploring and proposing deep learning models to detect social media-based disaster identification. For example, Yu et al. [19] found their CNN model to yield the best F-score (i.e., 80%) based on experiments conducted using three datasets, namely, Hurricane Harvey, Hurricane Sandy, and Hurricane Irma. A similar study using CNN was done by the authors of [20], who extracted location references from emergency tweets, with findings indicating an F-score of 96%. The authors further extended their work by incorporating a multi-modal technique using LSTM and found the combination of both text and images to produce the best F-score (i.e., 93%) compared to using only text (i.e., 92%) [21]. Another study based on the CrisisLexT26 dataset containing tweets related to 26 disasters, trained and tested using Bi-directional Gated Recurrent Units (GRU) and LSTM learning models, reported that both the models detected disaster-related tweets, with F-score values of 79% and 82% for LSTM and Bi-GRU, respectively.

Others explored conventional word embedding techniques, such as the authors of [2], who proposed a hybrid CNN model combining character and word embedding techniques (i.e., FastText) to detect disaster tweets using datasets related to hurricanes, floods, and wildfires. They found that character-based CNN performed the best across all the datasets, with an average F-score of 71%. Conversely, the authors of [27] proposed a multilayer perceptron model, which is a feed forward NN using Word2Vec embedding, to classify disasters using two earthquake datasets for training. The authors tested their model using a COVID-19 dataset and reported a weighted F-score of 85%. Although often reported to yield improved detection results, these conventional word embedding techniques are context-free; hence, the word "fire" would be assumed to have the same meaning, regardless of its use in a sentence [9,26]. To address this issue, the contextual embedding learning model BERT was proposed by Devlin et al. [28].

BERT is a pretrained transformer bidirectional training model developed to resolve language modeling and next sentence prediction in tasks involving natural language processing (NLP) [28]. Unlike the conventional word embedding techniques, such as FastText, GloVE, and Word2Vec, BERT evaluates text in two directions (i.e., left to right and vice-versa). Disaster-based studies incorporating BERT often reported improved classifications; for instance, a series of experiments using seven different catastrophic event datasets based on a multi-modal technique combining BERT and DenseNet yielded promising F-scores ranging from 66% to 88% [22]. The authors of [9] compared BERT-Bi-LSTM with traditional context-free embedding techniques using a Twitter dataset, and found the former exhibited the best results in prediction, with an F-score of 83%. The authors of [9] further extended their analysis to include more embedding techniques, such as GloVe, Skip-Gram, FastText, and other DNN models (RNN, CNN). Results generally indicate that BERT-based modeling yields the best results for disaster-prediction tasks [25]. Other studies implementing BERT include the detection of tweets linked to the Jakarta flood in 2020 [29], COVID-19 crisis communications [24], public datasets, such as crisisLexT26 and crisisNLP [23], etc.

Although BERT often yields good results on NLP tasks, it is, however, resource intensive [30]. Therefore, researchers began to explore simpler versions of BERT (or its variants) such as RoBERTa, TinyBERT, ELECTRA, and AlBERT, among others. However, a search of the disaster detection studies revealed very few studies that have utilized these variants. For instance, the authors of [14] proposed an ensemble-based strategy by combining RoBERTa, BERTweet, and CT-BERT models to detect COVID-19 related tweets and found their approach to produce the best F-score of 91%, outperforming the traditional machine learning and deep learning algorithms. The authors of [8], on the other hand, proposed a sentiment-aware contextual model named SentiBERT-BiLSTM-CNN for tweet-based disaster detection, with SentiBERT specifically used to extract sentimental contextual embeddings from a given tweet. The authors found their proposed model to outperform the rest of the models, with an F-score of 92.7%.

Table 1 provides the review of deep learning studies discussed in this section. In summary, the review shows that the majority of the studies on Twitter disaster detection were based on the traditional context-free embedding techniques, whereas those exploring the more robust transformer-based techniques were scant. Further, it can be observed that BERT remains to be largely explored in this regard, despite the promising results and performance of its variants [8,14]. The review, therefore, provides an insight into the gaps of AI-based Twitter disaster detection and helps to guide this study in exploring the transformers through deep learning models.

Table 1. Summary of deep learning studies in detecting tweets related to disasters.

References	Disaster	Algorithm	Word Embedding	F-Score (%)
[19]	Hurricane	CNN	Word2Vec	80
[20]	Earthquake	CNN	Bag-of-words, GloVe	96
[21]	Hurricane, wildfire, earthquake, flood	LSTM, CNN	GloVe	93
[31]	26 disasters	LSTM, bi-directional GRU	WordNet	79–82
[2]	Hurricane, flood, wildfire	CNN	GloVe, FastText	71
[27]	Earthquake	MLP	Word2vec	85
[24]	Earthquake, wildfire, flood	CNN	BERT, DenseNet	66–88
[8]	General (i.e., flood, fire, earthquake)	Bi-LSTM–CNN	SentiBERT	92.7
[23]	26 disasters	LSTM, CNN	BERT	71.86
[9]	General (i.e., flood, fire, earthquake)	Bi-LSTM	BERT	83.16
[14]	COVID-19 related disaster	-	RoBERTa, BERTweet, CT-BERT	91

CNN: Convolutional Neural Network; LSTM: Long Short-Term Memory; MLP: Multilayer Perceptron.

3. Materials and Method

Figure 1 depicts a general overview of the pipeline for disaster detection with several consecutive modules.

The pre-processed tweets act as input to the transformers, where contextual word embedding takes place. The output of the transformers are then fitted to a deep NN algorithm to form ensemble models, specifically NN, CNN, LSTM, and Bi-LSTM. The ensemble combination of the transformer and NN models then makes the final prediction, that is, whether a tweet is disaster or non-disaster related. These modules are elaborated in the subsequent sections.

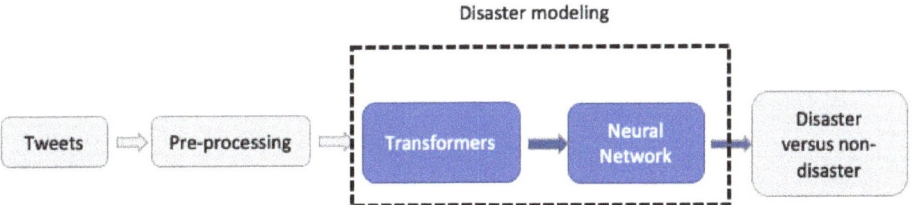

Figure 1. Disaster detection pipeline.

3.1. Twitter Dataset

A Twitter dataset available on Kaggle (https://www.kaggle.com/c/nlp-getting-started/data?select=train.csv, accessed on 23 December 2021) containing 7613 tweets regarding disasters was used in this study. The metadata included ID, keyword (i.e., unique words from the tweet), location (i.e., origin of tweet), and the actual text. The dataset also contained human labels identifying if the tweet pertains to a disaster or otherwise (i.e., binary labels). Specifically, the tweets were classified as 1 (i.e., disaster) or 0 (i.e., not a disaster), with examples of disasters communicated in the dataset including floods, storms, earthquakes, and fires. Table 2 provides some examples for both the disaster and non-disaster tweets. The dataset has been used by the authors of [8,9,25], as stated in Section 2.

Table 2. Sample tweets from the Kaggle disaster dataset (1—Disaster; 0—Non-disaster).

Original Tweets	Label
Our Deeds are the Reason of this #earthquake May ALLAH Forgive us all	1
#Flood in Bago Myanmar #We arrived Bago	1
Forest fire near La Ronge Sask. Canada	1
I love fruits	0
My car is so fast	0
Summer is lovely	0

A simple exploratory data analysis revealed the dataset to be balanced, that is, 42.9% (n = 3271) and 57.1% (n = 4342) for disaster and non-disaster, respectively. The average length of tweets was 12.5 words, with most of the disaster and non-disaster tweets ranging between 10 and 20 words. Analysis also shows that the disaster tweets are relatively longer than the non-disaster tweets [8]. Figure 2 shows an overview of the top words associated with the two labels. It can be observed that most of the disaster-related words, such as fire, storm, death, and flood, were found in the disaster tweets, while the other tweets contain more commonly used words, such as going, love, new, etc. Some disaster-related words, such as fire, burning, and blown, were found in both the labels, albeit with different frequencies. This clearly indicates the possibility of the words having different contextual meanings, hence, the importance of understanding them through the use of contextual word embedding techniques.

3.2. Data Pre-Processing

The next stage involved pre-processing the tweets in order to reduce the "noise" in the social media data. This included the removal of hashtags, punctuation marks, special characters, and stop words, among others. Further, all upper-cases were converted into lower-cases, similar to the methods used in [8,9,25]. The pre-processed tweets served as an input to the data modeling stage (see Figure 1), specifically, for the contextual word embedding (i.e., transformers).

Non-disaster   Disaster

Figure 2. Overview of the top words for disaster and non-disaster tweets.

3.3. Contextual Word Embedding (Transformers)

Six transformer-based contextual word embedding techniques were examined in the current study, including BERT (both the base/small and large variants), ELECTRA, Bert Expert, Talking-Heads Attention, and TN-Bert. The BERT is the original transformer, and is a base model (i.e., other variants were extended/modified from this) (see Figure 3). There are two main variants in BERT, BERT-base/small and BERT-large, consisting of 12 and 24 transformer blocks, respectively. BERT is a multi-head attention-based (i.e., each head performs separate computations that are aggregated at the end) language model that employs the transformer encoders and decoders to learn the contextual relationships between words [28]. The encoder reads the text input, while the decoder produces a prediction. In BERT, the bidirectional transformer NN acts as the encoder, converting each tokenized word into its numerical vector in order to translate words that are semantically related to embedding that is numerically close [8]. It specifically uses the Wordpiece embedding input for tokens, along with positional (i.e., the position of each token in a given sequence) and segment (i.e., when sentence pairs are used as input) embedding for each token. The final embedding is usually the sum of all the embedding (i.e., token, positional, and segment). BERT uses the masked language modeling (MLM) approach, in which tokens are randomly replaced with [MASK], and a model is trained to reconstruct the tokens that have been replaced. The embedded numerical vectors are then fed into the Softmax, which makes a final prediction. In this study, however, the Softmax layer is replaced with a deep NN model that makes the final prediction, in line with previous studies [9,22]. Although BERT has been shown to produce good results on NLP tasks, it is however, impractical for use on resource-limited devices, as it is computationally expensive [26,30]. This resulted in the emergence of BERT variants, such as TN-Bert, which is a compressed version of the original BERT architecture, using tensor networks. Previous experiments have shown the variant to be 37% smaller and 22% faster than BERT-base [32].

On the other hand, ELECTRA is identical to BERT, except there has an additional linear layer between the embedding layer and encoder. Unlike other models that are based on MLM pre-training, ELECTRA is a discriminator that replaces random tokens with fake tokens, akin to the technique adopted in the generative adversarial network (GAN), in which a generator is optimized to train the discriminator [30]. This approach is considered less costly and more efficient. In fact, ELECTRA is often touted to be one of the best variants, performing with a fraction of the computing power of BERT [30].

Other lesser-known variants include Talking Head, or Talking-Heads Attention, which is a new variation on the multi-head attention used in BERT, using linear projections across the attention-heads, before and after the Softmax operation. This variant has been shown to have better performance in MLM tasks, as well as question/answer tasks, despite having a small number of additional parameters and computation ability [33]. On the other hand, the BertExpert was developed using a fine-tuned collection of BERTs that are trained on eight different datasets, comprising six Wikipedia and BooksCorpus datasets and two

PubMed datasets, to improve its performance in the NLP [28]. The pre-trained word embedding produced by the transformers is then used as input to the NN pipeline for disaster detection.

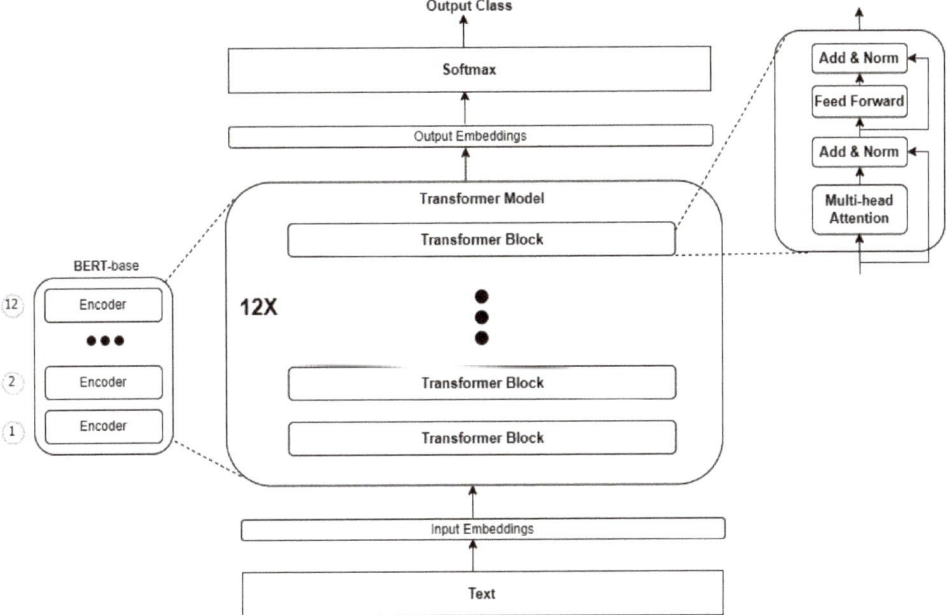

Figure 3. BERT-base architecture.

It is worth noting that since the variants were based on the BERT-base model, the word embedding technique does not differ from the base model; instead, the variants mainly differ in terms of simplicity (e.g., reduced number of layers). For example, the only difference regarding ELECTRA is the separation of the embedding size and the hidden size, compared to BERT [30].

3.4. Disaster Modeling

As the main focus of this paper is on the contextual word embedding techniques, this section presents only a brief overview of the DNN algorithms used. NN refers to a network in which all neurons in a layer are fully connected by weighted links to other neurons in the next layers. Inspired by the biological nervous system, NN generally has three layers, namely, input (i.e., receives and presents input pattern to the network), hidden (optional) (i.e., transforms input inside the network), and output (i.e., returns value corresponding to the prediction of the response variable). Activation functions define how the weighted sum of the input is transformed into an output, with popular functions, including Rectified Linear Activation (ReLU), Sigmoid, and Tanh, for the hidden layer, and Sigmoid and Softmax for the output layer. In this paper, the output of the transformer (e.g., BERT) encoders are fitted to NN with the following sequence of layers: a layer of 32 neurons, a dropout layer, and an output layer, with Sigmoid as the activation function [34–36]. It is worth noting that the NN model was used as a baseline for comparison with the DNN models.

CNN consists of convolution layers, a pooling layer, and fully connected output layers. The convolution layers apply filters with a specific kernel size to learn features from a given dataset, whereas the pooling layer serves as an intermediate layer to reduce the dimensions of the convolution layers output. The output layer contains activation functions to predict the final class of the input dataset [37]. We used a convolution layer with 256 filters and a window size of 3, 4, and 5-word vectors, with a kernel regularizer that applies an L1 regularization penalty with a value of 0.01, along with ReLU as the activation function, a pooling layer with max pooling (i.e., pool size = 4), and an output layer using Sigmoid.

On the other hand, LSTM can be viewed as an improvised version of RNN, consisting of a set of recurrently connected blocks (i.e., memory blocks) with three gates, that is, an input gate, a forget gate, and an output gate [38]. It is capable of learning order-dependence in sequence-prediction problems. We used an LSTM layer with 256 units and ReLU as the activation function. Sigmoid, on the other hand was used as the activation function for the output layer. The Bi-LSTM is similar to the LSTM; however, it processes input data in forward and backward directions [38]. The Bi-LSTM layer consists of 128 neurons, whereas the dense layer consists of 64 neurons. Tanh and ReLU were used as the activation functions for these two layers, respectively. Sigmoid was used for the output layer. All the NN models were executed using Adam as the optimizer, with a learning rate of 0.00003, and binary cross entropy as the loss function. Sigmoid was selected as the activation function for all the models, considering that the final prediction is based on binary labels. Table 3 shows the parameter setups used for all the models.

Table 3. Parameter setups for DNN models.

Models	Setup	Parameters
NN	Layers	3 (Neurons = 32)
	Dropout rate	0.1 *
	Activation Function	ReLU (Hidden) & Sigmoid (Output)
CNN	Layers	3 (Filters = 256; Kernel: 3–5)
	Dropout rate	0.3
	Activation Function	ReLU (Hidden) & Sigmoid (Output)
LSTM	Layers	3 (Neuron = 256)
	Dropout rate	0.3
	Activation Function	Tanh (Hidden) & Sigmoid (Output)
Bi-LSTM	Layers	LSTM(units = 128, activation = "tanh") Dense (units = 64, activation = "ReLU") Dense(units = 1, activation = "sigmoid")
	Dropout rate	0.3
	Activation Function	Tanh (LSTM), ReLU & Sigmoid

* Note: All the dropout rates were determined using the grid search approach, hence, the dissimilarity between NN and the rest of the models.

3.5. Evaluation and Experiments

Considering that Twitter disaster detection is a classification problem (i.e., disaster versus non-disaster), standard classification metrics were used to assess the effectiveness of the proposed models' performance [8,9,25]. These include precision, recall, F-score, accuracy and area under curve (AUC). As per the tweet labels that are binary in nature, a disaster (i.e., 1) is deemed as a positive class, while a non-disaster is a negative class. Therefore, true positive (TP) refers to the actual disaster tweets predicted as disasters, whereas false positive (FP) refers to tweets that are actually false, but predicted as true. A similar implication applies to true negative (TN) and false negative (FN). Using these notations, accuracy refers to the number of correctly predicted tweets among all of the tweets, and can be denoted using Equation (1) below:

$$Accuracy\ (Acc) = \frac{TP + TN}{TP + FN + TN + FP} \quad (1)$$

where TP—true positive; TN—true negative; FN—false negative; TN—true negative.

Precision reflects the proportion of TP over the total sample, whereas recall is the number of positive classes missed (i.e., proportion of the correctly identified TP over the sample predicted as positive by the model) [8,9]. Both these metrics can be determined using Equations (2) and (3) below.

$$Precision\ (P) = \frac{TP}{TP + FP} \quad (2)$$

$$Recall\ (R) = \frac{TP}{TP + TN} \quad (3)$$

F-score refers to the harmonic mean of recall and precision, and determined using Equation (4) below.

$$F - score = \frac{2 \cdot Precision \cdot Recall}{Precision \cdot Recall} \quad (4)$$

Finally, AUC provides an indication as to how well a model is capable of distinguishing between classes, with higher scores meaning the model works better at predicting positive classes as 1 (disaster) and negative classes as 0 (non disaster). It can be determined using Equation (5), as given below:

$$AUC = \frac{S_p - \frac{n_p(n_n+1)}{2}}{n_p n_n} \quad (5)$$

where S_p indicates the sum of all positive samples, n_p indicates the number of positive examples, and n_n indicates the number of negative samples.

All five metrics return a score between 0 and 1, with a higher score indicating a better detection/classification performance.

The training and testing were accomplished using an 80–20 split. Table 4 below depicts the descriptive statistics for the split data used for training (i.e., 80% = 6090). The average length of tweets was 14.9, while 7273 words have frequency >1. Figure 4 shows the word length distribution for disaster and non-disaster tweets. It can be observed that the disaster tweets are generally longer than non-disaster tweets, although most of them are between a word length of 10 to 20.

Table 4. Descriptive statistics for 80% training data.

Characteristics	n
Total training data	6090
Total positive data (or disaster tweets)	2617
Total unique words	27,083
Total unique words with frequency >1	7253
Avg. length of tweets	14.9
Median length of tweets	15.0
Maximum length of tweets	31
Minimum length of tweets	1

All the experiments and modeling were accomplished using Python 3.7.12 (with sklearn library) and TensorFlow 2.7.0, with a GPU NVIDIA Tesla P100.

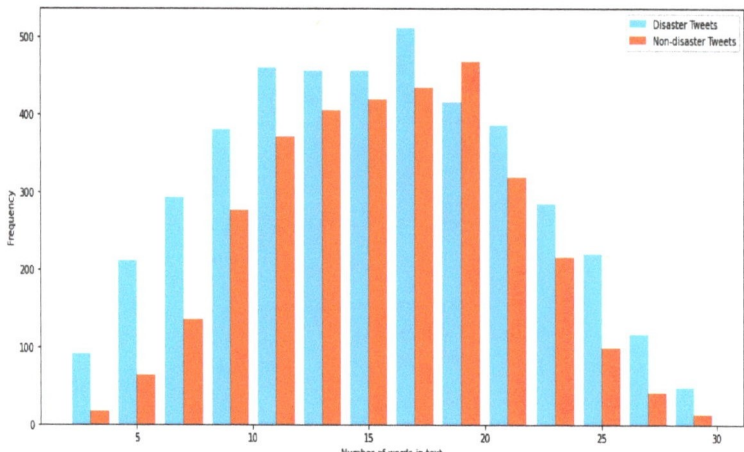

Figure 4. Word length distribution for disaster and non-disaster tweets (training data).

4. Results and Discussion

Table 5 depicts the results of the experiments for each of the ensemble models.

Table 5. Ensemble model performance results.

Model	Transformers	Accuracy	Precision	Recall	F-Score	AUC
NN	$BERT_{Large}$	0.82	0.83	0.73	0.78	0.86
	$BERT_{Small}$	0.82	0.81	0.76	0.78	0.88
	ELECTRA	0.83	0.80	0.79	0.79	0.89
	TN-BERT	0.82	0.87	0.69	0.77	0.88
	BERT Expert	0.83	0.81	0.77	0.79	0.89
	Talking Head	0.83	0.86	0.71	0.78	0.88
LSTM	$BERT_{Large}$	0.82	0.88	0.67	0.76	0.88
	$BERT_{Small}$	0.81	0.87	0.67	0.76	0.88
	ELECTRA	0.83	0.85	0.74	0.79	0.89
	TN-BERT	0.82	0.88	0.67	0.76	0.87
	BERT Expert	0.81	0.76	0.81	0.79	0.89
	Talking Head	0.82	0.84	0.72	0.77	0.88
CNN	$BERT_{Large}$	0.83	0.89	0.68	0.77	0.88
	$BERT_{Small}$	0.79	0.72	0.83	0.77	0.88
	ELECTRA	0.82	0.78	0.82	0.80	0.89
	TN-BERT	0.82	0.92	0.64	0.75	0.87
	BERT Expert	0.84	0.91	0.69	0.78	0.89
	Talking Head	0.83	0.87	0.72	0.79	0.88

Table 5. Cont.

Model	Transformers	Accuracy	Precision	Recall	F-Score	AUC
BiLSTM	$BERT_{Large}$	0.83	0.87	0.70	0.78	0.88
	$BERT_{Small}$	0.80	0.79	0.74	0.76	0.88
	ELECTRA	0.82	0.79	0.81	0.80	0.90
	TN-BERT	0.83	0.84	0.74	0.79	0.88
	BERT Expert	0.81	0.75	0.83	0.79	0.89
	Talking Head	0.84	0.87	0.74	0.80	0.89

The results generally indicate that all the models consistently perform well, with F-scores ranging from 76% to 80%, and accuracy scores from 79% to 83%. A similar observation was noted for AUC, which ranged between 86% and 90%. This supports previous findings showing that transformer-based contextual word embedding techniques improve disaster detection on social media [8,9,14,23–25]. This is probably due to the nature of the transformers, that is, the techniques take context of words into consideration, hence their ability to interpret ambiguous words in a sentence supersede the context-free embedding techniques, such as Word2Vec and GloVe [2,19,21].

Although the performance scores are only marginally different, an overall comparison between the ensembles revealed Bi-LSTM to yield the best performance across all five metrics, with scores ranging from 70% to 90%. Bi-LSTM is deemed to be an improvement over the previous DNN models, including LSTM (which is an improvement of RNN). Although this does not necessarily result in better detection performance, the bidirectional text processing employed by Bi-LSTM may also have contributed to its good performance, akin to BERT and its variants. A similar pattern was reflected by the authors of [9], who worked on the same dataset using BERT-small, for which the authors reported a slightly better performance with an F-score of 83% and accuracy of 85.6%.

Interestingly, the simpler and less complicated BERT variants are observed to yield comparable, and even superior results, to the original BERT (i.e., $BERT_{Large}$ and $BERT_{Small}$). The top two variants that yielded consistently good performance across all the metrics and NN models include ELECTRA and Talking Head, with the best performance noted in combination with Bi-LSTM (F-score$_{ELECTRA}$ = 80%; Accuracy$_{ELECTRA}$ = 82%; F-score$_{TalkingHead}$ = 80%; Accuracy$_{TalkingHead}$ = 84%). Table 6 provides a few sample tweets and the classification results for both of these models. To the best of our knowledge, these variants have yet to be explored by other researchers, including those focusing on disaster detection and management. Nevertheless, our findings, support the results reported by the respective developers, in which the variants were notably found to outperform most of the transformers, including the original BERT [29,32]. This finding is deemed novel, and promises to offer a feasible and cost-effective solution in detecting disasters via social media, without requiring intensive and expensive resources.

Table 6. Sample detection results for Bi-LSTM.

Sample Tweets	Prediction		True Label
	Talking Head	ELECTRA	
The summer program I worked for went the city pool we had to evacuate because one of my kids left a surprise. @jimmyfallon #WorstSummerJob	1	0	0
You are the avalanche. One world away. My make believing. While I'm wide awake.	0	0	0
Dorman 917-033 Ignition Knock (Detonation) Sensor Connector http://t.co/WxCes39ZTe http://t.co/PyGKSSSCFR	0	0	1

Table 6. Cont.

Sample Tweets	Prediction		True Label
	Talking Head	ELECTRA	
Christian Attacked by Muslims at the Temple Mount after Waving Israeli Flag via Pamela Geller- ... http://t.co/wGWiQmICL1	1	1	1
70 Years After Atomic Bombs Japan Still Struggles With War Past: The anniversary of the devastation wrought b ... http://t.co/vFCtrzaOk2	1	1	1
You are equally as scared cause this somehow started to heal you fill your wounds that you once thought were permanent.	0	0	0
@abcnews UK scandal of 2009 caused major upheaval to Parliamentary expenses with subsequent sackings and prison. What are we waiting for?	0	0	0
Expect gusty winds heavy downpours and lightning moving northeast toward VA now. http://t.co/jyxafD4knK	1	1	1
August 5: Your daily horoscope: A relationship upheaval over the next few months may be disruptive but in the ... http://t.co/gk4uNPZNhN	0	0	0
@BattleRoyaleMod when they die they just get teleported into somewhere middle of ocean and stays trapped in there unless they decides 2/6	0	0	0

5. Conclusions, Limitation and Future Direction

This study explored the use of transformer-based contextual word embedding with deep NN models to detect disaster-related communication on Twitter. The popular BERT model, along with its lesser-known variants, were explored by combining them with CNN, NN, LSTM, and Bi-LSTM. Experimental results show all the ensemble models to yield consistently good results, with F-scores ranging from 76% to 80%. Although only marginally different, ELECTRA and Talking Head variants produced the best results when combined with Bi-LSTM. Our results added value to the existing literature, as we showed that disaster detection is effective and efficient with the use of simpler and less complicated variants.

This study only used a single Twitter dataset ($n = 7613$). Additional experiments and analyses involving a larger dataset, and comparisons with similar datasets, including those from other social media platforms, such as Facebook, would be beneficial. This will help to establish the performance of the variants and NN models in detecting disaster through textual communications. Further, the study is also limited to communications in English. Social media platform users are diversified, with communication taking place in various languages, including Chinese, Hindi, and French, among others. Transformers, such as BERT, provide support in processing multi-language texts; hence, future studies should explore the performance of these techniques by using datasets that are not limited to English. Finally, the study is also limited by using a single modality (i.e., text). Communications on social media platforms often include images and videos as well; therefore, future studies can explore detecting disaster-related communication using a multi-modal input.

Author Contributions: Conceptualization, V.B.; Formal analysis, C.L.L. and R.L.; Funding acquisition, J.P.; Methodology, Z.S., L.L.T. and Y.F.; Project administration, V.B.; Draft revision: V.B., C.L.L. and Z.S.; Writing—original draft, V.B. All authors have read and agreed to the published version of the manuscript.

Funding: This research received no external funding.

Institutional Review Board Statement: Not applicable.

Informed Consent Statement: Not applicable.

Data Availability Statement: The data are available on Kaggle (https://www.kaggle.com/c/nlp-getting-started/data?select=train.csv, accessed on 23 December 2021).

Conflicts of Interest: The authors declare no conflict of interest.

References

1. DiCarlo, M.F.; Berglund, E.Z. Connected communities improve hazard response: An agent-based model of social media behaviors during hurricanes. *Sustain. Cities Soc.* **2021**, *69*, 102836. [CrossRef]
2. Roy, P.K.; Kumar, A.; Singh, J.P.; Dwivedi, Y.K.; Rana, N.P.; Raman, R. Disaster related social media content processing for sustainable cities. *Sustain. Cities Soc.* **2021**, *75*, 103363. [CrossRef]
3. Rhodan, M. Please Send Help: Hurricane Harvey Victims Turn to Twitter and Facebook. 2017. Available online: http://time.com/4921961/hurricane-harvey-twitter-facebook-social-media/ (accessed on 13 February 2022).
4. Son, J.; Lee, H.K.; Jin, S.; Lee, J. Content features of tweets for effective communication during disasters: A media synchronicity theory perspective. *Int. J. Inf. Manag.* **2019**, *45*, 56–68. [CrossRef]
5. Zhai, W.; Peng, Z.R.; Yuan, F. Examine the effects of neighborhood equity on disaster situational awareness: Harness machine learning and geotagged Twitter data. *Int. J. Disaster Risk Reduct.* **2021**, *48*, 101611. [CrossRef]
6. Karimiziarani, M.; Jafarzadegan, K.; Abbaszadeh, P.; Shao, W.; Moradkhani, H. Hazard risk awareness and disaster management: Extracting the information content of twitter data. *Sustain. Cities Soc.* **2022**, *77*, 103577. [CrossRef]
7. Robertson, B.W.; Johnson, M.; Murthy, D.; Smith, W.R.; Stephes, K.K. Using a combination of human insights and 'deep learning' for real-time disaster communication. *Prog. Disaster Sci.* **2019**, *2*, 100030. [CrossRef]
8. Song, G.; Huang, D.A. Sentiment-Aware Contextual Model for Real-Time Disaster Prediction Using Twitter Data. *Future Internet* **2021**, *13*, 163. [CrossRef]
9. Chanda, A.K. Efficacy of BERT embeddings on predicting disaster from Twitter data. *arXiv* **2021**, arXiv:2108.10698.
10. Chen, Z.; Lim, S. Social media data-based typhoon disaster assessment. *Int. J. Disaster Risk Reduct.* **2021**, *64*, 102482. [CrossRef]
11. Resch, B.; Usländer, F.; Havas, C. Combining machine-learning topic models and spatiotemporal analysis of social media data for disaster footprint and damage assessment. *Cartogr. Geogr. Inf. Sci.* **2018**, *45*, 362–376. [CrossRef]
12. Ragini, J.R.; Anand, P.R.; Bhaskar, V. Big data analytics for disaster response and recovery through sentiment analysis. *Int. J. Inf. Manag.* **2018**, *42*, 13–24. [CrossRef]
13. Neppalli, V.K.; Caragea, C.; Squicciarini, A.; Tapia, A.; Stehle, S. Sentiment analysis during hurricane sandy in emergency response. *Int. J. Disaster Risk Reduct.* **2017**, *21*, 213–222. [CrossRef]
14. Malla, S.; Alphonse, P. COVID-19 outbreak: An ensemble pre-trained deep learning model for detecting informative tweets. *Appl. Soft Comput.* **2021**, *107*, 107495. [CrossRef]
15. Nazer, T.H.; Morstatter, F.; Dani, H.; Liu, H. Finding requests in social media for disaster relief. In Proceedings of the 2016 IEEE/ACM International Conference on Advances in Social Networks Analysis and Mining (ASONAM), San Francisco, CA, USA, 18–21 August 2016; pp. 1410–1413.
16. Alam, F.; Ofli, F.; Imran, M. Descriptive and visual summaries of disaster events using artificial intelligence techniques: Case studies of Hurricanes Harvey, Irma, and Maria. *Behav. Inf. Technol.* **2019**, *39*, 288–318. [CrossRef]
17. Basu, M.; Shandilya, A.; Khosla, P.; Ghosh, K.; Ghosh, S. Extracting resource needs and availabilities from microblogs for aiding post-disaster relief operations. *IEEE Trans. Comput. Soc. Syst.* **2019**, *6*, 604–618. [CrossRef]
18. Mohanty, S.D.; Biggers, B.; Ahmed, S.S.; Pourebrahim, N.; Goldstein, E.B.; Bunch, R.; Chi, G.; Sadri, F.; McCoy, T.; Cosby, A. A multi-modal approach towards mining social media data during natural disasters—A case study of Hurricane Irma. *Int. J. Disaster Risk Reduct.* **2021**, *54*, 102032. [CrossRef]
19. Yu, M.; Huang, Q.; Qin, H.; Scheele, C.; Yang, C. Deep learning for real-time social media text classification for situation awareness–using hurricanes sandy, harvey, and irma as case studies. *Int. J. Digit. Earth* **2019**, *12*, 1230–1247. [CrossRef]
20. Kumar, A.; Singh, J.P. Location reference identification from tweets during emergencies: A deep learning approach. *Int. J. Disaster Risk Reduct.* **2019**, *33*, 365–375. [CrossRef]
21. Kumar, A.; Singh, J.P.; Dwivedi, Y.K.; Rana, N.P. A deep multi-modal neural network for informative twitter content classification during emergencies. *Ann. Oper. Res.* **2020**, 1–32. [CrossRef]
22. Madichetty, S.; Muthukumarasamy, S.; Jayadev, P. Multi-modal classification of twitter data during disasters for humanitarian response. *J. Ambient. Intell. Humaniz. Comput.* **2021**, *12*, 10223–10237. [CrossRef]
23. Naaz, S.; Ul-Abedin, Z.; Rizvi, D.R. Sequence Classification of Tweets with Transfer Learning via BERT in the Field of Disaster Management. *EAI Endorsed Trans. Scalable Inf. Syst.* **2021**, *8*, e8. [CrossRef]
24. Wang, Z.; Zhu, T.; Mai, S. Disaster Detector on Twitter Using Bidirectional Encoder Representation from Transformers with Keyword Position Information. In Proceedings of the 2020 IEEE 2nd International Conference on Civil Aviation Safety and Information Technology, Weihai, China, 14–16 October 2020; pp. 474–477.
25. Deb, S.; Chanda, A.K. Comparative analysis of contextual and context-free embeddings in disaster prediction from Twitter data. *Mach. Learn. Appl.* **2022**, *7*, 100253. [CrossRef]
26. Qui, X.; Sun, T.; Xu, Y.; Shao, Y.; Huang, X. Pre-trained Models for Natural Language Processing: A Survey. *arXiv* **2021**, arXiv:2003.08271.
27. Behl, S.; Rao, A.; Aggarwal, S.; Chadha, S.; Pannu, H.S. Twitter for disaster relief through sentiment analysis for COVID-19 and natural hazard crises. *Int. J. Disaster Risk Reduct.* **2021**, *55*, 102101. [CrossRef]

28. Devlin, J.; Chang, M.-W.; Lee, K.; Toutanova, K. *BERT: Pre-Training of Deep Bidirectional Transformers for BERT: Pre-training of Deep Bidirectional Transformers for*; NAACL-HLT 2019; Association for Computational Linguistics: Minneapolis, MI, USA, 2019; pp. 4171–4186.
29. Maharani, W. Sentiment Analysis during Jakarta Flood for Emergency Responses and Situational Awareness in Disaster Management using BERT. In Proceedings of the 2020 8th International Conference on Information and Communication Technology (ICoICT), Yogyakarta, Indonesia, 24–26 June 2020; pp. 1–5.
30. Clark, K.; Luong, M.T.; Le, Q.V.; Manning, C.D. ELECTRA: Pre-training Text Encoders as Discriminators Rather Than Generators. *arXiv* **2020**, arXiv:2003.10555.
31. Bhuvaneswari, A.; Thomas, J.T.J.; Kesavan, P. Embedded Bi-directional GRU and LSTM Learning Models to Predict Disasters on Twitter Data. *Procedia Comput. Sci.* **2019**, *165*, 511–516. [CrossRef]
32. Abadi, M.; Ashish, A.; Barham, P.; Eugene, B.; Chen, Z.; Davis, A.; Dean, J. TensorFlow: TN_BERT. 2021. Available online: https://tfhub.dev/google/tn_bert/1 (accessed on 28 December 2021).
33. Shazeer, N.; Lan, Z.Z.; Cheng, Y.; Ding, N.; Hou, L. Talking Heads Attention. *arXiv* **2020**, arXiv:2003.02436v1.
34. Zhao, Y.; Ren, S.; Kurthscde, J. Synchronization of coupled memristive competitive BAM neural networks with different time scales. *Neurocomputing* **2021**, *427*, 110–117. [CrossRef]
35. Alqatawna, A.; Álvarez, A.M.R.; García-Moreno, S.S.C. Comparison of Multivariate Regression Models and Artificial Neural Networks for Prediction Highway Traffic Accidents in Spain: A Case Study. *Transp. Res. Procedia* **2021**, *58*, 277–284. [CrossRef]
36. Bre, F.; Gimenez, J.; Fachinotti, V. Prediction of wind pressure coefficients on building surfaces using Artificial Neural Networks. *Energy Build.* **2018**, *158*, 1429–1441. [CrossRef]
37. Zhang, L.; Wang, S.; Liu, B. Deep learning for sentiment analysis: A survey. *WIREs Data Min. Knowl. Discov.* **2018**, *8*, e1253. [CrossRef]
38. Jang, B.; Kim, M.; Harerimana, G.; Kang, S.-U.; Kim, J. Bi-LSTM Model to Increase Accuracy in Text Classification: Combining Word2vec CNN and Attention Mechanism. *Appl. Sci.* **2020**, *10*, 5841. [CrossRef]

 mathematics

Article

Imbalanced Multimodal Attention-Based System for Multiclass House Price Prediction

Yansong Li *,†, Paula Branco † and Hanxiang Zhang

School of Electrical Engineering and Computer Science, Faculty of Engineering, University of Ottawa, Ottawa, ON K1N 6N5, Canada
* Correspondence: yli627@uottawa.ca
† These authors contributed equally to this work.

Abstract: House price prediction is an important problem for individuals, companies, organizations, and governments. With a vast amount of diversified and multimodal data available about houses, the predictive models built should seek to make the best use of these data. This leads to the complex problem of how to effectively use multimodal data for house price prediction. Moreover, this is also a context suffering from class imbalance, an issue that cannot be disregarded. In this paper, we propose a new algorithm for addressing these problems: the imbalanced multimodal attention-based system (IMAS). The IMAS makes use of an oversampling strategy that operates on multimodal data, namely using text, numeric, categorical, and boolean data types. A self-attention mechanism is embedded to leverage the usage of neighboring information that can benefit the model's performance. Moreover, the self-attention mechanism allows for the determination of the features that are the most relevant and adapts the weights used according to that information when performing inference. Our experimental results show the clear advantage of the IMAS, which outperforms all the competitors tested. The analysis of the weights obtained through the self-attention mechanism provides insights into the features' relevance and also supports the importance of using this mechanism in the predictive model.

Keywords: imbalance; multimodal; attention; house price prediction

MSC: 68T01; 68T07; 68T50

Citation: Li, Y.; Branco, P.; Zhang, H. Imbalanced Multimodal Attention-Based System for Multiclass House Price Prediction. *Mathematics* **2023**, *11*, 113. https://doi.org/10.3390/math11010113

Academic Editor: Daniel-Ioan Curiac

Received: 13 November 2022
Revised: 3 December 2022
Accepted: 21 December 2022
Published: 27 December 2022

Copyright: © 2022 by the authors. Licensee MDPI, Basel, Switzerland. This article is an open access article distributed under the terms and conditions of the Creative Commons Attribution (CC BY) license (https://creativecommons.org/licenses/by/4.0/).

1. Introduction

The problem of predicting house prices is relevant, and solving it has the potential to benefit both individuals buying homes and house sellers. Traditional models for house price prediction use exclusively numerical attributes. These attributes contain important information for predictive models, including the number of rooms or the number of floors. However, they usually disregard other information that is nowadays more frequently available in house descriptions. In this paper, we tackle a multiclass house prediction problem by developing a solution that uses multiple modes of data.

The first key characteristic of the problem we are tackling is related to the use of multimodal data. Thus, in the first stage, we need to determine how to extract and use all the different modes of the features. Moreover, we also need to determine if all features are equally important and useful and should be considered in the model's development. Many companies and sellers provide short descriptions of houses, making them available through advertising platforms. This text contains potentially important information that can be used together with other types of data to obtain a better prediction of the house price. As far as we know, multimodal house price prediction [1] is limited to using satellite images and numerical data as two modalities for price prediction. However, in most cases, satellite image data are unavailable, and concatenating heterogeneous numerical types of data as the same modality fails to capture the inherent structural information of the different numerical data types. We propose a multimodal attention mechanism to explore the underlying structural information of the text data and heterogeneous numerical data, introducing a "microscopic" multimodal learning paradigm in this way.

A second important characteristic of our problem concerns the imbalance typically present in this setting. We expect that the majority of houses will have a price that is closer to the average value, with a very small number having a price that is very high or low. This imbalance in the distribution of the classes may cause severe issues for the learning algorithm, especially if our goal is to be more accurate in predicting the most or least expensive house prices. We take into consideration this challenge that is naturally present in this domain and propose an oversampling strategy that is applied to all the data modalities.

Our main goal is to solve a multiclass prediction problem with an imbalance in the target class through a multimodal attention-based framework. To achieve this, we propose the IMAS, a solution that is able to address the class imbalance problem while using multimodal data and embedding an attention mechanism to ensure the best adaptation to the multiple features used. Multiple developments have emerged with the appearance of the self-attention mechanism in the transformer architecture. In particular, important multimodal applications have appeared in the fields of vision and language (e.g., [2,3]) and vision and audio (e.g., [4,5]). However, these applications do not focus on a "microscopic multimodal view", where not only the usage of text data and heterogeneous numeric data is considered but also numeric heterogeneous data are envisioned as different modalities. Moreover, these solutions have not yet been applied in a house price prediction context. Through an extensive experimental comparison, we compare the IMAS with several alternative solutions and show the clear advantage of our proposed system.

1.1. Problem Definition

We tackle the problem of house price prediction by using multiple feature modes, including numeric, boolean, categorical, and textual attributes. Let each one of these feature modes be represented by $X = \{X_{text}, X_{bool}, X_{cate}, X_{num}\}$, where X represents the aggregated set of all features, X_{text} represents the features to be extracted from the house description text, and the remaining X_{bool}, X_{cate}, and X_{num} represent the sets of the boolean, numeric, and categorical features extracted from the houses, respectively. We consider the house price, the problem's target variable, as a multiclass variable containing six different classes that correspond to six different ranges of house prices. We represent the target variable by Y. Our goal is to approximate an unknown function $Y = f(X_{text}, X_{bool}, X_{cate}, X_{num})$ based on a training dataset $\{\langle \mathbf{x}_i, y_i \rangle\}_{i=1}^{n}$. The house prices are represented by six different classes, i.e., $y_i \in \{class_1, class_2, \cdots, class_6\}$, which means we face a multiclass problem with six classes. Moreover, the class distribution is not balanced, i.e., some classes are well represented by many examples in the available data, whereas others are scarcely represented and have a much smaller number of examples.

1.2. Intuition for our Solution

By integrating multiple features into the construction of a model, we need to take into account the fact that we may be using irrelevant features and that some features may be more important than others. Thus, to effectively use all the available information, we must focus our attention on the most relevant characteristics of the data. To achieve this, we use the self-attention mechanism.

Being the current de facto method for building associations between data, the self-attention mechanism [6] can effectively analyze long-term sequential or structural information and dynamically assign weights from a global perspective to different data representations based on downstream task information. Accordingly, self-attention has also demonstrated advantages in more complex multimodal domains, especially in perceptual problems combining vision and text [7,8]. However, in some practical numerical analysis tasks, such as house price prediction, most prior works [1,9] only concatenate various numerical values as a "modal" to produce attention computations with other modals such as text and images and thus might not be able to capture all meaningful relationships between different types of numerical values. In addition, different numeric data types, such as boolean, discrete, and continuous variables, are inherently heterogeneous and permutation invariant. Simply concatenating different types of numerical values cannot capture the underlying structural information.

To overcome the limitations of the existing house price prediction pipeline, we propose the IMAS with multimodal attention, which introduces numerical-oriented multimodal learning that aims to explore the underlying structural information and produce a weighted fusion of different numerical values in an end-to-end fashion. In addition, we also provide a corresponding multimodal data augmentation technique that generates corresponding multimodal data based on house prices.

1.3. Main Contributions

The key aspect of our proposed IMAS is its adaptability to multimodal learning from both a macro perspective (text and numerical data) and a micro perspective (numerical, categorical, and boolean data), which are inherently heterogeneous and play different roles in house price prediction. The main contributions of this paper are as follows:

- we propose the IMAS, a new system to tackle the problem of multiclass house price prediction that is capable of handling multimodal data (textual, numerical, categorical, and boolean) while dealing with the class imbalance problem;
- we provide an extensive set of experiments, where we compare our proposed system with several alternative ways of dealing with the multimodal data;
- we show the advantage of the proposed system on a recent and large dataset that we collected and preprocessed;
- we provide an analysis of the IMAS in terms of the impact on the results of the different modes of features;
- we provide the code for reproducing our experiments to the research community at the following repository: https://github.com/Jackline97/Multimodal_House_Price. (accessed on 1 December 2022).

1.4. Organization

This paper is organized as follows. Section 2 presents an overview of the most relevant literature for house price prediction, covering the classical statistical-based hedonic models, standard machine learning models, deep learning-based models, and also models using more advanced Natural Language Processing (NLP) techniques. In Section 3, we describe our proposed IMAS system, providing details of its different components. Section 4 provides the experimental settings and describes the dataset used and Section 5 analyzes and discusses the results of our experiments. Finally, Section 6 concludes the paper.

2. Literature Review

This section provides an extensive overview of the three core topics related to our work: the statistical-based hedonic price models, machine learning models, and models that specifically make use of natural language processing techniques to tackle the house price prediction problem.

2.1. Statistical-Based Hedonic Models

Research on house prices has been an important topic since the 1970s, a time when the approaches used were based on traditional statistical methods originating from the economics field. In 1974, Rosen [10] presented the Hedonic Price Theory, a statistical method that has since become well known and widely used. This popular theory uses a set of attributes that can explain the house price for representing a house [11]. These attributes, such as the number of bedrooms or the number of bathrooms, are not equally important for determining the house price. Instead, they are ranked depending on their impact on the utility function of a house. This model assumes that the house's sale price is achieved through a market balance between home buyers' and sellers' utilities, given that both aim to maximize the house's utility function. The initial hedonic model took into account only the house's characteristics, disregarding other external factors [10]. Still, the hedonic model changed and evolved, and further external factors were included in the model for representing the house price. This was motivated by the confirmation that considering solely the initial characteristics proposed was insufficient for representing the house price. In effect, other external properties, such as the house's location, also affect the property value. Thus, given the strong relationship between the house price and its location, the hedonic price model was updated to also include the house's location as an attribute [12].

However, the development of a hedonic regression model has multiple constraints, which can lead to a diversity of relevant drawbacks. For instance, it requires a team of experts to manually study the data to develop a mathematical model. However, this is a time-consuming and expensive process. Moreover, this model is not able to handle nonlinearity [11] well and it does not allow for the use of unstructured textual information such as description texts.

More recently, the extraction of visual features and their usage as a complementary source of information for the models have also been considered. Some research works have shown that using visual information to represent the scenic characteristics of a house and its neighborhood has great potential for estimating the house price (e.g., [13–15]).

2.2. Standard Machine Learning Models

Many standard machine learning algorithms, ranging from the popular random forest algorithm to the boosting solution algorithm and support vector machine (SVM), to name a few, have been explored for predicting house prices. The majority of the proposed solutions use exclusively numerical house attributes.

SVMs were applied in the context of house price prediction for a large city in China [16]. Both a default SVM and an SVM using particle swarm optimization (PSO) to determine the best SVM parameters were tested, with the latter producing the best overall results for the predictive task. Random forest models were compared with the hedonic model and ordinary least squares (OLS) [17]. This comparison was carried out with house data from South Korea and showed a clear advantage of the random forest models for this task, which were able to better capture the nonlinearity of the house price prediction problem. House data from Karachi, a city in Pakistan, were used in a different study [18] that assessed the performance of a boosting algorithm to address the house price prediction task. In this case, the extreme gradient boosting (XGBoost) algorithm provided good results. Another study [19] compared multiple regression techniques for predicting house prices, including multiple linear regression, ridge regression, LASSO, elastic net, gradient boosting, and AdaBoost regression, on a public dataset (https://geodacenter.github.io/data-and-lab/KingCounty-HouseSales2015/ (accessed on 28 November 2022)) containing house sale prices from King County, USA. It was found that the gradient boosting algorithm provided the best solution.

However, the development of models for house price prediction has not been constrained by standard machine learning models. Moreover, other sources of data beyond numerical data have been explored and used to solve this task. The following sections discuss both the other models and the data sources that have been used in this domain.

2.3. Models Using Deep Learning Techniques

With the increasing volume of data, deep learning models have become a popular solution, typically displaying good results. Several deep learning solutions have been tested for tackling house price prediction.

Some of the proposed deep learning solutions involve using image data as a complementary source of features for the models. For instance, Zhao et al. [20] developed a new model that combines a convolutional neural network (CNN) and an XGBoost model. This was accomplished by replacing the CNN's last layer with the XGBoost model. The CNN extracts features from the images and the XGBoost algorithm predicts the house price using all the processed features (from images and numerical data). The proposed solution outperformed the multilayer perceptron and k-nearest neighbor models [20]. The system presented by Wang et al. [1] used three sources of data (satellite images, house transaction data, and public facility data) to extract house features, which were then processed by an attention mechanism to provide a price prediction.

Some proposed systems rely on a combination of standard machine learning algorithms and neural networks. This is the case for the work proposed by Varma et al. [21], where linear regression, random forest, and neural networks were incorporated for house price prediction. This was achieved by feeding the outputs of the linear regression and random forest models into the neural network as the input features. Other solutions exist that apply other neural networks, such as recurrent neural networks (RNNs) or long short-term memory (LSTM). For instance, Chen et al. [22] collected numerical features from four large cities in China, which were then used to train RNN and LSTM models. The results showed that the RNN and stacked LSTM outperformed the well-known autoregressive integrated moving average (ARIMA) model.

In the field of deep learning, other authors have sought to address the imbalance problem through specialized neural networks. For instance, in [23], a probabilistic neural network model was proposed that took into account the unbalanced representation of the problem classes to address the small sample and class imbalance problems in a medical data context. Another solution was presented in [24] involving classification through the use of neural-like structures in the geometric transformations model. This proposal also addressed the problem of class imbalance via a specialized model based on neural structures. Still, these methods were not applied to the house price prediction problem, nor did they consider the use of multiple modalities of data.

Although some advancements have been made in the particular domain of house price prediction, this is still an application area where research is in its infancy, especially with regard to the use of more advanced models and the use of other sources of data besides traditional numerical data. In this respect, in the next section, we discuss the research carried out in this domain that uses the textual information of houses.

2.4. Models Using Natural Language Processing Techniques

Besides traditional models and models using deep learning and processing images, there is another source of information that may help in the prediction of house prices. This alternative source of information is text and it can be found on multiple platforms, such as websites advertising houses for sale. Some researchers have started to explore house price prediction by applying text mining to house description data. An example is the work of Stevens [25] where multiple naïve Bayes, SVM, gradient boosting, and other methods were employed to solve the task of house price prediction. This researcher processed house description data using text mining techniques, including the term frequency-inverse document frequency (TF-IDF) and bag-of-words models. The results indicated a positive impact of using the information obtained from house description data, showing the potential of also using textual data for this problem.

Abdallah et al. [26] studied house price prediction by applying text mining to the titles and descriptions in real estate classifieds. A two-stage model was proposed using the structured numerical features in the first stage and the features obtained from the titles and descriptions in the second stage. Keywords were extracted using the TF-IDF technique and the authors showed that adding this information had a positive impact on the house price prediction model. This work confirmed the potential for considering the descriptive texts associated with houses to predict their prices. Two years later, Abdallah [27] extended the previous work by developing a system that identified the most influential keywords in real estate classifieds. Continuing the described trend of identifying relevant words for house price prediction, in 2020, Guo et al. [28] highlighted and ranked 29 Chinese keywords as critical data that could have a great influence on house prices. Three standard learning models (the generalized linear regression model, the elastic net model, and the random forest model) were evaluated. This work confirmed previous findings related to the importance of extracting relevant keywords from unstructured text data that can have a positive impact on the performance of the model. Still, alternative frameworks such as BERT were not included in any of the described research works.

Recently, text classification using deep learning has exhibited significant growth, with the newly developed solutions surpassing standard machine learning algorithms [29]. However, even though the new techniques have shown great potential, there is still a research gap concerning the study of these techniques in the particular application domain of house price prediction. This paper targets this gap by providing a study on alternative solutions for house price prediction that use both the more traditional numerical features and the description texts of houses. Instead of focusing on extracting relevant keywords, we seek to use the entirety of the description data from which features are extracted. Our goal is to show which techniques work better in this setting while taking into account the specificity of the domain, which includes imbalance domains.

2.5. Models Using Multimodal Data and Self-Attention

As human perception is inherently based on the multimodal environment, multimodal learning has been a fundamental step toward building comprehensive perceptual-cognitive abilities, thus contributing to more practical applications in our daily lives. Thanks to the exponential development of computation resources and over-parameterized deep learning models, the transformer established together with the self-attention mechanism has demonstrated tremendous potential in the multimodal learning domain, such as VideoBERT [2], VisualBERT [3], ImageBERT [30], and CLIP [8] in the vision and language field and AV-HuBERT [5] and LiRA [4] in the vision and audio field. These prior works introduced scalable multimodal fusion and translation paradigms that can robustly connect heterogeneous multimodal information based on downstream task supervision signals. To interpret the robustness of transformer architecture in multimodal learning, recent studies in the graph representation learning field [31,32] have shown that self-attention is intuitively a graph-style modeling, which can model arbitrary input sequences (multimodal information) as a fully-connected graph, thus helping transformers to adapt to a modality agnostic pipeline that is compatible with various modalities.

An area of research that is related to our application is the field of affective computing and sentiment analysis [33], where emotional information is detected, which is critical for many application domains. In the case of house price prediction, the presence of emotions in the text can lead to advancements, for instance, in the personalization of recommendations or the profiling of sellers or buyers. Still, we could not find any works in the particular context of house price prediction that carried out sentiment analysis. Some works exist, such as the "sentic blending" approach [34], which seeks to interpret the conceptual and affective information in natural language using different modalities. The authors proposed a scalable methodology for fusing multiple data modalities using a multidimensional vector space. The MuSe-Toolbox [35] is another interesting work where a Python toolkit is presented that creates multiple continuous and discrete emotion gold standards. In this sense, this research direction is also connected with our work.

However, multimodal learning has yet to be sufficiently explored in the house price prediction domain. To the best of our knowledge, only Wang et al. [1] have utilized the self-attention mechanism to produce multimodal learning on house price prediction. Nevertheless, their multimodal learning is based on abundant data resources from house satellite images and fails to capture the underlying structural information of the numerical data, which requires significant time and resources to collect data. In this work, we propose a generalizable multimodal attention framework to adapt the most common numerical-

3. Our Proposed Solution: The IMAS Framework

In this section, we present our solution for multimodal house price prediction, the IMAS framework. We discuss the key components of the system, but first, we begin with the introduction of some of the notations we use.

Let $\{(X_1, y_1), ..., (X_N, y_N)\}$ be a set of N samples with multimodal properties, where X_n refers to the n-th sample and y_n refers to the corresponding house price properties or labels. We consider the existence of four different modes in our data (text, boolean, categorical, and numerical) and denote by $X_n = \{X_{text}, X_{bool}, X_{cate}, X_{num}\}$ the n-th sample of size $M = [l, k, j, d]$ with $X_{text} = \{t_1, ...t_l\}$, where $t_i \in V$, $X_{bool} = \{b_1, ...b_k\}$, where $b_i \in \{0, 1\}$, $X_{cate} = \{c_1, ...c_j\}$, where $c_i \in \mathbb{Z}^+$ and $X_{num} \in \mathbb{R}^d$, respectively. We first introduce the encoder for each modality and then present the proposed multimodal self-attention learning-based method and corresponding data augmentation techniques for dealing with the imbalance classes.

3.1. Data Representation Extraction

The multilayer perceptron (MLP) [36] algorithm is widely adopted to encode continuous or discrete features into an informative representation through a linear or nonlinear transformation. Given a sample $X_n = \{X_{text}, X_{bool}, X_{cate}, X_{num}\}$, we construct MLP_{bool}, MLP_{cate}, and MLP_{num} to independently extract boolean embedding $X'_{bool} \in \mathbb{R}^c$, categorical embedding $X'_{cate} \in \mathbb{R}^c$, and numerical embedding $X'_{num} \in \mathbb{R}^c$. As for the textual data, we leverage one of the most canonical pre-trained language models (PLM) BERT f_{PLM} as our text encoder to extract the sequence embedding $X'_{text} \in \mathbb{R}^c$. Finally, our information sequence X'_n can be represented by

$$X'_n = \{X'_{text}, X'_{bool}, X'_{cate}, X'_{num}\} \quad (1)$$

We can observe this first step in the bottom left in Figure 1.

3.2. Multimodal Self-Attention Learning

After having the encoded sequences for each modality, we apply the self-attention step. One could simply concatenate all the multimodal features to obtain a fixed multimodal representation [37,38]. However, we take this representation a step further by using a multihead attention. As shown in Figure 1, we propose to model the dependencies between different types of modals with a self-attention mechanism [6]. This way, we can leverage the importance of different modalities of data contributing to the results. Specifically, given a set of information sequences X'_n, we would construct $W_q, W_k, W_v \in \mathbb{R}^{c \times c_m}$ to separately parameterize each attention $head_i$ and project inputs X'_n to $Q \in \mathbb{R}^{n \times c_m}$, $K \in \mathbb{R}^{n \times c_m}$, and $V \in \mathbb{R}^{n \times c_m}$. Finally, our classification head h_{CLS} is obtained through the following process:

$$head_i(Q, K, V) = \text{softmax}\left(\frac{QK^\top}{\sqrt{c_m}}\right)V \quad (2)$$

$$h'_n = \text{LayerNorm}(\text{Concat}(head_1, ..., head_h) + X'_n) \quad (3)$$

$$h_{CLS} = \text{softmax}(\text{Mean}(h'_n)W_o) \quad (4)$$

where $W_o \in \mathbb{R}^{n \times c}$, c represents the model dimension, h is the number of heads, and c_m is typically set to $\frac{c}{h}$, which indicates that each head is parameterized on a lower-dimensional space. h'_n is produced through a residual block followed by layer normalization [39]. Finally, our objective function is described by Equation (5).

$$\mathcal{L}_{task} = -\sum_{i=1}^{|Y|} y_i \log h_{CLS}, \quad (5)$$

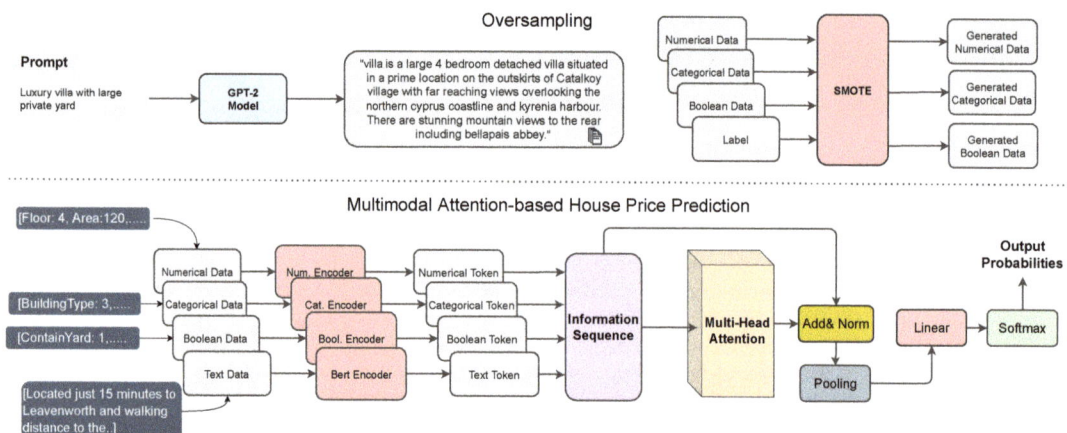

Figure 1. The proposed IMAS framework for house price prediction. Top: oversampling strategy applied to all types of features. Bottom: IMAS.

3.3. Data Augmentation for Imbalanced Class

To generate authentic multimodal data for an imbalanced class, we construct a generator for each modality of the data. This means that the synthetic text instances generated and the numerical, boolean, and categorical synthetic cases generated are implemented using two different strategies.

Regarding the text feature X_{text}, we utilize the auto-regressive-based model GPT2 [40] as a text generator f_{text} to generate the house description text. Specifically, we prepend a sequence of prompts $P = \{p_1, ..., p_l\}$ according to the house price ranges as the initial word sequence and factorize the joint probabilities of the generated text through

$$p(w_{1:T}|P) = \prod_{t=1}^{T}(w_t|w_{1:t-1}, P) \qquad (6)$$

where l is the length of the prompt and length T is generally determined *on the fly* until the <EOS> token is generated from f_{text}.

The new synthetic cases with the numerical, boolean, and categorical features are generated using the well-known SMOTE [41] method. This data preprocessing solution is capable of generating new cases by interpolating two cases from a given minority class and, thereby, expanding the decision border of that class. This is one of the most popular methods used for dealing with the class imbalance, mitigating the important issues of other, simpler methods such as random oversampling or random undersampling. SMOTE uses a seed example from the class of interest (a minority class) and one of its k-nearest neighbors is randomly selected. These two examples are then used to generate a new synthetic case by generating new feature values that are interpolated from the two cases' features. Equation (7) shows for a given feature a, the calculation of the difference between the values of that feature in the seed case and the selected neighbor, represented by *case* and *neig*, respectively. In Equation (8), the new feature for the new case (represented by *new*) is generated using the feature value of *case* and the $diff$ value obtained in Equation (7) to which a random value between 0 and 1 is added.

$$diff = case[a] - neig[a] \qquad (7)$$

$$new[a] = case[a] + random(0,1) \times diff \qquad (8)$$

For each new case, both synthetic data generation methods are used in parallel to obtain the complete information of the new case.

4. Materials and Methods

This section presents the dataset collected and used in this paper, descriptions of the different baselines considered, and all the experimental settings of the experiments carried out.

4.1. House Price Dataset

In this paper, we used a large amount of real estate data that we extracted and processed from the website of one of Canada's most popular real estate companies. This allowed us access to a large volume of houses containing the diversified information we needed. We selected the following five major Canadian cities: Ottawa, Toronto, Mississauga, Brampton, and Hamilton. The latter four cities are localized in the Greater Golden Horseshoe Region, a densely populated and industrialized region in Canada, containing over 20% of the Canadian population and over 54% of the population of Ontario (https://www12.statcan.gc.ca/census-recensement/index-eng.cfm, (accessed on 29 November 2022)). All five cities we selected for this study were in the top 10 Canadian municipalities with the largest populations in 2021.

This dataset includes (i) standard numerical features such as the number of rooms and number of bathrooms; (ii) categorical features such as the type of outdoor area (balcony, skylight, etc.); (iii) boolean features such as the indication of the existence or not of a parking garage; and (iv) text describing each property. The data collection was carried out through a web crawler that we implemented for this purpose. For each house listed on the real estate website, we collected different types of attributes. This allowed us to use a recent dataset with a vast number of examples and with all the information we required for our task.

We collected the advertised house selling prices, which we then categorized into six price ranges and used as our target variable. All types of houses were considered in the five locations selected including new dwellings and second-hand houses. The web scraping was carried out on a Windows 10 laptop with a Jupyter Notebook and Python 3. All the house information was extracted between May and June of 2021.

The raw data collected was cleaned and preprocessed into categorical, numerical, boolean, and text features. Let us first discuss how the categorical, numerical, and boolean features were treated. We applied multiple cleaning and preprocessing steps to this set of features. The most important steps included removing features with more than 50% of missing values or errors in the data collected, merging features with the same information, simplifying categorical features into more consistent classes, handling synonyms in categorical features, and uniforming numeric units. After these steps, we obtained a total of 85 features, excluding the text data. These 85 attributes were decomposed as follows regarding their type: 10 were numerical, 58 were boolean, and 17 were categorical.

Regarding the textual data extracted, we converted all abbreviations, acronyms, and their full word forms to one single format and fixed all typos and misspellings. Figure 2 shows an example of a textual description obtained for a house.

> **Description**
> INCREDIBLE VIEWS from this CORNER UNIT condo conveniently located in Britannia. Walking distance to a variety of walking paths, parks, transit & safety facilities. The unit offers TWO BALCONIES with stunning views of the sunrise & sunset! In addition to the RENOVATED FULL BATH, beautifully UPGRADED open-concept kitchen looking out to the mature nature surrounding the area. This building offers Incredible amenities, in-door salt water pool, guest suites, exercise room, squash court, billiards etc.

Figure 2. An example of the textual description found on a real estate website for a given house.

Finally, we categorized the target variable into six distinct classes. Table 1 shows the ranges and distributions of the house price classes we considered.

Table 1. Ranges and distributions of house price classes.

	Class 1	Class 2	Class 3	Class 4	Class 5	Class 6
Price Range	0–5×10^5	5×10^5–15×10^5	15×10^5–25×10^5	25×10^5–35×10^5	35×10^5–85×10^5	$\geq 85 \times 10^5$
Frequency	994	6397	1058	389	297	83
Classes Percentage	10.8%	69.4%	11.5%	4.2%	3.2%	0.9%

4.2. Experimental Settings

This section provides an overview of our experiments, focusing on the settings. We tested the IMAS algorithm with and without oversampling and provide the parameters used in Section 4.2.1. Section 4.2.2 presents the parameters of the augmentation strategy embedded in the IMAS. In Section 4.2.3, we present the details of the hardware and optimizer used in our experiments. Finally, the description of the four baselines considered, as well as the details of the different learning algorithms that each one used, are provided in Section 4.2.4, where we also discuss the performance assessment metrics evaluated.

4.2.1. Parameters of the IMAS Models

We begin by describing the IMAS parameter settings. The remaining baselines considered, as well as their respective parameter configurations, are described in Section 4.2.4. For testing the IMAS, we set up three independent MLPs with ReLU nonlinear activation functions as the boolean, categorical, and numerical encoders. Each output layer of these MLPs had the same number of channels ($c = 36$). As for the text encoder, we leveraged the BERT-based model (with 12 layers in total), with a learnable pooling layer and the tanh activation function targeting each batch's first <CLS> token to extract and downsample the text embeddings to the same dimension as the other features, i.e., $c = 36$. Finally, we prepend our text, boolean, categorical, and numerical features together as the final house information sequence. As for the multihead attention layer, we set the number of heads to 12 ($h = 12$) and the hidden dimension as $c_m = \frac{c}{h}$. The overall dropout rate in the BERT model and multihead attention layer was set to 0.3.

4.2.2. Data Augmentation

We used the GPT2-small model with 12 layers in total ($h = 12$) as the text generator and fine tuned the GPT2 with the house description and prompt information in Table 2. During the inference phase, we applied the nucleus sampling to obtain the generated text with $p = 0.7$, temperature $t = 0.9$, and a repetition penalty of 2. As for the boolean, categorical, and numerical feature generation, we applied the SMOTE method with the number of nearest neighbors set to the default of 5. SMOTE and GPT2 were applied to the selected minority classes (Class 3, Class 4, and Class 5). Moreover, it is known that a fully balanced dataset is not always optimal. Thus, we decided to augment the cases in these classes but opted to not completely balance all the classes, leaving these three minority classes still below the frequencies observed in the remaining classes. The intuition behind this was twofold: (i) a balanced dataset can be non-optimal; and (ii) a vast increase in the frequency of very scarce classes can result in overfitting. For these reasons, we opted to only augment the three selected minority classes with 500 more cases, leaving them with a total of 600 to 900 examples, whereas the other classes had between 1000 and 6000 original examples. The results of the data augmentation per class are shown in Table 3.

Table 2. Prompt information for text generation

Class	Prompt Info.
Class 1	tiny-sized apartment with shared public infrastructure.
Class 2	bachelor apartment with limited private infrastructure.
Class 3	family-applicable apartments with standard community services and private infrastructure.
Class 4	large and well-furnished apartment in a prosperous district.
Class 5	superior apartment with upscale customization services in the commercial center area.
Class 6	luxury villa with large private yard.

Table 3. Initial distributions of the 6 classes of house prices and their corresponding distributions after the application of SMOTE for oversampling.

	Class 0	Class 1	Class 2	Class 3	Class 4	Class 5
Initial Dist.	994	6397	1058	389	297	83
Dist. after Oversampling	994	6397	1058	889	797	583

4.2.3. Hardware and Optimizer

All of our models were trained with an NVIDIA RTX 2070 GPU. In all the experiments, we utilized the Adam optimizer and set $\beta1 = 0.9, \beta2 = 0.999, \epsilon = 1 \times 10^{-8}$. We trained the GPT2 generator with a learning rate of 5×10^{-4} and our multimodal attention-based model with a learning rate of 5×10^{-5}. The learning weight decay was explicitly set on a bias term with a ratio of 0.1. All batch sizes were set to 16, the epochs to 4, and the warm-up step to 100.

4.2.4. Baselines and Performance Assessment Metrics

We implemented four competitors (B1, B2, B3, and B4), which can use all or part of the features collected to evaluate the effectiveness of the IMAS. Figure 3 depicts the four baselines considered. The baselines selected for this study are as follows:

- **B1—Standard Machine Learning:** We implemented non-parametric supervised learning methods, including decision tree, SVM, naïve Bayes, random forest, and XGBoost to directly predict the house price range by concatenating the numerical, categorical, and boolean data. We set the splitter to "best," the criterion to Gini, and the minimum sample split to 2 for the decision tree. As for SVM, we used the radial basis function as the kernel function with the degree $k = 3$. We set the number of estimators to 100, learning rate to 1.0, max depth to 1 for XGBoost, minimum sample split to 2 for the random forest, lbfgs solver to logistic regression, and variance smoothing factor to 1e-9 for naïve Bayes. The detailed parameter settings of each of these learning algorithms are described in Appendix A.
- **B2—Multimodal Machine Learning:** To utilize the text data, we implemented unsupervised learning algorithms (Word2vec) to obtain the word embeddings. Furthermore, we concatenated the word embeddings with the numerical, categorical, and boolean features and fed them into the classical machine learning models as the initial multimodal machine learning pipeline. As for the Word2vec model, we adopted the continuous skip-gram architecture and trained the model with our collected house description data. The output word embedding dimension for both skip-grams was 300.
- **B3—Pretrained Language Model:** To fully explore the semantics of the house description data, we leveraged the pretrained BERT for sequence classification from Huggingface to directly fine tune our collected description data and infer the house price range. We applied the Adam optimizer and set the learning rate to 4e-5 and the epochs to 5 as the training hyperparameters.
- **B4—End2End Multimodal Learning:** To leverage the multimodal feature and combine it with the pretrained language model, we concatenated the extracted sentence embedding with the multimodal feature and fed them into a stack of linear layers to make the final prediction. The training regime was identical to the BERT model.

Regarding the performance assessment, we observed the overall accuracy and the F1 score calculated through macro averaging. The macro averaging version of the F1 score allows for a correct evaluation of the performance of multiclass classification problems in an imbalanced scenario [42]. Moreover, we also observed the accuracy to determine if an increase in the F1 would negatively impact the overall performance of the models.

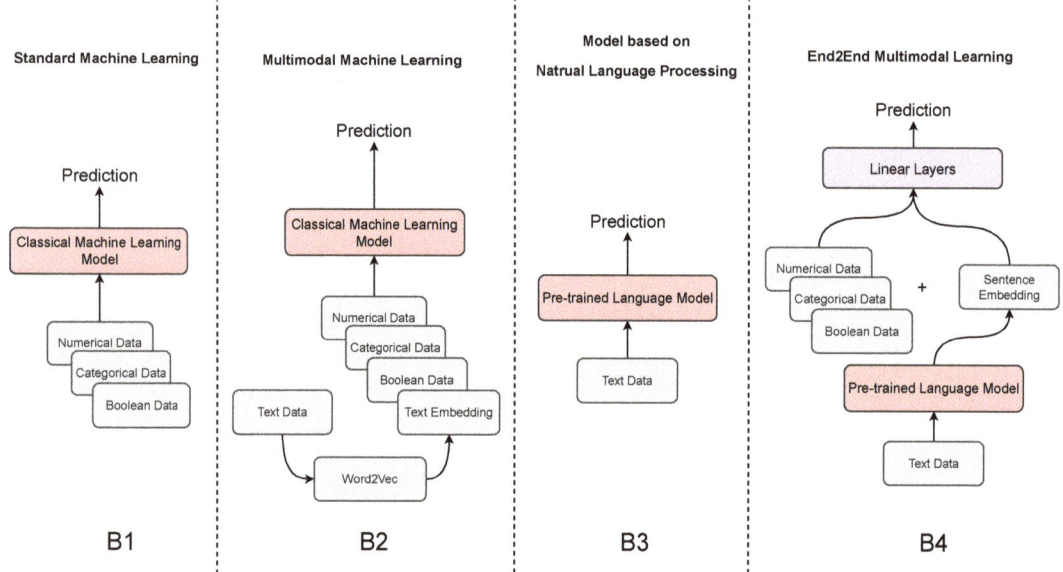

Figure 3. Four baseline alternatives for predicting house prices that incorporate multimodal features.

5. Analysis and Discussion of Results

This section presents and discusses the main results. We also provide an analysis of the impact of the attention mechanism and present an error analysis of our model.

5.1. Main Results

We tested the four baselines (B1 and B2 with two different machine learning algorithms) and we included our proposed IMAS with and without oversampling. Our main results are displayed in Table 4. If we compare the results of baselines B1 and B2, we observe a clear advantage for baseline B1 for all learning algorithms tested except naïve Bayes. The difference between B1 and B2 lies in the use of all textual, boolean, numerical, and categorical features on B2, whereas B1 did not use text data (cf. Figure 3). This shows a detrimental effect on the performance when using the house description text in these scenarios. In the case of naïve Bayes, both the results of B1 and B2 were very poor, showing that this classifier was not well suited for this task.

However, if we compare any of the results of B1 and B2 with the results of B3, we see that B3 provided more advantages in both accuracy and F1-score. Because B3 only used textual data, the conclusion is that these textual data might not be useless and should not be discarded without further consideration. The last baseline B4 used all features in a multimodal framework using a pretrained language model and all the remaining features. Overall, B4 provided the best results among the baseline alternatives that we considered in terms of accuracy and F1 score.

We observed that the IMAS without oversampling provided the best accuracy and F1 score compared to all the variants of the four baselines. However, when using the IMAS with oversampling, we obtained even higher accuracy and a higher F1 score, showing that this method was able to effectively use all the features available.

Table 4. Accuracy and F1 results of our baselines and two variants of the proposed IMAS method (with and without oversampling).

Baseline	Model Type	Data Type	Accuracy	F1 Score
B1	Decision Tree	$X_{num}, X_{bool}, X_{cat}$	0.69 ± 0.01	0.41 ± 0.01
B2		$X_{text}, X_{num}, X_{bool}, X_{cat}$	0.65 ± 0.02	0.37 ± 0.01
B1	Random Forest	$X_{num}, X_{bool}, X_{cat}$	0.73 ± 0.01	0.43 ± 0.01
B2		$X_{text}, X_{num}, X_{bool}, X_{cat}$	0.69 ± 0.02	0.29 ± 0.02
B1	Logistic Regression	$X_{num}, X_{bool}, X_{cat}$	0.72 ± 0.01	0.32 ± 0.01
B2		$X_{text}, X_{num}, X_{bool}, X_{cat}$	0.70 ± 0.01	0.19 ± 0.01
B1	Naïve Bayes	$X_{num}, X_{bool}, X_{cat}$	0.04 ± 0.02	0.07 ± 0.01
B2		$X_{text}, X_{num}, X_{bool}, X_{cat}$	0.16 ± 0.02	0.14 ± 0.02
B1	GBoost	$X_{num}, X_{bool}, X_{cat}$	0.72 ± 0.02	0.37 ± 0.01
B2		$X_{text}, X_{num}, X_{bool}, X_{cat}$	0.71 ± 0.01	0.36 ± 0.03
B1	SVM	$X_{num}, X_{bool}, X_{cat}$	0.71 ± 0.02	0.20 ± 0.01
B2		$X_{text}, X_{num}, X_{bool}, X_{cat}$	0.70 ± 0.01	0.19 ± 0.03
B3	BERT	X_{text}	0.73 ± 0.01	0.42 ± 0.01
B4	Multimodal Learning BERT	$X_{text}, X_{num}, X_{bool}, X_{cat}$	0.75 ± 0.01	0.45 ± 0.01
Our solution	IMAS without Oversampling	$X_{text}, X_{num}, X_{bool}, X_{cat}$	0.77 ± 0.01	0.45 ± 0.02
Our solution	IMAS with Oversampling	$X_{text}, X_{num}, X_{bool}, X_{cat}$	**0.78 ± 0.01**	**0.50 ± 0.01**

F1 score calculated using macro averaging.

5.2. Analysis of the Attention Mechanism and Standard Model's Insights

We inspected the attention weights obtained to better understand their impact and to obtain more insights into the IMAS solution. We computed the average attention weight matrix from the multihead attention layer of the IMAS system for each class and visualized the attention weights. Figure 4 shows the attention weight results for each of the classes per type of modal feature. As shown in this figure, we can clearly observe that the IMAS assigned the highest importance to the categorical embeddings in all cases (the lightest colored cells), which indicates that the most critical determinants of house prices in our dataset were derived from the categorical features. We also observed that the attention weights of the categorical features increased with the increase in the house price, i.e., as we moved from Class 1 (the least expensive houses) to Class 6 (the most expensive houses), the categorical features exhibited a higher weight. Moreover, the importance of the other modal features did not change significantly with the increase in price, which further illustrates the importance of the categorical features for the "high-priced" houses in our dataset. Finally, we also observed that the textual features had higher weights on lower-priced houses (Class 1), shifting slowly to a weight more similar to those of the other features as the house price increased. This shows that assigning the same importance to all features across the different house price classes is not a good option. In effect, by observing the attention map, we can clearly see that different features were more important for predicting houses with lower prices and this changed for houses with higher prices. This differentiated weighting of the features was not achieved with the standard models as they did not use the self-attention mechanism, which highlights the importance of considering this mechanism when predicting house prices. These results confirm that the attention mechanism is an important step in our solution. By assigning more attention weights to the most critical features, we can steer our IMAS system to focus on the most essential modalities, thus producing class-adapted and improved results.

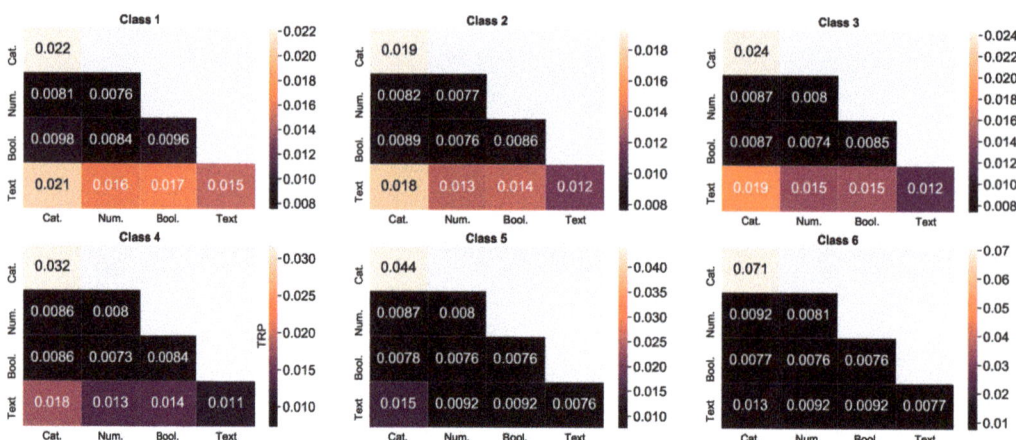

Figure 4. Heatmaps of the attention weights for each class's final layer in the multihead attention layer. Each row represents one modal from the input information sequence X'. Each column in a row represents the attention weight assigned to the specific modal. (Note: To better compare the attention weights across different classes, we removed the softmax activation function while extracting the attention weights from the multihead attention layers.)

Besides analyzing the attention mechanism, we also investigated the decision tree model to obtain more insights into the standard baseline models. In Figure 5, we can observe a decision tree model built with a maximum depth of 4. We did not include here the fully grown tree developed in this study as it became overly large and was extremely difficult to understand. For this reason, we opted to represent a decision tree with a maximum depth of 4. We can see that the features related to the characteristics of the bathrooms of the house were among the top features used in this model. Moreover, we also observed that the garage, bedrooms, type of finishing, laundry, city, heating, cooling, and type of house also appear in the features used in this tree. It is interesting to confirm that some classes never appeared in this model (Class 3), whereas other classes were represented in leaf nodes with a very small number of examples. For instance, Class 5, which was initially represented by 72 examples, ended up being classified on the right-most leaf node, where only 12 examples of that class were present. This confirms the difficulties of classifying some classes of our problem. Still, we must highlight that this is not the model learned in our study but a simplified model with limited depth that enables visualization of the tree.

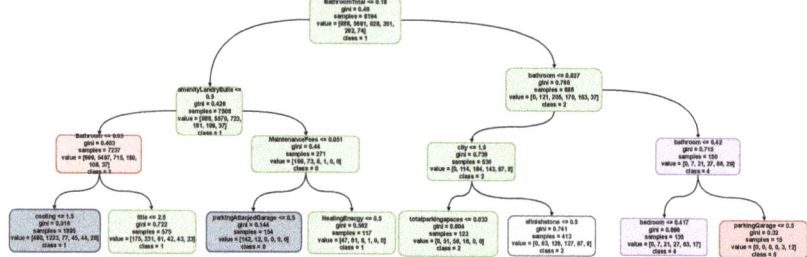

Figure 5. Graphical representation of a decision tree model built with a maximum depth of 4 to allow the interpretation of the results.

5.3. Error Analysis

We further analyzed the errors made by our model by observing the confusion matrix results of the IMAS on the test set, as shown in Figure 6. We verified that most of the errors mainly originated from Classes 1, 4, and 6, where the model misclassified a large number of Class 1 cases as Class 2; a large number of Class 4 cases as Class 3; and many Class 6 cases as Classes 5 and 4. We speculated that the problem was caused by the insufficient sample size and the close price range. However, we also observed that the majority of the errors were made in neighboring classes and thus huge mistakes, such as misclassifying a Class 1 case as a Class 6, were very rare. This confusion matrix also showed that further improvements may be possible and should directly target the fragilities observed in this matrix. We discuss these future developments in the following section.

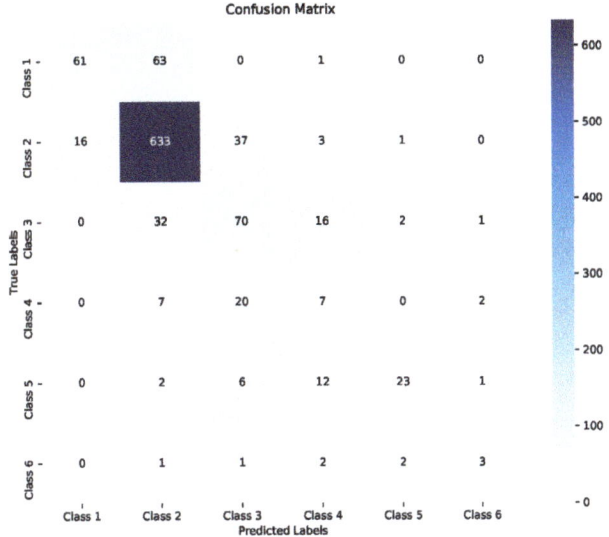

Figure 6. Confusion matrix results obtained for the IMAS with oversampling on the test set.

6. Conclusions

In this paper, we study solutions to deal with the multimodal problem of predicting house price classes. We implement several baseline alternatives, as well as a new algorithm, which we named the IMAS, which is able to effectively deal with this predictive problem while tackling the class imbalance issue. Our proposed solution comprises an oversampling strategy for multimodal data. Then, it goes a step further with the utilization of the four available modalities of features by using a self-attention mechanism to weight the different features, building an adapted solution that uses the features in a more efficient way.

Our results demonstrate that the proposed IMAS solution outperforms all the alternatives tested, showing a clear advantage in this context. The IMAS was able to achieve 78% accuracy and an F1 score of 50%, whereas the best alternative method obtained 75% accuracy and an F1 score of 43%. This shows that the IMAS is able to improve not only the overall accuracy of the model but also its performance in the more difficult and minority classes. Frequently, the improvement of the performance of the minority class is achieved at the cost of degrading the overall performance. Notably, our proposed IMAS is able to increase both results. This is a very interesting result that was achieved by making more intelligent use of the available data through the IMAS. Although the simple concatenation of different modalities is non-optimum, allowing the loss of important information, we show that the IMAS is able to leverage the most relevant features of the multiple modalities to obtain the best performance for each of the classes in the problem. We also provide an analysis of the weights obtained by our self-attention mechanism, showing that it provides adapted weights to the different classes and features. This is indeed a useful solution that allows for the consideration of the neighboring information in cases when inference is performed.

Using multiple modalities of data provides a useful solution that achieves high performance. However, the IMAS has limitations that should be taken into account, namely our proposed system requires more computational power and time to train. This can represent a limitation for end users that have lower computational resources. Another important aspect concerns the potential usage of even more modalities, such as house images, which we did not consider in this work.

We believe that building multimodal models for house price prediction is a promising avenue for future work, namely we consider that exploring the use of other oversampling strategies could bring advantages to the model by making it focus on the classes with higher misclassification errors. This is relevant because the underlying distribution of our target, the house price, was not balanced. Thus, exploring special-purpose methods to deal with this problem is important. Another interesting avenue is related to the decoupling of the representation and learning phases. Several works have shown that this can provide good results for long-tailed distributions (e.g., [43]), but so far, no work has studied this for house price prediction with the type of multimodal data that we used. This direction can become even more relevant if images are also included in the available data. Finally, embedding reinforcement learning into the IMAS framework could also be worth trying as an alternative solution. In effect, some work has been conducted in other application domains where multimodal data are used and reinforcement learning is able to help in building an improved model (e.g., [44]). Finally, we will also consider tackling this problem as a regression problem to observe the impact on the models of the different modalities and the self-attention mechanism.

Author Contributions: Conceptualization, Y.L. and P.B.; Software, Y.L.; Formal analysis, Y.L.; Visualization, Y.L.; Writing—original draft, Y.L. and P.B.; Data curation, H.Z.; Writing—review and editing, Y.L., P.B. and H.Z.; Supervision, P.B. All authors have read and agreed to the published version of the manuscript.

Funding: The work of P. Branco was undertaken, in part, thanks to funding from a Discovery Grant from NSERC.

Institutional Review Board Statement: Not applicable.

Informed Consent Statement: Not applicable.

Data Availability Statement: Not applicable.

Conflicts of Interest: The authors declare no conflicts of interest.

Appendix A

This Appendix provides the complete set of hyperparameters of the baseline models tested in our experiments, which are provided in Table A1.

Table A1. Hyperparameter settings for baseline models.

Baseline	Model Type	Parameter Setting
B1 B2	Decision Tree (DT)	**DT**: minimum sample split = 2, criterion = 'gini', splitter = 'best' **Word2Vec**: Skip-gram architecture with a hidden dimension of 300
B1 B2	Random Forest (RF)	**RF**: criterion = 'gini',min samples split = 2, max_features = 'sqrt' **Word2Vec**: Skip-gram architecture with a hidden dimension of 300
B1 B2	Logistic Regression (LR)	**LR**: penalty = 'l2', tolerance = 1e-4, max_iter = 1000, warm_start = True **Word2Vec**: Skip-gram architecture with a hidden dimension of 300
B1 B2	Naïve Bayes (NB)	**NB**: variance smoothing = 1e-9, type = 'Gaussian' **Word2Vec**: Skip-gram architecture with a hidden dimension of 300
B1 B2	XGBoost	**XGBoost**: loss = 'multinomial deviance', learning_rate = 0.1, n_estimators = 100, max_depth = 3 **Word2Vec**: Skip-gram architecture with a hidden dimension of 300
B1 B2	SVM	**SVM**: penalty = 'l2', Tolerance = 1e-4, solver = 'lbfgs', regularization term C = 1 **Word2Vec**: Skip-gram architecture with a hidden dimension of 300

References

1. Wang, P.Y.; Chen, C.T.; Su, J.W.; Wang, T.Y.; Huang, S.H. Deep learning model for house price prediction using heterogeneous data analysis along with joint self-attention mechanism. *IEEE Access* **2021**, *9*, 55244–55259. [CrossRef]
2. Sun, C.; Myers, A.; Vondrick, C.; Murphy, K.; Schmid, C. Videobert: A joint model for video and language representation learning. In Proceedings of the IEEE/CVF International Conference on Computer Vision, Seoul, Republic of Korea, 27 October–2 November 2019; pp. 7464–7473.
3. Li, L.H.; Yatskar, M.; Yin, D.; Hsieh, C.J.; Chang, K.W. Visualbert: A simple and performant baseline for vision and language. *arXiv* **2019**, arXiv:1908.03557.
4. Ma, P.; Mira, R.; Petridis, S.; Schuller, B.W.; Pantic, M. LiRA: Learning visual speech representations from audio through self-supervision. *arXiv* **2021**, arXiv:2106.09171.
5. Shi, B.; Hsu, W.N.; Lakhotia, K.; Mohamed, A. Learning audio-visual speech representation by masked multimodal cluster prediction. *arXiv* **2022**, arXiv:2201.02184.
6. Vaswani, A.; Shazeer, N.; Parmar, N.; Uszkoreit, J.; Jones, L.; Gomez, A.N.; Kaiser, Ł.; Polosukhin, I. Attention is all you need. *Adv. Neural Inf. Process. Syst.* **2017**, *30*, 5998–6008.
7. Dosovitskiy, A.; Beyer, L.; Kolesnikov, A.; Weissenborn, D.; Zhai, X.; Unterthiner, T.; Dehghani, M.; Minderer, M.; Heigold, G.; Gelly, S.; et al. An image is worth 16 × 16 words: Transformers for image recognition at scale. *arXiv* **2020**, arXiv:2010.11929.
8. Radford, A.; Kim, J.W.; Hallacy, C.; Ramesh, A.; Goh, G.; Agarwal, S.; Sastry, G.; Askell, A.; Mishkin, P.; Clark, J.; et al. Learning transferable visual models from natural language supervision. In Proceedings of the International Conference on Machine Learning, PMLR, Online, 18 July–24 July 2021; pp. 8748–8763.
9. Zhou, X.; Tong, W. Learning with self-attention for rental market spatial dynamics in the Atlanta metropolitan area. *Earth Sci. Inform.* **2021**, *14*, 837–845. [CrossRef]
10. Rosen, S. Hedonic prices and implicit markets: Product differentiation in pure competition. *J. Political Econ.* **1974**, *82*, 34–55. [CrossRef]
11. Limsombunchai, V. House price prediction: Hedonic price model vs. artificial neural network. In Proceedings of the New Zealand Agricultural and Resource Economics Society Conference, Blenheim, New Zealand, 25–26 June 2004; pp. 25–26.
12. Frew, J.; Wilson, B. Estimating the connection between location and property value. *J. Real Estate Pract. Educ.* **2002**, *5*, 17–25. [CrossRef]
13. Gebru, T.; Krause, J.; Wang, Y.; Chen, D.; Deng, J.; Aiden, E.L.; Fei-Fei, L. Using deep learning and Google Street View to estimate the demographic makeup of neighborhoods across the United States. *Proc. Natl. Acad. Sci. USA* **2017**, *114*, 13108–13113. [CrossRef]
14. Yao, Y.; Zhang, J.; Hong, Y.; Liang, H.; He, J. Mapping fine-scale urban housing prices by fusing remotely sensed imagery and social media data. *Trans. GIS* **2018**, *22*, 561–581. [CrossRef]
15. Chen, L.; Yao, X.; Liu, Y.; Zhu, Y.; Chen, W.; Zhao, X.; Chi, T. Measuring impacts of urban environmental elements on housing prices based on multisource data—a case study of Shanghai, China. *ISPRS Int. J.-Geo-Inf.* **2020**, *9*, 106. [CrossRef]
16. Wang, X.; Wen, J.; Zhang, Y.; Wang, Y. Real estate price forecasting based on SVM optimized by PSO. *Optik* **2014**, *125*, 1439–1443. [CrossRef]
17. Hong, J.; Choi, H.; Kim, W.s. A house price valuation based on the random forest approach: The mass appraisal of residential property in south korea. *Int. J. Strateg. Prop. Manag.* **2020**, *24*, 140–152. [CrossRef]
18. Ahtesham, M.; Bawany, N.Z.; Fatima, K. House Price Prediction using Machine Learning Algorithm-The Case of Karachi City, Pakistan. In Proceedings of the 2020 21st International Arab Conference on Information Technology (ACIT), Giza, Egypt, 28–30 November 2020; pp. 1–5.
19. Madhuri, C.R.; Anuradha, G.; Pujitha, M.V. House price prediction using regression techniques: A comparative study. In Proceedings of the 2019 International Conference on Smart Structures and Systems (ICSSS), Chennai, India, 14–15 March 2019; pp. 1–5.
20. Zhao, Y.; Chetty, G.; Tran, D. Deep learning with XGBoost for real estate appraisal. In Proceedings of the 2019 IEEE Symposium Series on Computational Intelligence (SSCI), Xiamen, China, 6–9 December 2019; pp. 1396–1401, 2019 International Conference on Smart Structures and Systems (ICSSS).
21. Varma, A.; Sarma, A.; Doshi, S.; Nair, R. House price prediction using machine learning and neural networks. In Proceedings of the 2018 Second International Conference on Inventive Communication and Computational Technologies (ICICCT), Coimbatore, India, 20–21 April 2018; pp. 1936–1939.
22. Chen, X.; Wei, L.; Xu, J. House price prediction using LSTM. *arXiv* **2017**, arXiv:1709.08432.
23. Izonin, I.; Tkachenko, R.; Greguš, M. I-PNN: An Improved Probabilistic Neural Network for Binary Classification of Imbalanced Medical Data. In Proceedings of the International Conference on Database and Expert Systems Applications, Vienna, Austria, 22–24 August 2022; pp. 147–157.
24. Tkachenko, R.; Doroshenko, A.; Izonin, I.; Tsymbal, Y.; Havrysh, B. Imbalance data classification via neural-like structures of geometric transformations model: Local and global approaches. In Proceedings of the International Conference on Computer Science, Engineering and Education Applications, Kiev, Ukraine, 18–20 January 2018; pp. 112–122.
25. Stevens, D. Predicting Real Estate Price Using Text Mining Automated Real Estate Description Analysis. HAIT Master's Thesis, Department of Communication and Information Sciences, Tilburg University, Tilburg, The Netherlands, July, 2014.

26. Abdallah, S.; Khashan, D.A. Using text mining to analyze real estate classifieds. In Proceedings of the International Conference on Advanced Intelligent Systems and Informatics, Cairo, Egypt, 24–26 October 2016; pp. 193–202.
27. Abdallah, S. An intelligent system for identifying influential words in real-estate classifieds. *J. Intell. Syst.* **2018**, *27*, 183–194. [CrossRef]
28. Guo, J.q.; Chiang, S.h.; Liu, M.; Yang, C.C.; Guo, K.y. Can machine learning algorithms associated with text mining from internet data improve housing price prediction performance? *Int. J. Strateg. Prop. Manag.* **2020**, *24*, 300–312. [CrossRef]
29. Minaee, S.; Kalchbrenner, N.; Cambria, E.; Nikzad, N.; Chenaghlu, M.; Gao, J. Deep learning–based text classification: A comprehensive review. *ACM Comput. Surv. (CSUR)* **2021**, *54*, 1–40. [CrossRef]
30. Qi, D.; Su, L.; Song, J.; Cui, E.; Bharti, T.; Sacheti, A. Imagebert: Cross-modal pre-training with large-scale weak-supervised image-text data. *arXiv* **2020**, arXiv:2001.07966.
31. Veličković, P.; Cucurull, G.; Casanova, A.; Romero, A.; Lio, P.; Bengio, Y. Graph attention networks. *arXiv* **2017**, arXiv:1710.10903.
32. Zhang, S.; He, X.; Yan, S. Latentgnn: Learning efficient non-local relations for visual recognition. In Proceedings of the International Conference on Machine Learning. PMLR, Long Beach, CA, USA, 10–15 June 2019; pp. 7374–7383.
33. Cambria, E.; Das, D.; Bandyopadhyay, S.; Feraco, A. Affective computing and sentiment analysis. In *A Practical Guide to Sentiment Analysis*; Springer: Cham, Switzerland, 2017; pp. 1–10.
34. Cambria, E.; Howard, N.; Hsu, J.; Hussain, A. Sentic blending: Scalable multimodal fusion for the continuous interpretation of semantics and sentics. In Proceedings of the 2013 IEEE Symposium on Computational Intelligence for Human-Like Intelligence (CIHLI), Singapore, 16–19 April 2013; pp. 108–117.
35. Stappen, L.; Schumann, L.; Sertolli, B.; Baird, A.; Weigell, B.; Cambria, E.; Schuller, B.W. Muse-toolbox: The multimodal sentiment analysis continuous annotation fusion and discrete class transformation toolbox. In Proceedings of the 2nd on Multimodal Sentiment Analysis Challenge, Virtual Event, 24 October 2021; pp. 75–82.
36. Rumelhart, D.E.; Hinton, G.E.; Williams, R.J. *Learning Internal Representations by Error Propagation*; Technical Report; California Univ San Diego La Jolla Inst for Cognitive Science: San Diego, CA, USA, 1985.
37. Ngiam, J.; Khosla, A.; Kim, M.; Nam, J.; Lee, H.; Ng, A.Y. Multimodal deep learning. In Proceedings of the ICML, Bellevue, DC, USA, 28 June–2 July 2011.
38. Gupta, T.; Schwing, A.G.; Hoiem, D. ViCo: Word Embeddings from Visual Co-occurrences. *CoRR* **2019**, *abs/1908.08527*.
39. Ba, J.L.; Kiros, J.R.; Hinton, G.E. Layer normalization. *arXiv* **2016**, arXiv:1607.06450.
40. Radford, A.; Wu, J.; Child, R.; Luan, D.; Amodei, D.; Sutskever, I. Language models are unsupervised multitask learners. *OpenAI Blog* **2019**, *1*, 9.
41. Chawla, N.V.; Bowyer, K.W.; Hall, L.O.; Kegelmeyer, W.P. SMOTE: Synthetic minority over-sampling technique. *J. Artif. Intell. Res.* **2002**, *16*, 321–357. [CrossRef]
42. Branco, P.; Torgo, L.; Ribeiro, R.P. A survey of predictive modeling on imbalanced domains. *ACM Comput. Surv. (CSUR)* **2016**, *49*, 1–50. [CrossRef]
43. Kang, B.; Xie, S.; Rohrbach, M.; Yan, Z.; Gordo, A.; Feng, J.; Kalantidis, Y. Decoupling representation and classifier for long-tailed recognition. *arXiv* **2019**, arXiv:1910.09217.
44. Gui, T.; Zhu, L.; Zhang, Q.; Peng, M.; Zhou, X.; Ding, K.; Chen, Z. Cooperative multimodal approach to depression detection in twitter. In Proceedings of the AAAI Conference on Artificial Intelligence, Honolulu, HI, USA, 27 January–1 February 2019; Volume 33, pp. 110–117.

Disclaimer/Publisher's Note: The statements, opinions and data contained in all publications are solely those of the individual author(s) and contributor(s) and not of MDPI and/or the editor(s). MDPI and/or the editor(s) disclaim responsibility for any injury to people or property resulting from any ideas, methods, instructions or products referred to in the content.

Article

Geo-Spatial Mapping of Hate Speech Prediction in Roman Urdu

Samia Aziz [1], Muhammad Shahzad Sarfraz [1], Muhammad Usman [1], Muhammad Umar Aftab [1] and Hafiz Tayyab Rauf [2,*]

[1] Department of Computer Science, National University of Computer and Emerging Sciences, Islamabad, Chiniot-Faisalabad Campus, Chiniot 35400, Pakistan
[2] Centre for Smart Systems, AI and Cybersecurity, Staffordshire University, Stoke-on-Trent ST4 2DE, UK
* Correspondence: hafiztayyabrauf093@gmail.com

Abstract: Social media has transformed into a crucial channel for political expression. Twitter, especially, is a vital platform used to exchange political hate in Pakistan. Political hate speech affects the public image of politicians, targets their supporters, and hurts public sentiments. Hate speech is a controversial public speech that promotes violence toward a person or group based on specific characteristics. Although studies have been conducted to identify hate speech in European languages, Roman languages have yet to receive much attention. In this research work, we present the automatic detection of political hate speech in Roman Urdu. An exclusive political hate speech labeled dataset (RU-PHS) containing 5002 instances and city-level information has been developed. To overcome the vast lexical structure of Roman Urdu, we propose an algorithm for the lexical unification of Roman Urdu. Three vectorization techniques are developed: TF-IDF, word2vec, and fastText. A comparative analysis of the accuracy and time complexity of conventional machine learning models and fine-tuned neural networks using dense word representations is presented for classifying and predicting political hate speech. The results show that a random forest and the proposed feed-forward neural network achieve an accuracy of 93% using fastText word embedding to distinguish between neutral and politically offensive speech. The statistical information helps identify trends and patterns, and the hotspot and cluster analysis assist in pinpointing Punjab as a highly susceptible area in Pakistan in terms of political hate tweet generation.

Keywords: natural language processing; machine learning; deep learning; spatial analysis

MSC: 68T07; 68T50

1. Introduction

The recent couple of years have seen drastic growth in social networks and the rate of content consumers. Social media platforms are used to share posts (Facebook) and tweets (Twitter) that can contain text, images, videos, emotions, etc., directly affecting the daily life of consumers. A significant and slippery type of such language is hateful speech: content that communicates a class's sentiment. Offensive speech has become a significant issue for everyone on the Web, where consumer-created content appears from the remark areas of information sites to ongoing talk meetings in vivid games. Such content can embarrass consumers and can furthermore support radicalization and incite violence [1]. Twitter is among the leading social media platforms. A 140-character post is called a tweet and can include spaces, emojis, URLs, and hashtags. According to the latest survey [2], 217 million active monetizable users and 500 million tweets are produced daily. Twitter restricts consumers from posting hateful and contemptuous substances [3].

The Urdu language has over 230 million speakers worldwide, including in the UAE, the UK, and the US. The overall active social media stats of Pakistani users are depicted in Figure 1. Urdu is the official language of Pakistan, a rank it imparts to English in a nation of 226 million people. Despite that, there are a few difficulties related to Urdu writing. The Urdu language comprises 40 letters. The standard consoles are intended to only deal with the 26 letters of English. This enormous gap between various alphabets makes it almost difficult to write Urdu letters using a standard English console. Urdu is a morphologically rich language that bears a shortfall of resources. It has a complex inflectional framework, a course of word improvement wherein things are added to the root word to demonstrate syntactic implications. Roman Urdu (RU) is the conventional name utilized for the Urdu language written in Roman script.

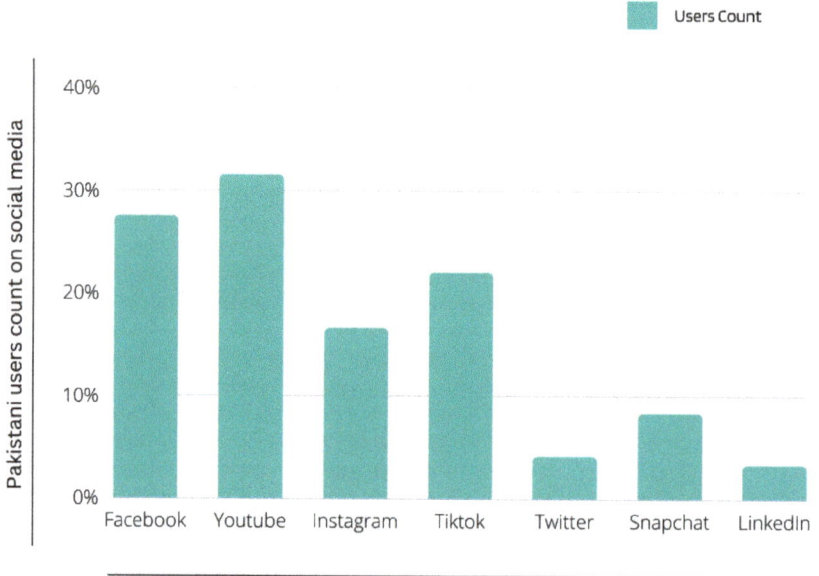

Figure 1. Active social media user stats of Pakistan based on each individual company's ad reach in the start of 2022.

Provided the volume of information growth of social media platforms, especially on Twitter, where users express their opinions, feelings, and surprising/devastating news in RU, they may also leave inappropriate content such as hate speech. The main parts of the problem statement in this research are that online hate speech can set off extreme occasions in society [4]. Current methods, such as word embeddings, are only available for English or asset-rich languages [5]. Present hate speech detection procedures do not perform unequivocally on the code-mixed imperfect, informal, and resource-poor languages [6].

The principal objective was classifying hate speech to identify and analyze data from social networks, especially Twitter, using standard machine learning methods for text classification and evaluation. The content on social media posted each minute is usually unrefined and represents one's beliefs; people express and judge others based on their choices, ultimately creating circumstances for others and even societies. For example, discussion on religion and politics almost always results in violence. For this research, the aim was to target offensive political speech written in RU script. The tweets were targeted based on infamous political keywords that could potentially contain RU data and offensive speech. The offensive speech data were obtained from Twitter. Several objectives designed for this research could help classify, predict, and geomap offensive speech written in RU. The main contributions of this research are as follows:

1. This research work contributes to a detailed analysis of current approaches employed for the classification of hate speech in Roman Urdu. It also presents a review of the literature on data sets developed by previous studies and a comparative analysis that highlights the strengths and weaknesses of these studies.
2. This research proposes a complete dataset of Roman Urdu political hate speech (RU-PHS) containing 5002 instances along with their labels and city-level location information.
3. To overcome the vast lexical structure of Roman Urdu, an algorithm for the lexical unification of Roman Urdu is proposed, by leveraging regular expressions.
4. A comparative analysis between conventional machine learning models, a feed-forward neural network, and a conventional neural network using dense word representations (i.e., TF-IDF, word2vec, and fastText) is presented for the classification and prediction of political hate speech.
5. A spatial data analysis of the RU-PHS dataset in terms of hotspots and clusters is conducted to predict future affected areas in Pakistan.

The paper is organized as follows: In Section 2, we discuss preliminary concepts of text classification, its applications, and state-of-the-art approaches with contemporary trends and open problems. This is followed by Section 3, in which a comprehensive review of the literature related to the scope of this research study is presented. Section 4 presents the proposed methodology for the said problems. Section 5 discusses the implementation, dataset description, and formulation process. Section 6 presents the spatial analysis and results of data points. Section 7 addresses the hyperparameter settings for the proposed models and evaluates their performance. Lastly, Section 8 presents the conclusions and future directions.

2. Preliminaries

2.1. Text Classification

Text or document classification organizes, structures, and sorts text into binary or multiple classes. Over the past several decades, text classification problems have been widely studied and addressed in a variety of real-life domains [7]. Researchers are now interested in developing applications that use text classifiers, especially given the recent advancements in natural language processing (NLP) and data mining.

Classifying text into different categories starts using plain raw text files stored on the disk. It then involves data cleaning, preprocessing, and transformation. The transformed data are then preprocessed for the machine learning algorithm; this step is known as feature engineering and converts words into features for training classification and predictive models. Figure 2 gives a classic representation of the training of a machine learning classifier to classify text. Labels are provided along with the text data to train a machine learning algorithm. The data preprocessing steps are performed, including tokenization, lower casing, stop word removal, stemming, and lemmatization.

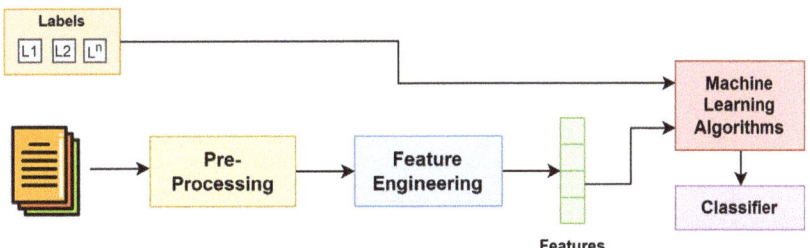

Figure 2. Training pipeline of text classification phenomena.

The feature engineering steps convert words into meaningful information such as frequencies using TF-IDF and one-hot encoding; for a dense representation, word2vec, fastText, and Glove word embeddings are used to capture contextual information. Once the features are extracted, they are passed to the ML models, which then learn to classify the data into given categories. Figure 3 represents the prediction process, where the ML model is not provided with labels to test what the model has learned from the training data.

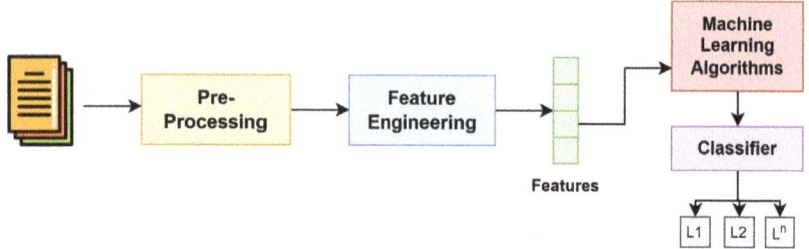

Figure 3. Prediction pipeline of text classification phenomena.

2.2. Sentiment Analysis

Sentiment analysis is the process of determining if a user-generated post is positive, negative, or objective. NLP is used in an emotion detection analysis system. Machine learning algorithms assign weighted sentiment values to entities, topics, documents, and categorizations within a statement or phrase. It helps corporations get an idea of how well or poorly their product or service is performing on the market by analyzing the general sentiment of reviews and conversations on social networks. Opinion research is also used to distinguish positive or hostile public sentiments communicated on sites about culture, race, or orientation that could cause viciousness and hostility between individuals of various backgrounds. The sentiment investigation task centers around distinguishing and extracting feelings from a message to a specific subject or item. A subtask of sentiment examination is the opinion order in light of specific polarities [8].

2.2.1. Fine-Grained

The fine-grained sentiment analysis model analyzes the sentence by dividing it into clauses or phrases. It helps to gain polarity precision. A phrase is divided into expressions or clauses, and every fragment is examined in association with others. We can recognize who discusses an item and what an individual discusses in their criticism. We can regulate a sentiment analysis across the subsequent polarity classes: neutral, positive, negative, and offensive. The fine-grained analysis is beneficent when analyzing reviews or ratings.

2.2.2. Aspect Based

The aspect-based sentiment analysis focuses on the features mentioned in a phrase that is later classified as an emotion. This model dives deeper and helps detect the specific aspects that people talk about in their posts.

2.2.3. Emotion Detection

The emotion detection sentiment analysis model goes way beyond just polarity count. It helps recognize emotions embedded in phrases such as happiness, sadness, frustration, anger, fear, panic, etc. This model utilizes lexicon-based approaches to analyze the word level that delivers a specific emotion. Some state-of-the-art classifiers also use strong artificial intelligence techniques. It is prescribed to involve machine learning over lexicons since individuals express feelings in many ways. For instance, the line "This movie is going to kill me" might communicate sensations of dread and frenzy.

2.2.4. Intent Analysis

As the name suggests, intent sentiment analysis helps detect a consumer's intentions. Based on consumers' shopping behaviors, are they interested in buying or are they just browsing? Precisely recognizing users' intent helps save organizations time and money. Thus, often, organizations pursue purchasers that want to avoid purchasing in the short term. An exact intent investigation can determine this obstacle. In this way, if a consumer has a history of buying things online, a corporation can target them with marketing. If they never buy online, time and assets can be saved by not advertising to those consumers.

3. Related Work

In this digital age, since web-based hate speech content began to become viral on various social media stages, additional research has been conducted on detecting, classifying, and predicting hostile speech. Nevertheless, only some text corpora have been produced in RU containing a minimal dataset. A prior work [4] introduced RU toxic comment identification. They presented an extensive corpus containing 72,000 labeled comments with a substantial interannotator agreement. They worked with existing machine learning methods that performed well for English language toxic datasets incorporating text classification techniques and recent deep-learning-based models. This study's principal challenge was the inaccessibility of pretrained word embeddings in RU, so they created different word embeddings utilizing Glove, word2vec, and fastText procedures. They achieved the highest scores in word embeddings utilizing the skip-gram model of fastText.

In [5], research work by Rizwan Ali Naqv et al. aimed to develop a Roman Urdu news classifier. For this, they scraped data from news websites and divided it into five classes: international news, health, sports, business, and technology. They collected a total of 735 news texts that belonged to the categories mentioned. This data set was collected in Urdu and later translated into RU using ijunoon.com. They faced the challenge of lexical variations of RU in this study. To handle this problem, they divided their test data set into two parts with lexical variations (real-world test data) and without lexical variations. To extract features from this news dataset, the study used (TF-IDF).

In addition to unsupervised machine learning techniques, studies such as that by Nobata et al. [9] introduced the utilization of supervised ML techniques for recognizing offensive speech. Of these research studies, the first research study gathered publicly available commentary from the financial and news domains and generated a body of offensive speech. Furthermore, research was carried out involving syntactic features and various kinds of embedding techniques. Moin Khan et al. [10] developed an RU corpus composed of over 5000 tweets, most of which were hate speech. They divided the tweets into hostile and neutral at first and further sorted the hostile tweets into offensive and hate speech. They involved a few supervised learning technique strategies for assessing the developed corpus. Logistic regression performed best in their study to distinguish between neutral and hostile sentences. Hammad Rizwan et al. [11] proposed a dataset named RUHSOLD with 10,012 tweets in RU and labeled them into five hate speech classes, including abusive, profane, sexism, religious hate, and normal. A novel approach, CNN-gram for offensive speech classification, was proposed and a comparative analysis of their proposed model was performed with various baseline models using the RUHSOLD dataset.

The study [12] examined several methods for classifying offensive speech on social media platforms. They introduced an integration of lexicon-based and machine-learning-based techniques for hate speech prediction. They notably used emotional information in a sentence to help get a better accuracy in offensive speech detection. They performed a statistical analysis to determine the critical correlation between the probability that the consumer would share comments related to the base class, and the tagged labels related to that class. The review achieved correlation coefficient values for racism and sexism of 0.71 and 0.76, respectively. Additional research by Muhammad Bilal et al. [13] on RU opinion mining evaluated three classification algorithms: naive Bayes, decision tree, and KNN. They extracted opinions from an online blog and labeled them positive and negative. These labeled data were further supplied to the models, and naive Bayes outperformed all the others in terms of accuracy, recall, precision, and F measures.

Various studies have generated Roman Urdu hate speech corpora and made them publicly available. Table 1 summarizes the Roman Urdu datasets generated along with their name, size, and language. A novel study [14] conducted research on generating a parallel corpus for Urdu and RU. They presented a large-scale RU parallel corpus named Roman-Urdu-Parl that contained 6.37 million Urdu and RU text pairs. These data were collected from various sources. The crowd-sourcing technique was used to annotate the data set. It contained a total of 42.9K unique words for RU and 43.8K unique words for Urdu. This study mainly focused on word representation learning and its machine transliteration and vector representation. Despite the traditional techniques to perform sentiment analysis, such as lexical normalization, word dictionary, and code transfer indication, a study [15], independent of these techniques, proposed a sentiment analysis using multilingual BERT (mBERT) and XLM-RoBERTa (XLM-R) models. They acquired the Twitter data set during the 2018 election named MultiSenti. It contained code-mixed English and RU. The dataset, after preprocessing, was divided into three classes that include positive, negative, and neutral. XLM-Roberta gave higher accuracy and F1 score for informal and under-resource languages such as code-mixed English and RU.

Roman Urdu datasets were acquired using different platforms. Table 2 gives a summary of the famous platforms used for this matter, in which Twitter has been used most frequently in research studies.

Table 1. Publicly available Urdu and Roman Urdu datasets along with their characteristics.

Ref.	Corpus	Language	Frequency	Type
[6]	DSL RU Sentiments	Roman Urdu	3241	Sentiments
[16]	RUT	Roman Urdu	72,000	Comments
[3]	HS-RU-20	Roman Urdu	5000	Tweets
[11]	RUHSOLD	Roman Urdu	10,012	Tweets
[13]	No Corpus Name	Roman Urdu	300	Opinions
[15]	MultiSenti	RU and English	20,735	Tweets
[17]	UCSA	Urdu	9601	Reviews
[18]	No Corpus Name	Roman Urdu	14,131	YouTube Comments
[19]	No Corpus Name	English	2577	Tweets
[20]	No Corpus Name	Roman Urdu	1000	Tweets
[21]	Aryan Urdu	English and RU	–	–
[22]	No Corpus Name	Roman Urdu	454	Reviews
[23]	UCI RUSA-19	Roman Urdu	20,229, 10,016	Sentences
[24]	UOD	Urdu RU	2171	YouTube Comments
[25]	TRAC-1 HS HOT	Hindi-English	12,000, 11,623	Sentences
[26]	RUED	Roman Urdu	20,000	Sentences
[27]	RUSA-19	Roman Urdu	10,021	Sentences
[28]	Roman Urdu (RU)	Roman Urdu	11,000	Reviews
[29]	No Corpus Name	Urdu	6025	Sentences
[30]	No Corpus Name	Roman Urdu	18,000	Sentences
[12]	Existing Dataset	English	24,782	Tweets
[31]	No Corpus Name	Urdu	6000	Sentences

Table 2. Summary of platforms used in the collection of datasets.

Ref.	Twitter	YouTube	Facebook	Yahoo	Formspring	Wikipedia	Slashdot
[3]				✓			
[32]		✓					
[33]	✓						
[34]		✓					
[35]				✓			
[36]	✓						
[37]	✓						
[38]							✓
[39]	✓						
[40]	✓						
[41]	✓						
[42]	✓	✓			✓		
[43]	✓						
[44]		✓					✓
[45]	✓						
[46]	✓					✓	
[47]							✓
[48]	✓						
[49]	✓						
[50]	✓						
[51]	✓						
[52]	✓						
[53]	✓						

Mukand [17] introduced a technique for extremity characterization of code-mixed data. The technique was based on a hypothesis, namely SCL (structural correspondence learning), used in domain adaptation. The transliteration oracle handled the problem with spelling variations. A transliteration oracle is a transliterate processor that converts strings based on the sound they represent from one writing system (such as Latin) to another (such as Arabic). The authors of the paper used two types of translation oracles—the first oracle, which accommodated spelling variations, and the second oracle, which was a translation between Urdu and English. Using a double metaphone algorithm, the first oracle completely switched all tokens to RU. Tokens that had the same metaphone code in both target and source languages were added into pivot pairs. The second oracle accomplished the interpretation between Urdu and English.

Research carried out by Kaur et al. [54] in 2014 proposed a hybrid approach for Punjabi text classification. This exploration utilized a number of naive Bayesian and N-gram methods. The elements of the N-gram method were extracted and then used as a training data set to train a naive Bayes classifier. The algorithm was then tested by providing testing data. The observation was made that the results from previously proposed frameworks and the current algorithm gave a promising number of clarifications. Studies have employed different techniques to solve these problems, and an analysis of the strengths and weaknesses of these studies are presented in Table 3. Another approach was used by Ashari et al. in [55] in which they classified using naive Bayes, decision tree, and KNN classifiers and proposed three classification models to design an alternative solution using WEKA as an information mining instrument. Their investigations showed that decision tree was the quickest and KNN computations took time, so it was a slow characterization strategy. The explanation they referenced was that, in the decision tree, there was no computation included. Characterization by adhering to the tree guidelines was faster than those that required computation in the NB and KNN classifiers.

Table 3. Analysis of studies on the classification of Urdu and Roman Urdu hate speech.

Ref.	Strengths	Weaknesses
[56]	Classification of Urdu sentences on document-level, lexicon-based sentiment analysis	No method to tackle implicit negation Noun phrases not considered
[57]	Utilized long short-term memory (LSTM) for polarity detection in Roman Urdu	No validation of data collection process, no data preprocessing method declared Methods were not transparent
[58]	806 Roman Urdu sentences collection, feature construction, and application on different multilingual classifiers	Limited dataset No structure of the dataset
[59]	Lexicon- and rule-based methods used to construct an RU classification algorithm, ML, and phonetic techniques used	Limited categorization of the dataset No normalizing of the dataset
[60]	15,000 roman Urdu sentences collected	The dataset contained biographies and was not general
[31]	22,000 sentences of RU were collected; supervised and unsupervised methods were used	Ambiguous combination of classifiers
[61]	1200 text documents of Urdu news were collected; performed a linguistic analysis	No character-level features used Needs evaluation on state-of-the-art semantic techniques
[62]	Existing values collated to different techniques	No dataset mentioned No classification methods mentioned
[63]	A massive dataset of 5 sentiments; use of lexical classifying techniques	Confusing representation of the dataset Lack of credible results
[64]	1000 reviews collected and various frameworks compared, i.e., Hadoop MapReduce	Limited dataset; classifiers were not general and were overfitting on the given dataset

In 2012, another study on sentiment analysis was carried out by Jebaseeli [65] in which they explored the use of three classifiers, namely, NB, KNN and RF, for the classification of sentiments as positive or negative about the machine learning structure for inspiration to dissect the ability of these three classifiers. In the study, a data set of 300 surveys was taken with a split of 100 positive, 100 negative, and 100 neutral surveys [65]. In the preprocessing step, customarily assembling words and just generally utilized words were taken out by utilizing the SVD approach. SVD was utilized to rate the significance of words. The resulting preprocessed information was utilized as responsibility estimation. In that examination, a degree of 55–60% accuracy was achieved. Gamallo [66] presented a set of NB classifiers to determine the polarization of English Twitter posts. Two naive classifiers were compiled: the baseline (designed to portray tweets as specific, negative, and neutral) and the binary classifier. The classifiers took into account phrases (nouns, verbs, adjectives, and adverbs), multiword, and polarities vocabulary from numerous roots. A related study[67] used a psychrometric deep learning model to classify the sentiments of tourists against the COVID-19 pandemic. The comments were collected from Twitter containing information about weather, health, holidays, seasonality, and economics. The proposed model used the PANAS (Positive and Negative Affect Scale) to classify these comments.

4. Proposed Methodology

4.1. Representing Words

The text data presented as input to any machine learning model and coming as output from it are converted to embeddings. These input and output embeddings of words are the parameters of the model, stored in lookup matrices W_i and W_o. Word embedding methods are employed to demonstrate words and connect humans mathematically—an artificial knowledge of learning.

Word embeddings learn text representations in an n-dimensional space, in which words can be represented in terms of frequency counts, i.e., TF-IDF or words with similar meanings have similar representations. Two similar words are represented by almost identical vectors very close together in a feature space, i.e., word2vec and fastText. These techniques are preferred depending on the data's status, size, and output preferences. Much work has recently been done with models representing words as functions of subword units. Table 4 shows the words and their decomposition patterns. In this work, we considered two word representations: words and decomposing them into N-grams of characters. This is required for most natural language processing problems. In this section, we present the three types of word representations developed to convert the exclusively collected dataset into vector representations.

Table 4. Word and subword decomposition example of word "Bhagora".

Representation	Decomposition
Word	Bhagora
Character	B+h+a+g+o+r+a
Character 2-gram	Bh+ha+ag+go+or+ra
Character 3-gram	Bha+hag+ago+gor+ora

4.1.1. TF-IDF

TF-IDF [68] is a quantitative tool that evaluates the relevance of a word in a collection of documents. This is accomplished by simply multiplying metrics: the number of times a word appears in a document and the word's inverse document frequency along a collection of documents. The higher the score, the more important that word is in that document. To put it mathematically, the TF-IDF score for the word w in document d of document set D is shown in Equation (1). Then, Equations (2) and (3) further drive the term frequency and document frequency.

$$tfidf(w,d,D) = tf(w,d) \cdot idf(w,D) \tag{1}$$

where:

$$tf(w,d) = \log(1 + \text{freq}(w,d)) \tag{2}$$

$$idf(w,D) = \log\left(\frac{N}{\text{count}(d \in D : w \in d)}\right) \tag{3}$$

4.1.2. word2vec

word2vec [69] is a predictive neural word embedding model that uses a neural network model to learn vector representations from a large corpus of text. It predicts the target word by computing the cosine similarity between vectors, i.e., by analyzing nearby words. The following Figure 4 represents how word vectors with similar meanings are clustered in close proximity in word2vec and how a one-hot encoding does not capture context at all.

$$\text{similarity}(Basketball, Handball) = \cos(\theta) = \frac{Basketball \cdot Handball}{\|Basketball\| \|Handball\|} \tag{4}$$

word2vec captures the similarity score between words using the cosine similarity equation when trained on a large corpus. In Figure 4, the vectors X, Y, and Z can be considered dimensions. Each word occupies a dimension for the one-hot encoding and has nothing to do with the rest of the words. Hence, all the words are independent of each other. In word2vec, the main goal is to have words occupy close spatial positions if they are contextually the same. Equation (4) calculates the similarity between such vectors, which is close to one, i.e., the cosine angle is close to zero. This is achieved by taking the product of both vectors, in this case, Basketball and Handball, and dividing it by the product of the lengths of both vectors.

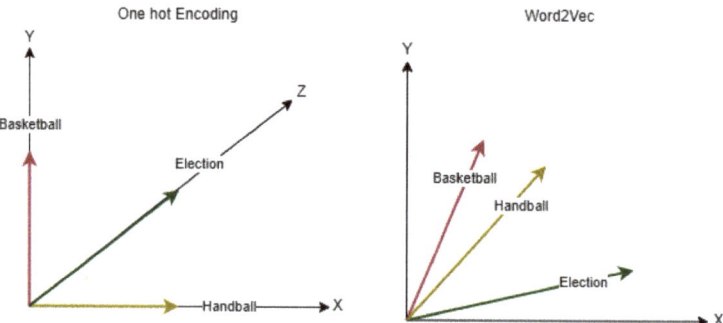

Figure 4. The representation of one-hot-encoded vectors vs. word2vec vectors.

There are two main architectures of word2vec that are used to learn distributed representations.

- Continuous bag-of-words (CBOW);
- Continuous skip-gram (CSG).

CBOW attempts to predict a word based on a window of surrounding context words, but the bag-of-word assumption is not affected by the sequence of context words, whereas continuous skip gram does the opposite. Based on the input word, the continuous skip-gram model predicts whether words that are surrounding a word also called context words. This model contains one hidden layer, which performs a dot product of the input vector and weight matrix and no activation function is used (see Figure 5). The output vector generated by the hidden layer and the weight matrix of the hidden layer is multiplied together with a softmax function to predict the probability of context words.

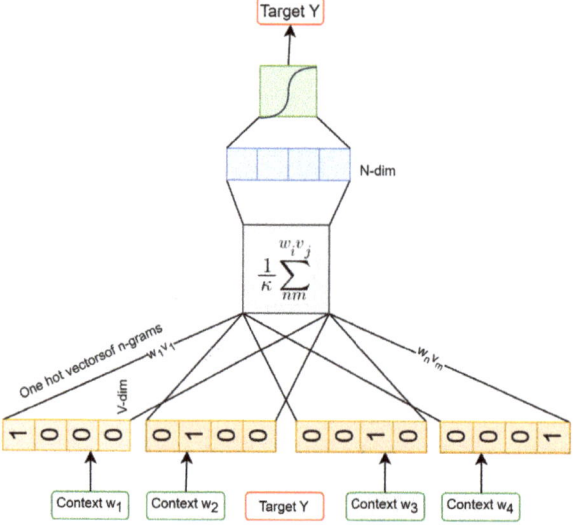

Figure 5. Roman Urdu word representations using continues bag of words model of fastText.

4.1.3. fastText

fastText [70] embeddings use subword-level knowledge to generate word vectors. Words are expressed as the sum of gram vectors after learning N-gram representations. This adds information at the subword level to the word2vec framework. This enables embeddings for understanding prefixes and suffixes. Similarly to word2vec, fastText learns the word vectors along with the N-grams that exist within each word, although these embeddings are computationally more expensive than word2vec.

4.2. Machine Learning for Political Hate Speech Detection

4.2.1. Feed-Forward Neural Network

A feed-forward neural network is the oldest and most fundamental type of artificial NN in which node links do not constitute a loop [71]. Feed-forward neural networks are made of an input layer, n numbers of hidden layers, and an output layer where the neurons of the input and hidden layers carry weights and the data only move in one direction, i.e., in a forward fashion (see Figure 6). In this case, the input or embedding layer takes the distributed representations V of words W generated by the word2vec and fastText models.

$$\mathbf{L} \in \mathbb{R}^{d_r \times |\mathcal{V}|} \tag{5}$$

It takes the vocabulary size and maximum input length of words in the vocabulary as embedding layer features. Vectors are denoted as $\mathbf{r} \in \mathbb{R}^{d_r}$ and are represented in practice by a lookup matrix L; see Equation (5). In this lookup matrix L, every row has a continuing vector that belongs to words existing in the vocabulary and is called the word embedding, represented as shown in Equation (6).

$$\mathbf{L} = [\mathbf{r}_j]_{j=1}^{|\mathcal{V}|} \tag{6}$$

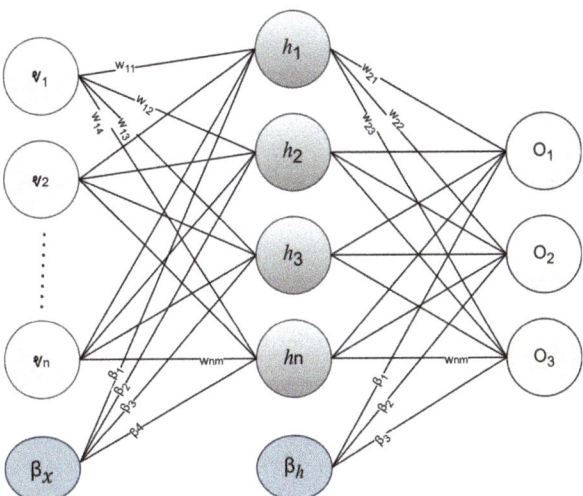

Figure 6. An abstract view of proposed feed forward neural network architecture.

After the input layer, where the data are fed to input neurons in the shape of feature vectors, the values and their assigned weights are then fed-forward to the hidden layers, where the magic happens. Each hidden layer transforms the values linearly with a weight metric W (shown in Equation (7)) and β as a bias vector $\beta^h \in \mathbb{R}^{dh}$.

$$W_{i,j}^h \in \mathbb{R}^{dn \times (n-1)dr} \tag{7}$$

This is then followed by applying an activation function (shown in Equation (8)) to induce nonlinearity into the network. It helps simulate whether the neuron fires or not, prevents overfitting, and speeds up the convergence. In Equation (8), $W_{i,j}^h$ represents the product of the input vectors and the weights of the hidden layer, and b^h represent the bias of the hidden layers h_t. Finally, in the output layer, these hidden representations are mapped to a probability distribution. This implies that we must assign a probability to every word in the dictionary.

$$h_t = \phi\left(W_{i,j}^h v_i + b^h\right) \tag{8}$$

4.2.2. Convolutional Neural Network

Convolutional neural networks (CNNs) [72] were initially developed to recognize digits, especially handwritten ones from images. The main functionalities of a CNN are convolutional and pooling layers to retrieve features from the input data. For Roman Urdu hate speech classification, we fine-tuned a 1D CNN model. The block diagram of the proposed architecture can be seen in Figure 7.

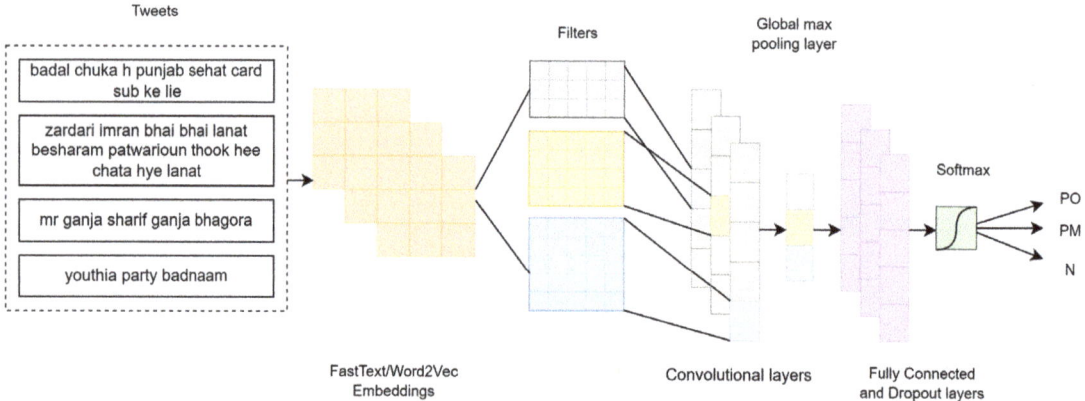

Figure 7. An abstract view of proposed 1-D convolutional neural network architecture.

A convolution layer is a sliding window that converts feature vectors from a fixed-size region. Pooling layers are typically used after a convolutional layer to reduce dimensionality and provide a fixed-length output. For example, max pooling takes the maximum value from the previous convolutional layer. The pooling output is usually passed to a fully connected layer, which is functionally equivalent to a typical multilayer perceptron neural network (MLP). For text classification tasks, a 1D array represents the text, and the architecture of the CNN becomes 1D convolutional and grouping operations. The CNN model used for classifying labeled Roman Urdu tweets contained five layers: the input layer as an embedding layer, a 1D convolutional layer, one global max pooling layer, and two dense layers. The input size had dimension 200, and the output had dimension 3. The CNN computed the operations' results and the loss function gradient using forward and backward propagation.

$$z_i = [\omega_1, \omega_2, \ldots \omega_{i+k}] \in \mathbb{R}^{k \times D} \tag{9}$$

Given a sequence of n words $w_1, w_2, \ldots w_n$, where each word belongs to the word vocabulary W_c and embedding vector with dimension D_c, the word embedding matrix is $C = \mathbb{R}^{D_c \times |W_c|}$. The sentences are passed to this embedding matrix and converted to vectors. The 1D convolution is produced by sliding a window of size k with the same convolutional filters and kernels in every sliding window throughout the sequence. With a dot product between the embedding vectors v and the weight w and the convolution of width k, the concatenated embedding vector of the ith sliding window is shown in Equation (9).

Since in forward propagation, the input data are fed to the neural network in the forward direction to calculate output vectors from input vectors at each layer l, the forward propagation in a one-dimensional convolutional network is shown in Equation (10).

$$s_n^l = \beta_n^l + \sum_{i=1}^{N^{l-1}} \text{conv}\left(\omega_{i=1}^{l-1}, o_i^{l-1}\right) \tag{10}$$

where β_n^l is the bias of the nth neuron at layer l, and o_i^{l-1} expresses the output of the ith neuron at layer $l-1$. For each sliding window i, the scaler values s_i are generated by applying convolutional filters to each of them, that is, $s_i = g(z_i.v) \in \mathbb{R}$. Features extracted from this layer are then passed to a 1D convolutional layer which in the implementation had a filter size of 5, i.e., $u_1, \ldots u_5$ multiplied by a matrix U and adding bias β^l at layer l. Each layer receives the input and calculates the output with an activation function which was a ReLu in this implementation (shown in Equation (11)).

$$s_i = g(z_i.U + \beta) \tag{11}$$

This output is then forwarded to the next layer in the network, along with the learning rate η, the weights of the kernel are updated using the following Equation (12).

$$\omega_{ik}^{l-1}(p+1) = w_{ik}^{l-1}(p) - \eta \frac{\partial \mathbb{E}}{\partial w_{ik}^{l-1}}(p) \tag{12}$$

Since the values assigned to the biases are learnable, just like the weights, the biases are also updated (shown in Equation (13)). p and $p+1$ represents the current state and next state. $\mathbb{E}$ represents the mean square error (MSE) between observed values and actual values at a given layer.

$$\beta_k^l(p+1) = \beta_k^l(p) - \eta \frac{\partial \mathbb{E}}{\partial \beta_k^l}(p) \tag{13}$$

This is followed by a pooling layer, i.e., a global max pooling. It combines all the resultant vectors produced by the convolutional layer into a one-dimensional feature vector. Max pooling is done by taking the max value from the resultant vector as shown graphically in Figure 7. This 1D vector captures the most important features from the sentence and maps them to classification labels. Furthermore, dropout layers are added, randomly dropping half of the neurons, a common method for reducing overfitting in neural networks, before passing through to the output layer, where a prediction is made.

5. Implementation

5.1. RU-PHS Dataset

To validate the effectiveness of our proposed methodology, a benchmark dataset was developed named Roman Urdu Political Hate Speech. This entire dataset contained a total of 5001 labeled Roman Urdu tweets. Each row contained text with its corresponding labels and their respective city-level locations. It did not contain any null values. The data set was categorized into three classes, PO, PM, and N, described in Table 5. Of the 5K tweets, 3028 were labeled as politically offensive, 1190 as politically medium, and 784 as neutral.

Table 5. Roman Urdu Political Hate Speech (RU-PHS) dataset characteristics

Labels	Full Form	#tweets	#Words
PO	Politically offensive	3028	273,379
PM	Politically medium	1190	80,322
N	Neutral	784	46,553

5.2. Preprocessing

Text data are typically unstructured, especially data scraped from social networks, as it is user-generated content. While Roman Urdu writing lacks rules and has no standard lexicon, users write a given word with their own set of rules with several spelling variations. This creates the need to normalize the data and transform it into a structured feature space. The data set was collected from the social media platform Twitter for this research work. The data set was based on trending political hate words from January 2022 to April 2022. Data were collected using an R script, and Twitter Python API was used to stream the data set, which allowed the use of the Twitter developer portal for us to retrieve tweet data.

The scraped data contained more than 30 columns of information for each tweet irrelevant to this investigation. Only the columns "Text" and "Location" were obtained from it. These data were further filtered based on the location, and only tweets from Pakistan were retained. Data were preprocessed using regular expressions (re) to remove @mentions, #Hashtags, URLs, Unicode characters, emojis, and white spaces and converted to lowercase. Furthermore, the dataset was imbalanced since the "politically medium" and "neutral" classes had comparatively fewer samples. To generate synthetic samples for the minority class, the SMOTE algorithm was used. SMOTE is an oversampling technique, which helps produce new samples by focusing on the feature set and interpolating between positive samples that lie together. The total sample distribution of the dataset was (5002, 3), and after SMOTE balancing, the total samples of all three classes were transformed to (9084, 3); only the minority classes were oversampled based on the max number of samples of the majority class, which was 3028.

5.2.1. Guideline Development

For the development of guidelines, we designed a constant procedure to form a strictly exhaustive set of guidelines to determine whether a given phrase or tweet was hate speech. The essential advantage of this guideline development was the consistent approach that would form with their use and lead to correct annotations. The following Table 6 highlights the first-level classification guidelines for offensive speech identification. There were two levels of classifications. The first level classified hate speech and neutral expressions. In the second-level classification for this research, we aimed to classify political hate speech into further three categories: neutral, medium, and offensive. An overall review of the scraped tweets after cleaning was conducted. It was revealed that there was a sizable number of unwanted tweets that were neither neutral nor offensive and did not lie under political hate speech. Since our primary focus was non-English data for this research, all the tweets were split into English and non-English content. A semiautomated technique of NLTK's language detection feature was developed to identify candidate corpus for further manual labeling of the data.

5.2.2. Data Annotation

In this step, machine classifiers were used to learn the characteristics of Twitter posts that represented the class to which they belonged to complete this subjective task using a large-scope data analysis critical for the volumes of data created. In the next step, we manually identified and annotated tweets using the guidelines developed, as machine learning classifiers needed to be fed more information to classify the data correctly. RU data needed predefined rules and regulations to write its roman counterpart, making it difficult to label the data automatically. Thus, the collected data were partly annotated using machine learning algorithms and partly annotated by a human annotator. The annotator was a native speaker of the Urdu language and a graduate. Figure 8 represents the taxonomy developed for the classification of hate speech.

Table 6. The set of class guidelines developed for data labeling.

Classes	Guidelines
Political hate speech	A tweet or phrase belonged to the "political hate speech" class if it met any or all of the following parameters: If a tweet had a hate term about a political figure, political party, government or if it targeted the followers of a specific political party. For example, "Ap ka baap nawaz bhagora chor h" translated in English as "Your father Nawaz is a truant and thief". Some other offensive terms could be "youthia" and "patwari" targeting the supporters of specific political parties.
Neutral	A tweet or phrase corresponded to the "neutral" class if it lacked any of the criteria mentioned for the political hate speech class, for example, "Wsa hi acha lgta ha mujha nawaz sharef" translated in English as "I just like nawaz sharef".
Offensive	A tweet or phrase that belonged to the "political hate speech" class was further classified as "offensive", if the tweet had abusive terms or symbols promoting hostility, igniting anger, or inciting harm to an individual political entity or a group of people that belonged to a political party or that supported a political profile. For example, "Bhounktey rahhooooo nawaz chor" translated in English as "Keep on barking nawaz thief".
Medium/little offensive	A tweet or phrase that belonged to the "political hate speech" class was further classified as "sarcasm/little offensive", if the tweet mocked and conveyed contempt against a political individual, political party, and supporter of a specific political profile yet if it did not contain explicit hate words. For example, "Bilkul thek kaha ap nay nawaz Shareef nay boht investment ki h hmare adliya pay" translated in English as "You are right, Nawaz shareef has invested a lot in our judiciary system".

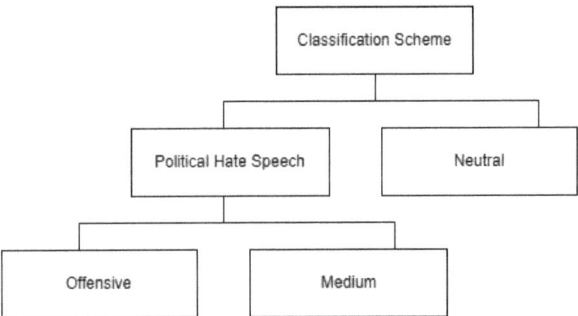

Figure 8. Taxonomy diagram of political hate speech classification.

5.2.3. Custom Stop Words

Stop words are known as conjunction terms or "Haroof e Jaar" in Urdu. A similar list of stop words is also present for Roman Urdu. The complete removal of stop words has the primary benefit of returning only relevant documents. We removed English stop words from our dataset using NLTK library's default list of 40 stop words. A predefined list of RU stop words was obtained from GitHub containing 100 words [18]. A custom list of stop words was extracted from the data set (RU-PHS). For this, we counted the frequency of the most commonly occurring words and sorted them in A–Z order using a Python script. For the next step, the standard stop words list was compared to the frequently occurring words list, and the stop word variants contained in the RU-PHS dataset were identified and removed.

5.2.4. Lexical Unification

Roman Urdu lacks standardization rules, especially user-generated data, which are always unstructured, e.g., inconsistent forms of writing words. Since the machine cannot comprehend that one word can be written with many variations, it takes each variation as a whole different word. This can also lead to biased and compromised results in the classification task. To overcome this problem and to map different variations of one word to a single string we proposed to remove vowels from words. The algorithm (shown in Algorithm 1) was designed to find instances of strings that occurred most frequently in the RU-PHS dataset and to remove vowels from those strings. Table 7 represents the transformation of word variations to a normalized form by pruning vowels.

Algorithm 1: RU Lexical Unification by Removing Vowels.

1. Read CSV file containing scraped data
2. Clean the data by removing
   a. @mentions, #hashtags, URLs, and Unicode characters.
   b. White spaces including from the start and end of the line.
   c. Non-English, numeric values, and special symbols.
3. Compute a list F of the most frequently occurring words
$$\sum_{i=1}^{n}(stringS)$$
4. Select strings with the highest frequency
$$\max\left[\sum_{i=1}^{n}(stringS)\right]$$
5. Create a list of vowels V
6. Compare each string to the list of vowels
   a. Convert strings to lowercase
   b. For each x in input string S
   c. If x is in V
       Replace it with empty space
       else
       Retain it as it is
7. Replace all instances of the original string in the CSV file with the resultant string.

Table 7. Words normalization using proposed lexical unification algorithm.

Words	Frequency	Normalized
Kampain	74	Kmpn
Kampein	65	Kmpn
Kampain	55	Kmpn
Kanpay	25	Knpy
Kanpein	15	Knpn
Kanpen	12	Knpn
kanpien	11	knpn

6. Spatial Data Analysis of Political Hate Speech

Spatial analysis is the process of modeling problems geographically, deriving results through information processing, and then exploring and examining those results. This kind of analysis has proven to be highly effective for assessing the geographic viability of specific locations for various applications, estimating and forecasting outcomes, interpreting and comprehending change, identifying meaningful patterns hidden in data, and much more. In this research, the exclusive political hate speech dataset (RU-PHS) was collected along with locations. The data set was collected only from Pakistan and contained city-level information on each tweet. The aim was to apply geospatial techniques on the dataset to predict hate speech.

6.1. Geocoding

For a geospatial analysis, first, the city-level locations were converted to latitude and longitude using the Python geopy module. Using third-party geocoders and other information sources, geopy makes it simple to find the coordinate information of addresses, cities, countries, and landmarks all over the world. Figure 9 gives a visual representation and it can be seen that most of the tweets were posted from the Punjab region of Pakistan. The city-level locations were replicated as we could only retrieve city-level information from tweets; thus, one point on the map might contain hundreds of points behind it, as it was the exact location for many other instances. This could be improved by obtaining the area-level information of the tweets to map them better and predict future locations. Tweet locations were visualized in ArcMap.

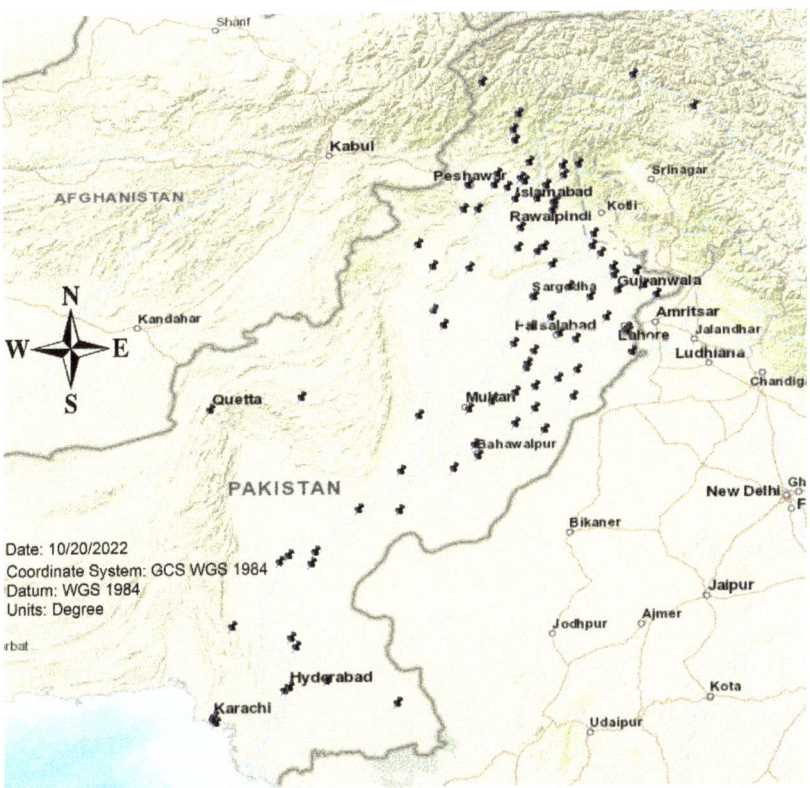

Figure 9. Visualization of city-level tweets' information over Pakistan's base map using ArcGIS.

6.2. Hotspot Analysis

A hotspot is considered an area with a higher concentration of events than would be anticipated from a random distribution of incidents. The analysis of point distributions or spatial layouts of points in space led to the development of hotspot detection [73]. The density of locations within a given area was compared to a complete spatial randomness model, which described the point events occurring at random (i.e., a homogeneous spatial Poisson process). Hotspot techniques evaluate the level of point event interaction to comprehend spatial patterns and assess the density of data points in a particular region. The following Figure 10 visualizes the hot and cold spots that were visualized using the information from the RU-PHS labels. The legend shown on the right side gives a summary of the mapped points. The blue points show the cold spots, and the red points show the hotspots with 99% probability.

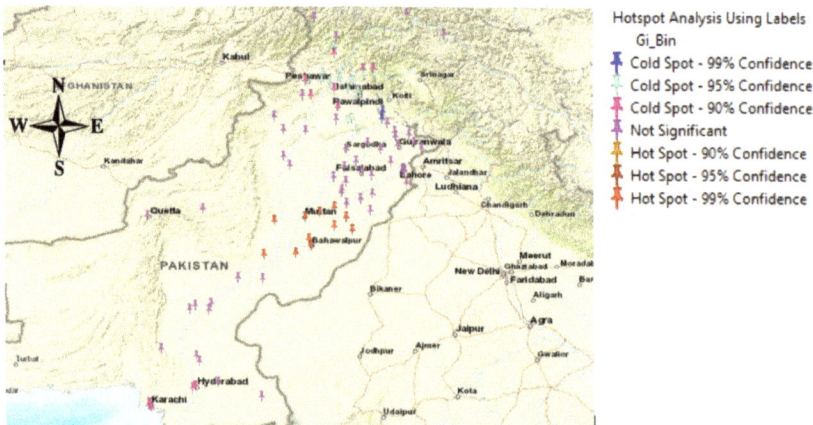

Figure 10. Visualization of hotspot analysis of tweets' labels over Pakistan's base map Using ArcGIS.

6.3. Cluster Analysis

A cluster and outlier analysis was used to validate and supplement the hotspot analysis because it could detect both groups and areas with anomalies. As a result, its findings highlighted aspects that may have been neglected in the hotspot analysis but were noteworthy, particularly in areas in which different types of subgroups coexisted. The results of this analysis (with a fixed bandwidth and a Euclidean distance of 6 miles) were very noticeable, particularly considering that the criteria were the same as in the hotspot analysis for ease of understanding and comparison purposes. Figure 11 shows the results of the cluster outlier analysis using the RU-PHS label information.

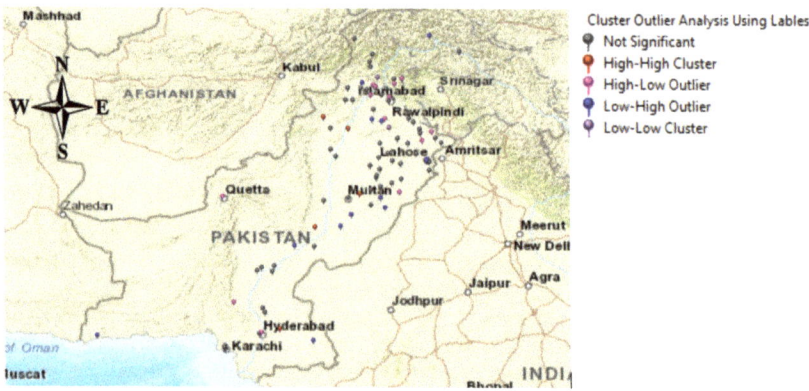

Figure 11. Visualization of cluster outlier analysis of tweets' labels over Pakistan's base map using ArcGIS.

6.4. Interpolation

To improve visual representation and provide guidance in decision making, the results were interpolated onto a continuous surface using an inverse distance weighted interpolation (IDW), as shown in Figure 12a for hotspot point data and Figure 12b for cluster outlier point data. The interpolation estimates values for raster cells based on a small set of sample data points. It could forecast null values about any geographic point data. The interpolation was used only for the visual representation; otherwise, the real statistical analysis took place feature by data. Displaying both the surface and true results of the hotspot analysis simultaneously was an excellent way to logically portray both the statistical results and the more approachable visualization.

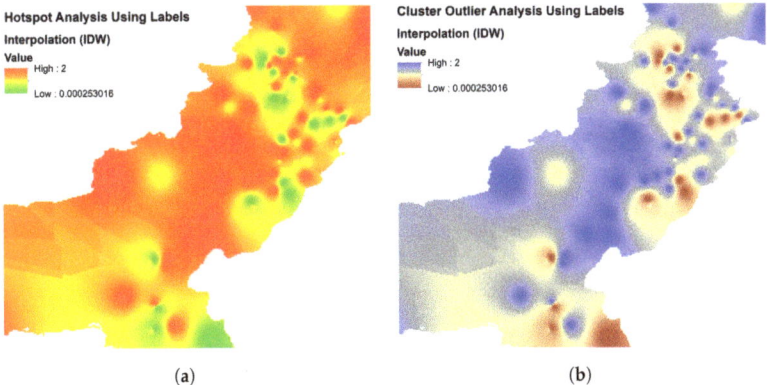

Figure 12. Inverse distance weighted interpolation results: (**a**) hotspot points data; (**b**) cluster outlier points data.

7. Results and Discussions

To test the effectiveness of our proposed methodology, we used the RU-PHS dataset developed and labeled by this research. Before the experiment, the data set was cleaned, lexically unified, lemmatized for English words, tokenized, and transformed by a SMOTE analysis since the data set suffered imbalance. We used TF-IDF vectorizer, word2vec, and fastText for dense vector representations of words. The aim was to classify political hate speech into three classes neutral (N), politically offensive hate (PO), and politically medium hate (PM). For the classification, conventional machine learning models were used to present a comparative analysis concerning deep neural networks.

7.1. Hyperparameters

The vocabulary size was 13,799; the input length was equal to the maximum number of tokens present in the sentence, and a low-rank projection of the co-occurrence statistics of each word concerning all other words was 50, i.e., the embedding dimension passed as the output dimension to the embedding layer. Similar embedding layer dimensions were leveraged for different vector embeddings. To experiment, the data were split into the typical 80%, 20% split, where 20% of the data were for testing and validating the proposed model. The feed-forward neural network consisted of five layers with ReLu as an activation function and softmax on the output layer to predict a multinomial probability distribution for multiclass classification. Table 8 presents the model summary of feed-forward neural network architecture for the classification of RU-PHS.

Table 8. Model summary of the fine-tuned feed-forward neural network.

Sr.	Layer	Type	Output Shape	Parameters	Activation
1	Input	Embedding	(None, 200, 50)	689,950	-
2	Hidden	Flatten	(None, 10,000)	0	-
3	Hidden	Dense	(None, 64)	640,064	ReLu
4	Hidden	Dense	(None, 32)	2080	ReLu
5	Output	Dense	(None, 3)	99	Softmax

Similarly, the convolutional neural network was implemented with 723,401 trainable parameters for 15 epochs. To measure the performance of both our classification models based on error and probability, the categorical cross-entropy was used as the loss function, since it is commonly used for multiclass classification tasks. To optimize stochastic gradient descent, the Adam optimizer was used as it provides more efficient neural network weights by running repeated cycles of adaptive moment estimation. The only difference was that the sequences of word embeddings went through several convolutional operations with kernel heights and then through a ReLu activation and a 1D global max pooling operation. Finally, the maximum values of the dense layers were concatenated and passed to a fully connected classification layer with a softmax activation. A detailed summary of the convolutional neural network model for the classification of RU-PHS is presented in Table 9.

Table 9. Model summary of the fine-tuned convolutional neural network.

Sr.	Layer	Type	Output Shape	Parameters	Activation
1	Input	Embedding	(None, 200, 50)	689,950	-
2	Hidden	Conv1D	(None, 196, 128)	32,128	Relu
3	Hidden	GlobalMaxPooling1D	(None, 128)	0	-
4	Hidden	Dense	(None, 10)	1290	Relu
5	Output	Dense	(None, 3)	33	Softmax

7.2. Model Training and Validation

The models were trained using the training data and the accuracy was used as the evaluation metric to check models' performance both in training accuracy and in validation accuracy. The models were trained with different numbers of epochs and the maximum validation accuracy achieved was 93% for the feed-forward neural network and 92% for the convolutional neural network for 14 epochs. Figure 13a,b gives a detailed insight into the training and validation accuracy for the feed-forward neural model with the continuous skip-gram vector representations of fastText.

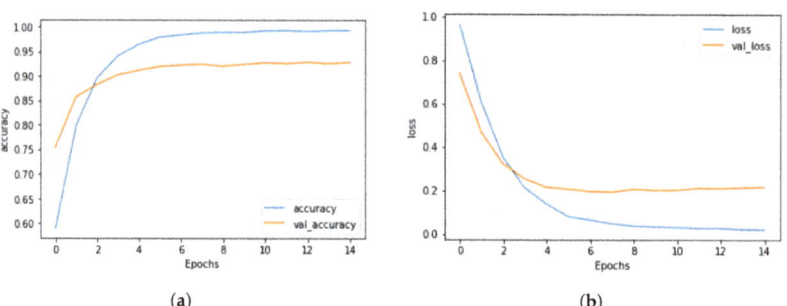

Figure 13. Accuracy and loss ROC curves of proposed feed forward neural network: (**a**) training and validation accuracy; (**b**) training and validation loss.

The training and validation curves in Figure 14a,b indicated that increasing the training epochs could improve the precision of the CNN model. However, when we increased the number of epochs, no increment was observed in the validation accuracy; on the other hand, the training accuracy was increased to 97–98%. This suggested that the model started to overfit. Since the dataset was small and the ideal number of epochs depended on the complexity of the dataset, no improvement was seen in the model by increasing the epochs. However, it could be seen that both training and validation accuracies increased with the same trend.

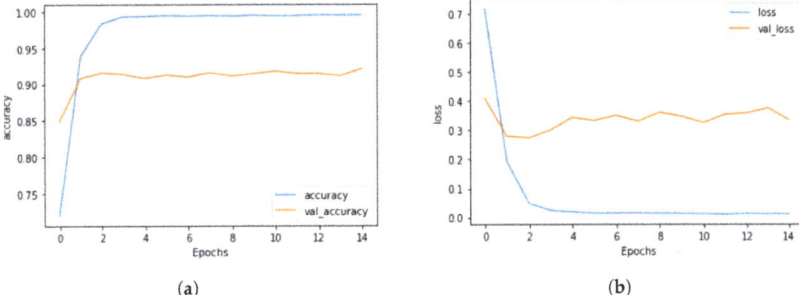

Figure 14. Accuracy and loss ROC curves of proposed convolutional neural network: (**a**) training and validation accuracy; (**b**) training and validation loss.

7.3. Accuracy

The standard accuracy metrics were used to measure the classification performance in the RU-PHS data set, i.e., accuracy, macroaveraged precision, macroaveraged recall, macroaveraged F1 score. Since the class imbalance was tackled, to let the classifier treat each class equally and to reflect the overall performance of the model with regard to the most frequent class labels, the macroaveraged scores was used.

In this section, we compare the overall performance of conventional machine learning models and neural networks for classifying tweets into politically offensive hate, politically medium hate, and neutral classes. Table 10 shows the accuracy scores of each model about various word representations techniques. In the Table 10, it can be seen that TF-IDF performed well with conventional machine learning models such as multinomial naive Bayes with 87% accuracy, linear SVM with 89% accuracy, random forest with 91% accuracy, and gradient boosting with 90% accuracy. Since it only calculated document correlation in the word-count space rather than using a similarity score, the accuracy outcomes could be promising in this problem.

On the other hand, the continuous skip-gram model for word2vec and fastText performed really well with regression models and the proposed neural networks achieving up to 93% accuracy. Details of test classification results of each class can also be seen in the confusion matrix shown in Figure 15a,b, where 0 refers to the "neutral" class, 1 refers to the "politically medium" class and 2 refers to the "politically offensive" class. In the CNN classification for the politically offensive class Figure 15a, only 39 comments were mislabeled as neutral and 60 as politically medium, while 764 comments were classified accurately as politically offensive. For the politically medium class, 871 were correctly labeled and only 29 and 48 were mislabeled as neutral and politically offensive, respectively. For the neutral class, 875 were correctly labeled as neutral and only 17 and 23 were mislabeled as politically medium and politically offensive, respectively. Similarly, in the feed-forward NN Figure 15b classification for the politically offensive class, 777 comments were classified accurately as politically offensive. Only 40 and 46 comments were mislabeled as politically medium and neutral, respectively. For the politically medium class, 870 were correctly labeled and only 45 and 33 were mislabeled as neutral and politically offensive, respectively. For the neutral class, 878 were correctly labeled as neutral, and only 15 and 22 were mislabeled as politically medium and politically offensive, respectively.

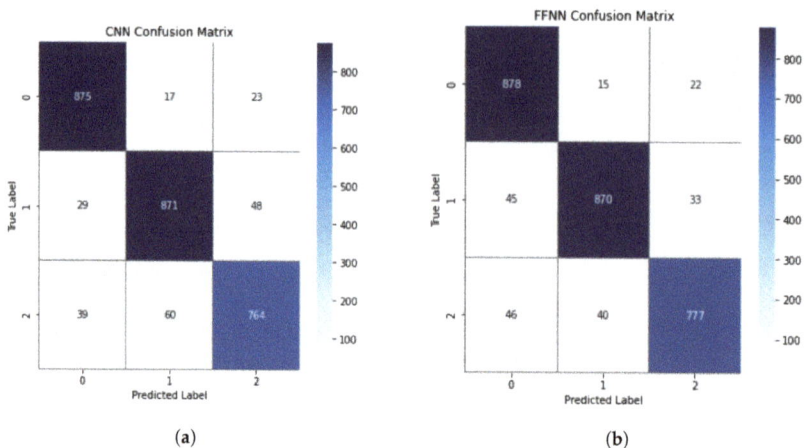

Figure 15. Confusion matrices for RU-PHS dataset classification: (**a**) CNN confusion matrix; (**b**) feed-forward NN confusion matrix.

Table 10. Summary of results achieved by conventional machine learning approaches and proposed neural network architectures with five different word representations. The results in bold are the best results out of five feature extraction techniques in each model. For example, highest accuracy achieved by TF-IDF using Multinomial NB. Similarly in Neural Networks FastText(CSG) achieved highest accuracy out of four other feature extraction techniques.

Technique	Classifier	Features	Accuracy (%)	Precision (%)	Recall (%)	F1-Score (%)
Bayes	Multinomial naïve Bayes	TF-IDF	**87**	**88**	**88**	**87**
		word2vec(CBOW)	50	57	51	52
		word2vec(CSG)	60	64	60	61
		fastText(CBOW)	66	70	67	66
		fastText(CSG)	69	72	70	69
SVM	Linear	TF-IDF	**89**	**90**	**90**	**90**
		word2vec(CBOW)	62	70	73	73
		word2vec(CSG)	70	75	70	70
		fastText(CBOW)	74	76	74	74
		fastText(CSG)	75	77	76	77
Random	Forest	TF-IDF	91	92	91	91
		word2vec(CBOW)	88	89	89	89
		word2vec(CSG)	91	92	92	92
		fastText(CBOW)	91	89	91	91
		fastText(CSG)	**93**	**92**	**93**	**93**
Regression	Gradient boosting	TF-IDF	90	91	91	91
		word2vec(CBOW)	91	90	91	91
		word2vec(CSG)	**92**	**92**	**92**	**92**
		fastText(CBOW)	90	91	94	91
		fastText(CSG)	90	90	92	92
	XgBoost	TF-IDF	84	86	85	85
		word2vec(CBOW)	70	74	70	70
		word2vec(CSG)	77	80	78	78
		fastText(CBOW)	82	84	83	83
		fastText(CSG)	**89**	**90**	**91**	**91**
Neural networks	Feed-forward neural network	word2vec(CBOW)	65	71	65	65
		word2vec(CSG)	72	77	72	72
		fastText(CBOW)	85	86	91	89
		fastText(CSG)	**93**	**90**	**92**	**93**
	Convolutional neural network	word2vec(CBOW)	70	75	71	71
		word2vec(CSG)	89	91	90	89
		fastText(CBOW)	85	88	89	89
		fastText(CSG)	**92**	**92**	**91**	**92**

From Table 10, it can be inferred that the proposed feed-forward neural network with the fastText continuous skip-gram model outperformed the baseline models and the convolutional neural network with a better classification convergence for the RU-

PHS dataset. The time taken to build the models is presented in Table 11, and since the architecture and hyperparameters for all the classification models were different and were fine-tuned for achieving maximum accuracy, this comparison in terms of time complexity gives some insight into the results obtained and the respective time consumed.

Table 11. Comparison of time performance of machine learning models on RU-PHS dataset

Classifier	MNB	LSVM	RF	GB	FFNN	CNN
Features	TF-IDF	TF-IDF	fastText(CSG)	W2V(CSG)	fastText(CSG)	fastText(CSG)
Time	2 s	6 s	80 s	60 s	17 s	20 s

8. Conclusions and Future Directions

This research work presented the automatic detection of political hate speech in Roman Urdu. Our significant contribution was to present an entire dataset of political hate speech from Twitter posts. The classification of Roman Urdu is challenging due to its vast lexical structure. To address this problem, we proposed an algorithm for unifying the RU-PHS dataset. In this work, we developed three different word representation techniques using TF-IDF, word2vec, and fastText to convert word-level information to vector representations. We explored the performance of seven machine learning models for the classification of the RU-PHS dataset. A comparison of the effectiveness of word representations with conventional machine learning techniques and the proposed neural networks was made. By analyzing the results from different equations, it was found that the skip-gram model of fastText, which works on character n-grams, achieved the highest empirical scores compared to word2vec, which takes into account the word n-grams. Overall, regression-based models achieved a promising accuracy but could not be considered the best approaches due to their time complexity. The proposed feed-forward neural network achieved a 93% accuracy with fastText vector representations on the RU-PHS dataset. After validation through various machine learning and deep learning methods, the dataset was mapped using the spatial information in ArcMap. The statistical information helped in the identification of trends and patterns, and the hotspot and cluster analysis assisted in pinpointing the highly susceptible areas in Pakistan. Due to a lack of resources, the information was only obtained at the city level. The results demonstrated that Punjab cities were the most affected and key locations of hate and sarcastic tweet generation.

For future work, we aim to develop a more robust algorithm for the lexical unification of Roman languages. We also consider collecting area-specific location information of tweets for a better predictability of affected regions. We also aim to train the proposed model for generic speech classification. Our dataset RU_PHS was made available for the research community to reproduce results. It will help in the development of more generic machine learning models for the detection of political hate speech in Roman Urdu.

Author Contributions: Conceptualization, S.A., M.U., M.U.A., M.S.S. and H.T.R.; methodology, S.A.; validation, M.U., M.U.A., M.S.S. and H.T.R.; formal analysis, M.U. and M.U.A.; investigation, M.U. and M.U.A.; data curation, S.A. and M.U.; writing—original draft preparation, S.A.; writing—review and editing, M.S.S., M.U., M.U.A. and H.T.R.; supervision, M.S.S. and H.T.R.; resources, M.S.S. and H.T.R. All authors have read and agreed to the published version of the manuscript.

Funding: This research received no external funding.

Data Availability Statement: The dataset shall be available through declaration from all authors

Conflicts of Interest: The authors declare no conflict of interest.

References

1. Gitari, N.D.; Zuping, Z.; Damien, H.; Long, J. A lexicon-based approach for hate speech detection. *Int. J. Multimed. Ubiquitous Eng.* **2015**, *10*, 215–230. [CrossRef]
2. Aslam, S. Twitter by the Numbers: Stats, Demographics & Fun Facts. 2022. Available online: https://www.omnicoreagency.com/twitter-statistics/ (accessed on 8 June 2022).
3. Djuric, N.; Zhou, J.; Morris, R.; Grbovic, M.; Radosavljevic, V.; Bhamidipati, N. Hate speech detection with comment embeddings. In Proceedings of the 24th International Conference on World Wide Web, Florence, Italy, 18–22 May 2015; pp. 29–30.
4. Saeed, H.H.; Ashraf, M.H.; Kamiran, F.; Karim, A.; Calders, T. Roman Urdu toxic comment classification. *Lang. Resour. Eval.* **2021**, *55*, 971–996. [CrossRef]
5. Naqvi, R.A.; Khan, M.A.; Malik, N.; Saqib, S.; Alyas, T.; Hussain, D. Roman Urdu news headline classification empowered with machine learning. *Comput. Mater. Contin.* **2020**, *65*, 1221–1236.
6. Mehmood, F.; Ghani, M.U.; Ibrahim, M.A.; Shahzadi, R.; Mahmood, W.; Asim, M.N. A precisely xtreme-multi channel hybrid approach for roman urdu sentiment analysis. *IEEE Access* **2020**, *8*, 192740–192759. [CrossRef]
7. Jiang, M.; Liang, Y.; Feng, X.; Fan, X.; Pei, Z.; Xue, Y.; Guan, R. Text classification based on deep belief network and softmax regression. *Neural Comput. Appl.* **2018**, *29*, 61–70. [CrossRef]
8. Dulac-Arnold, G.; Denoyer, L.; Gallinari, P. Text classification: A sequential reading approach. In Proceedings of the European Conference on Information Retrieval, Stavanger, Norway, 10–14 April 2011; Springer: Berlin/Heidelberg, Germany, 2011; pp. 411–423.
9. Bollen, J.; Gonçalves, B.; Ruan, G.; Mao, H. Happiness is assortative in online social networks. *Artif. life* **2011**, *17*, 237–251. [CrossRef] [PubMed]
10. Khan, M.M.; Shahzad, K.; Malik, M.K. Hate speech detection in roman urdu. *ACM Trans. Asian Low-Resour. Lang. Inf. Process. (TALLIP)* **2021**, *20*, 1–19. [CrossRef]
11. Rizwan, H.; Shakeel, M.H.; Karim, A. Hate-speech and offensive language detection in roman Urdu. In Proceedings of the 2020 Conference on Empirical Methods in Natural Language Processing (EMNLP), Online, 16–20 November 2020; pp. 2512–2522.
12. Martins, R.; Gomes, M.; Almeida, J.J.; Novais, P.; Henriques, P. Hate speech classification in social media using emotional analysis. In Proceedings of the 2018 7th Brazilian Conference on Intelligent Systems (BRACIS), Sao Paulo, Brazil, 22–25 October 2018; pp. 61–66.
13. Bilal, M.; Israr, H.; Shahid, M.; Khan, A. Sentiment classification of Roman-Urdu opinions using Naïve Bayesian, Decision Tree and KNN classification techniques. *J. King Saud Univ.-Comput. Inf. Sci.* **2016**, *28*, 330–344. [CrossRef]
14. Alam, M.; Hussain, S.U. Roman-Urdu-Parl: Roman-Urdu and Urdu Parallel Corpus for Urdu Language Understanding. *Trans. Asian Low-Resour. Lang. Inf. Process.* **2022**, *21*, 1–20. [CrossRef]
15. Younas, A.; Nasim, R.; Ali, S.; Wang, G.; Qi, F. Sentiment Analysis of Code-Mixed Roman Urdu-English Social Media Text using Deep Learning Approaches. In Proceedings of the 2020 IEEE 23rd International Conference on Computational Science and Engineering (CSE), Guangzhou, China, 29 December 2020–1 January 2021; pp. 66–71.
16. Wasswa, H.W. The Role of Social Media in the 2013 Presidential Election Campaigns in Kenya. Ph.D. Thesis, University of Nairobi, Nairobi, Kenya, 2013.
17. Mukund, S.; Srihari, R.K. Analyzing Urdu social media for sentiments using transfer learning with controlled translations. In Proceedings of the Second Workshop on Language in Social Media, Montreal, QC, Canada, 7 June 2012; pp. 1–8.
18. Tehreem, T. Sentiment analysis for youtube comments in roman urdu. *arXiv* **2021**, arXiv:2102.10075.
19. Aimal, M.; Bakhtyar, M.; Baber, J.; Lakho, S.; Mohammad, U.; Ahmed, W.; Karim, J. Identifying negativity factors from social media text corpus using sentiment analysis method. *arXiv* **2021**, arXiv:2107.02175.
20. Habiba, R.; Awais, D.M.; Shoaib, D.M. A Technique to Calculate National Happiness Index by Analyzing Roman Urdu Messages Posted on Social Media. *ACM Trans. Asian Low-Resour. Lang. Inf. Process. (TALLIP)* **2020**, *19*, 1–16. [CrossRef]
21. Hussain, A.; Arshad, M.U. An Attention Based Neural Network for Code Switching Detection: English & Roman Urdu. *arXiv* **2021**, arXiv:2103.02252.
22. Sadia, H.; Ullah, M.; Hussain, T.; Gul, N.; Hussain, M.F.; ul Haq, N.; Bakar, A. An efficient way of finding polarity of roman urdu reviews by using Boolean rules. *Scalable Comput. Pract. Exp.* **2020**, *21*, 277–289. [CrossRef]
23. Rana, T.A.; Shahzadi, K.; Rana, T.; Arshad, A.; Tubishat, M. An Unsupervised Approach for Sentiment Analysis on Social Media Short Text Classification in Roman Urdu. *Trans. Asian Low-Resour. Lang. Inf. Process.* **2021**, *21*, 1–16. [CrossRef]
24. Akhter, M.P.; Jiangbin, Z.; Naqvi, I.R.; Abdelmajeed, M.; Sadiq, M.T. Automatic detection of offensive language for urdu and roman urdu. *IEEE Access* **2020**, *8*, 91213–91226. [CrossRef]
25. Santosh, T.; Aravind, K. Hate speech detection in hindi-english code-mixed social media text. In Proceedings of the ACM India Joint International Conference on Data Science and Management of Data, Kolkata, India 3–5 January 2019; pp. 310–313.
26. Arshad, M.U.; Bashir, M.F.; Majeed, A.; Shahzad, W.; Beg, M.O. Corpus for emotion detection on roman urdu. In Proceedings of the 2019 22nd International Multitopic Conference (INMIC), Islamabad, Pakistan, 29–30 November 2019; pp. 1–6.
27. Mahmood, Z.; Safder, I.; Nawab, R.M.A.; Bukhari, F.; Nawaz, R.; Alfakeeh, A.S.; Aljohani, N.R.; Hassan, S.U. Deep sentiments in roman urdu text using recurrent convolutional neural network model. *Inf. Process. Manag.* **2020**, *57*, 102233. [CrossRef]
28. Mehmood, K.; Essam, D.; Shafi, K.; Malik, M.K. Discriminative feature spamming technique for roman urdu sentiment analysis. *IEEE Access* **2019**, *7*, 47991–48002. [CrossRef]

29. Mukhtar, N.; Khan, M.A. Effective lexicon-based approach for Urdu sentiment analysis. *Artif. Intell. Rev.* **2020**, *53*, 2521–2548. [CrossRef]
30. Majeed, A.; Mujtaba, H.; Beg, M.O. Emotion detection in roman urdu text using machine learning. In Proceedings of the 35th IEEE/ACM International Conference on Automated Software Engineering Workshops, Virtual Event, Australia, 21–25 December 2020; pp. 125–130.
31. Naqvi, U.; Majid, A.; Abbas, S.A. UTSA: Urdu text sentiment analysis using deep learning methods. *IEEE Access* **2021**, *9*, 114085–114094. [CrossRef]
32. Chen, Y.; Zhou, Y.; Zhu, S.; Xu, H. Detecting offensive language in social media to protect adolescent online safety. In Proceedings of the 2012 International Conference on Privacy, Security, Risk and Trust and 2012 International Confernece on Social Computing, Amsterdam, The Netherlands, 3–5 September 2012; pp. 71–80.
33. Xiang, G.; Fan, B.; Wang, L.; Hong, J.; Rose, C. Detecting offensive tweets via topical feature discovery over a large scale twitter corpus. In Proceedings of the 21st ACM International Conference on Information and Knowledge Management, Maui, HI, USA, 29 October–2 November 2012; pp. 1980–1984.
34. Dinakar, K.; Jones, B.; Havasi, C.; Lieberman, H.; Picard, R. Common sense reasoning for detection, prevention, and mitigation of cyberbullying. *ACM Trans. Interact. Intell. Syst. (TiiS)* **2012**, *2*, 1–30. [CrossRef]
35. Warner, W.; Hirschberg, J. Detecting hate speech on the world wide web. In Proceedings of the Second Workshop on Language in Social Media, Montreal, QC, Canada, 7 June 2012; pp. 19–26.
36. Wadhwa, P.; Bhatia, M. Tracking on-line radicalization using investigative data mining. In Proceedings of the 2013 National Conference on Communications (NCC), New Delhi, India, 15–17 February 2013; pp. 1–5.
37. Kwok, I.; Wang, Y. Locate the hate: Detecting tweets against blacks. In Proceedings of the Twenty-Seventh AAAI Conference on Artificial Intelligence, Bellevue, WA, USA, 14–18 July 2013.
38. Nahar, V.; Al-Maskari, S.; Li, X.; Pang, C. Semi-supervised learning for cyberbullying detection in social networks. In *Proceedings of the Australasian Database Conference*; Springer: Berlin/Heidelberg, Germany, 2014; pp. 160–171.
39. Burnap, P.; Williams, M.L. Hate speech, machine classification and statistical modelling of information flows on Twitter: Interpretation and communication for policy decision making. In Proceedings of the Internet, Policy & Politics, Oxford, UK, 26 September 2014.
40. Agarwal, S.; Sureka, A. Using knn and svm based one-class classifier for detecting online radicalization on twitter. In Proceedings of the International Conference on Distributed Computing and Internet Technology, Bhubaneswar, India, 5–8 February 2015; Springer: Berlin/Heidelberg, Germany, 2015; pp. 431–442.
41. Waseem, Z.; Hovy, D. Hateful symbols or hateful people? predictive features for hate speech detection on twitter. In Proceedings of the NAACL Student Research Workshop, San Diego, CA, USA, 12–17 June 2016; pp. 88–93.
42. Di Capua, M.; Di Nardo, E.; Petrosino, A. Unsupervised cyber bullying detection in social networks. In Proceedings of the 2016 23rd International conference on pattern recognition (ICPR), Cancun, Mexico, 4–8 December 2016; pp. 432–437.
43. Park, J.H.; Fung, P. One-step and two-step classification for abusive language detection on twitter. *arXiv* **2017**, arXiv:1706.01206.
44. Chen, H.; McKeever, S.; Delany, S.J. Abusive Text Detection Using Neural Networks. In Proceedings of the AICS, Dublin, Ireland, 7–8 December 2017; pp. 258–260.
45. Badjatiya, P.; Gupta, S.; Gupta, M.; Varma, V. Deep learning for hate speech detection in tweets. In Proceedings of the 6th International Conference on World Wide Web Companion, Perth, Australia, 3–7 April 2017; pp. 759–760.
46. Wiegand, M.; Ruppenhofer, J.; Schmidt, A.; Greenberg, C. Inducing a lexicon of abusive words–a feature-based approach. In Proceedings of the 2018 Conference of the North American Chapter of the Association for Computational Linguistics: Human Language Technologies, New Orleans, LA, USA, 1–6 June 2018; Long Papers; Association for Computational Linguistics: Cedarville, OH, USA, 2019; Volume 1, pp. 1046–1056.
47. Pawar, R.; Agrawal, Y.; Joshi, A.; Gorrepati, R.; Raje, R.R. Cyberbullying detection system with multiple server configurations. In Proceedings of the 2018 IEEE International Conference on Electro/Information Technology (EIT), Rochester, MI, USA, 3–5 May 2018; pp. 90–95.
48. Watanabe, H.; Bouazizi, M.; Ohtsuki, T. Hate speech on twitter: A pragmatic approach to collect hateful and offensive expressions and perform hate speech detection. *IEEE Access* **2018**, *6*, 13825–13835. [CrossRef]
49. Malmasi, S.; Zampieri, M. Challenges in discriminating profanity from hate speech. *J. Exp. Theor. Artif. Intell.* **2018**, *30*, 187–202. [CrossRef]
50. Pitsilis, G.K.; Ramampiaro, H.; Langseth, H. Effective hate-speech detection in Twitter data using recurrent neural networks. *Appl. Intell.* **2018**, *48*, 4730–4742. [CrossRef]
51. Fernandez, M.; Alani, H. Contextual semantics for radicalisation detection on Twitter. In Proceedings of the Semantic Web for Social Good Workshop (SW4SG) at International Semantic Web Conference 2018, Monterey, CA, USA, 9 October 2018,
52. Ousidhoum, N.; Lin, Z.; Zhang, H.; Song, Y.; Yeung, D.Y. Multilingual and multi-aspect hate speech analysis. *arXiv* **2019**, arXiv:1908.11049.
53. Zhang, Z.; Luo, L. Hate speech detection: A solved problem? the challenging case of long tail on twitter. *Semant. Web* **2019**, *10*, 925–945. [CrossRef]

54. Kaur, A.; Gupta, V. N-gram based approach for opinion mining of Punjabi text. In Proceedings of the International Workshop on Multi-Disciplinary Trends in Artificial Intelligence, Bangalore, India, 8–10 December 2014; Springer: Berlin/Heidelberg, Germany, 2014; pp. 81–88.
55. Ashari, A.; Paryudi, I.; Tjoa, A.M. Performance comparison between Naïve Bayes, decision tree and k-nearest neighbor in searching alternative design in an energy simulation tool. *Int. J. Adv. Comput. Sci. Appl. (IJACSA)* **2013**, *4*, 33–39. [CrossRef]
56. Syed, A.Z.; Aslam, M.; Martinez-Enriquez, A.M. Lexicon based sentiment analysis of Urdu text using SentiUnits. In Proceedings of the Mexican International Conference on Artificial Intelligence, Pachuca, Mexico, 8–13 November 2010; Springer: Berlin/Heidelberg, Germany, 2010; pp. 32–43.
57. Ghulam, H.; Zeng, F.; Li, W.; Xiao, Y. Deep learning-based sentiment analysis for roman urdu text. *Procedia Comput. Sci.* **2019**, *147*, 131–135. [CrossRef]
58. Khan, L.; Amjad, A.; Afaq, K.M.; Chang, H.T. Deep sentiment analysis using CNN-LSTM architecture of English and Roman Urdu text shared in social media. *Appl. Sci.* **2022**, *12*, 2694. [CrossRef]
59. Sharf, Z.; Rahman, S.U. Lexical normalization of roman urdu text. *Int. J. Comput. Sci. Netw. Secur.* **2017**, *17*, 213–221.
60. Sharf, Z.; Mansoor, H.A. Opinion mining in roman urdu using baseline classifiers. *Int. J. Comput. Sci. Netw. Secur.* **2018**, *18*, 156–164.
61. Sharjeel, M.; Nawab, R.M.A.; Rayson, P. COUNTER: Corpus of Urdu news text reuse. *Lang. Resour. Eval.* **2017**, *51*, 777–803. [CrossRef]
62. Dzakiyullah, N.R.; Hussin, B.; Saleh, C.; Handani, A.M. Comparison neural network and support vector machine for production quantity prediction. *Adv. Sci. Lett.* **2014**, *20*, 2129–2133. [CrossRef]
63. Bose, R.; Aithal, P.; Roy, S. Sentiment analysis on the basis of tweeter comments of application of drugs by customary language toolkit and textblob opinions of distinct countries. *Int. J.* **2020**, *8*, 3684–3696.
64. Suri, N.; Verma, T. Multilingual Sentimental Analysis on Twitter Dataset: A Review. *Int. J. Adv. Comput. Sci. Appl.* **2017**, *10*, 2789–2799.
65. Jebaseel, A.; Kirubakaran, D.E. M-learning sentiment analysis with data mining techniques. *Int. J. Comput. Sci. Telecommun.* **2012**, *3*, 45–48.
66. Gamallo, P.; Garcia, M.; et al. Citius: A Naive-Bayes Strategy for Sentiment Analysis on English Tweets. In Proceedings of the Semeval@Coling, Dublin, Ireland, 23–24 August 2014; pp. 171–175.
67. Peña, A.; Mesias, J.; Patiño, A.; Carvalho, J.V.; Gomez, G.; Ibarra, K.; Bedoya, S. PANAS-TDL: A psychrometric deep learning model for characterizing sentiments of tourists against the COVID-19 pandemic on Twitter. In *Proceedings of the Advances in Tourism, Technology and Systems: Selected Papers from ICOTTS20*; Springer: Berlin/Heidelberg, Germany, 2021; Volume 2, pp. 162–176.
68. Jing, L.P.; Huang, H.K.; Shi, H.B. Improved feature selection approach TFIDF in text mining. In Proceedings of the International Conference on Machine Learning and Cybernetics, Beijing, China, 4–5 November 2002; Volume 2, pp. 944–946.
69. Mikolov, T.; Sutskever, I.; Chen, K.; Corrado, G.S.; Dean, J. Distributed representations of words and phrases and their compositionality. *Adv. Neural Inf. Process. Syst.* **2013**, *26*, 1–9.
70. Bojanowski, P.; Grave, E.; Joulin, A.; Mikolov, T. Enriching Word Vectors with Subword Information. *Trans. Assoc. Comput. Linguist.* **2017**, *5*, 135–146. [CrossRef]
71. Zell, A. *Simulation Neuronaler Netze*; Addison-Wesley: Bonn, Germany, 1994; Volume 1.
72. Johnson, R.; Zhang, T. Effective use of word order for text categorization with convolutional neural networks. *arXiv* **2014**, arXiv:1412.1058.
73. Chakravorty, S. Identifying crime clusters: The spatial principles. *Middle States Geogr.* **1995**, *28*, 53–58.

Disclaimer/Publisher's Note: The statements, opinions and data contained in all publications are solely those of the individual author(s) and contributor(s) and not of MDPI and/or the editor(s). MDPI and/or the editor(s) disclaim responsibility for any injury to people or property resulting from any ideas, methods, instructions or products referred to in the content.

Article

AutoGAN: An Automated Human-Out-of-the-Loop Approach for Training Generative Adversarial Networks

Ehsan Nazari *, Paula Branco and Guy-Vincent Jourdan

School of Electric Engineering and Computer Science, University of Ottawa, Ottawa, ON K1N 6N5, Canada
* Correspondence: enaza030@uottawa.ca

Abstract: Generative Adversarial Networks (GANs) have been used for many applications with overwhelming success. The training process of these models is complex, involving a zero-sum game between two neural networks trained in an adversarial manner. Thus, to use GANs, researchers and developers need to answer the question: "Is the GAN sufficiently trained?". However, understanding when a GAN is well trained for a given problem is a challenging and laborious task that usually requires monitoring the training process and human intervention for assessing the quality of the GAN generated outcomes. Currently, there is no automatic mechanism for determining the required number of epochs that correspond to a well-trained GAN, allowing the training process to be safely stopped. In this paper, we propose AutoGAN, an algorithm that allows one to answer this question in a fully automatic manner with minimal human intervention, being applicable to different data modalities including imagery and tabular data. Through an extensive set of experiments, we show the clear advantage of our solution when compared against alternative methods, for a task where the GAN outputs are used as an oversampling method. Moreover, we show that AutoGAN not only determines a good stopping point for training the GAN, but it also allows one to run fewer training epochs to achieve a similar or better performance with the GAN outputs.

Keywords: generative adversarial models; automatic training

MSC: 68T01; 68T07

1. Introduction

Generative models are a crucial part of many important machine learning and computer vision algorithms. In recent years, they have been used in multiple applications with outstanding success (e.g., [1]). Generative Adversarial Networks (GANs) [2] are a subset of the generative models that have attracted the attention of the scientific community. GANs have also been used in a diversity of real-world applications involving data generation, such as image generation [3–7], image-to-image translation [8–10], image super resolution [11], video generation [12,13], music generation [14], graphs generation [15], or text generation [16]. They have also been applied to address other complex tasks, namely data de-identification [17], over-sampling [18,19], improving classification accuracy [20,21], dealing with missing values [22], trajectory prediction [23], or spatio-temporal prediction [24].

The procedure to train a GAN is more complex and challenging than training a standard learning algorithm [25,26]. In effect, to train a GAN, we do not aim at optimizing an objective function. Instead, the learning task is related to game theory, which is defined as a minimax problem in which two players compete against each other, one trying to maximize an objective function, while the other is trying to minimize it. The solution to this minimax problem could be the Nash equilibrium of the game [27]. However, finding the Nash equilibrium is a complex and difficult task when compared with optimizing an objective function [2,27].

Besides being a complex task, other important challenges arise when training a GAN. One of these challenges is the lack of a systematic criterion to evaluate when the GAN is already sufficiently trained for the task at hand as the training epochs take place. Several attempts have been made to address this critical problem, with a growing body of research being put forward through the proposal of multiple alternative measures. So far, no single measure has been identified as the gold standard method for use across multiple applications and/or data modalities. This leaves researchers and end-users with the problem of determining when to stop the GAN training process for a given task through a non-systematic trial-and-error procedure. In this paper, we focus on finding a systematic solution to the problem of when to stop training a GAN that can be used across different data modalities.

The currently existing metrics for addressing the described problem can be categorized into 'qualitative evaluation' and 'quantitative evaluation'. The former involve human judgment, while the latter are based on different mathematically defined distance functions. A commonly used qualitative method of evaluating when to stop training a GAN is through human visual inspection of the generated samples [1]. This is a very direct and intuitive way of evaluating the quality of images. Nevertheless, it is a very costly and time-consuming task that cannot be applied to tabular data. The visual inspection process was regulated and standardised in a more systematic manner [1,28–30]. However, this solution has multiple disadvantages that prevent it from being broadly adopted. Namely, the following issues were found: (i) in some domains (e.g., medical domain), it might be difficult for a human to learn what is realistic or not; (ii) there are limitations regarding the number of images that can be reviewed in a reasonable period of time; (iii) the reviewers' biases and opinions may be incorporated into the process [30]; and (iv) visual inspection methods are restricted to images and cannot be applied to tabular data.

Regarding quantitative evaluation solutions, several measures have been proposed for assessing GANs trained on image datasets. Inception Score (IS) [31] and the Fréchet Inception Distance (FID) [32] are relatively popular measures in this category. Their goal is to use a large, pre-trained model, the InceptionNet in this case, to derive a good metric of the quality of the generated images. Other solutions, such as the Fréchet Confidence and Diversity (FCD) score, exchange the use of the InceptionNet model with an Autoencoder. Still, all these solutions will output a score, and it will be the end-user's responsibility to decide whether the GAN's training process can be stopped. Other quantitative evaluation metrics are trained on both imagery and non-imagery data. For instance, in [8,33,34], measures based on classification accuracy are introduced. While quantitative measures do not encounter the same issues as direct human (qualitative) evaluation, they may not directly correspond to how humans view and judge generated samples [1].

A new type of GAN called Wasserstein GAN (WGAN) was proposed in [35] to remove the oscillatory behaviour observed on the loss values of GAN components. WGAN can be observed as a way of incorporating qualitative measures into the loss functions of a GAN. Plotting WGAN learning curves has multiple applications, including improving sample quality explanability, which can help with the problem of deciding when to stop training GANs. However, WGAN does not allow the comparison of results between different GAN architectures, the estimation of the Wasserstein distance may be inaccurate [35], and WGAN still requires human visual validation in imagery datasets when observing the loss values and GAN performance.

Overall, the qualitative measures proposed require human intervention during GAN training, while quantitative measurements that address certain shortcomings of qualitative measures still require human monitoring of the metric during training. Therefore, the human remains in the loop for both types of measures. Moreover, from a data modality perspective, we observe that qualitative measurements are exclusively applicable to GANs trained on imagery datasets. In addition, the majority of the popular quantitative measures are also tailored for imagery datasets. Consequently, not only are the possibilities for applying GANs to non-image datasets limited, but human inspection or supervision is still required. In this paper, we tackled these gaps by proposing a **human-out-of-the-loop algorithm, named AutoGAN, where the usage of quantitative measures is fully automated**. In a nutshell, AutoGAN starts the training of a GAN and evaluates the improvements achieved at each iteration using an oracle. Note that we use the term oracle in the classical sense of Computing Theory, that is, a machine that (via some black-box process) solves a decision problem in constant time (see, e.g., [36]). The oracle is a central component of the algorithm that encapsulates the end-user preferences for the task at hand. An oracle should provide a score for a given generator, which should correspond to the generator's ability to synthesize "better". This score should match the end-user goals and thus define the end-user's understanding of the notion of "better" samples. We provide several examples of oracle instances in this paper to illustrate the different oracles that can be used. AutoGAN will rely on the oracle outputs to assess the training of the GAN. Furthermore, it will allow the performance to deteriorate while waiting for the GAN to recover. This is necessary to deal with the known oscillatory behaviour of the GAN's performance. When no further improvements are observed for a certain number of consecutive iterations, the AutoGAN will return the overall best GAN model obtained during this process. AutoGAN requires minimal human intervention and is applicable to different data modalities (tabular and images). Our extensive experiments demonstrate a clear advantage of using AutoGAN, even when compared to GANs trained under a thorough human visual inspection of the generated images.

The key contributions of this paper are four-fold:

- Present a comprehensive review of the literature on: (i) multiple distances and performance measures that can be used to assess the performance of a GAN; and (ii) existing algorithms involving automation in GANs;
- Introduce the AutoGAN Algorithm, a new automatic human-out-of-the-loop approach for determining when to stop training a GAN that is applicable to a variety of data modalities, including imagery and tabular datasets;
- Provide an extensive experimental comparison using multiple imagery and tabular datasets that include multiple GAN evaluation metrics;
- Provide all of our code so that AutoGAN can be easily used and to allow the reproducibility of our research.

This paper is organized as follows. Section 2 describes the background and related works. In Section 3, we present our algorithm, AutoGAN, designed to solve the problem of automatically determining when to stop training a GAN. We also provide in this section a set of oracle instances that can be used in our AutoGAN Algorithm. In Section 4, we describe the experiments carried out, including the datasets considered and the settings used, while in Section 5, we present and discuss the main results of the experiments. Finally, Section 6 concludes the paper and provides some interesting future research avenues.

2. Background and Related Work

This section starts by providing a brief background on GANs. Then, we review multiple distance measures and provide a detailed explanation of how they can be used to evaluate the quality of GANs. Finally, we review related works on automation in GANs that involve a neural architecture search.

2.1. Generative Adversarial Networks

Generative Adversarial Networks are a system composed of two differentiable functions, the generator and the discriminator [2]. The generator receives a sample drawn from a multivariate distribution and maps it to a sample from another distribution. The discriminator's goal is to discriminate between the synthetic samples obtained through the generator and the real samples. In the first phase of each iteration of the learning procedure, the generator attempts to deceive the discriminator into accepting its outputs as actual data, while in the second phase, the discriminator attempts to discern between real and fake samples. The generator and discriminator are trained together, competing against each other, and thus we can think about them as adversarial in the game theory sense. If trained on an image dataset, after a significant number of repetitions, the generator will be able to produce samples that are nearly indistinguishable from the actual images, i.e., the generator will generate synthetic samples from the distribution of the dataset.

A simple vanilla GAN does not need the class labels of the examples; thus, it can be regarded as an unsupervised model. Other variants of GANs, such as the Conditional Generative Adversarial Networks (CGANs) [37], use the class labels during the training process as an extra input to both the generator and the discriminator. The advantage of CGANs is that, after training, the generator provides the ability to generate samples from a specific class, whereas in a vanilla GAN, that control is not present.

2.2. Relevant Distances and Performance Measures

Measuring the quality of a GAN is crucial. In this subsection, we study several measures that have been used to assess the quality of GANs, including some distances and other measures used for performance assessment. We will focus on three particular measures: the Kullback–Leibler divergence, the Wasserstein distance, and the F1-score. We include here the F1-score as an example of a potentially interesting performance assessment metric that is useful in many problems involving GANs due to their application to imbalanced domains. Other metrics could be used, but the F1-score is one of the most frequently applied.

The Kullback–Leibler (KL) divergence is a well-known statistical distance that measures how similar two given distributions are [38]. Consider two distributions P and Q, where p and q denote the probability densities of P and Q, respectively. The KL-divergence is defined as shown in Equation (1).

$$D_{\text{KL}}(P \parallel Q) = \int_{-\infty}^{\infty} p(x) \log\left(\frac{p(x)}{q(x)}\right) dx \tag{1}$$

An alternative way to compute the distance between two probability distributions is provided by the Wasserstein distance [39]. Let X and Y be two random variables with finite p-moments, $X \sim P$ and $Y \sim Q$. Assume that $J(P,Q)$ represents all joint distributions J for random variables (X,Y). The p-Wasserstein distance is defined in Equation (2).

$$W_p(P,Q) = \left(\inf_{J \in J(P,Q)} \int \|x-y\|^p dJ(x,y)\right)^{1/p} \tag{2}$$

where $p \geq 1$. A special case of this distance is when $p = 1$. This distance is called the Earth Mover or 1-Wasserstein distance. The 2-Wasserstein distance is also called the Fréchet distance.

To determine the performance of a model, one can take advantage of the F1-score. This metric depends on the notions of true positives (TP), true negatives (TN), false positives (FP) and false negatives (FN), which are the cases correctly classified from the positive and negative class and the cases that were incorrectly classified as positive or negative class cases, respectively. The F1-score is defined as the harmonic mean of the precision (cf. Equation (3) and recall (cf. Equation (4). When dealing with binary classification problems, typically the F1-score of the minority class (or positive class, or class of interest) is reported as shown in Equation (5). The F1-score can also be calculated for each class in the domain, and its macro- or micro-average variants can be used as the global F1-score on a multiclass problem.

$$\text{precision} = \frac{TP}{TP+FP} \tag{3}$$

$$\text{recall} = \frac{TP}{TP+FN} \tag{4}$$

$$\text{F1-score} = \frac{2 * \text{precision} * \text{recall}}{\text{precision} + \text{recall}} = \frac{2*TP}{2*TP+FP+FN} \tag{5}$$

2.3. From Distances and Measures to Experimental Configurations for Evaluating the Performance of GANs

Different distances and measures can be used to assess the performance of a GAN. However, the setting in which these distances or measures are used can also change substantially. This section discusses these configurations in terms of the experimental setting they advocate as well as their underlying assumptions. We will review six configurations, explaining in detail how they are used to assess the performance of GANs.

2.3.1. Classification Accuracy Score: Train on Synthetic Data, and Test on Real Data

Ravuri and Vinyals [33] argue that if we have a good and well-trained generative model that accurately captures the data distribution, then any downstream task should perform similarly regardless of whether it uses generated or original data. The authors train several class-conditional generative models, such as CGANs and variational auto-encoders (VAEs), on real and labeled data. Following this step, a classifier is trained on synthetic data and used to predict the label of real images. A performance assessment metric such as the F1-score can be used to evaluate the resulting model. This configuration, termed CAS-real, has also been studied in [34], where the authors state that this setting shows how diverse the samples generated by a GAN are. While we can apply CAS-real to GANs trained on both imagery and tabular data, it requires a multi-class, labeled dataset. Furthermore, it can only be used with conditional GANs, which might be a disadvantage in some deployment scenarios.

2.3.2. Classification Accuracy Score: Train on Real Data, and Test on Synthetic Data

If we assume that the images generated with a well-trained GAN are realistic, then the classifiers trained on real images should have no problem identifying the synthesized image correctly as well. This assumption was put forward by Isola et al. [8], motivating the configuration we termed CAS-syn. Compared to the previous CAS-real configuration, CAS-syn switches the roles of synthetic and real data, i.e., in CAS-syn, a classifier is trained on real data and tested on synthetic data, while the reverse happens for CAS-real, which uses real data on the training phase and synthetic data on the testing phase. CAS-syn has also been studied in [34], where the authors argue that the CAS-syn configuration can measure how well the generated samples approximate the unknown real distribution on image data. GANs trained with either imagery or tabular data can use this configuration. However, CAS-syn requires a multi-class labeled dataset, and it is only applicable to CGANs.

2.3.3. Inception Score

A different approach named the Inception Score (IS) is proposed by Salimans et al. [31]. To begin, the conditional label distribution $p(y, x)$ is computed by applying an InceptionNet model to each image produced by a GAN trained on the original dataset. The assumptions underlying this approach are that: (i) the GAN should generate images with high confidence for each label, i.e., $p(y|x)$ has a low entropy; and (ii) the GAN should produce varied images, i.e., the marginal $\int p(x = G(z)) \, dz$ has a high entropy. Based on these two requirements, the authors propose the use of the following metric $\exp[\mathbb{E}_{x \sim p_g} D_{KL}(p(y|x) || p(y))]$, which they claim has a direct correlation with human judgment. The expected value of KL-divergence is exponentiated to allow for an easier comparison.

Although this is an extensively used approach, several weaknesses of this configuration must be taken into account. In particular, the disadvantages of IS have been enumerated in [30] and include: (1) sensitivity to parameters and implementations of model parameters; (2) biased towards ImageNet dataset and InceptionNet models; (3) diversity within classes is not captured; (4) requires a high sample size to be reliable; (5) a high IS is achievable by inputting only one example per ImageNet class; and (6) it can only be used for GANs trained on certain imagery datasets because the InceptionNet model uses colored images as inputs, uses convolutional layers, and is trained in the ImageNet dataset. Therefore, IS cannot be used with either black-and-white images or tabular data.

Moreover, the usage of IS on GANs trained on colored images other than ImageNet can be misleading [40].

2.3.4. Confidence and Diversity Score

The methodology described for IS can be altered to obtain a different configuration named the Confidence and Diversity Score (CDS). In this setting, we carry out the following steps: (1) use a neural network classifier with an arbitrary architecture; and (2) train the classifier on the target dataset instead of the ImageNet dataset [41]. This modification allows this new score to be applicable to GANs trained on non-imagery and imagery data, whereas the IS is confined to a special area of imagery data. However, the CDS requires the data to be clustered into two or more classes and requires the class labels to be available in order to calculate the score, while the original IS does not require class labels of the target dataset.

2.3.5. The Fréchet Inception Distance

Heusel et al. [32] proposes to use the features extracted from both real (r) and generated data (g) to assess the quality of images created by a GAN. Typically, an InceptionNet model is trained on the ImageNet dataset, and the results of the last pooling layer prior to the output classification layer are used as the extracted features.

The extracted features from real (X_r) and generated (X_g) data are viewed as continuous multivariate Gaussian distributions, i.e., $X_r \sim \mathcal{N}(\mu_r, \Sigma_r)$ and $X_g \sim \mathcal{N}(\mu_g, \Sigma_g)$, where μ_r and μ_g are the means of X_r and X_g and Σ_r and Σ_g are the covariance matrices of the two distributions. The parameters of the two underlying distributions are then estimated and the Fréchet distance between the two distributions is calculated. The Fréchet Inception Distance (FID) is used to compare the similarity between two multivariate Gaussian distributions, and is calculated as shown in Equation (6) for X_r and X_g.

$$d^2 = |\mu_X - \mu_Y|^2 + tr(\Sigma_X + \Sigma_Y - 2(\Sigma_X \Sigma_Y)^{1/2}) \tag{6}$$

The smaller the FID is, the closer the two estimated distributions are; consequently, the better the GAN outputs are. Unlike IS, FID captures the diversity within classes [30]. FID, on the other hand, is highly biased [30]; and small samples sizes can result in an overestimation of the true FID [30]. Although both FID and IS are based on the InceptionNet, the IS uses the trained InceptionNet model as is, while the FID uses this model as a feature extractor. Given that the InceptionNet is trained on colored images (the imageNet dataset), this could make both IS and FID only applicable to gray-scale images. However, the FID has the potential to be more generic and could be applied to both colored and gray-scale images, given the fact that the InceptionNet is merely used as a feature extractor. We will test the versatility of FID by also testing it on black-and-white images in our experiments to confirm this hypothesis.

2.3.6. Fréchet Confidence and Diversity Score

Modifications to FID were proposed by Obukhov and Krasnyanskiy [41] to obtain the Fréchet Confidence and Diversity (FCD) score. In this version, the InceptionNet model is replaced by an auto-encoder model trained on the target data. After training the auto-encoder, the encoder is used as a feature extractor. Different sizes of the encoder's output layer, i.e., the number of extracted features, were investigated.

Given the results obtained in this work [41], the authors considered that while the FCD score has a correlation with the quality of generated images, the same does not happen for the generated tabular and non-imagery data. The authors based this conclusion on the fact that no correlation was observed with a reduction in the errors of the generator and the discriminator. However, the known oscillatory behaviour of the generator and discriminator [35] leads us to conclude that a decrease in the errors does not necessarily imply proper training. When we present our experimental results in Section 5, we will go over this in greater detail.

2.4. Algorithms Involving Automation in GANs

Regarding automation in GANs, several efforts have been made to search for the best generator architecture in GANs. The proposed neural architecture search methods have provided good outcomes as they outperform architectures that are manually designed on multiple tasks [42,43]. In this field, Wang et al. [44] presented an algorithm for an automated neural architecture search for deep generative models. On the other hand, Gong et al. [45] define the search space for the generator architectural variations and propose the usage of a Recurrent Neural Network (RNN) to guide the search process. This study used the IS as the reward and applied a multi-level search strategy to search for the neural architecture progressively. Still, several research avenues remain to be explored, such as increasing the search space and also extending this search to the discriminator, incorporating class labels, or testing the search on high resolution images.

The research with automation gives rise to other concerns, for instance, related to the model's size. Building on the neural architecture search solutions, Fu et al. [43] presented the AutoGAN-Distiller (AGD), the first AutoML framework dedicated to GAN compression. However, several aspects remain to be studied. One of the main problems when training a GAN with a specified architecture is determining when the GAN is well trained and when the process can be stopped. However, as far as we know, no effort has been made to automate the process of training a GAN for a given architecture. In effect, many applications dealing with images rely on domain experts to evaluate when the images being generated have the required quality and thus stop the training procedure of the GAN. A domain expert needs to define when the GAN has trained for a sufficient number of iterations and the training process stops with his input. Moreover, frequently, the generated images are analysed to obtain that answer, which is not only a time-consuming process but can also be biased and susceptible to the subjectivity of the expert. Finally, such inspection is not possible when non-imagery data is used. The AutoGAN solution that we present in the following section seeks to answer these questions.

3. Proposed AutoGAN Method

This section describes our proposed solution, AutoGAN, for automating the training process of GANs. We begin by defining the goals and requirements of AutoGAN and then proceed to the details of our algorithm. Finally, we provide a detailed illustration of several oracle instances, an important component of AutoGAN. Notice that the term oracle is used in the classical sense of Computing Theory, representing a machine that (via some black-box process) solves a decision problem in constant time (e.g., [36]).

3.1. Algorithm Goals and Requisites

The goal of our solution is to provide the end-user with a GAN model that is well trained for the specific target task. To achieve this, the end-user needs to provide the task requirements as well as the particular GAN architecture that needs to be trained. Besides providing these settings, which reflect the preferences for the task at hand, the end-user will have no more intervention in the AutoGAN algorithm. Our AutoGAN algorithm will use this information to output the trained GAN model given the provided end-user preferences. This way, the end-user obtains a trained model in a fully automated way, i.e., except for the design aspect there is no human intervention, such as, for instance, setting the number of epochs to run or inspecting the results at certain checkpoints to determine whether the training process can be stopped.

AutoGAN includes a critical component that we named the oracle. This oracle is defined by the end-user and should encapsulate the requirements of the tasks being addressed. It is the user's responsibility to define the correct oracle for the task he aims to solve. The oracle can be observed as a function that receives the GAN generator and outputs a score corresponding to the ability of the generator to synthesize high-quality samples. The oracle parameters are defined by the end-user. Section 3.3 contains a detailed description of several oracle instances that can be used with our AutoGAN algorithm in various contexts and with different goals.

3.2. The AutoGAN Algorithm

When deciding when to stop training a GAN on imagery datasets, a human is typically in the loop and visually inspects the GAN's output samples to make that decision. On tabular data, this inspection is impossible to be carried out, and thus the task becomes harder. Some metrics can be monitored, but a human should still be involved in the process of deciding when to stop training. Frequently, we observe that researchers limit the GAN training to an arbitrary number of epochs, leading to GAN models trained sub-optimally.

To address this problem, we propose a systematic approach, AutoGAN, that automates the training process involving a quantitative measure. Our solution eliminates humans from the process of deciding when enough epochs have been run and the training of the GAN can be stopped. AutoGAN is an automated human-out-of-the-loop approach for training GANs that allows an end-user to determine when to stop training a GAN in a fully automatic way and without the need of inspecting any data, images, or metrics.

The key idea of the AutoGAN algorithm is to allow the training of a GAN to continue even when the GAN output samples do not show any improvements after several training iterations. This means that AutoGAN aims to provide the GAN with sufficient opportunities to overcome potential local unfavorable points, allowing it to reach an improved model. AutoGAN depends on the end-user definition of an oracle instance. AutoGAN uses the oracle instance provided to assess the quality of the output samples in an iterative manner until no further improvement in the GAN is expected. For a certain iteration of GAN outputs, the oracle produces a scalar score that corresponds to the quantitative measure that the end-user considers suitable to be monitored to estimate the GAN's performance.

The pseudocode of our proposed solution is presented in Algorithm 1. We consider the four following inputs: (1) the maximum number of failed attempts, which encapsulates how long we are willing to wait without observing any improvements in the GAN; (2) the unit used for the training iterations; (3) an untrained GAN with a particular architecture; and (4) an instance of an oracle that contains the task requirements set by the end-user. After the initialization, the GAN is trained in an iterative way. At each iteration, the GAN is trained and evaluated using the oracle settings. If a better solution is found, then it is stored as the best GAN trained up to that moment, and the best score achieved is also recorded. If the GAN obtained is worse than the best GAN stored, then that solution is discarded and a new iteration is run. This local deterioration of the performance is expected to happen due to the known relationship between the generator and discriminator losses [26]. For this reason, we need to assume that a certain number of consecutive failed attempts will happen. However, when the maximum number of failed attempts is reached, i.e., when the GAN was trained for the maximum number of consecutive rounds set without improvements, then, the algorithm stops and provides the best model that was obtained.

3.3. Potential Oracle Instances

An important component of our algorithm concerns the definition of an oracle instance. This task, although being the end-user's responsibility, can be difficult and needs to be carefully considered as the evaluation of AutoGAN will depend on the oracle defined. Thus, the instantiation of the oracle is a crucial step. This section provides an illustration of multiple oracle instances that can be used in different contexts concerning specific data and GAN requirements. Namely, we will describe oracle instances that have different assumptions regarding the characteristics of the used data (e.g., modalities or availability of class labels) and the GAN architectures.

Algorithm 1 The AutoGAN algorithm

Input: *Max_failed_attempts*: The maximum number of failed attempts accepted;
Train_unit: The unit used for training iterations;
Untrained_GAN: The GAN architecture selected and not trained;
Oracle: The selected oracle instance;
Output: *best_GAN*: The trained GAN model

current_GAN ← *Untrained_GAN*
best_GAN ← *Untrained_GAN*
best_score ← −∞
failed_attempts ← 0
while *failed_attempts* ≤ *Max_failed_attempts* **do**
    Train *current_GAN* for one *Train_unit*
    score ← *oracle*(*current_GAN*)
    if *score* ≥ *best_score* **then**
        failed_attempts ← 0 ;   // the new trained GAN is better than the best known
        best_GAN ← *current_GAN*
        best_score ← *score*
    else
        failed_attempts ← *failed_attempts* + 1 ;   // the trained GAN is worst than the best known
    end
end
return *best_GAN*

As previously mentioned, an oracle is a function that maps a given generator into a score that corresponds to the generator's ability to synthesize "better" samples. The oracle instance should define what the end-user understands by the term "better" sample. For instance, in some cases, a "better sample" might be to approximate as closely as possible the distribution of the dataset. However, in other situations, a "better sample" can indicate the presence of more diversity in the data or even, in the case of images, higher quality and sharpness. Figures 1–6 provide an overview of the six oracle instances that we will describe in more detail in the next sections.

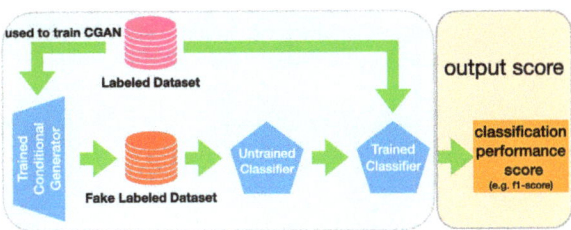

Figure 1. The architecture of an oracle instance based on CAS-real score.

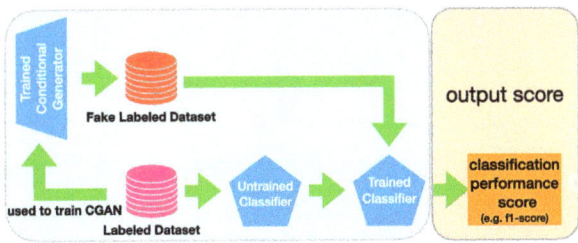

Figure 2. The architecture of an oracle instance based on CAS-syn score.

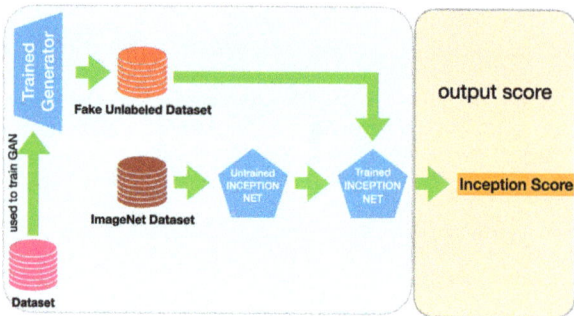

Figure 3. The architecture of the oracle based on IS.

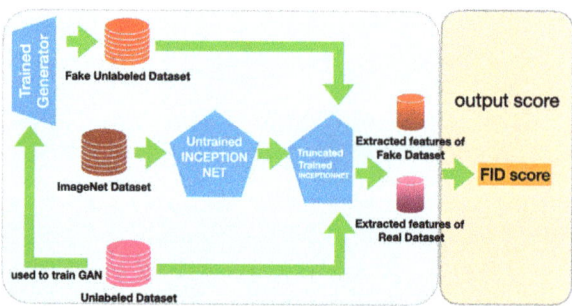

Figure 4. The architecture of an oracle instance based on FID Score.

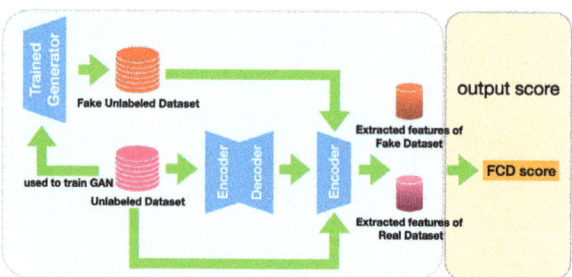

Figure 5. The architecture of an oracle instance based on FCD score.

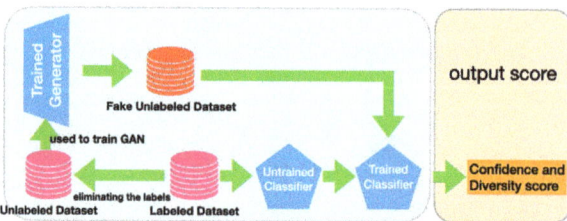

Figure 6. The architecture of an oracle instance based on Confidence and Diversity score.

The oracle instance used for a given task reflects the end-user preferences, and should be adapted to different deployment scenarios. Moreover, the oracle instance is not simply a metric or score used; it involves the entire architecture used to compute that score. For instance, a certain oracle instance may use only synthetic data to compute the desired score, while another oracle instance can use only real data to compute the same score. Other oracles may use some or all layers of a given neural network, while others might use a different classifier for that task. For this reason, the oracle entity encapsulates multiple settings that can and should be adapted to the specific task being solved, and thus, the oracle instances differ from other existing fixed solutions.

3.3.1. Oracle Instance Based on CAS-Real

This oracle begins by using the available labelled data to train a CGAN. Then, the CGAN is asked to generate a labelled dataset, which is fed to a classifier. The classifier is trained using the generated data. Finally, the trained classifier's performance is evaluated on the real labelled dataset. Any selected performance assessment metric can be used to evaluate the performance of the classifier. In our implementation, we selected the F1 score to be used because we decided to test this oracle instance in an imbalanced problem, and the F1 score is a suitable metric in this context. In this particular case, the higher the CAS-real score, the higher the quality of the GAN outputs. Figure 1 displays the key structure of the described oracle instance based on CAS-real.

3.3.2. Oracle Instance Based on CAS-syn

This oracle instance works in a similar way as the previous one that was based on CAS-real. The main difference concerns a change in the roles of real and synthetically generated data. This oracle starts by training a classifier with real labelled data. This same real data is also used to train a CGAN. Then, the generator of the CGAN is used to generate a synthetic test set utilized to assess the performance of the classifier. The trained classifier is tested on the generated labeled test set and the performance is recorded using a selected performance assessment metric. In our implementation, we used the F1 score because we tested this oracle in an imbalanced domain. In this case, the higher the CAS-syn score, the higher the quality of the GAN outputs. An overview of an oracle instance based on CAS-syn is shown in Figure 2.

3.3.3. Oracle Instance Based on Inception Score

In this oracle, the InceptionNet model is first trained on the ImageNet dataset, while the GAN is trained on the given real dataset. The GAN generator is then used to obtain new samples to be fed into the InceptionNet model. The IS is computed based on the output vectors of the model and used to assess the quality of the GAN. The higher the IS, the better the quality of the GAN outputs. This oracle can be used with both conditional and non-conditional GANs. An overview of the described oracle instance is displayed in Figure 3. We must highlight that this oracle based on IS is not applicable to tabular data or black and white images, as explained in Section 2.3.

3.3.4. Oracle Instance Based on Fréchet Inception Distance

This oracle instance also relies on the InceptionNet but uses a truncated version of this neural network architecture. The process starts with the training of the InceptionNet model on the ImageNet dataset. The target real dataset is used to train a GAN, whose generator is then used to obtain a certain number of fake samples. The real and fake data are given to the truncated version of the InceptionNet model to obtain their InceptionNet-represented features. Finally, the extracted features of both the fake and real data are used to calculate the FID score. The lower the FID score, the higher the quality of the GAN outputs. To obtain a positive correlation between the FID and performance in our implementation, we multiplied the FID score by minus one. This oracle can be used with both conditional and non-conditional GANs. Figure 4 shows the overview of an oracle instance based on FID.

3.3.5. Oracle Instance Based on Fréchet Confidence and Diversity Score

In [46], an extensive study is performed comparing different metrics to the original FID. The authors test several measurements that are based on the InceptionNet model pre-trained on different datasets. Other metrics were also tested using several self-supervised models that were used as feature extractors. Furthermore, the applicability of the FCD score on imagery and tabular data was investigated in [41].

This oracle instance is based on FCD and begins by training a GAN and an autoencoder using the available real dataset. Then, the GAN generator is used to generate new fake data. The real and generated data are given to the encoder so that we can obtain a new representation of their features. Finally, the extracted features of both real and generated data are used to calculate the FCD score. The lower the FCD score is, the higher the quality of the GAN outputs. Similar to the modified FID introduced in [41], we implemented an oracle using the FCD, as shown in Figure 5. We also included a minor implementation detail by multiplying the FCD score by minus one; this allowed us to observe a positive correlation between the FCD score and the quality of the outputs. This oracle instance can be used with both conditional and non-conditional GANs.

3.3.6. Oracle Instance Based on Confidence and Diversity Score

Since the introduction of the IS in [31], it has been widely used in the assessment of imagery generative models [4,9,47,48]. The InceptionNet model consists of 2D-convolutional networks, which are suitable for processing images. Moreover, IS is obtained via an InceptionNet model that is pre-trained on the ImageNet dataset. Therefore, as mentioned in [41], the application of the IS is not possible for real-valued tabular data.

By replacing the InceptionNet model with an arbitrary neural network classifier trained on the target dataset, the applicability of the Confidence and Diversity Score on imagery datasets is investigated in [41]. As shown in Figure 6, we built an oracle instance that uses the CDS to run tests on both imagery and tabular data. This oracle uses the end-user dataset to train both a neural network classifier and a GAN model. Then, the GAN's generator is used to obtain a certain number of synthetic samples that are used as the classifier's test set. Finally, the CDS is calculated based on the model's results on this test set. The higher the CDS, the better the quality of the GAN outputs. This oracle can be used with both conditional and non-conditional GANs.

3.3.7. Overview of the Oracle Instances and Their Characteristics

The different oracle instances described have multiple assumptions regarding the data and the GAN architecture, and thus can be used in diverse contexts. These instances serve as examples of possible oracle instances that can be used. However, the specific task requirements and the end-user preferences should drive the selection of the oracle instance to be used for a certain problem involving training a GAN. A comparison between the different oracle instances used in this paper is shown in Table 1. We observe that some oracles are only suitable for being used with CGANs (CAS-real and CAS-syn), while others can use any selected GAN. In terms of the required class labels, only FCD does not require the existence of labeled data during the training, while all the other alternatives discussed require those labels. We also verify that all oracles can be applied to imagery data, while only four of the implemented oracles are applicable to tabular data. Table 1 also displays the number of times the network/classifier in the oracle is required to train (column "train times"). The indication of "one time" means that it is trained in the beginning and no further training is necessary, and "multiple" means that a new training process is necessary after each change in the GAN weights. CAS-real is the only oracle instance that needs to have the training repeated multiple times to obtain the desired score. The remaining oracles only need to be trained once. By comparing all the six implemented oracle instances, we observe that the FCD is the most flexible, working for both tabular and image data while not requiring class labels and allowing the usage on any GAN architecture. We must also highlight that all oracle instances can be used with colored images and almost all can also be used with black-and-white images. Following some preliminary test, we observed that the oracle IS is not suitable for black-and-white images.

Table 1. A comparison between the requirements of the described oracle instances.

Oracle Instance	Required Labels		Type of GAN	Type of Data			Train Times	Metric	Source
	Labeled Data during Training	Labeled Data to Generate Score		Imagery Color	Imagery B & W	Tabular			
CAS-real	Required	Required	Requires a CGAN	✓	✓	✓	Multiple	F1-score	[33,34]
CAS-syn	Required	Not required	Requires a CGAN	✓	✓	✓	One time	F1-score	[8,34]
IS	Required	Not required	Any GAN	✓			One time	KL-divergence	[31]
FID	Required	Not required	Any GAN	✓	✓		One time	Fréchet distance	[32]
CDS	Required	Not required	Any GAN	✓	✓	✓	One time	KL-divergence	[41]
FCD	Not required	Not required	Any GAN	✓	✓	✓	One time	Fréchet distance	[41]

4. Experimental Evaluation

This section presents all the experiments carried out to observe the performance of our proposed AutoGAN algorithm. We begin by providing an overview of our experiments. Then, we describe the datasets used and provide the complete experimental settings. To allow the reproducibility of our results, all the code used in this paper is freely available to the research community at https://github.com/enazari/autoGAN (accessed on 8 February 2023).

4.1. Experiments' Overview

Our goal is to assess the ability of the AutoGAN algorithm (cf. Algorithm 1) in addressing the "when to stop training a GAN" problem. To verify whether a GAN is well-trained (or if the training process is automatically stopped at a good point), we use the GAN as an over-sampling tool under a class imbalance setting. Our assumption is that, if the GAN is conveniently trained, it will provide advantages similar to those of GANs that have been carefully trained with human intervention. This experimental setting allows us to inspect the effectiveness of our proposed solution in both imagery and tabular datasets.

The key structure of the experiments carried out is as follows. We start by assessing the performance of a certain classifier on a given imbalanced domain to observe the baseline performance (Initial method). Then, we train a GAN using different methods that will determine when the training should be stopped. Each one of these GAN models is then employed to generate new synthetic samples, which are used to balance the number of examples in the training set. The performance of the classifiers trained on the different balanced training sets is assessed and will determine whether the GANs generated high-quality synthetic data and thus were well trained. We must highlight that the synthetic cases are only used in the training set, and the test set is kept untouched and separated from the remaining data that are used exclusively to test the classifier. In particular, we are interested in observing whether AutoGAN is able to find a stopping iteration that leads to a well-trained GAN. If the outcomes of our proposed method are at least equal to those of the alternative methods, we may conclude that we have successfully addressed the quandary of when to stop training a GAN.

In our experiments, we use different alternative methods to decide when to stop training the GAN. The different alternatives tested depend on the type of dataset used (imagery or tabular). Overall, we tested the following four main alternatives: (i) **Initial**: a baseline where the original imbalanced dataset is used to train a classifier; (ii) **Fixed**: GAN trained for a fixed number of iterations, selected based on experiments from other research papers or experiments/guidelines where the GAN shows good results; (iii) **Manual**: GAN trained using human visual inspection to determine the number of iterations required to obtain a well-trained GAN; and (iv) **AutoGAN**: GAN automatically trained using the AutoGAN algorithm and one of the oracle instances defined in Section 3.3. We compare the performance obtained through these different methods against each other and the baseline (Initial).

To make the comparisons fair, we start the training process of a certain GAN and use the different alternative methods in parallel to determine when the process should stop, as shown in Figure 7. As a result, we obtain the final state of the GAN using different methods while following the same training process. The GAN's training process is only stopped after all tested methods provide a stopping signal. By testing our solution using this framework, we are able to assess the quality of GANs trained under several different processes on both imagery and tabular datasets. Moreover, we can also observe the number of epochs used by the different methods and their impact on the performance.

Figure 7. An example of when each alternative method might give the stop training signal to a given GAN.

We run three main experiments, which we describe briefly in Table 2. The first set of experiments is carried out on tabular datasets and involves the application of the initial, fixed, and AutoGAN methods. Given the nature of these datasets, a manual inspection is not possible as a human cannot visually inspect the quality of the generated tabular data. For the fixed method, we obtain the fixed number of stopping iterations to use to train the GAN from previous experiments in [19]. For the AutoGAN method, we are only able to apply four of the Oracles described in Section 3.3, namely CAS-real, CAS-syn, CDS, and FCD, which are the only ones applicable to tabular datasets. In the second and third sets of experiments, we use imagery datasets. We carried out extensive tests with a high number of imagery datasets in our second experiment, in which we applied the initial, fixed, and AutoGAN with six different oracles. Our third experiment was conducted on a smaller subset of the imagery datasets, for which we also tested the manual method besides all the other methods used for the second experiment. This third experiment could not have been run for all the imagery datasets due to the time required to run the manual method, which involves a human inspecting all the images generated by the GAN after each iteration to decide upon their quality. Being an extremely time-consuming task, we decided to run this method only for a subset of the imagery datasets. This allows us to include in our tests a frequently used method to assess the quality of the GAN while keeping the time to run our experiments manageable.

Table 2. Overall description of the three main experiences carried out. (* AutoGAN-IS was only used with imagery datasets that contain colored images).

Experiment	Experiment #1	Experiment #2	Experiment #3
Data Used	Tabular Data	Imagery Data 1	Imagery Data 2
Alternative Methods	Initial Fixed AutoGAN-CAS-real AutoGAN-CAS-syn AutoGAN-CDS AutoGAN-FCD	Initial Fixed AutoGAN-CAS-real AutoGAN-CAS-syn AutoGAN-CDS AutoGAN-FCD AutoGAN-FID AutoGAN-IS *	Initial Fixed Manual AutoGAN-CAS-real AutoGAN-CAS-syn AutoGAN-CDS AutoGAN-FCD AutoGAN-FID

4.2. Datasets

For our experiments, we considered four base tabular datasets and four base imagery datasets. For each of the base datasets, we created binary versions and obtained a total of 17 binary datasets. Figure 8 shows an overview of the eight base datasets and the binary versions created and used in this paper. The orange branches in this figure show the four base tabular datasets, upon which several binary datasets are built and are displayed in the red branches. Similarly, the blue branches show the four base imagery datasets, and their respective binary versions are represented in the purple branches. The dataset's names and the two classes selected for the binary task are shown in the red and purple branches. Overall, we consider a total of 17 binary datasets: 7 tabular and 10 imagery datasets.

The class imbalance setting we are creating assumes that the two classes of the predictive tasks are not represented with a similar frequency, i.e., one of the classes is represented by a higher number of examples (majority or negative class) in the available data, while the other one is poorly represented (minority or positive class). To create different class imbalance tasks with different characteristics, we generated multiple variants with a varying number of majority and minority class examples. For each of the 17 binary datasets, we create 16 variants by changing the imbalance ratio (the imbalance ratio is defined as the ratio between the number of minority class samples and the number of majority class samples) and the sample size. We used the same procedure described in [19] to obtain these variants of the datasets. Namely, we select a random sample of majority class examples matching a desired majority class count. A set of minority class examples is then randomly selected from the dataset and added to the previous majority class examples to obtain the required imbalance ratio. We considered all combinations of four majority class counts (100, 200, 500, and 1000) and four imbalance ratios (0.1, 0.2, 0.3, and 0.4). A total of 272 (17 binary datasets ×16 variants) imbalanced datasets are generated and used in our experiments.

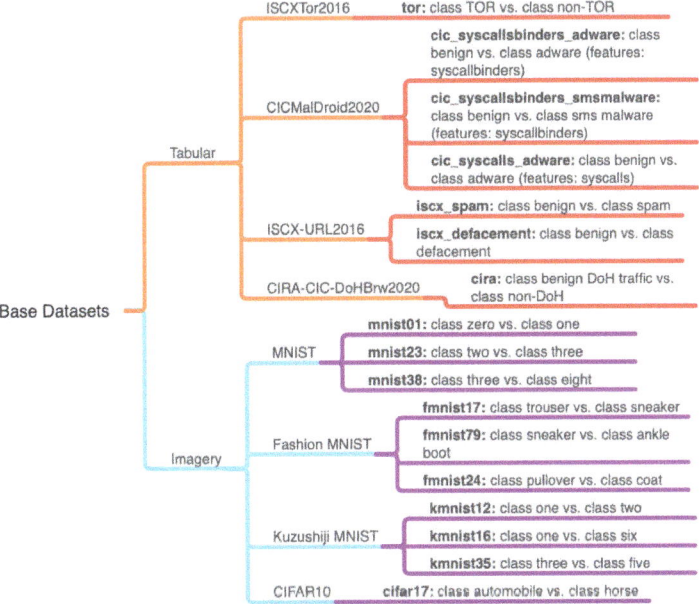

Figure 8. The base datasets (in blue and orange) used for creating 17 binary datasets (in red and purple). Dataset name and respective classes shown in the rightmost branch.

The following sections provide a more detailed description of the base tabular and imagery datasets as well as the 17 derived binary datasets that are used in our experiments.

4.2.1. Tabular Datasets

We used the same four base tabular datasets used in [19], namely ISCXTor2016 [49], CICMalDroid2020 [50], ISCX-URL2016 [51] and CIRA-CIC-DoHBrw2020 [52], which we transformed into seven different binary classification problems.

The ISCXTor2016 dataset [49] contains features extracted from network traffic using the ISCXFlowMeter. The binary classification dataset we named tor is derived from the target variable labels for TOR and non-TOR traffic.

The CICMalDroid2020 [50] dataset contains information about Android malware and includes the following five classes: benign, SMS malware, riskware, adware, and banking. The features are extracted from a total of 11,598 APK files and are grouped into two categories: (i) syscallbinders, which include the frequencies of system calls, binders, and composite behavior in a total of 470 features; and (ii) syscalls, which include the frequencies of system calls in a total of 139 features. Using the syscallsbinders features, we created two binary datasets: the cic-syscallsbinders-adware and the cic-syscallsbinders-smsadware. For the first one, only the instances with classes benign and adware were included, while for the second, only the instances with classes benign and sms malware were kept. We also created another binary dataset using the syscalls features. We named this dataset cic-syscalls-adware which includes the instances from adware and benign classes.

We obtained two binary datasets from the base dataset ISCX-URL2016 [51] (which contained five different classes): iscx-spam and iscx-defacement. The first one contains the cases from the classes benign and spam, and the second one contains the cases from the classes benign and defacement.

The last base tabular dataset considered is the CIRA-CIC-DoHBrw2020 [52], which has a target class with three labels: benign DoH traffic, malicious DoH traffic, and non-DoH traffic. We built a binary dataset that we named cira that includes only the benign DoH and non-DoH classes.

4.2.2. Imagery Datasets

In our experiments, we used the following four imagery base datasets: MNIST [53], Fashion-MNIST [54], Kuzushiji-MNIST [55], and CIFAR10 [56].

MNIST is a collection of 70,000 black-and-white images of 10 handwritten digits (i.e., 10 classes) with 28×28 pixels. We derived the following three binary datasets from the MNIST dataset: (1) mnist01: instances with classes zero and one are selected for this dataset; (2) mnist23: instances with digits (classes) two and three are selected for this dataset; and (3) mnist38: class three and class eight are chosen for this dataset. The different classes picked for these three binary datasets allow us to obtain a varying complexity of the predictive task, as we surmise that distinguishing between classes 0 and 1 is the simplest task while distinguishing between classes 3 and 8 can be observed as the most difficult task.

The Fashion-MNIST dataset contains 70,000 black-and-white images of 10 different clothing classes, each with 28×28 pixels. We derived three binary datasets from Fashion-MNIST by selecting different classes and using the same intuition used for the MNIST dataset to obtain tasks of different complexity. The following datasets were created: (1) fmnist17, using the classes trousers and sneakers; (2) fmnist79, using the classes sneaker and ankle boot; and (3) fmnist24, using the classes pullover and coat. We hypothesize that fmnist17 is the easiest of these tasks, fmnist79 has an intermediate complexity, and fmnist24 has the highest complexity of the three datasets.

Kuzushiji-MNIST dataset also contains 70,000 black and white images of 10 classes of handwritten Hiragana Japanese syllabary, each with 28×28 pixels. In this case, we also generated three different datasets by selecting two out of the 10 classes available in the original dataset. The following datasets were built: (1) kmnist12 with classes 1 and 2; (2) kmnist16 containing examples from classes 1 and 6; and (3) kmnist35 including cases from classes 3 and 5. We randomly selected the two classes used in each one of the cases.

Finally, we also derived one dataset from CIFAR10, a dataset containing 60,000 colored images of 10 classes of objects with $32 \times 32 \times 3$ pixels. We extracted automobile and horse classes to build our binary dataset, which we named cifar17.

4.3. Experimental Setting

Our three experiments, depicted in Figure 9, use 17 different base datasets, each with 16 variants with different imbalance ratios and sample sizes (see Section 4.2). For each experiment, we evaluated different alternative methods to provide a stopping signal to the GAN. We evaluate the method initial, which corresponds to using the original imbalanced training set, and the other alternatives, which correspond to using the images generated by the GAN stopped with a certain stopping signal to oversample the training set, making the two classes balanced. For these methods, we use different oracles with the AutoGAN algorithm and also use the fixed (a set number of iterations to train the GAN) and manual (a human manual inspection of the GAN images).

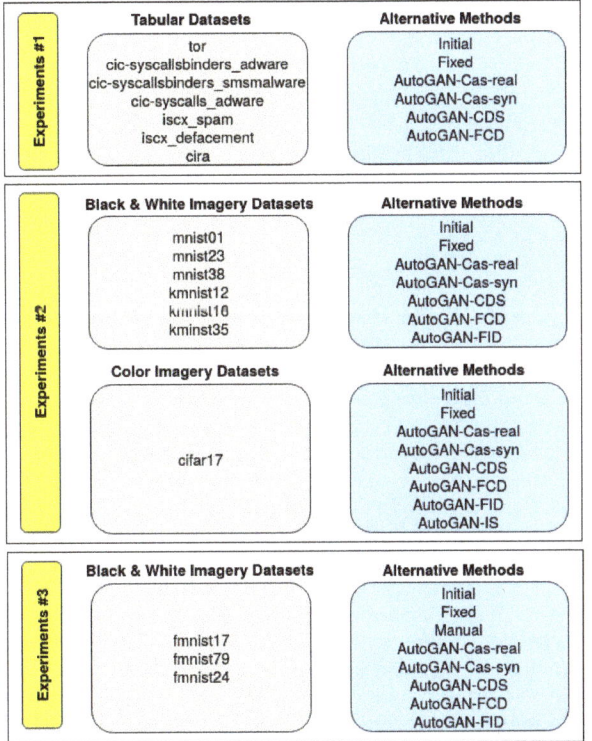

Figure 9. Detailed description of the three main experiments carried out.

One single GAN is trained until all methods give the stopping signal, as previously described and illustrated in Figure 7. We used a stratified five-fold cross-validation process. The F1-scores of both the minority and majority classes were recorded, irrespectively of the metric used internally by the AutoGAN algorithm. We report the average and standard deviation of the five-fold results. We also report the number of training iterations used for the GAN under each alternative method. This will allow us to observe the relationship between performance and the length of the required training. Finally, we analyse the Pearson correlation between the results of the different alternative methods for stopping the GAN training that we tested.

We selected a CGAN for our experiments. Two main architectures were considered: (i) fully connected hidden layers for both the discriminator and the generator; and (ii) convolutional layers for both the generator and discriminator. The output layer of the generator and the input layer of the discriminator were adapted to match the number of features in each dataset. Full details of the architectures are provided in the Appendix A.1.

The parameters used for AutoGAN with the oracles implemented are described in Appendix A.2. For the fixed alternative, we used the parameters used in [19] for the tabular datasets, while for the imagery datasets, we experimentally determined this value based on trial and error. For the manual alternative, we relied on the inputs from a human expert.

We selected a fully connected deep neural network for the classification task. The number of hidden layers and perceptrons used in each layer were adapted to each dataset. Full details on the network architecture are provided in Appendix A.3.

5. Results and Discussion

This section summarizes the main results and conclusion of the three experiments conducted.

5.1. Experiment #1: Tabular Datasets

We observed three different patterns in the results obtained from the tabular datasets. We present those patterns by showing the results of one dataset representative of the pattern. We will specifically discuss the results of the tor, iscx_defacement, and cira-based datasets. The detailed results of the remaining tabular datasets are provided in the Supplemental Material where additional figures (Figures S2–S9) and tables (Tables S1–S12, S33 and S34) are provided.

tor-based datasets

The results obtained on tor-based datasets exhibit a pattern that is also observed in the cic-syscallsbinders-adware, cic-syscallsbinders-smsmalware, and cic-syscalls-adware datasets. Figure 10 shows the average F1-scores for the minority class of the neural network trained on the different variants of the tor dataset (The corresponding results for the majority class can be observed in Figure S1 of the Supplemental Material). This figure demonstrates that all alternative methods applied to train the GAN produced better results than the initial setting (where no oversampling is applied). This demonstrates that, overall, all methods trained a GAN that generates images of comparable good quality. These results were aggregated by a majority class count and by imbalance ratio and are displayed in Figure 11 and Figure 12, respectively.

The following observations can be drawn from these results: (1) as an over-sampling technique, CGAN results in little or no deterioration of the majority class's F1-scores, whereas the minority class's F1-scores improve significantly; (2) as the difficulty factors (imbalance ratio and sample size) become more extreme, the classification task becomes more difficult, resulting in lower F1-scores; (3) if the initial F1 scores are lower, the amount of improvement obtained through CGAN over-sampling is greater; (4) the results of AutoGAN algorithm are relatively similar to that of the fixed setting in terms of F1-scores; and (5) AutoGAN algorithm achieves these results with a lower number of iterations for training the GAN when using three of the four tested oracles (FCD, CAS-real and CDS).

The stopping iterations displayed in the rightmost plot in Figures 11 and 12, show a clear difference in the oracle instances. For example, while the F1-scores of oracles CAS-real and CAS-syn in both minority and majority classes are similar, we observe that they stop at around 1000 and 2500 iterations, respectively. Furthermore, CAS-real achieves similar F1-scores to the fixed method while using a lower number of training iterations.

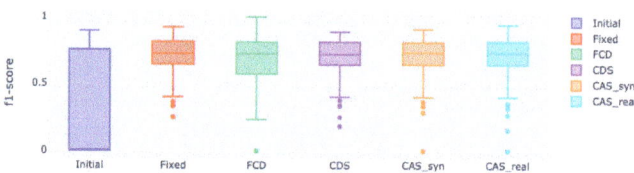

Figure 10. Box-plot of F1-scores of the minority class with different stopping methods for tor-based datasets.

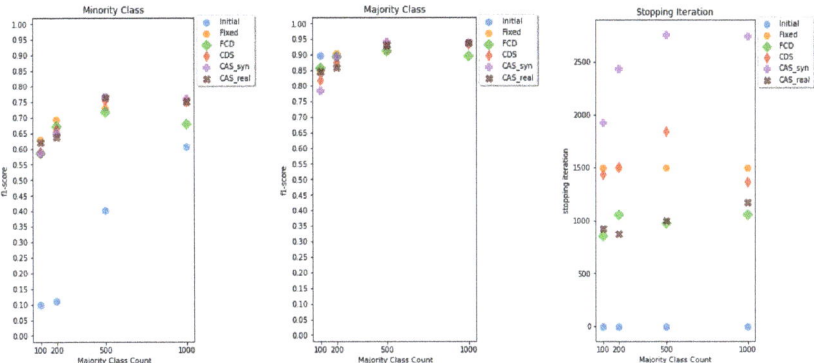

Figure 11. Average F1 results of tor-based datasets by majority class count for minority (**left**) and majority (**center**) classes, and average number of iterations until the training is stopped (**right**).

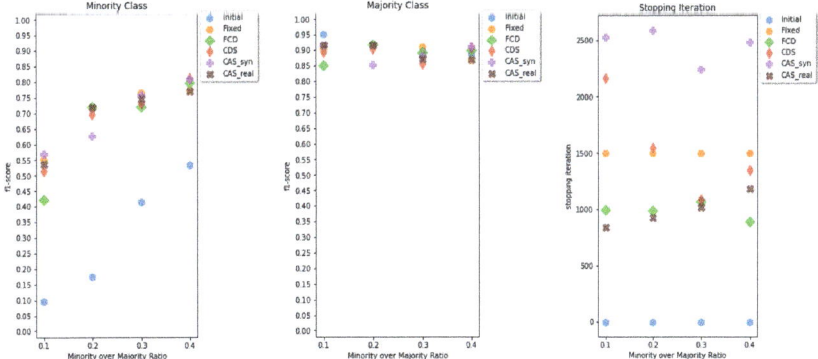

Figure 12. Average F1 results of tor-based datasets by imbalance ratio for minority (**left**) and majority (**center**) classes, and average number of iterations until the training is stopped (**right**).

iscx_defacement-based datasets

As the F1-score increases, the room for improvement shrinks, so that, after a certain point, fewer improvement opportunities are present. The experiments with iscx_defacement-based datasets, summarized in Figures 13 and 14, show no improvement when using any of the trained GANs when compared to the initial setting. The F1 results of the AutoGAN algorithm are also very close to the fixed setting. However, some differences are noticeable with regards to the number of iterations necessary for training the GAN. The fixed method used 1500 iterations, while, for instance, CDS consistently used fewer iterations.

cira-based datasets

The pattern observed in cira-based datasets was also observed in iscx-spam-based datasets. The three first observations identified in tor-based datasets are also present here (Figures 15 and 16). In addition, the results demonstrate that the performance outputs of the AutoGAN algorithm consistently surpass those of the fixed technique. Moreover, when compared against the fixed method, the results produced by AutoGAN with FCD and CDS Oracles are better while requiring fewer iterations. In fact, if we look at AutoGAN with FCD Oracle, the F1 performance achieved is among the best, despite the fact that it only took around 500 training iterations to stop the GAN (fixed used 1500 iterations).

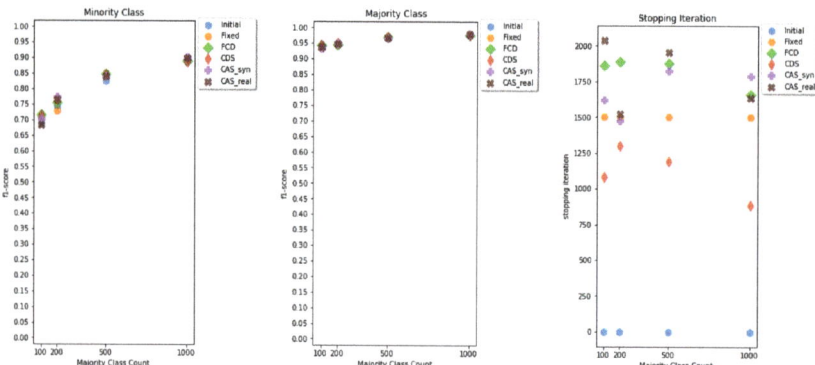

Figure 13. Average F1 results of iscx_defacement-based datasets by majority class count for minority (**left**) and majority (**center**) classes, and average number of iterations until the training is stopped (**right**).

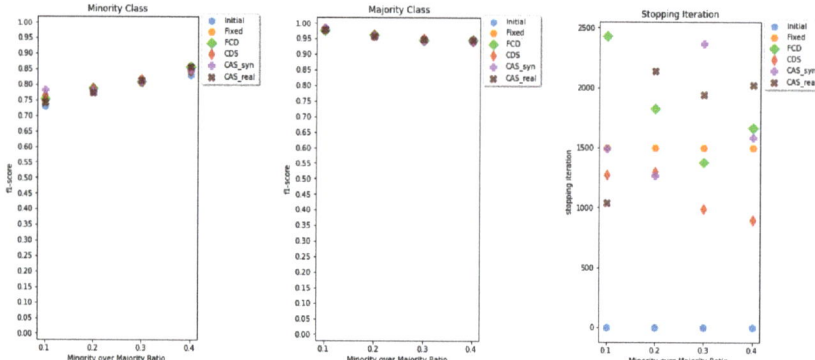

Figure 14. Average F1 results of iscx_defacement-based datasets by imbalance ratio for minority (**left**) and majority (**center**) classes, and average number of iterations until the training is stopped (**right**).

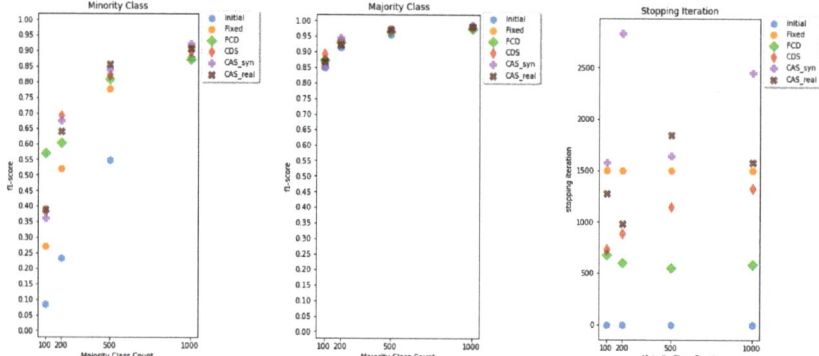

Figure 15. Average F1 results of cira-based datasets by majority class count for minority (**left**) and majority (**center**) classes, and average number of iterations until the training is stopped (**right**).

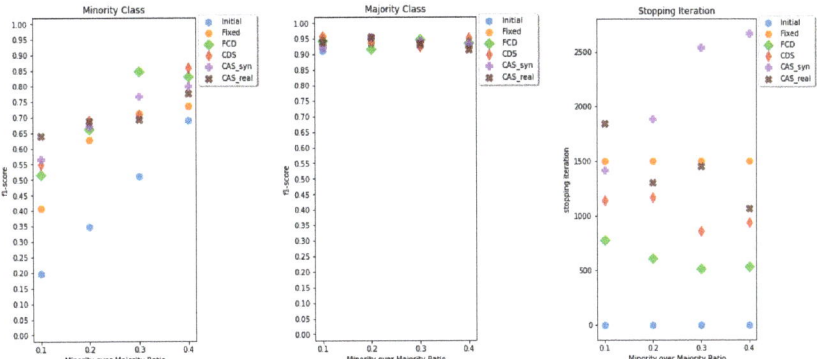

Figure 16. Average F1 results of cira-based datasets by imbalance ratio for minority (**left**) and majority (**center**) classes, and average number of iterations until the training is stopped (**right**).

5.2. Experiment #2: Imagery Datasets

5.2.1. Black-and-White Imagery Datasets

kmnist-based datasets

We selected kmnist-based datasets for showing the results of this experiment. Similar results were achieved with the mnist-based datasets. These additional results for mnist-based datsets are available in the Supplemental Material (Figures S12–S14 and Tables S21–S26). Figure 17 displays the results of all the variants of kmnist12 by imbalance ratio. As we can observe, all alternatives perform better than the initial method. Moreover, we also observe that all oracles tested in the AutoGAN algorithm perform similarly to the fixed alternative for both the minority and majority classes. However, there is a significant advantage to using AutoGAN when considering the number of training iterations. In fact, all the oracles tested use a much lower number of iterations than the fixed approach, although they achieve the same performance. The fixed approach was set to use more than 7000 iterations. The automatic method, on the other hand, uses between 1000 and 4000 iterations with the FCD and FID oracles. All the remaining oracles tested use a number of iterations between these two values. Further figures for Kmnit-based datasets are available in the Supplemental Material (Figures S10 and S11). Further detailed results for these datasets are available in Tables S27–S32.

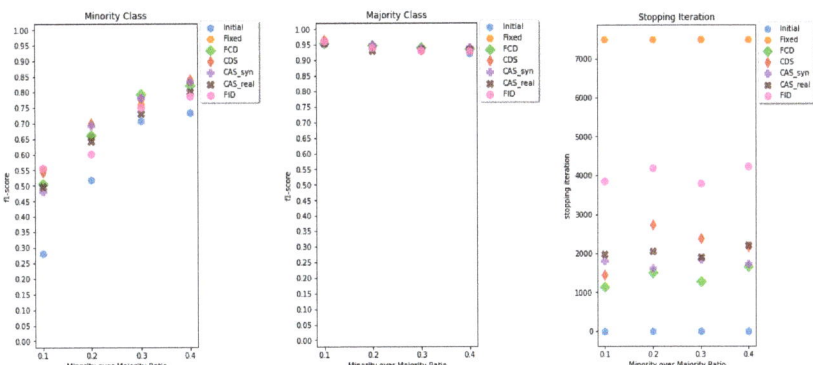

Figure 17. Average F1 results of kmnist12-based datasets by imbalance ratio for minority (**left**) and majority (**center**) classes, and average number of iterations until the training is stopped (**right**).

5.2.2. Color Imagery Datasets

cifar17 datasets

The results of the experiments on the 16 variants of the binary cifar17 dataset are shown in Figure 18. We do not observe a considerable improvement on the oversampling technique. However, in the most extreme case where the number of majority class count is 100, we observe improvements in the minority class with little effect on the majority class. In this case, the AutoGAN approach yields a similar performance to the fixed number of iterations, while, on average, requiring a much lower number of iterations for training (see Figure 18 on the right). Note that unlike black-and-white imagery datasets, we can also apply the IS oracle to this dataset. This shows that all the oracles tested use less training to achieve the same results. In effect, FID and FCD use approximately 5000 to 10,000 iterations, while the fixed method requires 20,000. These results also demonstrate the adaptability of our AutoGAN, which can increase the required training iterations dynamically without any human intervention. This is especially noticeable for CDS and IS oracles, which required a greater number of training iterations in the cases of the 100 and 200 majority class count. This number was not considered necessary for the other cases and was found automatically. Tables with the detailed results for cifar-based datasets are available in the Supplemental Material (Tables S19 and S20).

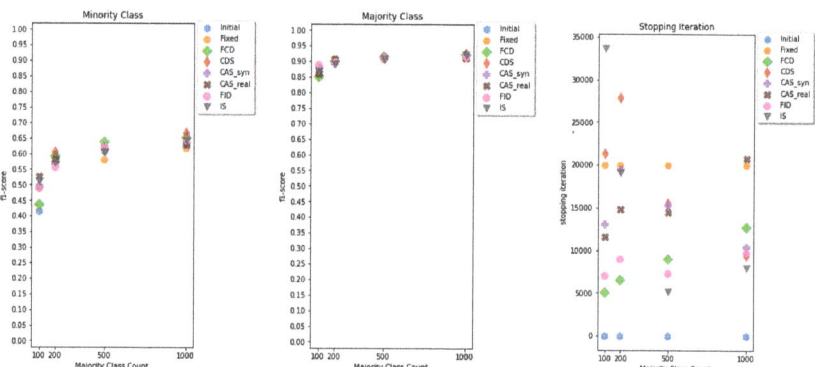

Figure 18. Average F1 results of cifar17-based datasets by imbalance ratio for minority (**left**) and majority (**center**) classes, and average number of iterations until the training is stopped (**right**).

5.3. Experiment #3: Imagery Datasets with Human Inspection

Fashion-MNIST-based datasets

The fmnist datasets was used to build three binary class problems: fmnist17, fmnist79, and fmnist24. We select the classes to obtain different difficulty levels for a human to visually distinguish between the two classes. The two classes are clearly distinguishable visually for the fmnist17 dataset, the task is more challenging for the fmnist79 dataset, and the fmnist24 dataset presents the most challenging task. The overall F1 results and training iterations required for these datasets are shown in Figure 19. Experiments indicate that the classification challenge for a neural network classifier is equivalent in difficulty to human visual classification. This can be observed on the leftmost plots of Figure 19, where the easiest task (top left plot) shows very high results for all methods, the intermediate task (middle left plot) shows some degradation of the performance across all methods, and the most difficult task (bottom left plot) displays much lower F1-scores for all methods. This shows clearly that, as the classification task becomes more difficult, the F1-score of the minority class deteriorates. GAN over-sampling offers the most benefits in the most difficult case, where there is significant room for improvement.

The following key observations can be drawn from these results: (1) in almost all cases, very little change in the performance of the majority class is observed; (2) AutoGAN results are very similar to the values obtained with the human manual inspection (human) and the fixed number of iterations (fixed); (3) when comparing the manual inspection with the fixed iterations, we observe that similar performance results are achieved with fewer iterations for the manual method; (4) AutoGAN algorithm, with any of the oracles tested, achieves the same performance results as manual method with a lower number of training iterations. This is in fact an outstanding result: AutoGAN is able to stop the training to obtain the same performance that we could obtain with a human inspection of the generated images, but it achieves this with less training. Additional detailed results are available for fmnist-based datasets in the Supplemental Material (Tables S13–S18).

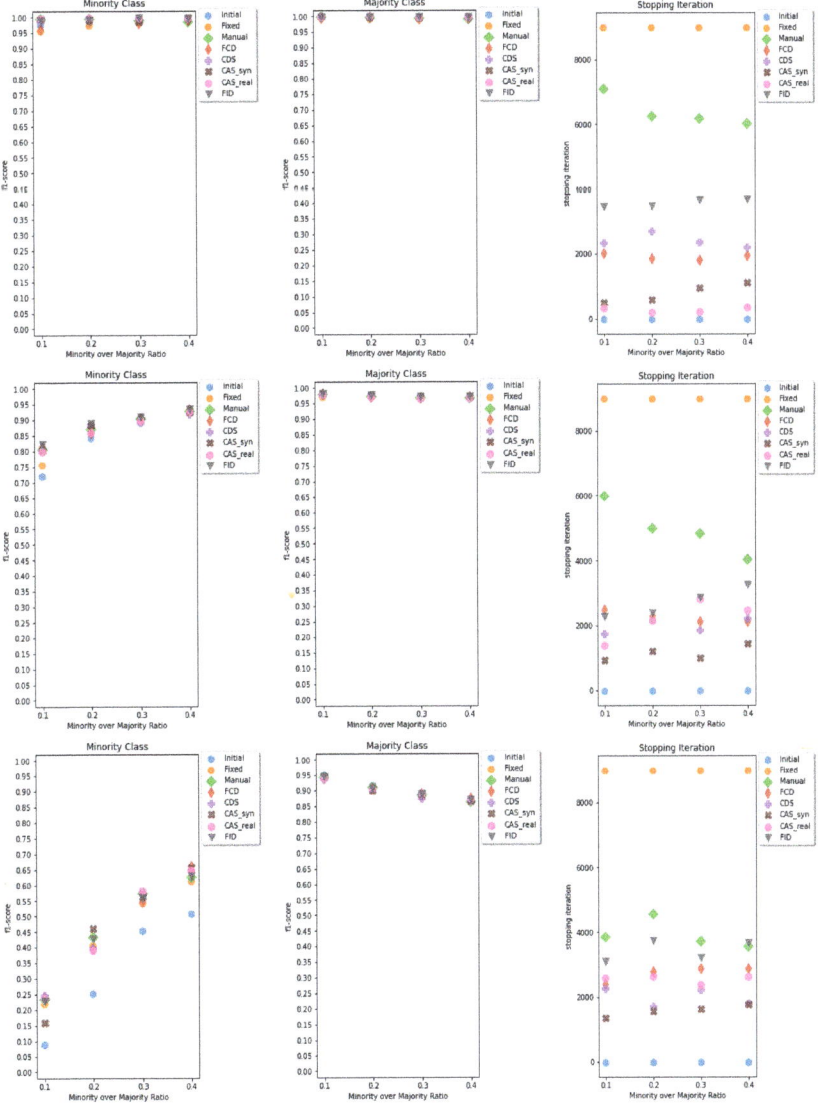

Figure 19. Average F1 results of fmnist17 (**top**), fmnist79 (**middle**), and fmnist24 (**bottom**)-based datasets by imbalance ratio for minority (**left**) and majority (**center**) classes, and average number of iterations until the training is stopped (**right**).

5.4. Correlation Analysis of the Methods Used for Stopping the GAN Training

We further studied the correlation between the different methods for stopping a GAN's training. We focused on the F1 results of the minority class. Our goal is to observe whether the results of AutoGAN with different oracles are similar to the other methods, including: initial, fixed, and manual. We computed the Pearson correlation between the F1 scores of four groups of experimental results. We considered the three main experiments carried out and formed four groups as follows: Group 1: includes all tabular datasets from experiment #1; Group 2: includes black-and-white imagery datasets from experiment #2 and the fmnist-based datasets; Group 3: includes colored imagery datasets used in experiment #2; and Group 4: includes only the fmnist-based datasets as they were tested with the manual option (experiment #3). Figures 20–23 show the correlation results and the corresponding dendrogram of the four groups described, respectively.

In Figures 20, 21, and 23, we observe that the initial method exhibits the lowest correlation with the remaining methods. However, for group 3, which contains the color imagery datasets, a different trend is shown, as displayed in Figure 22. We hypothesize that this difference can be explained by the over-sampling results (Figure 18); in the experiments where the initial results are sufficiently poor and the room for improvement is substantial, the GAN-oversampling demonstrates a significant improvement. In contrast, with cifar17-based datasets (group 3), GAN-oversampling yields negligible or no improvement. This lack of improvement from the initial results suggests that this might be linked to a higher correlation between the initial approach and the alternative methods.

When observing Figure 20, it is clear that all of the methods are clearly more separated from each other than from the initial. On the contrary, the figure highlights that the fixed exhibits more correlation with the other methods; namely, it is closer to the cluster containing CDS and CAS-syn.

Figure 21 shows the highest separation between initial and the remaining methods. We also observe that the fixed method is closer to FCD and FID for these experiments.

The correlation results of the group 3 (color imagery datasets) are the most surprising ones (Figure 22). Besides the fact that the initial method is not clearly separated from the remaining methods, we also observe a strong correlation between the IS and fixed. We must highlight that we only used IS in one color imagery base dataset (cifar17). Thus, these results might be biased towards the particular performance of these base datasets.

Finally, the correlation results observed in Figure 23 confirm that the fixed method is close to FID and FCD oracles. Moreover, these results highlight that the manual is very correlated with CAS-syn and also with CDS and CAS-real. This confirms the advantages of replacing a human's manual inspection of images with our AutoGAN algorithm, which can achieve results highly correlated with several of the oracles implemented and tested. Moreover, this is achieved with a lower number of training iterations, which brings benefits in terms of computational time and memory.

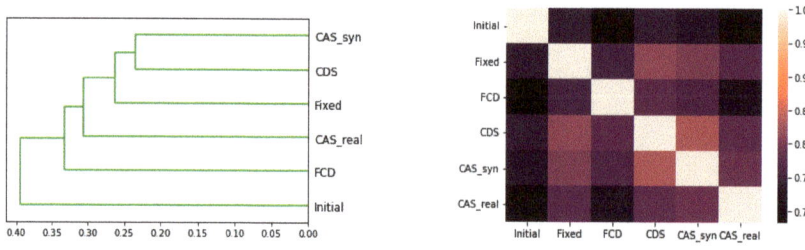

Figure 20. The Pearson correlation heatmap and dendrogram plots of the minority class of the experiments on all tabular datasets.

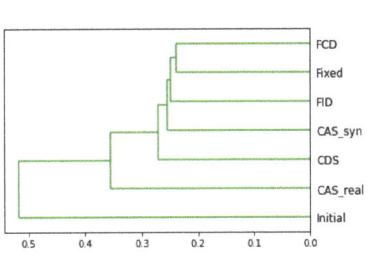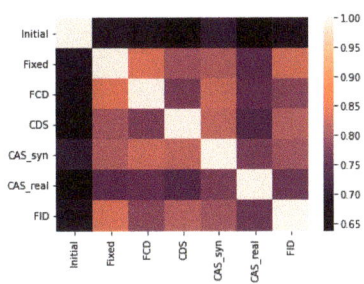

Figure 21. The Pearson correlation heatmap and dendrogram plots of the minority class of the experiments on all black-and-white imagery datasets (mnist-based, fmnist-based, and kmnist-based).

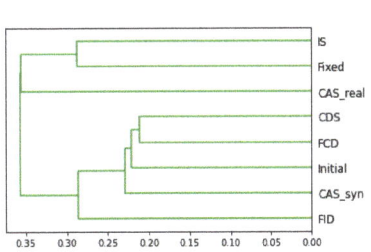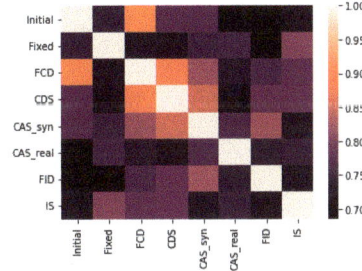

Figure 22. The Pearson correlation heatmap and dendrogram plots of the minority class of the experiments on color imagery datasets (cifar17-based).

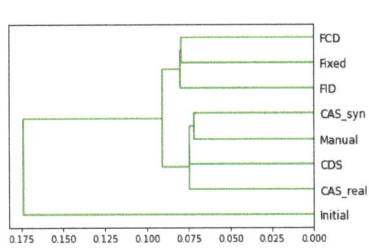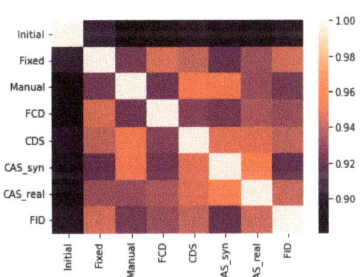

Figure 23. The Pearson correlation heatmap and dendrogram plots of the minority class of the experiments on fmnist-based datasets.

6. Conclusions

In this paper, we address the issue of when to stop training a GAN by combining quantitative measurements into an algorithm named AutoGAN. Our proposed AutoGAN is an "human-out-of-the-loop" solution, as it automatically decides when to stop training a GAN and requires minimal human monitoring or intervention during the GAN training process. The extensive set of experiments carried out on both tabular and imagery datasets show that AutoGAN achieves similar or superior results than all the alternative methods. Moreover, this solution provides gains in terms of the number of training iterations required, as it allows one to achieve a point of the GAN with fewer training iterations. Another key finding concerns the comparison with manual human inspection. In effect, we observe that AutoGAN consistently decides to stop the training at lower stages while ensuring that the data generated are of high quality.

Regarding our conclusions on tabular datasets, we must highlight that overall, the majority class performance is not affected while the minority class performance increases or is comparable. The performance results of the AutoGAN algorithm are relatively similar to those of running a fixed number of training iterations, but the AutoGAN algorithm achieves these results with a much lower number of training iterations.

On the imagery data, similar conclusions are reached, despite the fact that more oracles and alternatives for stopping the GAN's training process were tried. Overall, the Oracles tested with AutoGAN provided competitive results against the option of training the GAN for a fixed number of iterations but also against the option of training a GAN using manual human inspection. These results are remarkable, demonstrating that, in fact, the human inspection, when possible, is a time-consuming, subjective process that will require more training iterations to achieve the desired result.

Finally, our study of the Pearson correlation between the different methods demonstrates that, overall, the initial method has the lowest correlation with the remaining methods. The correlation between the oracles and the other methods varies greatly with the datasets tested. Thus, no global conclusion regarding the other method's correlation is provided.

In terms of future research directions, our proposed framework opens the way to shift several GAN applications from the image domain to the tabular data domain, as no supervision is required to train the GAN. An interesting future research direction could explore, for instance, the transferability of image-to-image translation to tabular-to-tabular translation, or image de-noising to tabular data de-noising. AutoGAN can assist with these new tasks as it allows any GAN to be trained for tabular data without human intervention. Another relevant research aspect could involve using AutoGAN to address the problem of mode collapse and vanishing gradients. In fact, our early experiments demonstrate that the scores obtained by oracle instances for GAN suffering from mode collapse show heavy oscillations; on the contrary, we do not observe such behaviour when the mode collapse problem is not present. Facing the potential problem of detecting overfitting in the GAN's generator can also be investigated in the future. We hypothesize that specific oracle instances and/or modifications to the AutoGAN algorithm would be necessary to achieve this goal.

Supplementary Materials: The following supporting information can be downloaded at: https://www.mdpi.com/article/10.3390/math11040977/s1.

Author Contributions: Conceptualization, E.N., P.B. and G.-V.J.; Methodology, E.N., P.B. and G.-V.J.; Software, E.N.; Formal analysis, E.N.; Visualization, E.N.; Writing—original draft, E.N. and P.B.; Data curation, E.N.; Writing—review and editing, E.N., P.B. and G.-V.J.; Supervision, P.B. and G.-V.J. All authors have read and agreed to the published version of the manuscript.

Funding: The work of E.N., P.B. and G.-V.J. was undertaken, in part, thanks to funding from Discovery Grants from NSERC.

Institutional Review Board Statement: Not applicable.

Informed Consent Statement: Not applicable.

Data Availability Statement: The base datasets we use are publicly available. Our code includes a function to generate the different imbalanced versions we created. By running this function on the base datasets, all our versions will be obtained.

Conflicts of Interest: The authors declare no conflict of interest.

Appendix A. Implementation Details

Appendix A.1. Details of the CGAN

The general architecture of GAN for all tabular data and black and white imagery data remains similar throughout all experiments. We used a fully connected conditional GAN architecture based on the code available on https://github.com/eriklindernoren/Keras-GAN/tree/master/cgan (accessed 8 February 2023). The only difference between the GANs is the output layer of the generator and the input layer of the discriminator, which match the dimension of the specific dataset being used. Tables A1 and A2 show the architectures of the generator and the discriminator for a dataset with 784 features, in this particular case, the fmnist-based datasets.

For cifar10-based datasets, a different architecture for both the generator and the discriminator is used. Tables A3 and A4 show the architecture details of the generator and the discriminator, respectively.

Table A1. The architecture of the generator used for the fmnist-based datasets.

Explanation	Layer	Output
Input1: noise	1	100 Neurons
Input2: class label	1	1 Neuron
transforming class label into 100	2	100 Neurons
multiply transformed class label with input noise	3	100 Neurons
Dense	4	100 Neurons
Dense	5	1024 Neurons
Dense	6	784 Neurons

Table A2. The architecture of the discriminator used for the fmnist-based datasets.

Explanation	Layer	Output
Input	1	784 Neurons
Dense	2	512 Neurons
Dense	3	512 Neurons
Dense	4	512 Neurons
Dense	5	1 Neuron

Table A3. The architecture of the generator used for the cifar10-based datasets.

Explanation	Layer	Output
Input1: noise	1	100 Neurons
Input2: class label	1	1 Neuron
Transforming class label into 100	2	100 Neurons
Multiply transformed class label with input noise	3	100 Neurons
Dense	4	4096 Neurons
Reshape to (4, 4, 256)	5	(4, 4, 256)
Conv2DTranspose: filters: 128; kernel shape: (4, 4)	6	(8, 8, 128)
Conv2DTranspose: filters: 128; kernel shape: (4, 4)	7	(16, 16, 128)
Conv2DTranspose: filters: 128; kernel shape: (4, 4)	8	(32, 32, 128)
Conv2D: filters: 3; kernel shape: (3, 3)	9	(32, 32, 3)
Reshape to 3072	10	3072 Neurons

Table A4. The architecture of the discriminator used for the cifar10-based datasets.

Explanation	Layer	Output
Input1: the image	1	3072 Neurons
Input2: class label	1	1 Neuron
Transforming class label into 100	2	100 Neurons
Multiply transformed class label with input noise	3	100 Neurons
Reshape to (32, 32, 3)	4	(32, 32, 3)
Conv2D: filters: 64; kernel shape: (3, 3)	5	(32, 32, 64)
Conv2D: filters: 128; kernel shape: (3, 3)	6	(16, 16, 128)
Conv2D: filters: 128; kernel shape: (3, 3)	7	(8, 8, 128)
Conv2D: filters: 256; kernel shape: (3, 3)	8	(4, 4, 256)
Flatten	9	4096
Dense	10	1 Neuron

Appendix A.2. Parameters Used for AutoGAN Algorithm

The hyper-parameters of AutoGAN Algorithm that were used across all the experiments are the following:

- The number of accepted failed attempts: 15;
- Iterations unit: 100;
- The number of generated samples per class for calculating the scores = 500.

The parameters of each oracle that we implemented and tested with the AutoGAN algorithm are as follows:

- Oracle CAS_syn:
    - The number of hidden layers for the classifier = 2;
    - The number of perceptrons for the classifier = 100;
    - The number of training epochs for the classifier = 100;
    - Optimizer: adam;
    - Batch size: 32.
- Oracle CAS_real:
    - The number of hidden layers for the classifier = 2;
    - The number of perceptrons for the classifier = 100;
    - The number of training epochs for the classifier = 100;
    - Optimizer: adam;
    - Batch size: 32.
- Oracle CDS:
    - The number of hidden layers for the classifier of CDS = 2;
    - The number of perceptrons for the classifier of CDS = 100;
    - The number of training epochs for the classifier of CDS = 100;
    - Optimizer: adam;
    - Batch size: 32.
- Oracle FCD:
    - The autoencoder consists of 6 layers of sizes: 784, 784×2, 784, 784/2 (the bottleneck), 784×2, 784;
    - Optimizer = 'adam';
    - Loss = 'mse';
    - The number of training epochs for the autoencoder = 200.

Appendix A.3. Classifier Details

The classifier used in our experiments is a fully connected deep neural network. For each base dataset, different numbers of the hidden layer and different numbers of perceptrons are used according to the difficulty of the problem. Moreover, the input layer of each neural network is altered to match the feature number of the datasets. The activation functions used are rectified linear units.

- Tor-based datasets: one hidden layer of 10 perceptrons;
- cic_syscallsbinders_adware-based datasets: two hidden layers of 20 perceptrons;
- cic_syscallsbinders_smsmalware-based datasets: two hidden layers of 20 perceptrons;
- cic_syscalls_adware-based datasets: two hidden layers of 100 perceptrons;
- iscx_spam-based datasets: two hidden layers of 20 perceptrons;
- iscx_defacement: two hidden layers of 100 perceptrons;
- cira-based datasets: one hidden layer of 10 perceptrons;
- mnist-based, fashion-mnist-based, Kuzushiji-mnist-based, and cifar10-based datasets: one hidden layers of five perceptrons.

References

1. Borji, A. Pros and Cons of GAN Evaluation Measures. *arXiv* **2018**, arXiv:1802.03446. [CrossRef]
2. Goodfellow, I.J.; Pouget-Abadie, J.; Mirza, M.; Xu, B.; Warde-Farley, D.; Ozair, S.; Courville, A.; Bengio, Y. Generative Adversarial Networks. *arXiv* **2014**, arXiv:1406.2661. [CrossRef]
3. Brock, A.; Donahue, J.; Simonyan, K. Large Scale GAN Training for High Fidelity Natural Image Synthesis. *arXiv* **2018**, arXiv:1809.11096. [CrossRef]
4. Karras, T.; Aila, T.; Laine, S.; Lehtinen, J. Progressive Growing of GANs for Improved Quality, Stability, and Variation. *arXiv* **2017**, arXiv:1710.10196. [CrossRef]
5. Karras, T.; Laine, S.; Aila, T. A Style-Based Generator Architecture for Generative Adversarial Networks. *arXiv* **2018**, arXiv:1812.04948. [CrossRef]
6. Karras, T.; Aittala, M.; Laine, S.; Härkönen, E.; Hellsten, J.; Lehtinen, J.; Aila, T. Alias-Free Generative Adversarial Networks. *arXiv* **2021**, arXiv:2106.12423. [CrossRef]
7. Karras, T.; Laine, S.; Aittala, M.; Hellsten, J.; Lehtinen, J.; Aila, T. Analyzing and Improving the Image Quality of StyleGAN. *arXiv* **2019**, arXiv:1912.04958. [CrossRef]
8. Isola, P.; Zhu, J.Y.; Zhou, T.; Efros, A.A. Image-to-Image Translation with Conditional Adversarial Networks. *arXiv* **2016**, arXiv:1611.07004. [CrossRef]
9. Zhu, J.Y.; Park, T.; Isola, P.; Efros, A.A. Unpaired Image-to-Image Translation using Cycle-Consistent Adversarial Networks. *arXiv* **2017**, arXiv:1703.10593. [CrossRef]
10. Emami, H.; Aliabadi, M.M.; Dong, M.; Chiniam, R.D. SPA-GAN: Spatial Attention GAN for Image-to-Image Translation. *IEEE Trans. Multimed.* **2021**, *23*, 391–401. [CrossRef]
11. Ledig, C.; Theis, L.; Huszar, F.; Caballero, J.; Cunningham, A.; Acosta, A.; Aitken, A.; Tejani, A.; Totz, J.; Wang, Z.; et al. Photo-Realistic Single Image Super-Resolution Using a Generative Adversarial Network. *arXiv* **2016**, arXiv:1609.04802. [CrossRef]
12. Tulyakov, S.; Liu, M.Y.; Yang, X.; Kautz, J. MoCoGAN: Decomposing Motion and Content for Video Generation. *arXiv* **2017**, arXiv:1707.04993. [CrossRef]
13. Munoz, A.; Zolfaghari, M.; Argus, M.; Brox, T. Temporal Shift GAN for Large Scale Video Generation. *arXiv* **2020**, arXiv:2004.01823. [CrossRef]
14. Dong, H.W.; Hsiao, W.Y.; Yang, L.C.; Yang, Y.H. MuseGAN: Multi-track Sequential Generative Adversarial Networks for Symbolic Music Generation and Accompaniment. *arXiv* **2017**, arXiv:1709.06298. [CrossRef]
15. Bojchevski, A.; Shchur, O.; Zügner, D.; Günnemann, S. NetGAN: Generating Graphs via Random Walks. *arXiv* **2018**, arXiv:1803.00816. [CrossRef]
16. Guo, J.; Lu, S.; Cai, H.; Zhang, W.; Yu, Y.; Wang, J. Long Text Generation via Adversarial Training with Leaked Information. *arXiv* **2017**, arXiv:1709.08624. [CrossRef]
17. Park, N.; Mohammadi, M.; Gorde, K.; Jajodia, S.; Park, H.; Kim, Y. Data synthesis based on generative adversarial networks. *Proc. VLDB Endow.* **2018**, *11*, 1071–1083. [CrossRef]
18. Nazari, e.; Branco, P. On Oversampling via Generative Adversarial Networks under Different Data Difficult Factors. In Proceedings of the International Workshop on Learning with Imbalanced Domains: Theory and Applications, Online, 17 September 2021; PMLR 2021; pp. 76–89.
19. Nazari, E.; Branco, P.; Jourdan, G.V. Using CGAN to Deal with Class Imbalance and Small Sample Size in Cybersecurity Problems. In Proceedings of the 2021 18th International Conference on Privacy, Security and Trust (PST), Auckland, New Zealand, 13–15 December 2021; IEEE: New York, NY, USA, 2021; pp. 1–10. [CrossRef]
20. Pennisi, M.; Palazzo, S.; Spampinato, C. Self-improving classification performance through GAN distillation. In Proceedings of the 2021 IEEE/CVF International Conference on Computer Vision Workshops (ICCVW), Montreal, BC, Canada, 11–17 October 2021; pp. 1640–1648. [CrossRef]
21. Chaudhari, P.; Agrawal, H.; Kotecha, K. Data augmentation using MG-GAN for improved cancer classification on gene expression data. *Soft Comput.* **2020**, *24*, 11381–11391. [CrossRef]
22. Luo, Y.; Cai, X.; Zhang, Y.; Xu, J.; Yuan, X. Multivariate Time Series Imputation with Generative Adversarial Networks. In *Advances in Neural Information Processing Systems*; Bengio, S., Wallach, H., Larochelle, H., Grauman, K., Cesa-Bianchi, N., Garnett, R., Eds.; Curran Associates, Inc.: Montreal, QC, Canada, 2018; Volume 31.
23. Gupta, A.; Johnson, J.; Fei-Fei, L.; Savarese, S.; Alahi, A. Social GAN: Socially Acceptable Trajectories with Generative Adversarial Networks. *arXiv* **2018**, arXiv:1803.10892. [CrossRef]
24. Saxena, D.; Cao, J. D-GAN: Deep Generative Adversarial Nets for Spatio-Temporal Prediction. *arXiv* **2019**, arXiv:1907.08556. [CrossRef]
25. Mescheder, L.; Geiger, A.; Nowozin, S. Which Training Methods for GANs do actually Converge? *arXiv* **2018**, arXiv:1801.04406. [CrossRef]
26. Daskalakis, C.; Ilyas, A.; Syrgkanis, V.; Zeng, H. Training GANs with Optimism. *arXiv* **2017**, arXiv:1711.00141. [CrossRef]
27. Goodfellow, I. NIPS 2016 Tutorial: Generative Adversarial Networks. *arXiv* **2017**, arXiv:1701.00160. [CrossRef]

28. Zhou, S.; Gordon, M.L.; Krishna, R.; Narcomey, A.; Fei-Fei, L.; Bernstein, M.S. HYPE: A Benchmark for Human eYe Perceptual Evaluation of Generative Models. *arXiv* **2019**, arXiv:1904.01121. [CrossRef].
29. Salimans, T.; Goodfellow, I.; Zaremba, W.; Cheung, V.; Radford, A.; Chen, X.; Chen, X. Improved Techniques for Training GANs. In *Advances in Neural Information Processing Systems*; Lee, D., Sugiyama, M., Luxburg, U., Guyon, I., Garnett, R., Eds.; Curran Associates, Inc.: Barcelona, Spain, 2016; Volume 29.
30. Borji, A. Pros and Cons of GAN Evaluation Measures: New Developments. *arXiv* **2021**, arXiv:2103.09396. [CrossRef].
31. Salimans, T.; Goodfellow, I.; Zaremba, W.; Cheung, V.; Radford, A.; Chen, X. Improved Techniques for Training GANs. *arXiv* **2016**, arXiv:1606.03498. [CrossRef].
32. Heusel, M.; Ramsauer, H.; Unterthiner, T.; Nessler, B.; Hochreiter, S. GANs Trained by a Two Time-Scale Update Rule Converge to a Local Nash Equilibrium. *arXiv* **2017**, arXiv:1706.08500. [CrossRef].
33. Ravuri, S.; Vinyals, O. Classification Accuracy Score for Conditional Generative Models. *arXiv* **2019**, arXiv:1905.10887. [CrossRef].
34. Shmelkov, K.; Schmid, C.; Alahari, K. How good is my GAN? In Proceedings of the European Conference on Computer Vision (ECCV), Munich, Germany, 8–14 September 2018.
35. Arjovsky, M.; Chintala, S.; Bottou, L. Wasserstein GAN. *arXiv* **2017**, arXiv:1701.07875. [CrossRef].
36. Papadimitriou, C.H. *Computational Complexity*; Addison-Wesley: Reading, MA, USA, 1994.
37. Mirza, M.; Osindero, S. Conditional Generative Adversarial Nets. *arXiv* **2014**, arXiv:1411.1784. [CrossRef].
38. Kullback, S. *Information Theory and Statistics*; Courier Corporation: New York, NY, USA, 1997.
39. Ramdas, A.; Garcia, N.; Cuturi, M. On Wasserstein Two Sample Testing and Related Families of Nonparametric Tests. *arXiv* **2015**, arXiv:1509.02237. [CrossRef].
40. Barratt, S.; Sharma, R. A Note on the Inception Score. *arXiv* **2018**, arXiv:1801.01973. [CrossRef].
41. Obukhov, A.; Krasnyanskiy, M. Quality Assessment Method for GAN Based on Modified Metrics Inception Score and Fréchet Inception Distance. In *Software Engineering Perspectives in Intelligent Systems*; Silhavy, R., Silhavy, P., Prokopova, Z., Eds.; Springer International Publishing: Cham, Switzerland, 2020; pp. 102–114.
42. Tan, M.; Chen, B.; Pang, R.; Vasudevan, V.; Sandler, M.; Howard, A.; Le, Q.V. Mnasnet: Platform-aware neural architecture search for mobile. In Proceedings of the IEEE/CVF Conference on Computer Vision and Pattern Recognition, Long Beach, CA, USA, 16–17 June 2019; pp. 2820–2828.
43. Fu, Y.; Chen, W.; Wang, H.; Li, H.; Lin, Y.; Wang, Z. Autogan-distiller: Searching to compress generative adversarial networks. *arXiv* **2020**, arXiv:2006.08198.
44. Wang, H.; Huan, J. Agan: Towards automated design of generative adversarial networks. *arXiv* **2019**, arXiv:1906.11080.
45. Gong, X.; Chang, S.; Jiang, Y.; Wang, Z. Autogan: Neural architecture search for generative adversarial networks. In Proceedings of the IEEE/CVF International Conference on Computer Vision, Seoul, Republic of Korea, 27–28 October 2019; pp. 3224–3234.
46. Morozov, S.; Voynov, A.; Babenko, A. On Self-Supervised Image Representations for {GAN} Evaluation. In Proceedings of the International Conference on Learning Representations, Virtual Event, 3–7 May 2021.
47. Isola, P.; Zhu, J.Y.; Zhou, T.; Efros, A.A. Image-To-Image Translation with Conditional Adversarial Networks. In Proceedings of the IEEE Conference on Computer Vision and Pattern Recognition (CVPR), Honolulu, HI, USA, 21–26 July 2017.
48. Gulrajani, I.; Ahmed, F.; Arjovsky, M.; Dumoulin, V.; Courville, A.C. Improved Training of Wasserstein GANs. In *Advances in Neural Information Processing Systems*; Guyon, I., Luxburg, U.V., Bengio, S., Wallach, H., Fergus, R., Vishwanathan, S., Garnett, R., Eds.; Curran Associates, Inc.: Long Beach, CA, USA, 2017; Volume 30.
49. Habibi Lashkari, A.; Draper Gil, G.; Mamun, M.S.I.; Ghorbani, A.A. Characterization of Tor Traffic using Time based Features. In Proceedings of the 3rd International Conference on Information Systems Security and Privacy—ICISSP, Porto, Portugal, 19–21 February 2017; INSTICC; SciTePress: Setubal, Portugal, 2017; pp. 253–262. [CrossRef].
50. Mahdavifar, S.; Abdul Kadir, A.F.; Fatemi, R.; Alhadidi, D.; Ghorbani, A.A. Dynamic Android Malware Category Classification using Semi-Supervised Deep Learning. In Proceedings of the 2020 IEEE Intl Conf on Dependable, Autonomic and Secure Computing, Intl Conf on Pervasive Intelligence and Computing, Intl Conf on Cloud and Big Data Computing, Intl Conf on Cyber Science and Technology Congress (DASC/PiCom/CBDCom/CyberSciTech), Online Event, 17–22 August 2020; pp. 515–522. . [CrossRef].
51. Mamun, M.S.I.; Rathore, M.A.; Lashkari, A.H.; Stakhanova, N.; Ghorbani, A.A. Detecting Malicious URLs Using Lexical Analysis. In *Network and System Security*; Chen, J., Piuri, V., Su, C., Yung, M., Eds.; Springer International Publishing: Cham, Switzerland, 2016; pp. 467–482.
52. MontazeriShatoori, M.; Davidson, L.; Kaur, G.; Habibi Lashkari, A. Detection of DoH Tunnels using Time-series Classification of Encrypted Traffic. In Proceedings of the 2020 IEEE DASC/PiCom/CBDCom/CyberSciTech, Online Event, 17–22 August 2020; pp. 63–70. [CrossRef].
53. Deng, L. The mnist database of handwritten digit images for machine learning research. *IEEE Signal Process. Mag.* **2012**, *29*, 141–142. [CrossRef].
54. Xiao, H.; Rasul, K.; Vollgraf, R. Fashion-MNIST: A Novel Image Dataset for Benchmarking Machine Learning Algorithms. *arXiv* **2017**, arXiv:1708.07747. [CrossRef].

55. Clanuwat, T.; Bober-Irizar, M.; Kitamoto, A.; Lamb, A.; Yamamoto, K.; Ha, D. Deep learning for classical japanese literature. *arXiv* **2018**, arXiv:1812.01718.
56. Krizhevsky, A. *Learning Multiple Layers of Features from Tiny Images*; Technical Report; Computer Science-University of Toronto: Toronto, ON, Canada, 2009.

Disclaimer/Publisher's Note: The statements, opinions and data contained in all publications are solely those of the individual author(s) and contributor(s) and not of MDPI and/or the editor(s). MDPI and/or the editor(s) disclaim responsibility for any injury to people or property resulting from any ideas, methods, instructions or products referred to in the content.

Article

Imbalanced Ectopic Beat Classification Using a Low-Memory-Usage CNN LMUEBCNet and Correlation-Based ECG Signal Oversampling

You-Liang Xie [1] and Che-Wei Lin [1,2,3,4,*]

1. Department of Biomedical Engineering, College of Engineering, National Cheng Kung University, Tainan 701, Taiwan
2. Medical Device Innovation Center, National Cheng Kung University, Tainan 701, Taiwan
3. Institute of Gerontology, College of Medicine, National Cheng Kung University, Tainan 701, Taiwan
4. Institute of Medical Informatics, College of Electrical Engineering and Computer Science, National Cheng Kung University, Tainan 701, Taiwan
* Correspondence: lincw@mail.ncku.edu.tw

Abstract: *Objective*: This study presents a low-memory-usage ectopic beat classification convolutional neural network (CNN) (LMUEBCNet) and a correlation-based oversampling (Corr-OS) method for ectopic beat data augmentation. *Methods*: A LMUEBCNet classifier consists of four VGG-based convolution layers and two fully connected layers with the continuous wavelet transform (CWT) spectrogram of a QRS complex (0.712 s) segment as the input of the LMUEBCNet. A Corr-OS method augmented a synthetic beat using the top K correlation heartbeat of all mixed subjects for balancing the training set. This study validates data via a 10-fold cross-validation in the following three scenarios: training/testing with native data (CV1), training/testing with augmented data (CV2), and training with augmented data but testing with native data (CV3). *Experiments*: The PhysioNet MIT-BIH arrhythmia ECG database was used for verifying the proposed algorithm. This database consists of a total of 109,443 heartbeats categorized into five classes according to AAMI EC57: non-ectopic beats (N), supraventricular ectopic beats (S), ventricular ectopic beats (V), a fusion of ventricular and normal beats (F), and unknown beats (Q), with 90,586/2781/7236/803/8039 heartbeats, respectively. Three pre-trained CNNs: AlexNet/ResNet18/VGG19 were utilized in this study to compare the ectopic beat classification performance of the LMUEBCNet. The effectiveness of using Corr-OS data augmentation was determined by comparing (1) with/without using the Corr-OS method and (2) Next-OS data augmentation method. Next-OS augmented the synthetic beat using the next heartbeat of one subject. *Results*: The proposed LMUEBCNet can achieve a 99.4% classification accuracy under the CV2 and CV3 cross-validation scenarios. The accuracy of the proposed LMUEBCNet is 0.4–0.5% less than the performance obtained from AlexNet/ResNet18/VGG19 under the same data augmentation and cross-validation scenario, but the parameter usage is only 10% or less than that of the AlexNet/ResNet18/VGG19 method. The proposed Corr-OS method can improve ectopic beat classification accuracy by 0.3%. *Conclusion*: This study developed a LMUEBCNet that can achieve a high ectopic beat classification accuracy with efficient parameter usage and utilized the Corr-OS method for balancing datasets to improve the classification performance.

Keywords: ectopic beat classification; MIT-BIH; AAMI; low memory usage; convolutional neural network (CNN); data augmentation; signal processing; image processing

MSC: 68T07; 92B20; 92C55; 94A12; 94A08; 68U10

Citation: Xie, Y.-L.; Lin, C.-W. Imbalanced Ectopic Beat Classification Using a Low-Memory-Usage CNN LMUEBCNet and Correlation-Based ECG Signal Oversampling. *Mathematics* **2023**, *11*, 1833. https://doi.org/10.3390/math11081833

Academic Editors: Alvaro Figueira and Francesco Renna

Received: 15 March 2023
Revised: 2 April 2023
Accepted: 4 April 2023
Published: 12 April 2023

Copyright: © 2023 by the authors. Licensee MDPI, Basel, Switzerland. This article is an open access article distributed under the terms and conditions of the Creative Commons Attribution (CC BY) license (https:// creativecommons.org/licenses/by/ 4.0/).

1. Introduction

Ectopic beats are a type of cardiac arrhythmias, with the excessive supraventricular ectopic activity being correlated with an increased risk of stroke, and the ablation of ventricular ectopic beats has been proven to improve cardiomyopathy [1]. Arrhythmia is caused by abnormalities of electrical impulses generation and/or conduction and ectopic beats are a type of cardiac arrhythmias [2]. To automatically recognize an ectopic beat (single heartbeat) is essential for arrhythmia diagnosis. Classification of normal/ectopic beat can be categorized into five classes: non-ectopic beats (N), supraventricular ectopic beats (S), ventricular ectopic beats (V), a fusion of ventricular and normal beats (F), and unknown beats (Q), based on the ANSI/AAMI EC57:2012 standard [3]. The ANSI/AAMI EC57 standard is published by Association for the Advancement of Medical Instrumentation (AAMI) and it provides the standard for testing and reporting the performance of the cardiac rhythm analysis algorithm. Ectopic beat classification is one of the testing items. The ECG databases such as the MIT-BIH (Massachusetts Institute of Technology—Boston's Beth Israel Hospital) arrhythmia database and the AHA (American Heart Association) ECG database are recommended by EC57 to be used to evaluate the ectopic beat classification performance.

Machine learning (ML) is good for handling multi-dimensional and multi-variety data and is thus appropriate to process the high-dimensional feature vector extracted from the ECG database to classify ectopic beats. ML classifiers such as the neural network (NN) and support vector machine (SVM) have been found to be effective for ectopic beat detection using morphological and interval-based features. When extracting different features including higher order statistics (HOSs), Gaussian mixture modeling (GMM), or wavelet packet entropy (WPE) from the RR interval and then classifying using decision trees (DTs) or random forest (RF), a 94% accuracy can be obtained in ectopic beat classification [4,5]. A combination of feature engineering techniques such as combining a discrete cosine transform (DCT)/discrete wavelet transform (DWT)/principal component analysis (PCA)/independent component analysis (ICA) to extract features and classify by various classifiers such as a k-nearest neighbor (k-NN), NN, SVM, support vector machine and radial basis function (SVM-RBF), and probabilistic neural network (PNN), can achieve accuracies of around 98% to 99% in the classification task [6–8].

Deep learning (DL) outperforms ML in many classification problems due to its ability to execute feature engineering by itself. 1D/2D/3D convolutional neural networks (CNNs) have been employed to classify ectopic beats with respect to ECG expressed in 1D/2D/3D forms [9]. In the time domain 1D signal data, Acharya et al. used a 1D-CNN model with three convolution layers and three fully connected layers, then balanced the dataset using the standard deviation and Z-score, finally achieving 94.03% in overall accuracy [10]. Wang et al. and Romdhane et al. used a self-designed 1D-CNN to classify ectopic beats within a 0.9 s to 10 s time-window and obtained an accuracy over 98% [11,12]. Yao et al. applied a gated recurrent unit (GRU) and six VGG-based local feature extraction modules (LFEM) to a 1D-CNN and achieved an overall accuracy of 99.61% in a training/test ratio of 8/2 [13]. In the 2D CNN for ectopic beat classification, Al Rahhal et al. and Xie et al. utilized the continuous wavelet transform (CWT) and STFT to generate a spectrogram, then applied the pre-trained VGG16 CNN and a self-designed 31-layer CNN classifier and achieved a high accuracy [14,15]. Zhai et al. applied a dual-beat coupling matrix with 73 by 73 pixels for generating features and a CNN that consisted of three convolution layers with two FC layers for classification, finally achieving an overall accuracy of 96.07% (50% training and 50% testing) [16]. Sellami et al. used a nine-layer CNN (one convolution with four residual modules (two convolutions)) to classify a single beat, two beats, and three beats. Next, they applied batch-weighted loss to overcome the imbalance between classes and achieved an overall accuracy of 99.5% and an average sensitivity of 94.7% [17]. For applying a 3D CNN in ectopic beat classification, Li et al. extracted and formulated the three-dimensional features including the single heartbeat segment, RRI ratios, and beat-to-beat correlations, and classified the three-dimensional features using the 3D-CNN, obtaining an overall accuracy of 91.44% (50% training and 50% testing) [18].

The low-memory-usage models such as KecNet/LiteNet are designed for the execution of the deep learning network in the portable device, with satisfactory performance but lower power consumption/memory usage [19,20]. A deeper CNN architecture generally can extract more features, but not all of them can be significantly trained [21,22], and this might increase the memory usage/complexity/training time [23]. Lu et al. utilized KecNet, a lightweight network that can classify N/S/V/F/Q classes with a 99.31% accuracy. It is only 0.11% slightly lower in accuracy but reduces 80% of the parameter count compared to using GoogleNet [19]. LiteNet developed by He et al. reduces more than half of the parameter count compared to using AlexNet, and only decreases 0.02% of the F1-score in the N/S/V/F/Q classification task [20].

The problem of data imbalances occurred in our daily activities, especially in the physiological signals. The imbalanced dataset makes minority classes easily obtain poor results, since the model usually fits majority classes in training tasks [24–26]. More and more research has been addressing the imbalanced dataset problem using data augmentation methods or oversampling methods [27]. Data imbalance conditions can be found in many arrhythmia databases such as the MIT-BIH arrhythmia ECG database. Non-ectopic beats (N), supraventricular ectopic beats (S), ventricular ectopic beats (V), a fusion of ventricular and normal beats (F), and unknown beats (Q), are 90,586/2781/7236/803/8039, respectively, in the MIT-BIH arrhythmia ECG database. Class N accounted for more than half of the database (82.8%), while S and V are only 2.5% and 6.6%, respectively [16]. The following data augmentation methods are widely used in different studies to solve the data imbalance problem: (1) random oversampling (ROS), (2) random undersampling (RUS), (3) the synthetic minority oversampling technique (SMOTE), (4) cost-sensitive learning, (5) generative adversarial networks (GANs), and (6) augmentation with cropping images [28]. The above methods used for solving the imbalanced dataset problem, in particular ROS and RUS, might cause overfitting and underfitting in the deep learning field with an increase in the minority class and a decrease in the majority class. The GAN algorithm includes a generator network and a discriminator network to balance the dataset with augmented figures. However, GANs might consume enormous computational resources with their two convolutional architectures. Based on the above reasons, the data augmentation method based on the SMOTE becomes the best choice in this study. In the above studies for balancing databases, correlation is hardly taken into consideration [29–33]. The traditional SMOTE algorithm only uses Euclidean distance to find k-nearest samples, whereas the correlation coefficient is also an important factor in obtaining the nearest samples for generating synthetic data and avoiding some noise or outliers [34–38].

This paper aims to develop a low-memory-usage ectopic beat classification convolutional neural network (LMUEBCNet) which can achieve more than 99% accuracy for discriminating N/S/V/F/Q classes in the MIT-BIH arrhythmia ECG database. The parameter usage in the LMUEBCNet is expected to be less than 10% of the AlexNet/ResNet18/VGG19 method. This study proposed a data-level oversampling (OS) approach called correlation-based oversampling (Corr-OS), which is modified from the SMOTE method and considers the correlation and relevance between ECG heartbeats to deal with data imbalance conditions.

The rest of the paper is organized as follows: Section 2 presents the related works that provide an overview of recent works for ectopic beat classification using low-memory-usage CNNs and oversampling methods. Section 3 describes the methods developed in this paper. Section 4 shows the experimental results. Discussions and conclusions of this work are given in Sections 5 and 6.

2. Related Works

2.1. Low-Memory-Usage Convolutional Neural Network for Ectopic Beat Classification

Mathunjwa et al. transformed 2 s ECG recordings into recurrence plot image and classified using a self-developed CNN. Noisy and ventricular fibrillation are classified in the first stage and normal AFib/VPC/APC are classified in the second stage. Mathunjwa et al. compared the performance of their self-designed network to ResNet (18/34/50/101/152 layers)/AlexNet/VGG-16/19 and concluded that a deeper CNN is not guaranteed to achieve higher ectopic beat classification accuracy. The customized CNN for ectopic beat classification can not only obtain higher classification accuracy, but also uses smaller memory usage/parameters to do so [21]. Lu et al. developed a KecNet 1-D CNN with a special sync-conv layer and only three convolution layers to classify N/S/V/F/Q and achieved a 99.31% accuracy. KecNet consumed only around 20% of parameters and only decreased accuracy by 0.1% when compared to using GoogLeNet [19] for ectopic beat classification. He et al. used a LiteNet 1-D CNN with a lighter inception structure and a residual structure to recognize N/S/V/F/Q, achieving an accuracy of 98.8%. LiteNet saved 60% of parameters and only decreased accuracy by 0.2% when compared with GoogLeNet [20]. LiteNet achieves higher classification accuracy than GoogLeNet in ectopic beat classification while consuming less power.

2.2. Oversampling Data Augmentation for Ectopic Beat Classification

Bernardo et al. utilized a self-designed 1-D CNN classifier with ROS to balance the dataset and reached an average macro F1-score of 0.98 and an 0.98 F1-score for all classes (N/S/V/F/Q) [39]. Zhang et al. applied ROS and RUS to balance the dataset of the hybrid time-frequency 2-D image with the ResNet-101 CNN classifier; they achieved average accuracies of 99.62% using ROS and 94.57% using ROS with RUS [40]. Acharya et al. balanced the dataset using the standard deviation and Z-score and generated all classes so that they had an equal number to the N class (90,592 images), achieving a significant improvement from 89.03% to 94.03% in overall accuracy using a 1D-CNN [10]. Lu et al. used 25 PQRST samples as features and extracted 200 features from a CNN (input signal images). Then, they applied several balancing methods, such as ROS, RUS, cluster centroids (CC), near miss (NM), edited nearest neighbors (ENNs), repeated edited nearest neighbors (RENNs), the neighborhood cleaning rule (NCR), and a one-sided selection (OSS). Finally, using ROS with a RF classifier obtained a highest accuracy of 99.96% [29]. Mousavi et al. used the SMOTE method to balance the dataset with a CNN auto-encoder and a bidirectional recurrent neural network (BiRNN) to classify the N/S/V/F classes and achieved an accuracy of 99.92% [30]. Ahmad et al. utilized the SMOTE method to oversample S/V/F/Q classes and obtained 30,000/20,000/20,000/10,000 samples, respectively. Next, using a AlexNet CNN and self-designed simpler CNN to extract the Gramian angular field (GAF), recurrence plot (RP), and Markov transition field matrix (MTF) features with the SVM classifier, finally achieved an accuracy of 99.7% [41]. Shaker et al. applied a GAN as the balancing method and a 1-D CNN with three inception modules and three FC layers for classification. They achieved an overall accuracy of above 98.0% and a sensitivity of over 97.7% [31].

3. Methods

The proposed ectopic beat classification algorithm consists of windowing processing, oversampling, feature generation, and a LMUEBCNet classifier. The flowchart of the proposed algorithm is shown in Figure 1. The windowing processing segments raw ECG signal into consecutive 0.712 s windows. The minority classes (S/V/F/Q) are augmented via the proposed correlation-based oversampling (Corr-OS) method. Corr-OS is generated by the interpolation of one ECG segment and a segment in the same class with a top K ($K = 1 \sim 5$) high correlation value. The time domain ECG signal is transformed into a time–frequency spectrogram (represented as figures) using the continuous wavelet transform (CWT) in feature generation. The difference between the N class and V/S class can be enhanced with the help of time–frequency transformation. The LMUEBCNet with low memory usage is composed of two convolution layers, two VGG-based convolution blocks, and two fully connected layers.

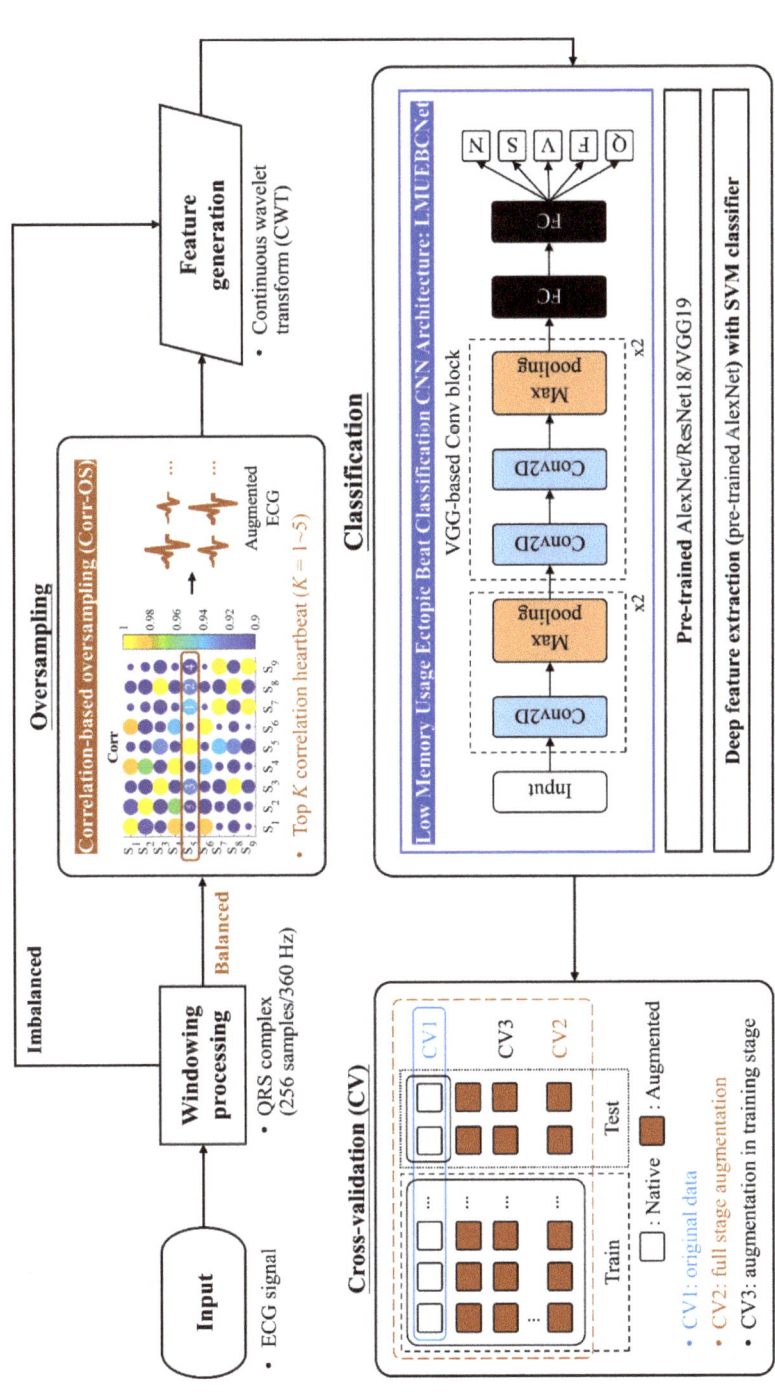

Figure 1. Flowchart of the proposed algorithm.

3.1. Windowing Processing

Windowing processing was applied for splitting a continuous ECG signal into ECG windows in order to easily analyze the ectopic beats. Each window segment consists of 0.712 s ECG readings which are centered with the R wave point that is extracted from each QRS complex. This study used the symbols of the MIT-BIH arrhythmia database downloaded from the PhysioBank ATM as the center and extended 0.356 s left/right (127 samples before and 128 samples after the R peak; sampling rate: 360 Hz).

3.2. Feature Generation: Continuous Wavelet Transform (CWT)

The continuous wavelet transform (CWT) is used to emphasize the difference between N/S/V/F/Q classes from the point of view of the time–frequency spectrum [42,43]. The computation of the CWT is expressed using Equation (1):

$$C(a,b) = \int_{-\infty}^{\infty} s(t) \frac{1}{\sqrt{a}} \psi\left(\frac{t-b}{a}\right) dt, \ a \epsilon R^+ - \{0\}, b \epsilon R, \quad (1)$$

$$\text{Morlet wavelet}: \ \psi(x) = e^{-x^2} \cos\left(\pi \sqrt{\frac{2}{\ln 2}} x\right) \quad (2)$$

where $s(t)$ is the signal, a is the scale, b is the translation, $\psi(t)$ is the mother wavelet shown in Equation (2), $\psi_{a,b}(t)$ is the scaled and translated wavelet, and C is the 2D matrix of the wavelet coefficients. The Morlet wavelet setting of a is two divided by the sampling rate (360 Hz), and b is zero in this study.

Time–frequency analysis is based on the classical Fourier analysis and assumes that signals are infinite in time or periodic, while many signals in practice are of a short duration and change substantially over their duration [4]. The CWT is non-redundant and efficient enough for accurate reconstruction by continuously varying the translation and scaling the parameters of the wavelet. The relationship between scale and frequency in the CWT was also explored as a band-pass filter. Wavelet analysis allows low-frequency information to be more accurate for long intervals and high-frequency information to be more accurate for short intervals. Figure 2 shows the original ECG signals for five classes (N/S/V/F/Q) and the time–frequency spectrogram after transformation.

3.3. LMUEBCNet Classifier and Performance Comparison to Existing CNNs

3.3.1. Low-Memory-Usage Ectopic Beat Classification Network: LMUEBCNet

LMUEBCNet is a neural network architecture that comprises of two convolutional layers, two VGG-based convolution blocks, and two fully connected layers. The first convolutional layer uses max pooling to downsample by a stride of 2. The second convolutional layer and two VGG-based convolution blocks are capable of extracting deeper features. Each VGG-based convolution block consists of two convolutional layers with the same padding. To avoid overfitting and reduce the parameters, a dropout of 0.25 is applied after ReLU activation of each convolutional/VGG block, for a total of four times. Additionally, a max pooling with a stride of 2 is applied after each dropout layer for denoising. Finally, all the extracted features are connected using fully connected layers with a softmax activation function.

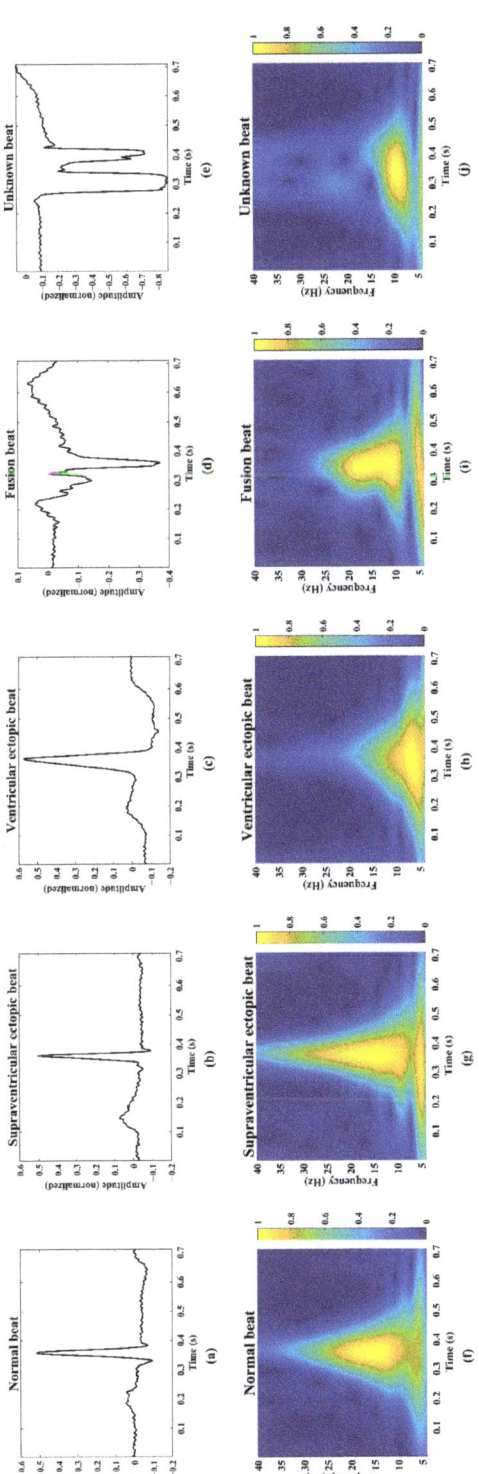

Figure 2. ECG signal of the QRS complex of (**a**) normal, (**b**) ventricular ectopic, (**c**) supraventricular ectopic, (**d**) fusion, and (**e**) unknown beats, and the CWT of the QRS complex of (**f**) normal, (**g**) ventricular ectopic, (**h**) supraventricular ectopic, (**i**) fusion, and (**j**) unknown beats.

LMUEBCNet's design incorporates 3 × 3 convolutional layers to achieve high performance while minimizing computational time. Unlike popular architectures such as AlexNet and VGG-16/19 [44], which employ 5 convolutional layers and 3 fully connected layers, this study proposes a new architecture with only 4 convolutional layers and 2 fully connected layers. This architecture reduces the number of parameters and model size. Table 1 displays the proposed LMUEBCNet architecture. The above approach provides a way of designing CNN architectures for embedded systems with limited memory, such as the ARM STM32F7 series, which requires only a maximum flash memory of 1 MB to 2 MB. The last convolutional layer has a maximum of 7 × 7 × 12 parameters, and the output parameters are set to C (number of classes) × 16 × 3 (number of channels).

Table 1. Proposed LMUEBCNet architecture compared with VGG19 [44].

	Layer	Filter Numbers		Output Size		Kernel Size	Stride	
		VGG19	LMUEBCNet	VGG19	LMUEBCNet		VGG19	LMUEBCNet
	Input			224 × 224 × 3		-	-	
1	Convolution	64 64	6	224 × 224 × 64	112 × 112 × 6	3 × 3	1	2
	Max Pooling	-	-	112 × 112 × 64	56 × 56 × 6	2 × 2	2	
2	Convolution	128 128	8	112 × 112 × 128	56 × 56 × 8	3 × 3	1	
	Max Pooling	-	-	56 × 56 × 128	28 × 28 × 8	2 × 2	2	
3	Convolution	256 256 256	12 12	56 × 56 × 256	28 × 28 × 12	3 × 3	1	
	Max Pooling	-	-	28 × 28 × 256	14 × 14 × 12	2 × 2	2	
4	Convolution	512 512 512	12 12	28 × 28 × 512	14 × 14 × 12	3 × 3	1	
	Max Pooling	-	-	14 × 14 × 512	7 × 7 × 12	2 × 2	2	
5	Convolution	512 512	-	14 × 14 × 512	-	3 × 3	1	-
	Max Pooling	-	-	7 × 7 × 512	-	2 × 2	2	-
6	FC	-	-	4096	-	-	-	-
7	FC	-	-	4096	1 × 1 × (C * × 48)	-	-	-
Output	FC	-	-	1000	C *	-	-	-

* C: number of the class.

3.3.2. Performance Comparison to Existing CNNs: Pre-Trained AlexNet/ResNet18/VGG19

This study compared the performance of the proposed LMUEBCNet with existing CNNs by following these techniques: (1) transfer learning using pre-trained AlexNet/ResNet18/VGG19 and (2) deep feature extraction with AlexNet and classification via a SVM classifier. The training process of the CNNs in this research was using the MATLAB® 2019 CNN toolbox [45,46]. The pre-trained CNN models have been trained on approximately 1.2 million images from the ImageNet Dataset [47].

AlexNet [48] is a popular CNN architecture used in computer vision, comprising of five convolutional layers with ReLU or pooling layers, two fully connected layers, and one output (fully connected) layer. The architecture's design, featuring five convolutional layers and three fully connected layers, has demonstrated high accuracy in image classification tasks on ImageNet. Due to its success, AlexNet has become a popular choice for deep learning researchers who use CNNs and GPUs to accelerate the learning process.

The Residual net (ResNet) [49] series have 18/34/50/101/152 convolution layers in their architectures. This study chose an 18-layer ResNet (ResNet18) to compare the performance of ectopic beat classification. The degradation problem for the increased depth of the network is solved by introducing a deep residual learning framework. The original mapping will be recast to $F(x) + x$, and it can be implemented by using a feedforward neural network with quick connections.

VGG16 and VGG19, developed by the Visual Geometry Group at the University of Oxford [44], are CNN architectures based on AlexNet's five convolutional layers and three fully connected layers. VGG16 has sixteen layers, with thirteen convolutional layers and three fully connected layers, while VGG19 has nineteen layers, with sixteen convolutional layers and three fully connected layers. The deeper architectures of the VGG models results in an increased model weight and computation time. However, for a single crop and similar layers, VGG outperforms AlexNet in prediction accuracy.

Transfer learning is a useful technique where layers from a pre-trained network on a large dataset can be fine-tuned on a new dataset. Fine-tuning the network can be faster and easier than building and training a new network from scratch. The pre-trained network has already learned many image features, but fine-tuning allows it to learn features specific to the new dataset [50]. In this study, pre-trained models such as AlexNet, ResNet18, and VGG19 were utilized with input image sizes of $227 \times 227 \times 3$ pixels for AlexNet and $224 \times 224 \times 3$ pixels for ResNet18 and VGG19. The classification output size was set to five classes, and all training curves converged to approximately 100%.

Deep feature extraction with AlexNet and classification via a SVM classifier was also used in this study for evaluating the performance. A pre-trained network can be used as a feature extractor by taking the layer activations as features. Feature extraction is a quick, easy way to take advantage of deep learning without having to spend time and effort training a complete network. The present study used a pre-trained network, AlexNet, as a feature generator to extract the learned image features and used these features to train the support vector machine (SVM) classifier [51]. The trained model has better generalization performance and achieves more advanced classification accuracy compared with other alternatives.

3.4. Oversampling Method: Correlation-Based Oversampling (Corr-OS)

This study proposes a novel correlation-based oversampling (Corr-OS) method to augment new beats by identifying the top K ($K \in \mathbb{N}$) correlation coefficient beats from all beats. In contrast to the traditional synthetic minority oversampling technique (SMOTE) methods that rely on k-nearest neighbors [52], the proposed method considers the importance of the original signal and identifies the most similar heartbeat based on the correlation coefficient between heartbeats [34,35]. The pseudo-code for the Corr-OS method is presented in Algorithm 1. The method involves collecting all segments of the MIT-BIH arrhythmia database records in the same class, calculating the correlation coefficient between each segment, and selecting the K highest correlation values. The proposed method then augments the artificial signals by interpolating the target segment with the segment of the highest correlation value and the target segment with the segment of the second-highest correlation value. For example, when $K = 2$, the augmented signal will be interpolated by the target segment with the segment of the highest correlation value and the target segment with the segment of the second-highest correlation value.

While random oversampling (ROS) and random undersampling (RUS) are commonly used to address binary class data imbalance problems, ROS can lead to overfitting. In multi-class datasets, the synthetic minority oversampling technique (SMOTE) is widely used to generate artificial samples through interpolating the minority samples and reducing overfitting [27,28]. However, most SMOTE methods use Euclidean distance to search for the k-nearest neighbors without considering the signal's correlation [32,33,53]. In this study, the proposed Next-OS method augments the synthetic data by selecting the beat and the next beat with the minimum Euclidean distance from one subject. The pseudo-code for the Next-OS method is presented in Appendix A Algorithm A1. Although the morphology of heartbeats differs among healthy individuals, the baseline of adjacent heartbeats has low variation, making it suitable for use in the proposed method. The proposed method finds all heartbeats with the same ectopic type in one record, except the segments where the R peak is too close to the beginning or end of the records. If there is no other heartbeat with the same ectopic type next to the target heartbeat, the method goes back to the first heartbeat of the record. Some augmented beats may be missing in the data that are too close to the end in the Next-OS method.

Algorithm 1. Pseudo-code of *Corr-OS()*

1: **Inputs:** Symbol (downloaded from PhysioBank ATM) array of the subject: S
        30-min ECG Lead II signal of the subject: ecg
        Total number (beats) of the class: n
        Total number (beats) of the majority class: N_{maj}
        Total number (beats) of the minority class: N_{minor}
        Dilation of the CWT: $a = 0.1$
        Translation of the CWT: $b = 0$

2: **Method:**
    for h = 1 to nS (total number of subjects)
      for i = 1 to n (total number (beats) of the record)
        S_R = sampling rate = 360 Hz in this study
        L = data length
        if $(S[i] < $ S_R $\times 0.35)$ **or** $(S[i] > L - $ S_R $\times 0.36)$ ⎫
          continue   Windowing
        else   processing
          $T[h][i] = ecg[S[i] - ($S_R$ \times 0.35): S[i] + (S_R \times 0.36)]$
        end if
    end
    for i = 1 to n ⎫
      for j = 1 to n
        $Local\_Corr[j]$ = Correlation Coefficient of $T[i]$ and $T[j]$
      end   Find top K
      for k = 1 to K ($K \in \mathbb{N}$: define by user)   correlation
        $Corr[i][k] = k + 1$ order of $Local\_Corr$ (the maximum is self-correlation, of each beat
        $Local\_Corr[1]$ = 1)
      end
    end
    for i = 1 to n ⎫
      L = round to the nearest integer of $(N_{maj}/N_{minor})-1$
      for j = 1 to K ($K \in \mathbb{N}$: defined by user)
        for k = 1 to L/K Generate
          δ = random numbers where $\delta \in [0, 1]$ Corr-OS
          $NewT[(j-1)\left(\frac{L}{2}\right) + k][256] = T[i][256] + (Corr[i][j] - T[i][256]) \times \delta$ beat
        end
      end
    end

3: **Output:** Array for Corr-OS beats: $NewT$
           CWT matrix: C

3.5. Cross-Validation (CV)

This study utilized the following three cross-validation methods for validating original (native) data and augmented data. The schematic diagram of three CV methods is shown in Figure 1 in the left bottom block (CV part). To obtain more reliable and steady predictions and reduce overfitting in deep learning, Zheng et al. applied various augmentation processes in different stages: augmentation in training stage, augmentation in testing stage, full stage data augmentation, and no data augmentation [54].

- CV1—original data: training/testing with native data; it can represent the baseline of the classification performance.
- CV2—full stage augmentation: training/testing with augmented data; it can represent the overall classification performance for all augmented data.
- CV3—augmentation in training stage: training with augmented data but testing with native data; it can represent the real-world case classification performance. It was only using augmented data for training that can avoid training similar images to cause overfitting. Santos et al. proposed a method that utilizes cross-validation during oversampling rather than k-fold cross-validation (randomly separate) after oversampling [55]. The testing data only kept the original data subset, and the oversampling data were not used in the training set. The present study regarded every single heartbeat as different data numbers (not subject-related).

In k-fold cross-validation, the original samples are randomly divided into k equal-sized subsamples [56]. One of the k subsamples is then selected as the verification data, while the remaining $k - 1$ subsamples are used for training. This process is repeated k times, with each subsample used exactly once as the verification data. The results are then averaged to produce a single estimate. This method offers an advantage over repeated random subsampling, as all observations are used for training and verification, and each observation is used only once for verification purposes. Typically, 10-fold cross-validation is used when k is an unfixed parameter. For example, if k equals 10, all the data are divided into ten folders, and the first folder is used for testing while the remaining data are used for training. The process is then repeated ten times, with each folder used once for testing until all the data have been tested. The final result is the mean of every calculation.

4. Experiments and Results

4.1. MIT-BIH Arrhythmia Database

PhysioNet provides free web access to large collections of recorded physiological signals and related open-source software. In this study, the MIT-BIH arrhythmia database and the INCART 12-lead arrhythmia database from PhysioNet were utilized for training and testing the proposed DL algorithm [57]. The MIT-BIH arrhythmia database comprises over 4000 long-term Holter recordings obtained by the Beth Israel Hospital Arrhythmia Laboratory between 1975 and 1979 [58]. The database includes 23 records chosen randomly from this set and 25 records selected from the same set. Each of the 48 records is slightly over 30 min long, with the upper signal being a modified limb lead II (MLII) obtained by placing electrodes on the chest in most records. The records also contain annotations transcribed from paper chart recordings.

The present study utilized the Association for the Advancement of Medical Instrumentation (AAMI) classes, which classify fifteen types of MIT-BIH heartbeats into five classes: N (non-ectopic beats), S (supraventricular ectopic beats), V (ventricular ectopic beats), F (fusion beats), and Q (unknown beats), as shown in Table 2. The MIT-BIH arrhythmia database records have a sampling rate of 360 Hz, and all 48 records are approximately 30 min long. The records contain symbols that classify heartbeats into different arrhythmia types based on the occurrence time of the R peak. The proposed method chose 127 samples before and 128 samples after the R peak from these symbols. The N class includes 90,586 beats, the S class includes 2781 beats, the V class includes 7235 beats, the F class includes 803 beats, and the Q class includes 8039 beats.

Table 2. Sample numbers in the MIT-BIH arrhythmia database and class description using the AAMI standard.

AAMI Class	MIT-BIH Symbol	MIT-BIH Heartbeat Types	Numbers	(%)
N (Non-ectopic beats)	N	Normal beat	75,015	68.543
	L	Left bundle branch block beat	8071	7.375
	R	Right bundle branch block beat	7255	6.629
	j	Nodal (junctional) escape beat	229	0.209
	e	Atrial escape beat	16	0.015
S (Supraventricular ectopic beats)	A	Atrial premature beat	2546	2.326
	a	Aberrated atrial premature beat	150	0.137
	J	Nodal (junctional) premature beat	83	0.076
	S	Supraventricular premature beat	2	0.002
V (Ventricular ectopic beats)	V	Premature ventricular contraction beat	7129	6.514
	E	Ventricular escape beat	106	0.097
F (Fusion beats)	F	Fusion of ventricular and normal beat	802	0.733
Q (Unknown beats)	Q	Unclassifiable beat	33	0.030
	/	Paced beat	7024	6.418
	f	Fusion of paced and normal beats	982	0.897
	Total:		109,443	100%

In this study, thirty-three augmentations were performed for every two beats in the S class, twelve augmentations were performed for every two beats in the V class, one hundred ten and one hundred thirteen augmentations were performed for every two beats in the F class, and eleven augmentations were performed for every two beats in the Q class. The total numbers for each minority class were brought closer to that of the majority class, N. The data numbers of the Next-OS and Corr-OS algorithms are shown in Table 3, representing the total number of heartbeats from all records that were randomly separated into ten folds using K-fold CV (K = 10).

Table 3. Data numbers in the dataset used in the experiments.

Class	Original Data Number	Ratio (Majority/Class)	Total Number after Oversampling	
			Next-OS	Corr-OS
N (majority)	90,586	1	90,586	90,586
S	2781	32.6	91,773	91,773
V	7236	12.5	87,013	94,068
F	803	112.8	88,802	90,739
Q	8039	11.3	88,439	88,429

4.2. Results

4.2.1. Calculating Error between Native/Augmented Segments Using Differences Plot

The augmented beats can be generated by the raw data of different beats. Note that the amplitude in Figures 3 and A6 are normalized amplitudes. The differences ($Difference = Signal_{oversampling} - Signal_{original}$) between the original signal and the augmented signal of the "A" symbol for the two oversampling methods are shown in Figure 3. The differences between Next-OS (Figure 3a) and Corr-OS (Figure 3b) (K = 1) are narrow, and Corr-OS keeps the baseline of the ECG compared with Next-OS. Using the top two (Figure 3c) and top five (Figure 3d) correlated beats of the Corr-OS method can generate more diverse signals than Next-OS (Figure 3a) and Corr-OS (Figure 3b) with K = 1. The first column of Figure 3a shows the raw ECG segment. The last two columns represented the augmented segments with different colors and the differences from the raw segment. The difference became larger when the K of Corr-OS increased. We then augmented different level variation segments for evaluating the performance of Next-OS and Corr-OS (K = 1~5). As shown in

Figure A6, the Corr-OS beats can be generated from the raw data of the beat and the next beat. Note that the amplitude in Figure A6 is the normalized amplitude. The difference between the original signal and the Corr-OS augmented signal of the F class (fusion beat) and the Q class (unknown beat) might be larger than that for the S class and the V class. This is because fusion beats and unknown beats might comprise a mixture of multiple diseases.

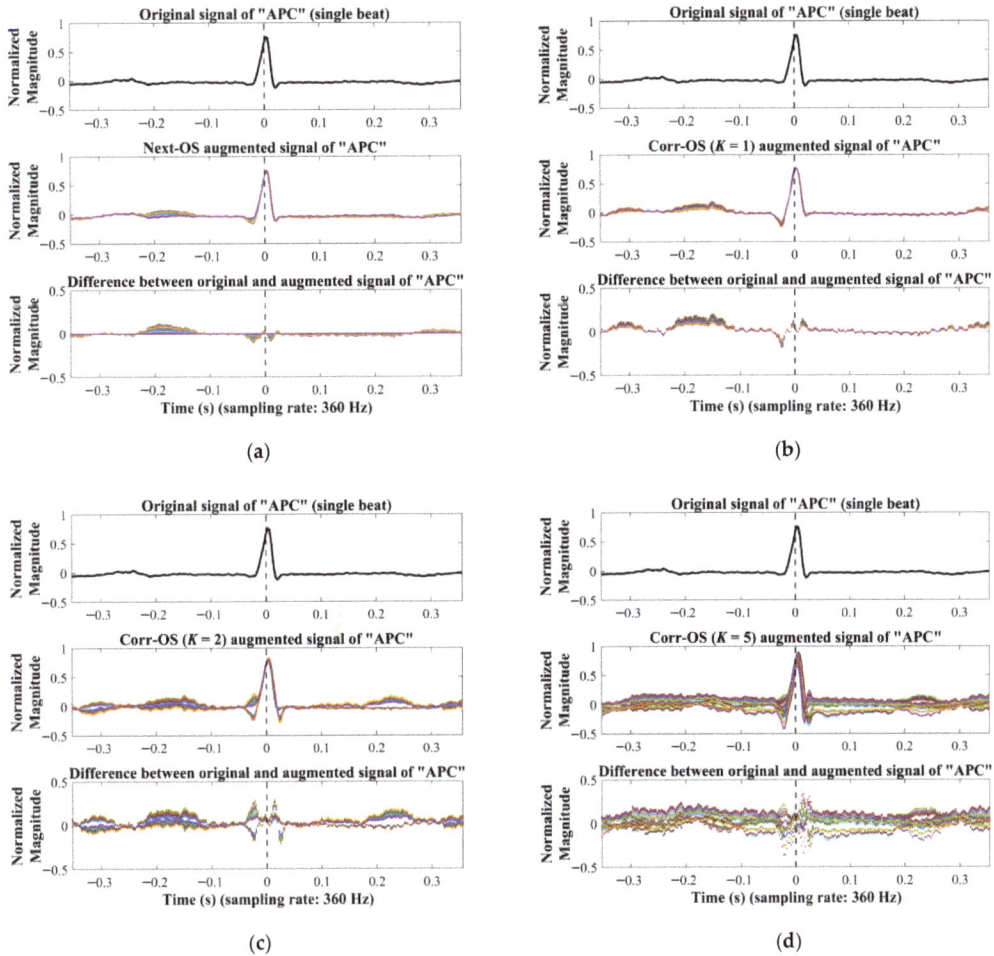

Figure 3. Differences between native and augmented ECG segments (symbol A, atrial premature beats) generated by the (a) Next-OS (next beat) and Corr-OS (top K correlation beats) algorithms with (b) $K = 1$, (c) $K = 2$, and (d) $K = 5$ (figure adapted from [59]).

4.2.2. Classification Performance between LMUEBCNet with Existed Models Using Corr-OS/Next-OS Methods under CV1/CV2/CV3

All the classification results were shown in Table 4 (CV1 and CV2) and Table 5 (CV3). The sensitivity and precision of each class are shown in Tables A1–A3. The total accuracy of classifying five AAMI classes using deep feature extraction with AlexNet and SVM classifier under CV1 (native dataset) achieved 99.4%.

Table 4. Classification performance between LMUEBCNet with existing models using native/Corr-OS/Next-OS dataset under CV1/CV2.

Data Augmentation		Classifier	F1-Score					Total Acc.	F1-Score		Memory Usage (MB)
			N	S	V	F	Q		Macro	Weighted	
Native (CV1 *)		SVM	99.9	94.1	96.7	87.0	98.9	99.4	95.3	94.5	N/A
		AlexNet	100.0	95.3	97.3	88.8	99.3	99.6	96.1	95.6	45.1
		ResNet18	100.0	94.2	96.8	87.1	98.9	99.5	95.4	94.6	39.8
		VGG19	100.0	95.9	97.5	89.3	99.2	99.6	96.4	96.1	496.0
		LMUEBCNet	99.9	90.1	94.8	81.7	98.1	99.1	92.9	90.8	1.1
Augmented (CV2 *)	Next-OS	AlexNet	99.6	99.9	99.6	99.8	99.8	99.7	99.7	99.7	45.7
		ResNet18	99.6	99.8	99.6	99.8	99.8	99.7	99.7	99.7	40.2
		VGG19	99.6	99.9	99.6	99.8	99.9	99.8	99.8	99.8	496.0
	Corr-OS (K = 1)	AlexNet	100.0	99.9	99.8	99.8	99.9	99.9	99.9	99.9	47.3
		ResNet18	100.0	99.9	99.9	99.9	99.9	99.9	99.9	99.9	41.8
		VGG19	100.0	99.9	99.8	99.9	99.9	99.9	99.9	99.9	499.3
		LMUEBCNet	99.7	99.4	98.9	99.4	99.7	99.4	99.4	99.4	2.6
	Corr-OS (K = 2)	AlexNet	100.0	99.8	99.6	99.8	99.8	99.8	99.8	99.8	-
		ResNet18	100.0	99.8	99.7	99.9	99.8	99.9	99.9	99.9	-
		VGG19	100.0	99.8	99.6	99.8	99.9	99.8	99.8	99.8	-
		LMUEBCNet	99.5	98.2	97.6	98.6	99.4	98.7	98.7	98.7	-
	Corr-OS (K = 3)	AlexNet	100.0	99.7	99.4	99.7	99.8	99.7	99.7	99.7	-
		ResNet18	100.0	99.7	99.6	99.8	99.9	99.8	99.8	99.8	-
		VGG19	100.0	99.7	99.4	99.7	99.8	99.7	99.7	99.7	-
		LMUEBCNet	99.4	98.3	97.4	98.4	99.4	98.6	98.6	98.6	-
	Corr-OS (K = 4)	AlexNet	100.0	99.6	99.3	99.7	99.8	99.7	99.7	99.7	-
		ResNet18	100.0	99.8	99.7	99.9	99.8	99.8	99.8	99.8	-
		VGG19	100.0	99.7	99.4	99.7	99.8	99.7	99.7	99.7	-
		LMUEBCNet	99.7	98.2	97.5	98.3	99.4	98.6	98.6	98.6	-
	Corr-OS (K = 5)	AlexNet	100.0	99.5	99.1	99.6	99.7	99.6	99.6	99.6	-
		ResNet18	100.0	99.5	99.2	99.7	99.7	99.6	99.6	99.6	-
		VGG19	100.0	99.5	99.0	99.5	99.7	99.6	99.6	99.6	-
		LMUEBCNet	99.7	98.0	97.1	98.1	99.3	98.4	98.5	98.5	-

* CV1: original data; CV2: full stage augmentation.

The LMUEBCNet (memory usage: 1.1 MB) under CV1 (native) can achieve a 92.9% macro F1-score, with the F1-scores for each class being 99.9%, 90.1%, 94.8%, 81.7%, and 98.1%, respectively. After data augmentation, the LMUEBCNet under Corr-OS ($K = 1$) in CV2 (full stage) can achieve a 99.4% F1-score with a 6.5% improvement in comparison to native dataset, and the F1-scores for each class were 99.7%, 99.4%, 99.3%, 99.4%, and 99.7%, respectively. The LMUEBCNet under Corr-OS ($K = 5$) in CV3 (training stage) can achieve a 96.1% macro F1-score with a 3.2% improvement in comparison to the native dataset, and the F1-scores for each class were 99.9%, 95.8%, 97.6%, 87.9%, and 99.3%, respectively. The PR curve of the F class using the LMUEBCNet can be improved after applying Corr-OS, as shown in Figure 4a–c. The ROC curve of the LMUEBCNet achieved an AUC of almost 1 for all classes, as shown in Figure 4d–f. The confusion matrix of the LMUEBCNet using different cross-validation methods (CV1, CV2, and CV3) is shown in Figures 4d–f and A1.

Table 5. Classification performance between LMUEBCNet with existing models using Corr-OS/Next-OS dataset under CV3.

Data Augmentation		Classifier	F1-Score					Total Acc.	F1-Score		Memory Usage (MB)
			N	S	V	F	Q		Macro	Weighted	
	Next-OS	AlexNet	99.2	97.0	92.7	84.2	98.9	98.6	94.4	96.5	45.7
		ResNet18	99.5	95.8	96.3	80.7	99.5	99.0	94.4	95.8	40.2
		VGG19	99.5	95.9	95.7	85.5	99.5	99.0	95.2	95.9	496.0
Corr-OS	(K = 1)	AlexNet	100.0	98.5	98.9	94.6	99.6	99.8	98.3	98.5	47.1
		ResNet18	100.0	98.3	98.9	94.6	99.6	99.8	98.3	98.3	41.7
		VGG19	100.0	98.4	99.0	94.7	99.6	99.8	98.4	98.5	499.3
		LMUEBCNet	99.9	95.3	97.3	89.9	99.1	99.4	96.3	95.6	2.4
	(K = 2)	AlexNet	100.0	98.7	99.0	95.4	99.7	99.8	98.6	98.7	-
		ResNet18	100.0	98.5	99.1	95.8	99.6	99.8	98.6	98.6	-
		VGG19	100.0	98.8	99.2	95.7	99.7	99.9	98.7	98.8	-
		LMUEBCNet	99.8	93.9	97.0	88.6	99.1	99.3	95.7	94.4	-
	(K = 3)	AlexNet	100.0	98.9	99.2	96.0	99.6	99.8	98.7	98.9	-
		ResNet18	100.0	98.5	99.0	96.1	99.6	99.8	98.6	98.5	-
		VGG19	100.0	98.9	99.2	95.7	99.7	99.8	98.7	98.9	-
		LMUEBCNet	99.7	93.3	97.0	87.7	98.7	99.2	95.3	93.8	-
	(K = 4)	AlexNet	100.0	98.6	99.1	95.7	99.6	99.8	98.6	98.7	-
		ResNet18	100.0	96.2	97.0	90.8	99.4	99.6	96.7	96.4	-
		VGG19	100.0	99.0	99.1	95.4	99.7	99.8	98.6	99.0	-
		LMUEBCNet	99.9	96.0	97.4	88.1	99.2	99.5	96.1	96.1	-
	(K = 5)	AlexNet	100.0	98.8	99.1	95.6	99.7	99.8	98.6	98.8	-
		ResNet18	100.0	98.9	99.2	96.5	99.7	99.9	98.9	98.9	-
		VGG19	100.0	99.0	99.2	95.0	99.7	99.9	98.6	98.9	-
		LMUEBCNet	99.9	95.8	97.6	87.9	99.3	99.5	96.1	96.0	-

AlexNet (memory usage: 45.1 MB) under CV1 (native) can achieve a 96.1% F1-score, with the F1-scores for each class being 100.0%, 95.3%, 97.3%, 88.8%, and 99.3%, respectively. After data augmentation, AlexNet under Corr-OS ($K = 1$) in CV2 (full stage) can achieve a 99.9% F1-score with a 3.8% improvement in comparison to the native dataset, and the F1-scores for each class were 100.0%, 99.9%, 99.8%, 99.8%, and 99.9%, respectively. AlexNet under Next-OS in CV2 (full stage) can achieve a 99.7% F1-score, with the F1-scores for each class being 99.6%, 99.8%, 99.6%, 99.8%, and 99.8%, respectively. AlexNet under Corr-OS ($K = 5$) in CV3 (training stage) can achieve a 98.6% macro F1-score, with a 2.5% improvement in comparison to the native dataset, and the F1-scores for each class were 100.0%, 98.8%, 99.1%, 95.6%, and 99.7%, respectively. AlexNet under Next-OS in CV3 (training stage) can achieve a 94.4% F1-score, with the F1-scores for each class being 99.2%, 97.0%, 92.7%, 84.2%, and 98.9%, respectively.

ResNet18 (memory usage: 39.8 MB) under CV1 (native) can achieve a 95.4% macro F1-score, with the F1-scores for each class being 100.0%, 94.2%, 96.8%, 87.1%, and 98.9%, respectively. After data augmentation, ResNet18 under Corr-OS ($K = 1$) in CV2 (full stage) can achieve a 99.9% F1-score with a 4.5% improvement in comparison to the native dataset, and the F1-scores for each class were 100.0%, 99.9%, 99.9%, 99.9%, and 99.9%, respectively. ResNet18 under Next-OS in CV2 (full stage) can achieve a 99.7% F1-score, with the F1-scores for each class being 99.6%, 99.9%, 99.6%, 99.8%, and 99.9%, respectively. ResNet18 under Corr-OS ($K = 5$) in CV3 (training stage) can achieve a 98.6% macro F1-score with a 3.2% improvement in comparison to the native dataset, and the F1-scores for each class were 100.0%, 98.9%, 99.2%, 96.5%, and 99.7%, respectively. ResNet18 under Next-OS in CV3 (training stage) can achieve a 94.4% F1-score, with the F1-scores for each class being 99.5%, 95.8%, 96.3%, 80.7%, and 99.5%, respectively.

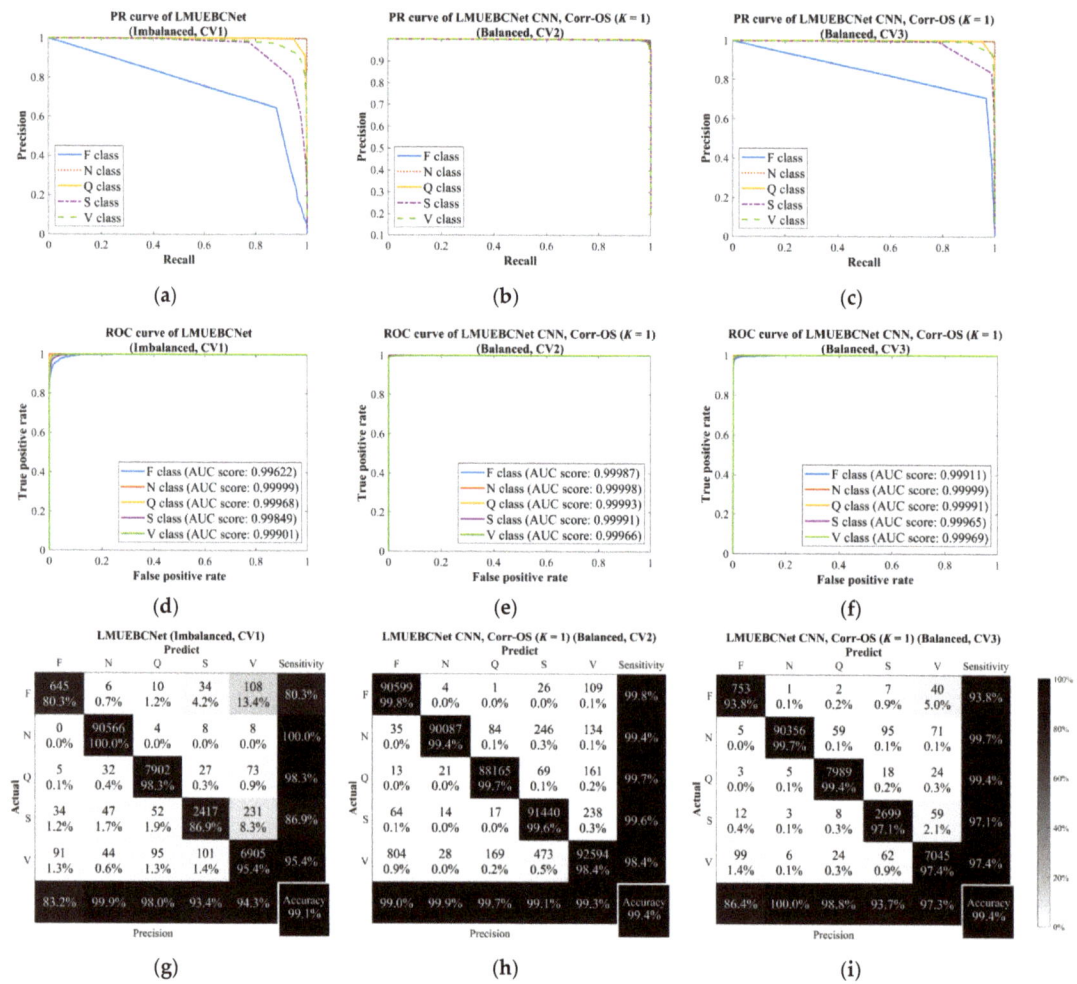

Figure 4. ROC curves and AUC scores of LMUEBCNet in (**a**) CV1, (**b**) CV2 of Corr-OS ($K = 1$), and (**c**) CV3 of Corr-OS ($K = 1$); PR curves of LMUEBCNet in (**d**) CV1, (**e**) CV2 of Corr-OS ($K = 1$), and (**f**) CV3 of Corr-OS ($K = 1$); confusion matrix of LMUEBCNet in (**g**) CV1, (**h**) CV2 of Corr-OS ($K = 1$), and (**i**) CV2 of Corr-OS ($K = 1$).

VGG19 (memory usage: 496.0 MB) under CV1 (native) can achieve a 96.4% macro F1-score, with the F1-scores for each class being 100.0%, 95.9%, 97.5%, 89.3%, and 99.2%, respectively. After data augmentation, VGG19 under Corr-OS ($K = 1$) in CV2 (full stage) can achieve a 99.9% F1-score with a 3.5% improvement in comparison to the native dataset, and the F1-scores for each class were 100.0%, 99.9%, 99.8%, 99.9%, and 99.9%, respectively. VGG19 under Next-OS in CV2 (full stage) can achieve a 99.8% F1-score, with the F1-scores for each class being 99.6%, 99.9%, 99.6%, 99.8%, and 99.9%, respectively. VGG19 under Corr-OS ($K = 5$) in CV3 (training stage) can achieve a 98.6% macro F1-score with a 2.2% improvement in comparison to the native dataset, and the F1-scores for each class were 100.0%, 99.0%, 99.2%, 95.0%, and 99.7%, respectively. VGG19 under Next-OS in CV3 (training stage) can achieve a 95.2% F1-score, with the F1-scores for each class being 99.5%, 95.9%, 95.7%, 85.5%, and 99.5%, respectively.

The confusion matrices of all classifiers are shown in Figures A1–A5. The AUC scores of AlexNet, ResNet18, and VGG19 for the imbalanced dataset are all about 0.99. The AUC scores of AlexNet, ResNet18, VGG19, and LMUEBCNet for the balanced dataset almost achieved a score of 1.

5. Discussion

The discussion/comparison based on the above classification results and existing literature can be described in the following five parts: (1) performance and memory/parameter usage of the LMUEBCNet vs. existing CNNs; (2) improvement using Corr-OS data augmentation method; (3) implications for different cross-validation methods; (4) classification performance compared with the existing literature; (5) limitations.

5.1. Accuracy/F1-Score Performance and Memory Usage of LMUEBCNet vs. Existing CNNs

The LMUEBCNet, with only 1% of VGG19's parameters, achieved an overall accuracy of 99.1%, which is close to that of VGG19, as shown in Figure 5. Compared to other VGG-like architectures, such as VGG8 [38], the LMUEBCNet can save a significant amount of memory usage while maintaining high performance. Deeper CNNs, such as VGG19 and ResNet18, may slightly improve or maintain a similar performance to AlexNet, but they significantly increase the memory usage of the saved model. AlexNet, with 12.8M parameters, achieved a total accuracy of 99.5% and a weighted F1-score of 94.6%. ResNet18, with 11.8M parameters, achieved a total accuracy of 99.5% and a weighted F1-score of 94.6%. VGG19, with over 100M parameters, achieved a total accuracy of 99.6% and a weighted F1-score of 96.4%. The classification performance of machine learning (ML) using deep feature extraction with AlexNet and the SVM classifier (total accuracy of 99.4% and weighted F1-score of 94.5%) is slightly lower than that of deep learning (DL) using the AlexNet CNN (total accuracy of 99.6% and weighted F1-score of 95.6%).

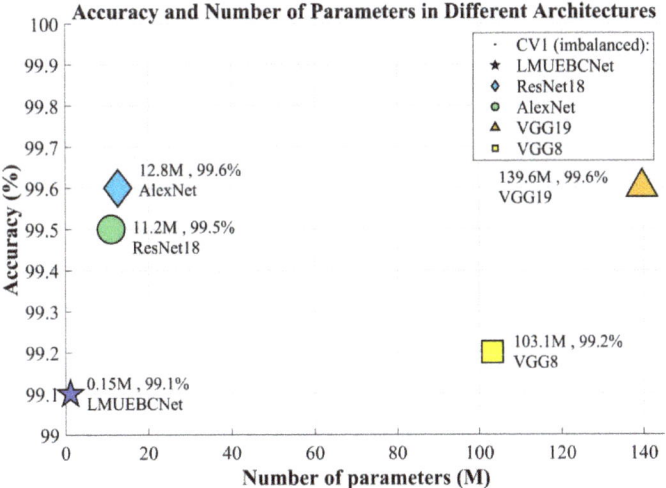

Figure 5. Total accuracy and the number of parameters in different CNN architectures.

The total generation time for oversampling the ECG signals from the original imbalanced dataset to the balanced dataset was only about 100 s. However, considerable effort is required for processing CWT spectrograms, which is still lower than the time required for algorithmic augmentation methods such as the GAN. The proposed LMUEBCNet only requires 1 MB of memory, while AlexNet/ResNet18/VGG19 need to reserve 40 to 500 MB of memory. The LMUEBCNet can save 50% to 70% of training time due to its low memory usage while maintaining a high accuracy of over 99.0%, whereas using VGG19 requires

6 h for training in CV2/CV3. All the training processes were performed on the TWCC supercomputer with NVIDIA Tesla V100 32GB GPU. To avoid possible overfitting, this study set the max epochs in training options and stopped before the loss began to increase.

5.2. Improvement in Accuracy/F1-Score/Sensitivity Using Corr-OS/Next-OS Methods

The LMUEBCNet achieved an accuracy of 99.4% using Corr-OS ($K = 1$) in CV2/CV3, with a 0.3% improvement in comparison to CV1 (native). Balancing the dataset using oversampling methods improved both the sensitivity and accuracy in CV2 and CV3. Next-OS and Corr-OS improved the average sensitivity in CV2 and CV3, resulting in a more balanced performance in all classes, rather than obtaining a result where the majority class is significantly higher than others. After balancing the dataset, the AUC scores of the five classes almost reached 1, and the PR curve of the minority classes, shown in Figure 4a–f, improved after applying oversampling methods (Next-OS and Corr-OS). In the VGG19 CNN, the total accuracy increased from 99.6% to 99.8% (Next-OS) and 99.9% (Corr-OS, $K = 1$), with sensitivity for the S/V/F/Q classes improving by about 5.0%/1.7%/13.7%/0.5%, respectively, in CV2. However, the sensitivity of the N class decreased in the Next-OS dataset. Using VGG19 with Next-OS in CV3 only improved the sensitivity of each class but resulted in poor precision, with the weighted F1-score decreasing to 95.9% from 96.1% (native), and the F1-score of the V/F classes decreasing by 1.8%/3.8%, respectively.

The improvement can be observed in standard deviations (Stds.) of 10-fold cross-validation under CV1/CV2/CV3, as shown in Figure 6. The Std. of the pre-trained AlexNet/ResNet18/VGG19 CNN under the native dataset ranged between 0.06% to 0.11%, whereas the Std. of the augmented datasets (Next-OS and Corr-OS) was less than 0.05% in CV2, and the Std. was about 0.04% and 0.05% in CV3. The Std. of the proposed low-memory-usage LMUEBCNet CNN was lower than 0.3% in CV1/CV2/CV3.

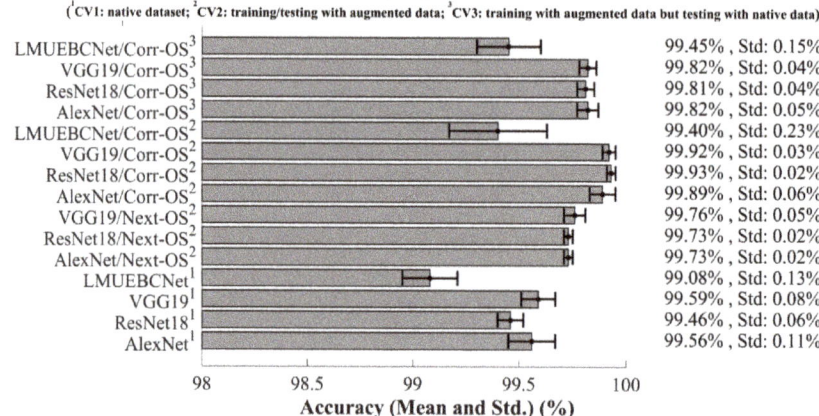

Figure 6. Standard deviation and total accuracy of LMUEBCNet/AlexNet/ResNet18/VGG19 using native/Next-OS/Corr-OS ($K = 1$) dataset in CV1/CV2/CV3.

5.3. Implications for Different Cross-Validation Methods (CV1/CV2/CV3)

CV1 was used as a baseline to validate the native dataset. The baseline accuracy/F1-score of the LMUEBCNet was 99.1%/92.9%. Cross-validation using CV2 provides an overall performance evaluation of all augmented data. However, training/testing with augmented data may result in over-optimism. The LMUEBCNet achieved a higher accuracy/F1-score up to 99.4%/99.4% in CV2. CV3 better fits the actual use scenario, and the results are slightly lower than CV2. The accuracy/F1-score of the LMUEBCNet in CV3 are 99.4%/96.3%, respectively. Training with augmented data in CV3 and testing with native data helps evaluate the performance of classification results, ensuring that the testing images are never considered in the training set. The PR curve shown in Figure 4b confirmed that CV2 is more optimistic, as the sensitivity, precision, and F1-score were always higher than CV3 for all CNN classifiers. In CV2, high similarity ECG images may appear in both the training/testing set, leading to over-optimism in 10-fold CV. Different from overfitting, Figure 3 shows that the augmented ECGs are not the same as the original ECG signal. Furthermore, a max epoch setting was used in this study to avoid overfitting during the learning task.

5.4. Classification Accuracy/F1-Score Performance Compared with the Existing Literature

Compared to previous studies using feature generation and machine learning or deep learning, Table 6 shows that the proposed LMUEBCNet with Corr-OS ($K = 1$) in CV2/CV3 achieved higher F1-scores than other methods. The VGG19 CNN achieved a 99.5% accuracy (native) in CV1 and a 99.9% accuracy (Corr-OS, $K = 5$) in CV3 for classifying N, S, V, F, and Q. Compared to Elhaj's study [60], the VGG19 CNN in both CV2/CV3 showed higher total accuracy, F1-scores, and sensitivity for the N and V classes. The LSTM is commonly used in non-CNN deep learning algorithms. Ronald et al. proposed a RNN-based algorithm and achieved nearly a 100% accuracy with the ECG-ID and MIT-BIH arrhythmia database by training and testing on only 9/18 segments per subject [61]. Darmawahyuni et al. utilized the LSTM with forward and backward pass weight to learn the balanced weights of the majority and minority classes with an imbalance ratio of five times [62]. In contrast, the present study randomly separated all segments into ten folds, losing the time correlation and thus making LSTM not the best choice. The proposed method using the oversampling (Next-OS and Corr-OS) algorithm to balance the dataset achieved higher sensitivity (around 100%) for a balanced dataset than in the other literature. Overall, the results presented in this study outperformed the literature for N/S/V/Q classes in CV3 with a fairer cross-validation method.

Table 6. Comparison with the existing literature (10-fold cross-validation).

Work	Features and Balanced Methods		Classifier	Sensitivity (%)					Total Acc. (%)	Macro F1-Score	Memory Usage
				N	S	V	F	Q			
[59]	PCA + DWT + HOS + ICA		SVM-RBF	98.9	100	98.9	100	100	98.9	-	-
[10]	Std., Z-score	Native	Nine-layer CNN	88.4	85.3	92.7	88.2	95.5	89.1	69.3	-
		Augmented		91.5	90.6	94.2	96.1	97.8	94.0	94.1	-
[16]	Signal images (batch-weighted loss)		Nine-layer CNN	99.9	90.8	99.1	90.2	93.3	99.5	96.9	-
[63]	LSTM-based auto-encoder		SVM	99.8	77.9	97.1	32.0	73.1	98.6	82.9	-
[40]	Hybrid time–frequency diagram, ROS + RUS		ResNet-101	99.5	90.2	98.7	85.0	99.5	98.5	96.0	-
Proposed method	CWT	Native	VGG19 CNN	100.0	95.0	98.1	86.2	99.4	99.6	96.4	496.0 MB
			LMUEBCNet CNN	100.0	86.9	95.4	80.3	98.3	99.1	92.9	1.1 MB
		Next-OS (CV2 *)	VGG19 CNN	99.6	99.8	99.6	99.9	99.8	99.8	99.8	496.0 MB
		Corr-OS ($K = 1$) (CV2 *)	ResNet18 CNN	100.0	99.9	99.9	99.9	99.9	99.9	99.9	41.8 MB
			LMUEBCNet CNN	99.3	99.6	98.5	99.8	99.4	99.4	99.4	2.6 MB
		Corr-OS, ($K = 1$) (CV3 *)	AlexNet CNN	100	98.3	99.1	94.8	99.6	99.8	98.3	47.0 MB
			ResNet18 CNN	100	98.5	98.9	93.8	99.6	99.8	98.3	41.6 MB
			VGG19 CNN	100	98.3	99.0	94.6	99.7	99.8	98.4	499.0 MB
			LMUEBCNet CNN	99.7	97.1	97.4	93.8	99.4	99.4	96.3	2.4 MB

* CV3: augmentation in training stage.

5.5. Limitation

The first limitation of this study is the lack of a subject-level cross-validation (CV) method. While leave-one-subject-out (LOSO) CV is recommended for real-world ECG detection, it was not feasible in this study due to time constraints. The second limitation is that the proposed LMUEBCNet still cannot outperform pre-trained models (AlexNet/ResNet18/VGG19) with limited parameters. However, despite these limitations, this study provides valuable evaluation results using 10-fold CV on the MIT-BIH arrhythmia database. The results show that the proposed low memory usage LMUEBCNet CNN with the Corr-OS oversampling method outperforms the existing literature in terms of accuracy, F1-score, and sensitivity for the N/S/V/Q classes in both CV2 and CV3.

6. Conclusions and Future Works

The proposed LMUEBCNet algorithm achieves high ectopic beat classification accuracy with efficient parameter usage and utilizes Corr-OS to balance the dataset, resulting in improved classification performance. It requires lower computational effort and is therefore more feasible for implementation on resource-constrained mobile devices such as embedded systems. The LMUEBCNet achieved an accuracy of 99.4% using Corr-OS ($K = 1$) in both CV2 and CV3, which is better than most previous studies using the MIT-BIH arrhythmia database. VGG19 with larger parameters under Corr-OS ($K = 1$) in CV3 achieved better results for ventricular ectopic beat (V) and supraventricular ectopic beat (S) detection, with a sensitivity of 99.0% and 98.3%, respectively.

Due to the lack of medical resources, human power, and poor internet connectivity in resource-scarce areas, edge computing devices are a suitable solution. The proposed LMUEBCNet algorithm requires only about 1 MB of memory and is easily portable into embedded systems with limited memory size. The future work is to convert the LMUEBCNet model into an embedded system for more convenient applications.

Author Contributions: Conceptualization, Y.-L.X. and C.-W.L.; methodology, Y.-L.X. and C.-W.L.; software, Y.-L.X.; validation, Y.-L.X.; investigation, Y.-L.X. and C.-W.L.; resources, C.-W.L.; writing—original draft preparation, Y.-L.X.; writing—review and editing, C.-W.L.; supervision, C.-W.L. All authors have read and agreed to the published version of the manuscript.

Funding: This research was funded by the Ministry of Science and Technology (Taiwan), grant No. 108-2628-E-006-003-MY3.

Institutional Review Board Statement: Not applicable.

Informed Consent Statement: Not applicable.

Data Availability Statement: Not applicable.

Conflicts of Interest: The authors declare no conflict of interest.

Appendix A

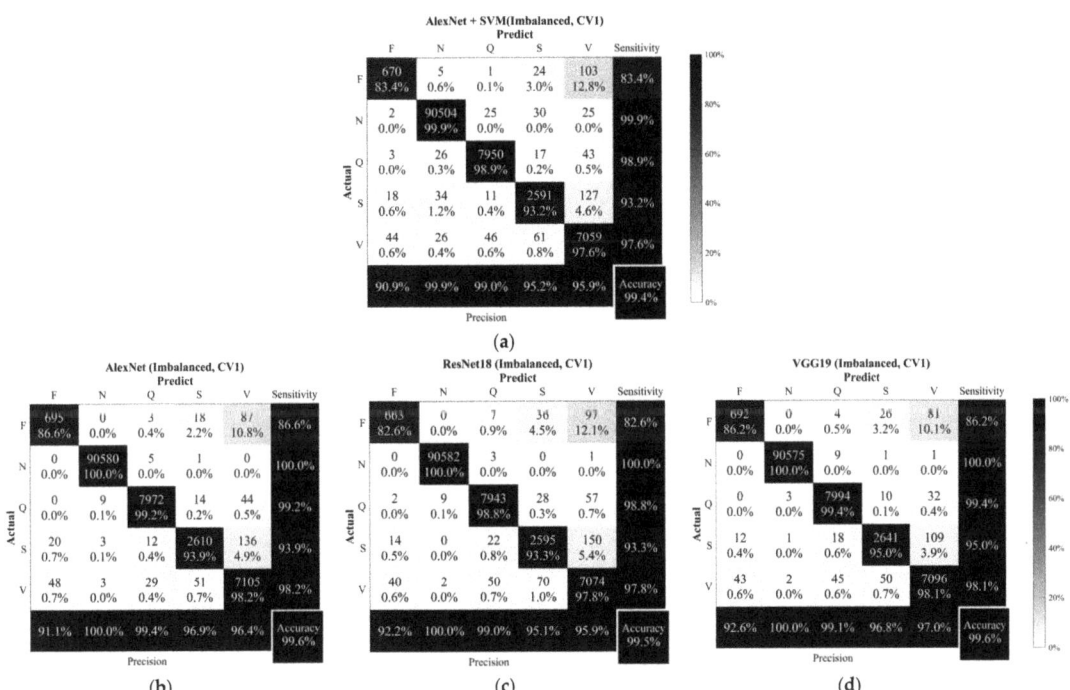

Figure A1. Confusion matrix of (**a**) AlexNet + SVM, (**b**) AlexNet, (**c**) ResNet18, and (**d**) VGG19 for the CV1 (imbalanced dataset).

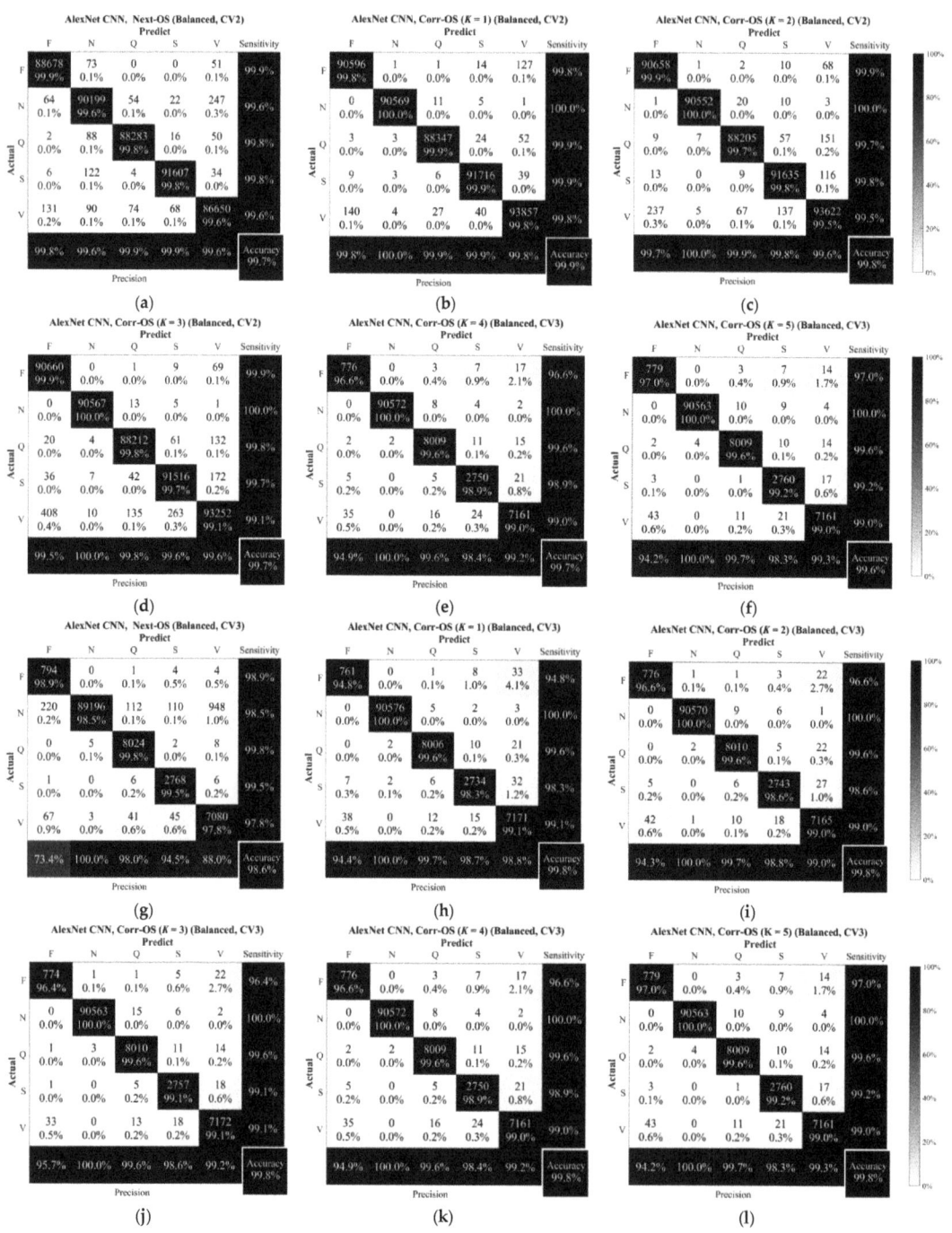

Figure A2. Confusion matrix of AlexNet using CV2 for (**a**) Next-OS, (**b**) Corr-OS ($K = 1$), (**c**) Corr-OS ($K = 2$), (**d**) Corr-OS ($K = 3$), (**e**) Corr-OS ($K = 4$), and (**f**) Corr-OS ($K = 5$); using CV3 for (**g**) Next-OS, (**h**) Corr-OS ($K = 1$), (**i**) Corr-OS ($K = 2$), (**j**) Corr-OS ($K = 3$), (**k**) Corr-OS ($K = 4$), and (**l**) Corr-OS ($K = 5$).

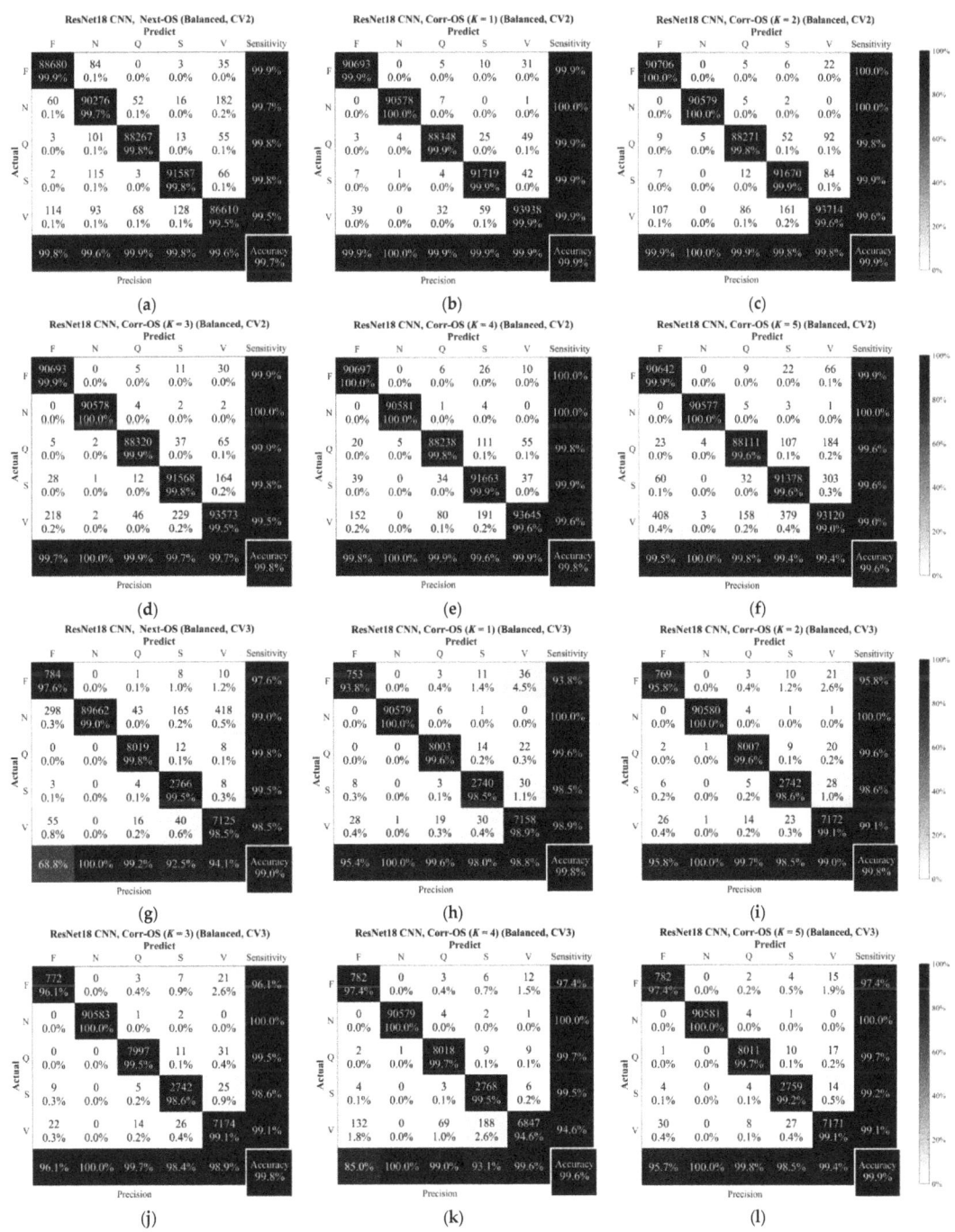

Figure A3. Confusion matrix of ResNet18 using CV2 for (**a**) Next-OS, (**b**) Corr-OS ($K = 1$), (**c**) Corr-OS ($K = 2$), (**d**) Corr-OS ($K = 3$), (**e**) Corr-OS ($K = 4$), and (**f**) Corr-OS ($K = 5$); using CV3 for (**g**) Next-OS, (**h**) Corr-OS ($K = 1$), (**i**) Corr-OS ($K = 2$), (**j**) Corr-OS ($K = 3$), (**k**) Corr-OS ($K = 4$), and (**l**) Corr-OS ($K = 5$).

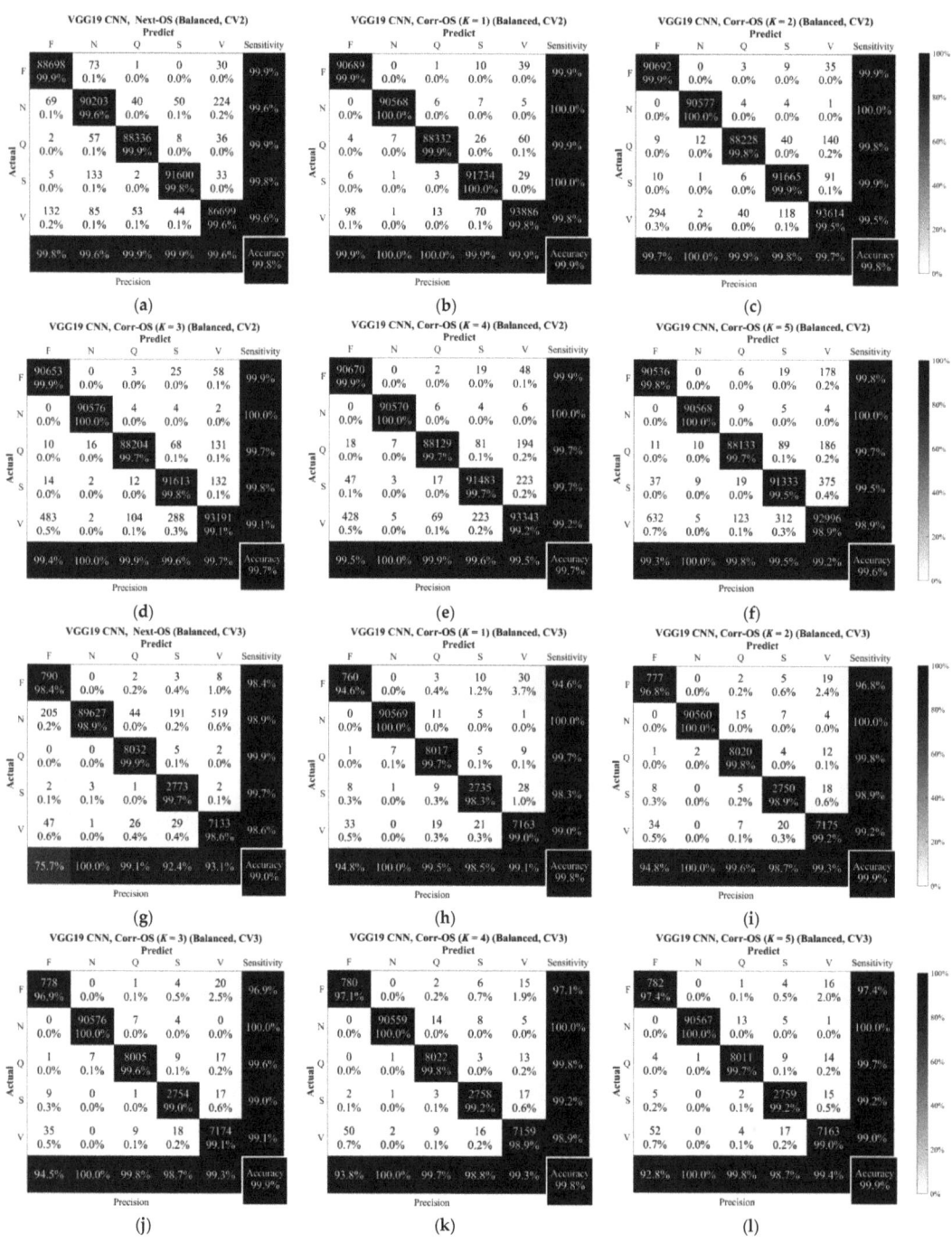

Figure A4. Confusion matrix of VGG19 using CV2 for (**a**) Next-OS, (**b**) Corr-OS ($K = 1$), (**c**) Corr-OS ($K = 2$), (**d**) Corr-OS ($K = 3$), (**e**) Corr-OS ($K = 4$), and (**f**) Corr-OS ($K = 5$); using CV3 for (**g**) Next-OS, (**h**) Corr-OS ($K = 1$), (**i**) Corr-OS ($K = 2$), (**j**) Corr-OS ($K = 3$), (**k**) Corr-OS ($K = 4$), and (**l**) Corr-OS ($K = 5$).

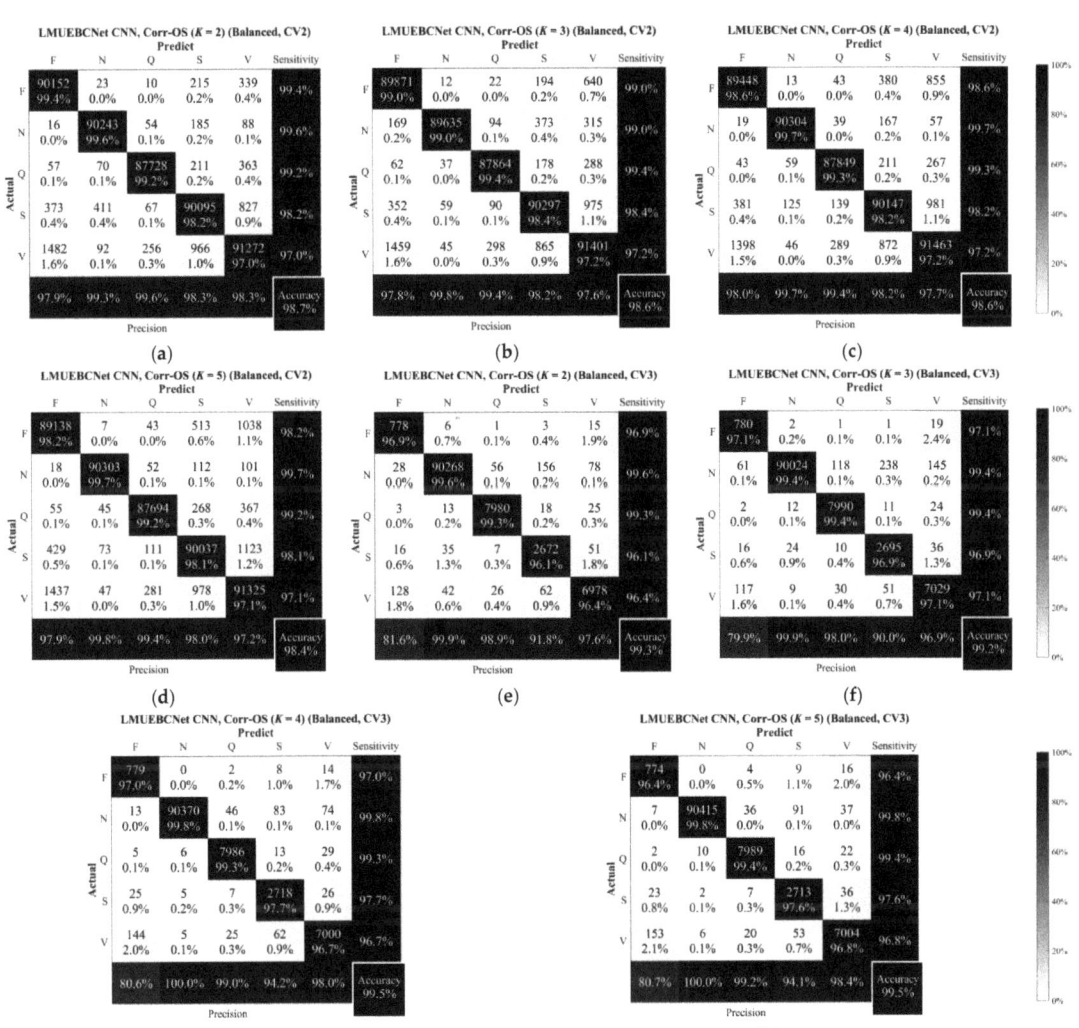

Figure A5. Confusion matrix of LMUEBCNet using CV2 for (**a**) Corr-OS ($K = 2$), (**b**) Corr-OS ($K = 3$), (**c**) Corr-OS ($K = 4$), and (**d**) Corr-OS ($K = 5$); using CV3 for (**e**) Corr-OS ($K = 2$), (**f**) Corr-OS ($K = 3$), (**g**) Corr-OS ($K = 4$), and (**h**) Corr-OS ($K = 5$).

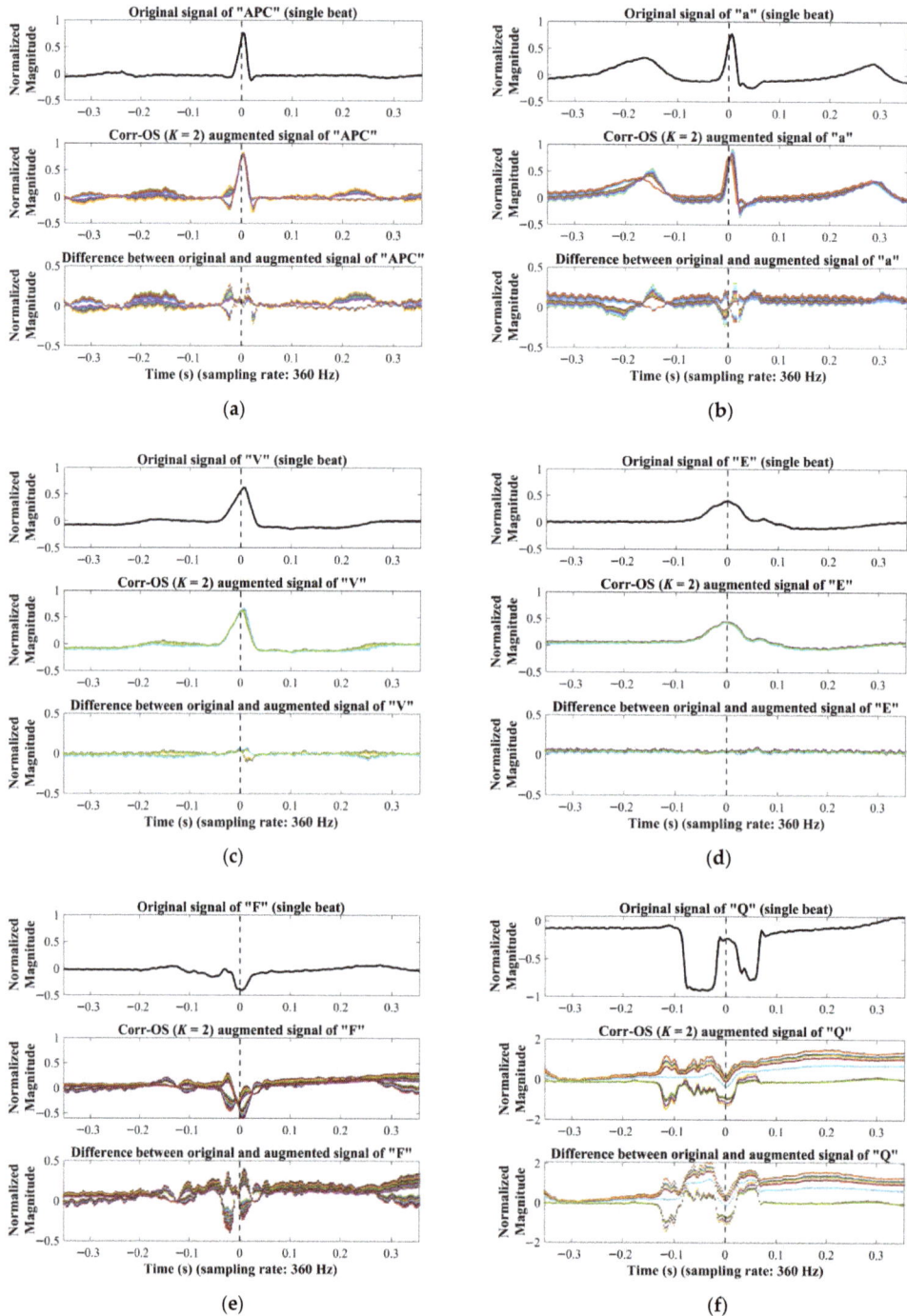

Figure A6. Differences between native and augmented ECG segments generated by Corr-OS ($K = 2$) of (**a**) symbol A, (**b**) symbol a, (**c**) symbol V, (**d**) symbol E, (**e**) symbol F, and (**f**) symbol Q (figure adapted from [59]).

Algorithm A1. Pseudo-code of Next-OS()

1: **Inputs:** Symbol (downloaded from PhysioBank ATM) array of the subject: S
   30-min ECG Lead II signal of the subject: ecg
   Total number (beats) of the majority class: N_{maj}
   Total number (beats) of the minority class: N_{minor}
   Dilation of the CWT: $a = 0.1$
   Translation of the CWT: $b = 0$

2: **Method:**
   for h = 1 to nS (total number of subjects)
      for i = 1 to n (total number (beats) of the record)
         S_R = sampling rate = 360 Hz in this study
         L = data length
         if $(S[i] < S\_R \times 0.35)$ or $(S[i] > L - S\_R \times 0.36)$
            continue
         else
            $T[i] = ecg[S[i] - (S\_R \times 0.35) : S[i] + (S\_R \times 0.36)]$
            if $i == n$
               $T[i+1] = ecg[S[1] - (S\_R \times 0.35) : S[1] + (S\_R \times 0.36)]$ ⎫
            else   ⎬ Generate
               $T[i+1] = ecg[S[i+1] - (S\_R \times 0.35) : S[i+1] + (S\_R \times 0.36)]$ ⎭ Next-OS
            end if   beat
            $AugN$ = round to the nearest integer of $(N_{maj}/N_{minor}) - 1$
            for j=1 to $AugN$
               δ = random numbers where $\delta \in [0,1]$
               $NewT[h][i][j] = T[i] + (T[i+1] - T[i]) \times \delta$
            end
         end if
      end
   end

3: **Output:** Array for Next-OS beats: $NewT$
   CWT matrix: C

Table A1. Sensitivity/precision of LMUEBCNet with existing models using native/Corr-OS/Next-OS dataset under CV1.

Data Augmentation	Classifier	N Sen.	N Pre.	S Sen.	S Pre.	V Sen.	V Pre.	F Sen.	F Pre.	Q Sen.	Q Pre.	Avg. Sen.
Native (CV1)	SVM	99.9	99.9	93.2	95.2	97.6	95.9	83.4	90.9	98.9	99.0	94.6
	AlexNet	100.0	100.0	93.9	96.9	98.2	96.4	86.6	91.1	99.2	99.4	95.6
	ResNet18	100.0	100.0	93.3	95.1	97.8	95.9	82.6	92.2	98.8	99.0	94.5
	VGG19	100.0	100.0	95.0	96.8	98.1	97.0	86.2	92.6	99.4	99.1	95.7
	LMUEBCNet	100.0	99.9	86.9	93.4	95.4	94.3	80.3	83.2	98.3	98.0	92.2

Table A2. Sensitivity/precision of LMUEBCNet with existing models using native/Corr-OS/Next-OS dataset under CV2.

Data Augmentation		Classifier	N		S		V		F		Q		Avg. Sen.
			Sen.	Pre.	Sen.	Pre.	Sen.	Pre.	Sen.	Pre.	Se.	Pre.	
Augmented (CV2)	Next-OS	AlexNet	99.6	99.6	99.8	99.9	99.6	99.6	99.9	99.8	99.8	99.9	99.7
		ResNet18	99.7	99.6	99.8	99.8	99.5	99.6	99.9	99.8	99.8	99.9	99.7
		VGG19	99.6	99.6	99.8	99.9	99.6	99.6	99.9	99.8	99.9	99.9	99.8
	Corr-OS (K = 1)	AlexNet	100.0	100.0	99.9	99.9	99.8	99.8	99.8	99.8	99.9	99.9	99.9
		ResNet18	100.0	100.0	99.9	99.9	99.9	99.9	99.9	99.9	99.9	99.9	99.9
		VGG19	100.0	100.0	100.0	99.9	99.8	99.9	99.9	99.9	99.9	100.0	99.9
		LMUEBCNet	99.4	99.9	99.6	99.1	98.4	99.3	99.8	99.0	99.7	99.7	99.4
	Corr-OS (K = 2)	AlexNet	100.0	100.0	99.8	99.8	99.5	99.6	99.9	99.7	99.7	99.9	99.8
		ResNet18	100.0	100.0	99.9	99.8	99.6	99.8	100.0	99.9	99.8	99.9	99.9
		VGG19	100.0	100.0	99.9	99.8	99.5	99.7	99.9	99.7	99.8	99.9	99.8
		LMUEBCNet	99.6	99.3	98.2	98.3	97.0	98.3	99.4	97.9	99.2	99.6	98.7
	Corr-OS (K = 3)	AlexNet	100.0	100.0	99.7	99.6	99.1	99.6	99.9	99.5	99.8	99.8	99.7
		ResNet18	100.0	100.0	99.8	99.7	99.5	99.7	99.9	99.7	99.9	99.9	99.8
		VGG19	100.0	100.0	99.8	99.6	99.1	99.7	99.9	99.4	99.7	99.9	99.7
		LMUEBCNet	99.0	99.8	98.4	98.2	97.2	97.6	99.0	97.8	99.4	99.4	98.6
	Corr-OS (K = 4)	AlexNet	100.0	100.0	99.5	99.5	99.0	99.5	99.8	99.5	99.7	99.8	99.7
		ResNet18	100.0	100.0	99.9	99.6	99.6	99.9	100.0	99.8	99.8	99.9	99.8
		VGG19	100.0	100.0	99.7	99.6	99.2	99.5	99.9	99.5	99.7	99.9	99.7
		LMUEBCNet	99.7	99.7	98.2	98.2	97.2	97.7	98.6	98.0	99.3	99.4	98.6
	Corr-OS (K = 5)	AlexNet	100.0	100.0	99.6	99.4	98.9	99.4	99.8	99.4	99.6	99.8	99.6
		ResNet18	100.0	100.0	99.6	99.4	99.0	99.4	99.9	99.5	99.6	99.8	99.6
		VGG19	100.0	100.0	99.5	99.5	98.9	99.2	99.8	99.3	99.7	99.8	99.6
		LMUEBCNet	99.7	99.8	98.1	98.0	97.1	97.2	98.2	97.9	99.2	99.4	98.4

Table A3. Sensitivity/precision of LMUEBCNet with existing models using Corr-OS/Next-OS dataset under CV3.

Data Augmentation		Classifier	N		S		V		F		Q		Avg. Sen.
			Sen.	Pre.	Sen.	Pre.	Sen.	Pre.	Sen.	Pre.	Sen.	Pre.	
Next-OS		AlexNet	98.5	100.0	99.5	94.5	97.8	88.0	98.9	73.4	99.8	98.0	98.9
		ResNet18	99.0	100.0	99.5	92.5	98.5	94.1	97.6	68.8	99.8	99.2	98.9
		VGG19	98.9	100.0	99.7	92.4	98.6	93.1	98.4	75.7	99.9	99.1	99.1
Corr-OS	(K = 1)	AlexNet	100.0	100.0	98.3	98.7	99.1	98.8	94.8	94.4	99.6	99.7	98.4
		ResNet18	100.0	100.0	98.5	98.0	98.9	98.8	93.8	95.4	99.6	99.6	98.2
		VGG19	100.0	100.0	98.3	98.5	99.0	99.1	94.6	94.8	99.7	99.5	98.3
		LMUEBCNet	99.7	100.0	97.1	93.7	97.4	97.3	93.8	86.4	99.4	98.8	97.5
	(K = 2)	AlexNet	100.0	100.0	98.6	98.8	99.0	99.0	96.6	94.3	99.6	99.7	98.8
		ResNet18	100.0	100.0	98.6	98.5	99.1	99.0	95.8	95.8	99.6	99.7	98.6
		VGG19	100.0	100.0	98.9	98.7	99.2	99.3	96.8	94.8	99.8	99.6	98.9
		LMUEBCNet	99.6	99.9	96.1	91.8	96.4	97.6	96.9	81.6	99.3	98.9	97.7
	(K = 3)	AlexNet	100.0	100.0	99.1	98.6	99.1	99.2	96.4	95.7	99.6	99.6	98.8
		ResNet18	100.0	100.0	98.6	98.4	99.1	98.9	96.1	96.1	99.5	99.7	98.7
		VGG19	100.0	100.0	99.0	98.7	99.1	99.0	96.9	94.5	99.8	99.8	98.9
		LMUEBCNet	99.4	99.9	96.9	90.0	97.1	96.9	97.1	79.9	99.4	98.0	98.0
	(K = 4)	AlexNet	100.0	100.0	98.9	98.4	99.0	99.2	96.6	94.9	99.6	99.6	98.8
		ResNet18	100.0	100.0	99.5	93.1	94.6	99.6	97.4	85.0	99.7	99.0	98.2
		VGG19	100.0	100.0	99.2	98.8	98.9	99.3	97.1	93.8	99.8	99.7	99.0
		LMUEBCNet	99.8	100.0	97.7	94.2	96.7	98.0	97.0	80.6	99.3	99.0	98.1
	(K = 5)	AlexNet	100.0	100.0	99.2	98.3	99.0	99.3	97.0	94.2	99.6	99.7	99.0
		ResNet18	100.0	100.0	99.2	98.5	99.1	99.4	97.4	95.7	99.7	99.8	99.1
		VGG19	100.0	100.0	99.2	98.7	99.0	99.4	97.4	92.8	99.7	99.8	99.1
		LMUEBCNet	99.8	100.0	97.6	94.1	96.8	98.4	96.4	80.7	99.4	99.2	98.0

References

1. Tsao, C.W.; Aday, A.W.; Almarzooq, Z.I.; Alonso, A.; Beaton, A.Z.; Bittencourt, M.S.; Boehme, A.K.; Buxton, A.E.; Carson, A.P.; Commodore-Mensah, Y.; et al. Heart Disease and Stroke Statistics—2022 Update: A Report From the American Heart Association. *Circulation* **2022**, *145*, e153–e639. [PubMed]
2. Stronati, G.; Benfaremo, D.; Selimi, A.; Ferraioli, Y.; Ferranti, F.; Dello Russo, A.; Guerra, F. Incidence and predictors of cardiac arrhythmias in patients with systemic sclerosis. *Europace* **2022**, *24* (Suppl. S1), euac053-124. [CrossRef]
3. ANSI/AAMI EC57; Testing and Reporting Performance Results of Cardiac Rhythm and ST Segment Measurement Algorithms. ANSI: New York, NY, USA, 2012. Available online: https://webstore.ansi.org/standards/aami/ansiaamiec572012r2020 (accessed on 7 April 2022).
4. Afkhami, R.G.; Azarnia, G.; Tinati, M.A. Cardiac arrhythmia classification using statistical and mixture modeling features of ECG signals. *Pattern Recognit. Lett.* **2016**, *70*, 45–51. [CrossRef]
5. Li, T.; Zhou, M. ECG classification using wavelet packet entropy and random forests. *Entropy* **2016**, *18*, 285. [CrossRef]
6. Desai, U.; Martis, R.J.; Nayak, C.G.; Sarika, K.; Nayak, S.G.; Shirva, A.; Nayak, V.; Mudassir, S. Discrete cosine transform features in automated classification of cardiac arrhythmia beats. In *Emerging Research in Computing, Information, Communication and Applications*; Springer: New Delhi, India, 2015; pp. 153–162.
7. Martis, R.J.; Acharya, U.R.; Min, L.C. ECG beat classification using PCA, LDA, ICA and discrete wavelet transform. *Biomed. Signal Process. Control.* **2013**, *8*, 437–448. [CrossRef]
8. Yang, W.; Si, Y.; Wang, D.; Guo, B. Automatic recognition of arrhythmia based on principal component analysis network and linear support vector machine. *Comput. Biol. Med.* **2018**, *101*, 22–32. [CrossRef]
9. Ebrahimi, Z.; Loni, M.; Daneshtalab, M.; Gharehbaghi, A. A review on deep learning methods for ECG arrhythmia classification. *Expert Syst. Appl. X* **2020**, *7*, 100033. [CrossRef]
10. Acharya, U.R.; Oh, S.L.; Hagiwara, Y.; Tan, J.H.; Adam, M.; Gertych, A.; San Tan, R. A deep convolutional neural network model to classify heartbeats. *Comput. Biol. Med.* **2017**, *89*, 389–396. [CrossRef]
11. Wang, H.; Shi, H.; Chen, X.; Zhao, L.; Huang, Y.; Liu, C. An improved convolutional neural network based approach for automated heartbeat classification. *J. Med. Syst.* **2020**, *44*, 35. [CrossRef]
12. Romdhane, T.F.; Pr, M.A. Electrocardiogram heartbeat classification based on a deep convolutional neural network and focal loss. *Comput. Biol. Med.* **2020**, *123*, 103866. [CrossRef]
13. Yao, G.; Mao, X.; Li, N.; Xu, H.; Xu, X.; Jiao, Y.; Ni, J. Interpretation of electrocardiogram heartbeat by CNN and GRU. *Comput. Math. Methods Med.* **2021**, *2021*, 6534942. [CrossRef] [PubMed]
14. Al Rahhal, M.M.; Bazi, Y.; Al Hichri, H.; Alajlan, N.; Melgani, F.; Yager, R.R. Deep Learning Approach for Active Classification of Electrocardiogram Signals. *Inf. Sci.* **2016**, *345*, 340–354. [CrossRef]
15. Xie, Q.; Tu, S.; Wang, G.; Lian, Y.; Xu, L. Feature enrichment based convolutional neural network for heartbeat classification from electrocardiogram. *IEEE Access* **2019**, *7*, 153751–153760. [CrossRef]
16. Zhai, X.; Tin, C. Automated ECG classification using dual heartbeat coupling based on convolutional neural network. *IEEE Access* **2018**, *6*, 27465–27472. [CrossRef]
17. Sellami, A.; Hwang, H. A robust deep convolutional neural network with batch-weighted loss for heartbeat classification. *Expert Syst. Appl.* **2019**, *122*, 75–84. [CrossRef]
18. Li, F.; Xu, Y.; Chen, Z.; Liu, Z. Automated heartbeat classification using 3-d inputs based on convolutional neural network with multi-fields of view. *IEEE Access* **2019**, *7*, 76295–76304. [CrossRef]
19. Lu, P.; Gao, Y.; Xi, H.; Zhang, Y.; Gao, C.; Zhou, B.; Zhang, H.; Chen, L.; Mao, X. KecNet: A light neural network for arrhythmia classification based on knowledge reinforcement. *J. Health Eng.* **2021**, *2021*, 6684954. [CrossRef]
20. He, Z.; Zhang, X.; Cao, Y.; Liu, Z.; Zhang, B.; Wang, X. LiteNet: Lightweight neural network for detecting arrhythmias at resource-constrained mobile devices. *Sensors* **2018**, *18*, 1229. [CrossRef]
21. Mathunjwa, B.M.; Lin, Y.T.; Lin, C.H.; Abbod, M.F.; Sadrawi, M.; Shieh, J.S. ECG Recurrence Plot-Based Arrhythmia Classification Using Two-Dimensional Deep Residual CNN Features. *Sensors* **2022**, *22*, 1660. [CrossRef]
22. Khan, A.; Sohail, A.; Zahoora, U.; Qureshi, A.S. A survey of the recent architectures of deep convolutional neural networks. *Artif. Intell. Rev.* **2020**, *53*, 5455–5516. [CrossRef]
23. Dey, M.; Omar, N.; Ullah, M.A. Temporal Feature-Based Classification Into Myocardial Infarction and Other CVDs Merging CNN and Bi-LSTM From ECG Signal. *IEEE Sens. J.* **2021**, *21*, 21688–21695. [CrossRef]
24. Tsinalis, O.; Matthews, P.M.; Guo, Y. Automatic sleep stage scoring using time-frequency analysis and stacked sparse autoencoders. *Ann. Biomed. Eng.* **2016**, *44*, 1587–1597. [CrossRef]
25. Amrane, M.; Oukid, S.; Gagaoua, I.; Ensarİ, T. Breast cancer classification using machine learning. In Proceedings of the 2018 Electric Electronics, Computer Science, Biomedical Engineerings' Meeting (EBBT), Istanbul, Turkey, 18–19 April 2018; pp. 1–4.
26. Gu, Y.; Ge, Z.; Bonnington, C.P.; Zhou, J. Progressive Transfer Learning And Adversarial Domain Adaptation For Cross-domain Skin Disease Classification. *IEEE J. Biomed. Health Inform.* **2019**, *24*, 1379–1393. [CrossRef] [PubMed]
27. He, H.; Garcia, E.A. Learning from imbalanced data. *IEEE Trans. Knowl. Data Eng.* **2009**, *21*, 1263–1284.
28. Johnson, J.M.; Khoshgoftaar, T.M. Survey on deep learning with class imbalance. *J. Big Data* **2019**, *6*, 27. [CrossRef]
29. Lu, W.; Hou, H.; Chu, J. Feature fusion for imbalanced ECG data analysis. *Biomed. Signal Process. Control.* **2018**, *41*, 152–160. [CrossRef]

30. Mousavi, S.; Afghah, F. Inter-and intra-patient ECG heartbeat classification for arrhythmia detection: A sequence to sequence deep learning approach. In Proceedings of the ICASSP 2019–2019 IEEE International Conference on Acoustics, Speech and Signal Processing (ICASSP), Brighton, UK, 12–17 May 2019.
31. Shaker, A.M.; Tantawi, M.; Shedeed, H.A.; Tolba, M.F. Generalization of convolutional neural networks for ECG classification using generative adversarial networks. *IEEE Access* **2020**, *8*, 35592–35605. [CrossRef]
32. Pandey, S.K.; Janghel, R.R. Automatic detection of arrhythmia from imbalanced ECG database using CNN model with SMOTE. *Australas. Phys. Eng. Sci. Med.* **2019**, *42*, 1129–1139. [CrossRef]
33. Bhattacharyya, S.; Majumder, S.; Debnath, P.; Chanda, M. Arrhythmic heartbeat classification using ensemble of random forest and support vector machine algorithm. *IEEE Trans. Artif. Intell.* **2021**, *2*, 260–268. [CrossRef]
34. Rao, K.N.; Reddy, C. An efficient software defect analysis using correlation-based oversampling. *Arab. J. Sci. Eng.* **2018**, *43*, 4391–4411. [CrossRef]
35. Devi, D.; Biswas, S.K.; Purkayastha, B. Correlation-based oversampling aided cost sensitive ensemble learning technique for treatment of class imbalance. *J. Exp. Theor. Artif. Intell.* **2022**, *34*, 143–174. [CrossRef]
36. Fahrudin, T.; Buliali, J.L.; Fatichah, C. Enhancing the performance of smote algorithm by using attribute weighting scheme and new selective sampling method for imbalanced data set. *Int. J. Innov. Comput. Inf. Control.* **2019**, *15*, 423–444.
37. Jiang, Z.; Pan, T.; Zhang, C.; Yang, J. A new oversampling method based on the classification contribution degree. *Symmetry* **2021**, *13*, 194. [CrossRef]
38. Zhang, Q.; Shen, Y.; Yi, Z. Video-based traffic sign detection and recognition. In Proceedings of the 2019 International Conference on Image and Video Processing, and Artificial Intelligence, SPIE, Shanghai, China, 23–25 August 2019; pp. 284–291.
39. Breve, B.; Caruccio, L.; Cirillo, S.; Deufemia, V.; Polese, G. Visual ECG Analysis in Real-world Scenarios. In Proceedings of the 27th International DMS Conference on Visualization and Visual Languages (DMSVIVA2021), Pittsburgh, PA, USA, 29–30 June 2021; pp. 46–54.
40. Zhang, Y.; Li, J.; Wei, S.; Zhou, F.; Li, D. Heartbeats Classification Using Hybrid Time-Frequency Analysis and Transfer Learning Based on ResNet. *IEEE J. Biomed. Health Inf.* **2021**, *25*, 4175–4184. [CrossRef] [PubMed]
41. Ahmad, Z.; Tabassum, A.; Guan, L.; Khan, N.M. ECG heartbeat classification using multimodal fusion. *IEEE Access* **2021**, *9*, 100615–100626. [CrossRef]
42. Time-Frequency Analysis. Available online: https://bit.ly/30tdZlo (accessed on 10 January 2022).
43. Du, P.; Kibbe, W.A.; Lin, S.M. Improved Peak Detection in Mass Spectrum by Incorporating Continuous Wavelet Transform-based Pattern Matching. *Bioinformatics* **2006**, *22*, 2059–2065. [CrossRef] [PubMed]
44. Szegedy, C.; Liu, W.; Jia, Y.; Sermanet, P.; Reed, S.; Anguelov, D.; Erhan, D.; Vanhoucke, V.; Rabinovich, A. Going Deeper with Convolutions. In Proceedings of the IEEE Conference on Computer Vision and Pattern Recognition, Boston, MA, USA, 7–12 June 2015; pp. 1–9.
45. Deep Learning Toolbox. Available online: https://bit.ly/2XFBgPf (accessed on 10 January 2022).
46. Pretrained Deep Neural Networks. Available online: https://bit.ly/2NKknna (accessed on 10 January 2022).
47. ImageNet. Available online: http://image-net.org/index (accessed on 10 January 2022).
48. Krizhevsky, A.; Sutskever, I.; Hinton, G. ImageNet Classification with Deep Convolutional Neural Networks. *Adv. Neural Inf. Process. Syst.* **2012**, 1106–1114. [CrossRef]
49. Kaiming, H.; Zhang, X.; Ren, S.; Sun, J. Deep Residual Learning for Image Recognition. In Proceedings of the IEEE Conference on Computer Vision and Pattern Recognition, Las Vegas, NV, USA, 27–30 June 2016; pp. 770–778.
50. Transfer Learning Using AlexNet. Available online: https://bit.ly/2XPhmFV (accessed on 10 January 2022).
51. Çinar, A.; Tuncer, S.A. Classification of normal sinus rhythm, abnormal arrhythmia and congestive heart failure ECG signals using LSTM and hybrid CNN-SVM deep neural networks. *Comput. Methods Biomech. Biomed. Eng.* **2021**, *24*, 203–214. [CrossRef]
52. Chawla, N.V.; Bowyer, K.W.; Hall, L.O.; Kegelmeyer, W.P. SMOTE: Synthetic minority over-sampling technique. *J. Artif. Intell. Res.* **2002**, *16*, 321–357. [CrossRef]
53. Chiu, C.C.; Lin, T.H.; Liau, B.Y. Using correlation coefficient in ECG waveform for arrhythmia detection. *Biomed. Eng. Appl. Basis Commun.* **2005**, *17*, 147–152. [CrossRef]
54. Zheng, Q.; Yang, M.; Tian, X.; Jiang, N.; Wang, D. A full stage data augmentation method in deep convolutional neural network for natural image classification. *Discret. Dyn. Nat. Soc.* **2020**, *2020*, 4706576. [CrossRef]
55. Santos, M.S.; Soares, J.P.; Abreu, P.H.; Araujo, H.; Santos, J. Cross-validation for imbalanced datasets: Avoiding overoptimistic and overfitting approaches [research frontier]. *IEEE Comput. Intell. Mag.* **2018**, *13*, 59–76. [CrossRef]
56. Cross-Validation (Statistics). Available online: https://bit.ly/2cEQ6Oz (accessed on 10 January 2022).
57. Moody, G.B.; Mark, R.G. The impact of the MIT-BIH Arrhythmia Database. *IEEE Eng. Med. Biol. Mag.* **2001**, *20*, 45–50. [CrossRef] [PubMed]
58. Goldberger, A.; Amaral, L.; Glass, L.; Hausdorff, J.; Ivanov, P.C.; Mark, R.; Mietus, J.E.; Moody, G.B.; Peng, C.K.; Stanley, H.E. PhysioBank, PhysioToolkit, and PhysioNet: Components of a new research resource for complex physiologic signals. *Circulation* **2000**, *101*, e215–e220. [CrossRef]
59. Raj, S.; Ray, K.C. A personalized arrhythmia monitoring platform. *Sci. Rep.* **2018**, *8*, 11395. [CrossRef]
60. Elhaj, F.A.; Salim, N.; Harris, A.R.; Swee, T.T. Arrhythmia Recognition and Classification Using Combined Linear and Nonlinear Features of ECG Signals. *Comput. Methods Programs Biomed.* **2016**, *127*, 52–63. [CrossRef]

61. Ronald, S.; Kuo, C.-C.J. ECG-based biometrics using recurrent neural networks. In Proceedings of the 2017 IEEE International Conference on Acoustics, Speech and Signal Processing (ICASSP), New Orleans, LA, USA, 5–9 March 2017.
62. Darmawahyuni, A.; Nurmaini, S.; Sukemi; Caesarendra, W.; Bhayyu, V.; Rachmatullah, M.N.; Firdaus. Deep learning with a recurrent network structure in the sequence modeling of imbalanced data for ECG-rhythm classifier. *Algorithms* **2019**, *12*, 118. [CrossRef]
63. Hou, B.; Yang, J.; Wang, P.; Yan, R. LSTM Based Auto-Encoder Model for ECG Arrhythmias Classification. *IEEE Trans. Instrum. Meas.* **2020**, *69*, 1232–1240. [CrossRef]

Disclaimer/Publisher's Note: The statements, opinions and data contained in all publications are solely those of the individual author(s) and contributor(s) and not of MDPI and/or the editor(s). MDPI and/or the editor(s) disclaim responsibility for any injury to people or property resulting from any ideas, methods, instructions or products referred to in the content.

MDPI
St. Alban-Anlage 66
4052 Basel
Switzerland
www.mdpi.com

Mathematics Editorial Office
E-mail: mathematics@mdpi.com
www.mdpi.com/journal/mathematics

Disclaimer/Publisher's Note: The statements, opinions and data contained in all publications are solely those of the individual author(s) and contributor(s) and not of MDPI and/or the editor(s). MDPI and/or the editor(s) disclaim responsibility for any injury to people or property resulting from any ideas, methods, instructions or products referred to in the content.

www.ingramcontent.com/pod-product-compliance
Lightning Source LLC
LaVergne TN
LVHW070450100526
838202LV00014B/1697